Markets for Managers

For other titles in the Wiley Finance series, please see www.wiley.com/finance

Markets for Managers

A Managerial Economics Primer

ANTHONY J. EVANS

WILEY

Library of Congress Cataloging-in-Publication Data

Evans, Anthony John, 1981–
   Markets for managers : a managerial economics primer / Anthony J. Evans.
      pages cm. – (The Wiley finance series)
   Includes bibliographical references and index.
   ISBN 978-1-118-86796-9 (hardback)
  1. Managerial economics. I. Title.
   HD30.22.E84 2014
   338.5024′658–dc23
                                   2014022437

A catalogue record for this book is available from the British Library.

ISBN 978-1-118-86796-9 (hardback/paperback)   ISBN 978-1-118-86794-5 (ebk)
ISBN 978-1-118-86795-2 (ebk)   ISBN 978-1-118-86793-8 (ebk)

Cover design by Wiley
Cover image: Image #150258983 Abstract image made of interlocking triangles in yellow, orange and brown. © Shutterstock.

Set in 10/12pt Times by Aptara Inc., New Delhi, India
Printed in Great Britain by CPI Group (UK) Ltd, Croydon, CR0 4YY

Contents

Preface

I have been fortunate to learn economics from some of the best teachers in the world. When I first stepped into a classroom to teach, in 2006, I felt overwhelmed by the task of condensing so much of the wonder of economics into such a short space of time. I still do.

This book originates from the lecture notes I've used in the classroom. It reflects the courses I've followed (in particular those of Malcolm Walter, Arthur Thomas, Peter Boettke and Jeffrey Rogers Hummel), and textbooks I've read. Although I've tried to provide extensive references I am probably guilty of oversight. I don't claim any originality or expert skills at synthesis. I have utilised lots of quotes and links to emphasise that I see myself as a guide, rather than a guru. Most books aimed at time poor professionals have an easy to communicate (i.e. simple) central idea that is presented in a counterintuitive way with well-written anecdotes. This book takes a step back. It is for people who enjoy 'pop economics', but want something more substantial. It fills in some of the holes, and stretches out a broad and serious look at the discipline of economics.

I cannot hope to replicate the content and delivery of a Managerial Economics course in book form. What I have tried to do is provide a substitute for the passive element of a formal MBA. If you want an overview of key concepts, embedded in examples, then this book is enough. But to really understand the material you need to discuss it, and apply it. These are the activities I like to spend class time doing, and they cannot be replicated on the page. New technologies are making learning cheaper, and with fewer barriers, and I hope this book can play a role, but only as a complement to other sources of information and other methods of learning.

I wish to offer special thanks to the following for commenting on early versions of the text: Toby Baxendale, Tom Clougherty, Othman Cole, Lana Dojčinović, Colleen Haight, David Howden, Stephen Lai, Benjamin Powell, Randolph Quirk, David Skarbek, Robert Thorpe, Terence Tse, Wolf von Laer and Nikolai Wenzel.

In October 2013 I made a visit to Washington DC for a manuscript workshop, and appreciate the time and help of Paul Dragos Aligica, T. Clark Durant, Matthew Mitchell, Nick Schandler, Ionut Sterpan and Vlad Tarko. In particular, Nick has accompanied this book from its earliest inception all the way through spotting typos on the final draft.

In November 2013 I held a manuscript focus group in London, and received exceedingly useful comments and feedback from Sam Bowman, Anton Howes, Robert C. Miller and Ben Southwood. It was held under the auspices of a Kaleidic Economics quarterly meeting and I thank all of the members for their collegiate backing.

I also want to acknowledge the support and advice provided by my friends and family. This book has required periods of fixation and I could not have done that without Faith. As a student, I thought of myself as a vorticist economist, writer and coach. But being a son, husband and father is my arcadia.

Finally, the primary motivation for writing this book is to provide a resource for my students. It is to them that I dedicate this work.

Introduction

'Managers can't just employ economists, they must become economists.'
—Shlomo Maital[1]

I magine that it is 1910 and you are presented with the following list of problems:[2]

1. To build and maintain roads adequate for use of conveyances, their operators and passengers.
2. To transport physically a person from Manchester to Washington DC in around 8 hours.
3. To convey instantly the visual replica of an action, such as a football match, to devices that people can fit in their pocket.
4. To find a way for women to be able to have sex without having children, or to have children without having sex.
5. To increase the average span of life by 30 years.

Put in this way, doesn't the first item seem easiest? And indeed this is the one that governments were committed to achieving. But with dubious success. In comparison, as John Sparks said, 'the other problems would have seemed fantastic and quite likely would have been rejected as the figments of someone's wild imagination.' And yet all of those have been accomplished. We barely give them a second thought.

This isn't to ignore the role that government plays in the medical and engineering achievements of modernity, but it is telling that the greatest achievements tend to stem from the creativity and tenacity of free individuals. Not from central planning, but from decentralised experimentation. This book will provide the economic ammunition for the argument that great things happen when people are free to try. Managerial Economics helps us to understand the policy framework that is required for this to happen, and the toolkit that can then be used to create genuine value. I hope to engender a profound respect for the use of markets as a means to solve complex social issues.

If this book has a unifying theme it is that markets are incredible. We use them every day, and largely take them for granted. The *poetry* of economics is to marvel at the mundane. This book helps you to see markets in a new light. To appreciate how they operate, and to reflect on their results. We are totally familiar with markets, but they are remarkable accomplishments of human interaction. Indeed the *science* of economics is to make the mundane intelligible. To use the economic way of thinking to discover the strengths of markets and the conditions that are needed for them to work. This book will help you to understand how markets function and how they impact managerial decision making. But we will also go beyond this. We will see how managers can use markets as a management tool – both in terms of internalising the insights into their daily actions, and in terms of adopting processes that can be applied across the organisation. I want to show you how markets generate social prosperity, but also how managers can use markets – and the principles on which they rest – to generate value.

By covering the key foundations of economic analysis we can apply them to specific concepts such as economic value added (EVA), price discrimination and value-based pricing. But the aim is to keep an eye on the bigger picture – biographies of famous economists, the seminal books and articles, and key moments in economic history. We will look at how examples of market failure, such as monopolies, asymmetric information and behavioural anomalies, are well understood by economists and can in fact strengthen the case for markets. My own predisposition will shine through and it will be obvious that I want to evangelise, as well as explain markets. But the reason I weigh in on key debates is in an effort to help the reader weigh up both sides. I wish to present arguments that I find compelling, alongside a charitable interpretation of those I don't. Ultimately I have enough respect for you as reader to make up your own mind. I wrote this book to act as an input in your decision making. Don't take my word for it. Consider markets.

NOTES

1. Maital, S. (2011) *Executive Economics: Ten Essential Tools for Managers*, Free Press, p. 5.
2. Based on Sparks, J.C. (1977) If men were free to try, *The Freeman*, 1 February. UK life expectancy figures from 'Chapter 4: Mortality, 2010-based NPP Reference Volume' Office for National Statistics, 29 March 2012 [http://www.ons.gov.uk/ons/dcp171776_253938.pdf, accessed 7 October 2013].

CHAPTER 1

Incentives Matter

'The theory of economics does not furnish a body of settled conclusions immediately applicable in policy. It is a method rather than a doctrine, an apparatus of mind, a technique of thinking which helps its possessor to draw correct conclusions.'

—John Maynard Keynes[1]

In early 1998, day care centres around Haifa, in Israel, had a problem. It was a problem common to many of us who have looked after children for a living: late parents.[2] After a long day being responsible for other people's children, by 4pm the teachers were ready to go home. And they weren't being paid for staying any longer. But invariably some parents would be late, and someone would have to stay behind and wait with the child. But one day some social scientists turned up (or rather, sent their research assistants) and made a suggestion: why not fine the parents for being late? It is a solution any economist would give.

Over the next few weeks things carried on as normal, as the researchers gathered data before making any changes. Then, they adopted a policy where any parent who was more than 10 minutes late would pay a $3 fine. But instead of reducing lateness, the number of late pickups more than doubled. The incentive backfired.

As an economist, I've heard this example a lot. It's often used to show economists that assuming people's behaviour can be manipulated with financial incentives is naïve and narrow minded. Indeed there is some truth to this. Just because originally there was no fine doesn't mean that there was no incentive to be on time. The social norm is to be on time, and late parents probably felt guilty. Once the arrangement moved from the social to a financial realm, parents realised they could 'buy' the right to be late. Indeed they weren't just buying the right to be late, but also the ability to not feel guilty about it. In fact, maybe the lesson of the day care experiment is not that economists overstate their subject matter, but that non-economists understate it. After all, the average monthly cost was about $380. A good economist would suggest that the fine was set at a price that was too low! If the goal was to reduce lateness, raise the fine. And even more importantly, discovering the point at which the fine has an effect will help the day care centre to know just how valuable the parents consider their time to be. This whole experiment might help them to discover which opening hours best suit their customers. Clearly the parents are willing to pay the teachers to stay later. Far from demonstrating the failure of markets, this example is like a cursory foray into their magic.

We tend to think that economics is the study of the economy, and indeed this is an important application. But economics isn't a subject matter; it's a way of thinking. The essence of the economic way of thinking is to understand how incentives and institutions affect people's behaviour. In terms of management, economics can give us important clues about why behaviour may be generating bad outcomes. Understanding concepts such as opportunity cost, price elasticity and price discrimination are tools that managers can use to improve a company's performance. But economics does more than this. It provides us with a way of thinking about human action. Economics is the study of society, and the tools with which we understand social behaviour are of direct relevance to management.

1.1 MANAGERIAL INDIVIDUALISM

In their excellent textbook *Managerial Economics*, Luke Froeb and Brian McCann offer the following guide to decision making: when you see an outcome that you deem to be undesirable, ask yourself three questions:[3]

1. Who made the bad decision?
2. Did they have the information they needed?
3. Did they have the right incentives?

All too often the first question isn't even asked, and failure is put down to some collective problem that is ill defined and impossible to alter. The main insight of managerial economics is to focus on the information and incentive mechanisms that help guide decision making. If you do not even know who is making the bad decision, there's little hope of finding out why they did so. This book intends to explore the information channels and incentive mechanisms that create value. It will focus on how markets can be utilised to help solve these problems.

The reason why economists make individual choice the centre of analysis is because we posit that only individuals choose.[4] This is not the same thing as saying that only individuals matter, or that 'society' is nothing more than a group of individuals. It stems from a concept called 'methodological individualism', which Jon Elster defines as 'the doctrine that all social phenomena (their structure and their change) are in principle explicable only in terms of individuals – their properties, goals and beliefs'.[5] We can talk about how 'Heinz have decided to build a new factory' but according to methodological individualism the literal interpretation that the company itself made the decision is false. Families, businesses and nations might have common interests and work together to achieve shared goals, but it is only as individuals that we make decisions. This doesn't imply that social phenomena aren't important. On the contrary, it is precisely because we wish to understand social phenomena that we see it through the lens of individual choice. We need to understand the preferences and constraints of individual members, to see how collective decisions get made, because social entities are the result of individual action.

This is why the first question – identifying the decision maker – is so important. It is only then that we can look into the circumstances in which the decision was made and what their objectives were. Economics helps to reveal the information and incentive systems within which we operate. The crucial point is that although these institutions influence our choices, we also have choices about how to shape them. In short there's a feedback mechanism between individuals and institutions, but with us in the driving seat. Institutions are, as John Commons defines them, 'collective action in control, liberation and expansion of individual action'.[6]

In this book we will make two key behavioural assumptions:

1. **The rationality assumption – incentives affect behaviour (at the margin)**

    The idea that incentives matter seems obvious but is often counterintuitive. My brother-in-law enjoys adventure and on a recent skiing trip realised that he was travelling faster than 30mph. My parents were worried that he might hurt himself if he crashed, so they bought him a helmet. Guess what? The next day he promptly reached 58mph! All safety equipment has a curious potential to backfire, because it alters your incentives to take risks. Although helmets mean that you are less likely to be injured if you have an accident, they also affect the probability of having an accident in the first place. In the case of skiing a helmet reduces the cost of an accident. All else being equal, this makes you more willing to risk having one. This may not be a large effect, and perhaps if you wore a helmet you'd think that you'd be just as careful as without. But the helmet is incentivising you to be more reckless, not less. Not only this, but it can affect other people's behaviour. If you wear a helmet you also reduce the cost to other people of them crashing into you. At the margin, it could lead to more accidents.[7]

    Think of the difference between Rugby and American Football. Both are similar sports but one key difference is that the players of the latter wear helmets. Which one do you think has the most neck and spinal injuries? The obvious answer would be Rugby, because they don't wear hard protection.[8] But because of this they face a higher cost of putting their head into a dangerous situation. Maybe they are less likely to enter tackles headfirst? Indeed not only do American Footballers face a higher rate of neck and head injuries, there are calls by some to *ban* helmets for this very reason.[9] A 2013 book on the subject claimed that in 1999 the NFL paid compensation to retired players after accepting they had suffered brain damage.[10] Since the year 2000 neurosurgeons have been warning the league that the sport was causing depression, dementia and brain damage.[11]

2. **The self-interest assumption – people pursue their own self-interest**

    Again, to economists this assumption is self-evident and trivial. Maybe we don't really know what other people's interests are. Either way, we put our own interests ahead of the interests of others. This does *not* imply that we are narrowly selfish. It doesn't mean that we're motivated by material possessions, or monetary gains. The welfare of your children, or colleagues, may be your primary goal. Your self-interest may well be altruistic. But it's what drives your economic decision making. As Gary Becker said,

    > *I have tried to pry economists away from narrow assumptions about self-interest. Behaviour is driven by a much richer set of values and preferences. Individuals maximise welfare as they conceive it, whether they be selfish, altruistic, loyal, spiteful, or masochistic.*[12]

The implications of these assumptions are crucial to management. Forget trying to 'motivate' people. Forget about coaching. The goal of management is really quite simple – to change behaviour you need to change what is in people's self-interest to pursue. You need to change incentives. Achieving that goal is where it gets difficult.

It may well be the case that some people are narrowly selfish, but acknowledging that people respond predictably to incentives does not condone any behaviour that results from it.

These assumptions are merely devices to make the world around us more intelligible. Indeed we can make a distinction between *positive* and *normative* analysis. Economists are often guilty of slipping between the two, and it's important to try to keep them separate. Positive analysis refers to what *is*. For example the claim that 'wearing helmets can increase the number of accidents' is a positive statement. Normative analysis refers to what *ought to be*. If I told you that 'people shouldn't wear helmets' I'd be making a normative statement. The proper role of the economist is to limit themselves to making positive claims about society. Having said this, positive claims only take us so far. Indeed the reason many of us engage in economic analysis is not only to understand the world, but to try to make it a better place. So normative analysis is important as well. The point is that when we move from positive to normative we introduce ethical and moral opinions. Traditionally economists were also moral philosophers, and we shouldn't shy away from ethical questions. The key point is that economists have no specialist claims when it comes to moral questions. Therefore our main function is to provide the positive analysis that helps to inform other people's moral decisions. Indeed we need to be really careful about calling things 'good' or 'bad'. The limits of economics are that we cannot make such judgements. But what we can do is point out a logical framework that – when combined with other disciplines – helps us to do so.

The danger is that economists slip in their normative analysis (i.e. their opinions) under the gravitas of their expertise.[13]

To get around this problem, the role of economist in public policy discussion, and the role of managerial economist when consulting, is to leave their own ethical opinions at the door. Instead, they should(!) engage in positive analysis that takes the policy goals of the policy maker or manager as given. In other words, it is not for the economist to say that minimum wages are good or bad. But we can tell you what the effects might be and leave it for you to decide if this is consistent with your goals. Therefore before we can even ask 'who made the bad decision?' we need to be clear about who is deeming it to be 'bad'. You? Or the person that makes the decision?[14]

What I mean by 'managerial individualism' is the idea that all corporate phenomena emerge from the actions and interactions of individual employees who are making choices in response to expected additional costs and benefits, *as they perceive them*. This last point is critical, because incentives are not an objective fact but a subjective interpretation.[15] We act when the *expected* marginal benefits exceed the *expected* marginal costs. One of the biggest misconceptions about economists is that when we talk about 'costs' and 'benefits' we're referring to a monetary value. But there is nothing financial about saying people respond to incentives.

A famous example is the idea that when you pay people to donate blood (as opposed to relying on voluntary donations) people donate less.[16] This seems to be a serious blow to the economist's claim that 'incentives matter'. But the mechanism is that financial rewards interfere with the positive feeling that comes from believing that you are doing a good deed. In which case the problem isn't that incentives don't matter, it's that the *type* of incentive matters a lot. Plenty of evidence suggests that offering money for the completion of tasks can reduce performance. Not only because it reduces intrinsic motivations, but also because it can encourage free riding,[17] cause people to choke under pressure,[18] or even because workers don't believe it is credible.[19] I remember once being told about a 'generous incentive package' but the conditions under which it applied were completely out of touch with my realistic targets. I lost confidence in my manager, and my performance fell.

Few of us are primarily motivated by money. The reason economists have a tendency to focus on money is simply because we are all motivated by it to *some* extent. Imagine offering your employees that reach specific targets a choice between the following 'rewards'

- Time off
- Social recognition and praise
- Cash
- Promotion/higher status

We don't need to claim that everyone would prefer cash. It's quite possible that some people will be more motivated by other items on the list (and indeed my own impression is that time off is the best motivational device of all). The job of a manager is to understand what motivates your employees, and chucking a £5 note at them is probably less appreciated than positive and constructive feedback. But it is difficult to know what truly motivates people, and the fact people are motivated by different things makes this even harder. In terms of incentives, money is indeed a lowest common denominator, but that's exactly why it is so useful.

The rest of this chapter focuses on consumer theory. When we wish to understand public policy, the decision maker is the politician. To understand management, the decision marker is the manager. To understand consumer theory, we need to focus on the consumer.

The consumer is central to economic analysis, because of consumer sovereignty. This is sometimes referred to 'consumer is king', which might be a useful phrase for salespeople but is meaningless jargon. It implies that firms should bend over backwards to satisfy the whims of their customers, and if you believe that a market economy will deliver this then you'll be disappointed. What consumer sovereignty means is that in a market economy, it is consumers who, as a group, decide upon how resources are managed. The 'economic problem' is deciding what is to be produced, how it will be produced and who it will be produced for. In a centrally planned economy it is state bureaucrats who decide. In a market economy it is consumers.

1.2 DEMAND CURVES

The starting point of economic analysis is that people place different valuations on the same things. Although this seems fairly obvious, it's a relatively new insight. For economists prior to the late nineteenth century 'value' was an inherent property of a good – it was something that could be determined independently of the person doing the 'determining'. Indeed even now when you ask people what drives 'value' you will notice that they fall back on old myths. One is that value stems from labour, the other is that it stems from scarcity. A simple counter example can destroy each of them.

Myth 1: Value stems from labour hours

It may seem churlish for me to demolish the foundation of pre-twentieth century economic thought (and indeed drive a stake through the heart of Marxism) with a single paragraph, but the amount of labour hours put into the production of goods and services does not determine their final value. Whether I've spent 3 months of hard toil crafting this chapter or rattled it up over a few cans of Natty Ice has no bearing on whether it is of value to you.

This may seem odd, because it's common in many industries for the price of something to reflect the amount of time it took to make. For example I pay my accountant based on how long it takes to prepare my tax return. But this is only because I'm using time as a proxy for his cost. And this is independent of the value being created. I'm only willing to pay him for his time because I deem the value he creates to be worth more. There is evidence that more firms are trying to look at value directly. In April 2009 Coca-Cola announced that they would start paying the advertising agents they hire based on specific results achieved rather than hours worked. This is known as 'value-based' compensation, and Proctor and Gamble are another large firm to move away from paying based on labour hours and towards paying based on performance.[20] When we focus on value it is output that matters, not inputs.

Myth 2: Value stems from scarcity

The notion that value stems from scarcity is both totally wrong and obviously correct. It is wrong in the sense that we only value things that serve a purpose. Counter examples help to explain this. Brain tumours are (thankfully) quite rare. They are scarce. But that doesn't make them highly valuable. It is true that scarcity can influence the *price* of a good, but that is because it affects the costs (and therefore the supply curve). But this chapter is referring to *value* – the demand curve. Indeed by definition any economic good is a scarce good. It is obviously correct that for a good to be valuable it must be scarce, but that's only because if it wasn't scarce it wouldn't be an economic good. Air isn't scarce, therefore it isn't a good. Scarcity is a necessary but not sufficient condition to determine something's value. In economics it's a fact of life. It's taken as a given. To explain the source of value we need to look elsewhere.

So if labour hours and scarcity don't explain value, what does? *Value is subjective and stems from the alleviation of pressing needs.* As long as we accept that we live in a world of scarcity, all economic decisions involve tradeoffs. The term 'need' is therefore a little misleading. We have a long list of pressing needs and there's always going to be a point at which you'd switch to satisfying other ones. For example we tend to think that basic human needs include shelter, or indeed electricity. But we only 'need' electricity in an abstract sense. If we 'needed' electricity we wouldn't see people reducing their usage when the cost increases. In every economic decision, we exercise choice. If electricity becomes more expensive we conserve more (for example by switching off lights when not in use), or use alternatives (which could be as simple as an extra layer of clothing). Everyone, no matter how poor, will be willing to give up *some* of one good if they're offered *enough* of other goods. Even in extreme situations people engage in tradeoffs based on their own interpretation of what constitutes their interests. You and I may rank food as being a basic need that we cannot do without. But across the world there are people going hungry because they have prioritised other needs. There's no universal hierarchy of needs that we all subscribe to. Life is about tradeoffs, not absolutisms. We have an infinite list of pressing needs, but only finite means with which to satisfy them. Therefore we rank-order our preferences and apply successive units of our budget to acquire the less and less urgent desires. Because we live in a world of scarcity, we satisfy our most pressing needs first.

So it is the alleviation of pressing needs that we 'value', not the 'commodities' themselves. This is what we mean by subjective, as opposed to objective, value. 'Goods' are simply the things that alleviate our pressing needs, and there is nothing inherently valuable about them. Indeed the distinction between tangible products and intangible services is somewhat false, because the *only* thing we value is the service of satisfying our pressing needs. As Steven Horwitz says, 'physical goods are only means to the fulfilling of various subjectively valued ends, so a good does not need to provide physically observable services to be valuable.'[21] Or, as James Bryant Quinn put it so succinctly,

Products are a happy way of capturing services.[22]

The lesson for management is to lead on benefits (i.e. how a product helps to satisfy the customer's pressing needs) rather than features (i.e. a description of the physical product). The value of the product derives from the service being provided, not the product itself.

It's important to see that this isn't economists imposing their value system on others, it's economists arguing that we all have our own personal value system and that economics helps to draw them together. Economists are essentially blasé about what something is worth. As Publilius Syrus, put it in the first century BC 'a thing is worth whatever a buyer will pay for it'. End of discussion! Those lengthy arguments in the pub about whether Fernando Torres is worth £50m are resolved by the economist's glib yet correct answer that if someone is willing to pay that much, he apparently is. We can disagree on whether *we* think he's worth that, but economics allows us to transcend arguments about personal taste to reflect those tastes in a non-arbitrary manner. The fact someone was willing to pay £50m tells us something useful.

The first law of demand states that price and quantity demanded are inversely related. This is because as the consumption of a good increases, the satisfaction derived from consuming more of the good (per unit of time) will eventually decline. The technical term for this phenomenon is the law of diminishing marginal utility (DMU). The term 'utility' just means our subjectively determined benefits. The greater the quantity of the good we consume, the greater we expect our *total* utility to be. But additional units can only be put to less valuable uses, so *marginal* utility must fall. We can use pizza as an example. Over a particular range the more slices of pizza we eat the happier we feel. As the quantity consumed rises so does total utility. But the first slice tastes better than the second. And the third slice brings even less pleasure. Marginal utility declines. The term 'satiation' refers to the point at which marginal utility becomes zero, and total utility stops increasing. If you consume more than this point marginal utility is negative, and you become less and less happy. The common term for this is 'vomiting'. When marginal utility becomes negative you would be willing to pay money *not* to consume additional units. Pizza is no longer a good, it becomes a 'bad'. DMU is a simple, but powerful concept. It states that the more you have of something, the less you value additional units. The rate of DMU will be different for different goods, and we would expect DMU to be more pronounced for perishable or sickly goods. Since you can store toilet roll you would probably be willing to pay a similar amount of money for a sixth roll as for the first. Therefore non-perishable (i.e. durable) goods tend to have a low rate of DMU. Conversely, I once bought a roast chicken from a supermarket at 8pm and was offered a second one for just 50p. But even though I had paid £5 for the first one another wasn't much use to me. The man behind the deli counter thought it was a bargain. I thought it was worthless. MU diminished rapidly.

Similarly, you might be willing to treat yourself and pay £10 for a slice of rich chocolate torte in a fancy restaurant, but are unlikely to want to pay the same amount for another one.

Ultimately our consumption choices are all relative – they depend on a relative comparison between the marginal utility and the price. More formally, consumers maximise their total utility when the final dollar spent on every good purchased provides the same marginal utility per dollar spent.[23] In other words, if we're choosing between beer and pizza and a beer costs twice as much, we'd purchase both items such that the marginal utility of the last beer is exactly twice as high as the marginal utility of the last slice of pizza. This is an equilibrium condition, because if it doesn't hold there's an incentive to change behaviour. For example, if the price of pizza rises for some reason then the ratio of marginal utility of pizza to the price of pizza will be lower than the ratio of marginal utility of beer to the price of beer. This means that you're gaining more marginal utility per pound spent from beer, implying that you should reallocate some of your budget from pizza to beer. If you do so, and your consumption of beer increases, the marginal utility will fall. Ultimately you will keep drinking until the two ratios are equal once more.

The concept of marginal value was a breakthrough in economic thought because it solved a perennial mystery: why are people willing to pay more for diamonds than they are for water? As Adam Smith himself put it,

> *Nothing is more useful than water; but it will purchase scarce anything ... A diamond, on the contrary, has scarce any value in use; but a very great quantity of other goods may frequently be had in exchange for it.*[24]

We've mentioned already that value stems from the ability to satisfy our pressing needs. We all recognise that water is essential for life and that by contrast diamonds are largely decorative.[25] Surely survival is a more pressing need than a nice piece of jewellery? And yet people save up for months to buy an engagement ring. It's tempting to explain this paradox by saying that diamonds are scarcer, but scarcity isn't enough. Lots of things are 'scarce' but if they don't fulfil our needs they're not valuable. The solution lies in the fact that we always act on the margin. In other words we're never asked to choose between 'water' and 'diamonds'. Rather, we choose been *additional* units of water and *additional* units of diamonds. We don't buy the concept of diamonds, we buy some amount more than we currently own. Therefore the value we place on goods comes from the needs that are satisfied by additional units. Because most of us consume a lot of water, *additional* units of water would only be put to satisfy minor needs. By contrast most people don't have many diamonds at all, so additional diamonds are highly sought after. There are diminishing marginal returns to both, but at any moment in time we're higher up the scale when it comes to diamonds. Our willingness to pay is based on marginal value, and not some intrinsic property contained within the good.

Economics textbooks tend to define the demand curve as the relationship between price and quantity – i.e. that as the price of a good falls we wish to purchase, have, use or consume more of it. This is true. But the underlying reason that demand curves slope downwards is because the more we have of a good the less we value additional units.

The fact that demand curves slope downwards helps to explain the concept of **consumer surplus**. This is defined as the difference between what you *do* pay for a good or service (i.e. the price) and the maximum that you would have been *willing* to pay. It makes sense to say that we'd only ever buy something if it's worth more to us than the price we pay, but this has a nice outcome that is worth dwelling on. Every purchase that we make delivers consumer surplus.

When I paid £380,000 for my house it seemed like an awful lot of money, and I was pretty certain that the person who sold it would have accepted quite a bit less. But I also knew that I would have happily paid over £400,000. That difference constitutes my consumer surplus. In one famous example people were asked how much access to the internet was worth to them.[26] When you think about it, so much of our utility comes from consumer surplus. People often criticise companies that charge prices that are higher than the cost of production (i.e. for making 'excessive' profits), but the other side of the coin is that consumers are *always* paying a price less than they value the good ('excessive' utility?).

One of the most common complaints about demand curves is that they oversimplify reality, but this is actually their primary strength. It's important here to underline the fact that demand curves *only* show the relationship between price and quantity. If any other variable changes, the demand curve will *shift*. In reality, of course, such change is ubiquitous. But that doesn't make demand curves irrelevant; it just means we have to be careful how much we can attribute to them.

The language we tend to use is that changes in price will affect *quantity demanded* (i.e. a movement along a demand curve). Changes in any variable other than price will affect *demand* (i.e. cause a shift in the entire demand curve). Examples of non-price factors that will cause a demand curve to shift include:

- Income
- The price of related goods
- The number of consumers
- Expectations about future price movements
- Changes in preferences.

If any of the above changes, our original demand curve becomes outdated.

We can split a price change into two underlying effects – if the price of a good falls there are two reasons why we'd consume more:

- Substitution effect – we can switch consumption from other goods

    If the price of a good falls it becomes cheaper relative to other goods, therefore we consume more of it (we substitute or 'switch' from the relatively expensive to the relatively cheap). This demonstrates why relative prices matter.
- Income effect – we can afford more

    If the price of a good falls our real income rises (we now have more income available for consumption) and so we can afford to consume more. Note that unlike the substitution effect (which is always negative) the income effect is ambiguous. More income may mean we wish to consume more of a good, but it may mean we wish to consume less.

A decent microeconomics course will make it clear that the first law of demand doesn't imply that people *always* respond to price changes, just that there is a *possible* price change that *will* create a change in behaviour. This helps us to deal with some common (but misguided) criticisms of the first law of demand.

1. Is there a little whore in all of us?

    Many people are uncomfortable with the implication that *everything* has a price. When Kerry Packer was bidding for the voting rights to screen ICC Cricket, he famously said 'There's a little bit of the whore in all of us, gentlemen. What's your price?'[27] I do think that this is a valid assumption to make about human behaviour, and the problem isn't that it's *inaccurate*, it's that it is *regrettable*. Non-economists might accept that in practice people do respond to incentives, but such incentives elicit socially harmful outcomes. I don't see it this way, because the assumption is simply saying that *people will be at the table* and since this will always expand the menu of choices, it's an improvement (or what economists refer to as a **Pareto Gain**). It just means that we're all influenced by price to some degree. If someone inherits their mother's house, they might claim that it has infinite value to them. The self-interest assumption says that there is a price at which they'd sell it. Why? Because the consumer has many competing preferences, and in a world of scarcity we make tradeoffs. Hence selling the house – at the right price – might make enough money to pay for the kids to go to university. Suddenly it's not a choice between mum's old house vs. not mum's old house; it's the house vs. an education. Regardless of whether it's sold or not (quite possibly its value is so very high there isn't an amount of alternative goods that can bid it away), surely it's selfish *not* to consider selling? If there's the slightest shred of altruism within your own preferences, there *must* be a possible price that would get you to sell. All economists are saying is that people will come to the table: nothing is off limits, we're all open to negotiation. And therefore this is welfare-enhancing, by expanding our menu of choice.

2. Luxury goods

A common response is that if prices signal quality, a luxury brand would fear that a reduction in price would signal a reduction in quality and therefore create a *fall* in quantity demanded. This seems intuitively plausible, but does it undermine the first law of demand? No, because it confuses a change in *demand* with a change in *quantity demanded*. If a company drastically alters its reputation, it's created a different product. The first law of demand (as represented on a demand curve) applies to the relationship between price and quantity demanded, for a given product. Therefore any other events (any non-price events) are exogenous and represent a shift in the curve. It may be true that Skoda has raised the price of their cars since the 1990s and more people have bought them. But both of these stem from a *shift* in the demand curve, and not a movement along it. It's possible that the quality of a Skoda has remained constant throughout (but it's worth considering whether this is likely, and if not why not) and the rise in demand is *purely* due to a price hike and its corresponding quality signal. But this is an abstract point and rests on an assumption that price is used as an accurate indication of quality. If the consumer *knows* the quality of the product, there's no reason why a rise in price would lead to a rise in quantity demanded. For any given Skoda, if the price rises you're less likely to wish to buy one. For Skoda cars as a whole, an increase in price *might* alter the type of product it is, if consumers don't know the quality. But this simply means that *tastes have changed*, and therefore the curve has shifted. 'Luxury goods' behave the same way as any other.

It is also worth recognising that although consumers may believe that high prices signal high quality, the opposite may also hold. Restaurants that have lower prices may generate large queues, which signals high quality to potential customers. In addition, Tyler Cowen suggests a link between the cheapness of ethnic food and the quality. He argues that in many neighbourhoods the immigrant population are more likely to frequent cheap restaurants, and this requires them to be authentic. If you want high quality Chinese food you want to find a restaurant were local Chinese people eat.[28]

3. Giffen goods

A 'Giffen good' is, by definition, a good where the income effect dominates the substitution effect. In other words it constitutes so much of your shopping basket that price changes have a massive effect on your real income. So if it's highly 'inferior' (i.e. demand falls as income rises) a fall in price can induce a *rise* in quantity demanded. But again changes in real income mean that the demand curve has shifted. And if it shifts, the self-interest assumption hasn't been violated. This provides the theoretical support for the empirical fact that Giffen goods are so hard to find.[29]

So all three of these theoretical objections to the law of demand fail to hold, and I think there are three reasons why people assert them:

1. Forgetting the 'ceteris paribus' condition

This is a Latin term that roughly means 'all else equal'. The real world is complex with many changes occurring at the same time. When we make a theoretical statement such as 'if price falls quantity demanded will rise' it rests on a number of assumptions – and the point of this chapter is to explain what they are. But perhaps the biggest assumption is that this is the only effect we are considering. In the real world many other events will coincide with a price cut. There may be a recession, a competitor could cut their prices, a hurricane could destroy your supply chain in the night. The term 'ceteris paribus' is simply a quick way of saying 'assuming that there's no recession, competitors' prices remain unchanged, there's no adverse weather conditions, etc.'. You may think that this severely weakens the applicability of a theoretical statement, and that's true. Economics cannot make perfect predictions. But it does mean that you have to be very careful about using real events to 'prove' or 'disprove' economic theory. We cannot say that quantity demanded will always go up after a price cut. But we can say that it will be higher than it would have been without one. Ceteris paribus.

2. A misunderstanding of the nature of theory

A theoretical premise is not refutable by evidence – it can only be refuted by better theory. Therefore if we define a normal good as one where demand rises if income rises, and then label coffee a normal good, evidence (hypothetical or otherwise) that a rise in income leads to a *fall* in demand for coffee is irrelevant. In that case, coffee isn't a normal good. It doesn't mean that normal goods don't exist. Consider the three primary colours of red, blue and yellow. In real life we never see these three colours on their own, since we're always viewing some combination of them. Evidence of a green object doesn't mean that blue and yellow don't exist; it just means they're not always observable and fixed.

3. Confusion between prices and revenues

A firm isn't interested in charging as high a price as possible – revenues are what matter. A simple monopolist's cost structure will show that even if she had enough market power to triple her price, this would lead to an increase in costs and probably *reduce* profits. Therefore it's wrong to apply the laws of demand to firm behaviour, because the laws of demand focus on how consumers respond to prices. However firms don't care about *prices,* only *revenue* (and how revenue and cost correspond to generate profit). In fact, it's likely that a monopolist would increase profit by *lowering* prices (depending on the elasticity of the demand curves).

1.3   ELASTICITY

DMU tells us that demand curves will *always* slope downwards. But even though all demand curves slope downwards, they will do so to different degrees. The **elasticity** of an economic variable refers to its *responsiveness* to changes. Therefore the price elasticity refers to the response of quantity demanded to changes in price, and reflects the slope of the demand curve. There are several ways to calculate the price elasticity of demand, but generally speaking we can divide the percentage change in quantity demanded by the percentage change in price. This will give us a negative number (due to the first law of demand) and reflect the extent of the responsiveness. If the elasticity is greater than 1 (i.e. changes in price lead to an even bigger change in quantity demanded) we can label it an 'elastic' good. If the elasticity is between 0 and 1 (i.e. the change in price is proportionally bigger than the resulting change in quantity demanded) then it is 'inelastic'.

For example, if Honda raised the price of a CR-V by 10% there would probably be a large fall in quantity demanded as people switched to similar cars from other companies. Let's imagine they sell 20% fewer cars as a result. In this case we can say that the price elasticity of demand is −2. If all SUV manufacturers raised their prices, we'd expect a less pronounced impact on demand. Maybe it would only fall by 5%. In which case we could say that the SUV market as a whole has a price elasticity of −0.5. The slope of the demand curve is only an indicator of the elasticity, and different sections of the demand curve will have different slopes. But generally speaking:

- An elastic demand curve is very flat (small changes in price lead to large changes in quantity demanded)
- An inelastic demand curve will be very steep (even a large change in price has a small effect on quantity demanded).

Many factors will influence the price elasticity, but we can list some of the main ones:

1. Substitutes

    The reason we'd expect the demand for Honda CR-Vs to be reasonably price elastic is because it's a competitive market with plenty of close substitutes. This means it's relatively easy for the substitution effect to kick in. But we can make two important points about substitutes. Firstly, *substitutes are subjectively determined.* In the same way that value is subjective, what constitutes a substitute is too. If I have fond memories of a previous Honda that I owned I will be less sensitive to price changes than someone who has never driven one before. In the example above I then talked about the entire SUV market. But maybe you would be happy with a large saloon instead. Whilst substitutes are subjectively determined, they are also *degrees of substitutability.* We can put these into four categories. Think of them as having the product at the core of expanding concentric circles, with broader and broader degrees of substitutability.

    - Product form – are goods that have the same features (i.e. they 'look' the same). In our example this might be different Honda dealers, or possibly Ford Kas, Toyota Rav 4s or a VW Tiguan.
    - Product category – these only have similar features and could even be thought of as the entire industry. We might add Volvo XC60s, Audi Q5 or Mercedes M class.

- Generic – are goods that fulfil the same customer needs, and are to be interpreted more broadly. To some extent other modes of transport can be considered a substitute for buying a car
- Budget – this reflects the fact that all goods and services are competing for the consumer's income.

2. Share of total budget

If your spending on a certain good constitutes a small part of your budget, you're unlikely to care much about price changes. Things like matches, toothpicks or salt are items we spend very little on over the course of a year, and even if the price doubled you might not even notice.

3. Search costs

The greater the hassle of finding alternatives the less responsive your demand will be to price changes. The internet has made searching far cheaper than previously and makes it easier to compare prices from different sellers. This makes demand more responsive to price changes

This all sounds quite abstract and we need to look at some direct managerial implications. The problem is that it's very hard in the real world to calculate the price elasticity of goods that you sell. But this makes it all the more important to develop an intuitive understanding of the factors that influence elasticity. The reason for this is because elasticity will determine the effect that a change in price has on total revenue. Total revenue is simply price multiplied by quantity. And we know from the first law of demand that there's an inverse relationship between the two. So if you lower prices, then you should expect to sell more. But there are two outcomes here. On the one hand you will be receiving less money per unit sold. But on the other hand you'll sell more units. It is the elasticity that will tell us which effect dominates.

If the good is elastic, then demand is highly responsive to changes in price. Therefore the additional units sold compensate for the fact that you're selling them at a lower price. Total revenue will go up. But if prices are increased, the opposite effect occurs and total revenue falls. Do not raise prices for elastic products!

If the good is inelastic, then demand is going to be less responsive. In this case a price cut will not lead to a large increase in sales and so total revenue falls. For inelastic goods you generally want to raise prices, because the additional revenue per item offsets the small fall in quantity demanded. An understanding of elasticity is crucial for any basic pricing strategy.

The **2nd law of demand** is that elasticity increases over time. We can demonstrate this by considering what happens when fuel prices rise. In the short term there may not be a massive effect, because it will be quite inelastic. But remember that we demand petrol to satisfy our pressing needs, and some of these needs will be more pressing than others. If petrol becomes more expensive we stop satisfying the least pressing needs first. Maybe you cut down on unnecessary journeys and improve your energy efficiency by taking the golf clubs out of the boot, driving at 55mph, or only going to the supermarket once a week. The more time that passes the easier it is to find substitutes. You start getting the train to work, or get taxis when you need to go to the airport. Over the medium term if fuel prices remain high you will consider buying a more fuel-efficient car. You wouldn't go out and buy a new car as soon as fuel prices went up, but higher fuel prices could mean that fuel efficiency is something you consider when you do come round to replacing it. If more time elapses we might expect more permanent solutions. You may start working from home more, or move house to reduce your commute. The bottom line is that substitutes are everywhere, but can be costly to find (after all there's a reason you've chosen to use a car in the first place). If the price of a good rises then consumers will reduce their consumption by a larger amount in the long run than in the short run. This is because the more time you have to deal with a price change, the easier it is to adapt (and therefore the less costly it is). Elasticity increases over time. And indeed rising fuel prices are market signals to encourage people to make this steady transition away from fossil fuels.

Changes in price are not the only thing that will influence demand. Indeed there's an 'elasticity' for any variable that influences a consumer's marginal value. We can look at two of the main ones:

- Income elasticity

    This is the responsiveness of demand to changes in income, and is calculated by the percentage change in quantity demanded divided by the percentage change in income. Intuitively you may think that the more income you have, the greater your demand will be. And for many goods this is the case. There would be a positive income elasticity, and we call them 'normal' goods. (If the income elasticity is greater than 1 we tend to call them 'superior'.) But think about low quality products that have obvious, higher standard alternatives. For example you may buy reasonably cheap cuts of meat, or low quality wine. But if your income rises you may decide to switch to rump steak and champagne. For some goods you'll therefore consume *less* if your income rises. In this case the income elasticity would be negative, and we label these goods as 'inferior'.

    Things like new cars, private education, donations to environmental goods and swimming pools are all highly income elastic. As income rises the demand for these goods expands even more rapidly and therefore spending on them rises as a proportion of income.

    A really important implication of this is that recessions are not necessarily bad for business. This is because falling incomes will only lead to falling demand if the good is a normal one. If the good is inferior (i.e. the cheap cuts of meat or the cheap wine) demand will rise.

- Cross price elasticity

    This is the responsiveness of demand to changes in price of an alternative good, and is calculated by dividing the percentage change in the quantity demanded of one good with the percentage change of price of another good. If the cross price elasticity is positive it means that when the price of good X goes up, the demand for good Y will. This implies that the two goods are **substitutes**. We've discussed previously how consumers can respond to price changes by switching to an alternative, and here's how we determine the substitution effect. Substitutes are two goods that provide a similar function. Typical examples include hamburgers and tacos; Coke and Pepsi; butter and margarine; ball point pen and felt tip pen. If the price of the former goes up, we'd expect people to switch to the latter.

    However not all goods act as alternatives to each other. Some goods need to be used with another product. If the cross price elasticity is negative it means that if the price of Y goes up the demand for X will fall. This is because fewer people will demand Y and therefore fewer people will demand X. We call such goods **complements**, and define them as goods that are consumed jointly. Typical examples include burgers and fries; hats and gloves; window frames and glass panels; cars and petrol. If the price of the former goes up, we'd expect people to buy less of both. Companies don't have to make money across all product lines – they can give away things for free if they encourage the purchase of complementary goods.

My local Honda dealer does not understand the difference between substitutes and complements. Within a year of buying a new CR-V they sent me details of special offers on an even newer CR-V. But to me they are close substitutes. The fact that I'd already bought one did not mean I would be interested in another. In fact, it took me three years to find a plastic cargo liner that would fit perfectly into the boot. Since this is a complement to a CR-V, this is the type of product the dealer should have been attempting to sell me.

The Alchian-Allen effect (also known as the **third law of demand**) claims that if you add a per unit levy to the prices of two substitute goods, the relative consumption of the higher priced good will rise. This can be directly applied to travel expenses. Imagine that the price of a standard train ticket from London to Liverpool is £40, whilst a first class ticket is £60. One way of viewing this is that the first class ticket is 1.5 times as expensive as travelling on standard. Now, imagine that the travel agent that makes the booking charges a flat rate of £10 per booking. The standard ticket is now £50, and first class is £70. The relative price of the first class ticket has now *fallen* to 1.4 times standard. First class travel has become relatively cheaper. Ceteris paribus, we would expect a shift from standard to first class.[30]

Consider Table 1.1, which shows a number of different goods down the middle column. We can add substitutes on the left hand side and complements on the right. The fact that you may disagree with some of these demonstrates that preferences are subjective.

Just because we've introduced some technical terms, and formulas, do not start to think that our object of study has become more objective. The extent to which goods are complements or substitutes still depends on our subjective judgement about their ability to satisfy the same pressing needs. Some people express a strong preference for Coke over Pepsi and vice versa. We can have a legitimate disagreement about whether they're 'the same'. We might use data relating to actual purchases and calculate a cross price elasticity, but this stems from the subjective judgement of consumers and is not an inherent property of the good. Today we may consider olives and hummus to be complements, because there can be no great dinner party without them. Tomorrow we may decide that we only need one or the other. Diversity of opinion is what makes markets tick.

We will finish this chapter by stating four postulates that will hold for the rest of the book. We have derived them sequentially, and they logically follow from each other. They sound obvious, but the trick of applying economics to complex situations is retaining a clear understanding of the logic of microeconomics.

1. People have preferences
2. More of a good is preferred to less
3. People are willing to substitute one good for another
4. Marginal value falls as you consume more.

TABLE 1.1 Cross price elasticity spectrum

Substitute	Good	Complement
Blu Ray player	DVD player	Television
Pepsi	Coca Cola	Hot dog
Olives	Hummus	Pitta bread
Water	Wine	Water

NOTES

1. Keynes, J.M. (1922) Introduction to the Cambridge Economic Handbook Series in Robertson, D.H., *Money*, Cambridge University Press.
2. The Israeli day care experiment was published as Gneezy, U. and Rustichini, A. (2000) A Fine is a Price, *The Journal of Legal Studies*, **29** (1), 1–17.
3. See Froeb, L.M. and McCann, B.T. (2008) *Managerial Economics*, Thomson South Western (2nd edition), p. viii. At the time of writing the most recent edition of the book is Froeb, L.M., McCann, B.T., Ward, M.R. and Shor, M. (2013) *Managerial Economics*, Thomson South Western (3rd edition).
4. For more detail on the concept of methodological individualism (with references) see Evans, A.J. (2010) Only Individuals Choose, in Boettke, P.J. (ed.) *Handbook on Contemporary Austrian Economics*, Edward Elgar.
5. Elster, J. (1982) Marxism, Functionalism and Game Theory, *Theory and Society*, **11**, 453.
6. Commons, J.R. (1931) Institutional Economics, *American Economic Review*, **21**, 648–657.
7. This is known as the Peltzman effect, which 'arises when people adjust their behavior to a regulation in ways that counteract the intended effect of the regulation'. Peltzman, S. (2004) Regulation and the Natural Progress of Opulence, *American Enterprise Institute*, vii. [http://www.aei.org/files/2005/05/16/files/2005/05/16/Peltzman-Lecture.pdf, accessed 24 September 2013].

   Another interesting application is bicycle helmets. According to UCL Professor John Adams mandatory helmets have three negative unintended consequences: (i) they encourage cyclists to take more risks; (ii) they encourage motorists to drive closer to them; (iii) they discourage cycling. In a study published by the *British Medical Journal*, Dorothy Robinson found that whilst people who wear helmets tend to have fewer injuries than non-wearers, there is no obvious relationship between enforced helmet laws and reductions in head injuries. She says,

   'The lack of obvious benefit from helmet laws may be because helmets ... are not designed for forces often encountered in ... serious crashes that cause most head injuries requiring hospital admission. Helmets may also encourage cyclists to take more risks, or motorists to take less care when they encounter cyclists.' Robinson, D.L. (2006) No clear evidence from countries that have enforced the wearing of helmets, *BMJ*, **332** (7543), 722–725.

   In the UK there were 122 cyclists killed on the roads in 2013 and it is unknown how many were wearing helmets. [See Gallagher, P. (2013) Hats on for cyclists? With deaths at a five-year high – calls for helmets to be made compulsory are getting louder. But not everyone agrees, *The Independent*, 4 August.] But even if none of them were wearing helmets, helmets are more useful at protecting the head from minor concussions, rather than life threatening ones. According to Martin Gibbs, from *British Cycling*, 'the majority of fatalities involve forces far in excess of the capabilities of helmets, such as those involving HGVs' (ibid.). I cannot find a single case where someone has died from head injuries whilst not wearing a helmet, that a helmet could have been reasonably expected to prevent. Indeed one of the common sources for a reduction in cycle accidents is a greater prevalence of cyclists, and so raising the cost and inconvenience of cycling may be generating accidents that otherwise wouldn't exist. What makes the issue all the more emotive is the campaign to make bicycle helmets mandatory for children. The risk for children is even more negligible than for adults, accounting for less than 1% of cycle deaths. [See Reported Road Casualties, Great Britain 2011, *Department for Transport* https://www.gov.uk/government/uploads/system/uploads/attachment_data/file/9280/rrcgb2011-complete.pdf, accessed 7 October 2013.] Again, there is no evidence that helmet laws have reduced deaths amongst children. But there *is* evidence that ill-fitting helmets have caused deaths amongst children via strangulation. See Byard, R.W., Cala, A., Ritchey, D. and Woodford N. (2011) Bicycle helmets and accidental asphyxia in childhood, *Medical Journal of Australia*, **194** (1), 49.
8. Some rugby players elect to wear skullcaps that provide more head protection, but I am not aware of any studies that consider whether this impacts their susceptibility to head injuries.

9. Albergotti, R. and Wang, S. (2009) Is it time to retire the football helmet? *Wall Street Journal*, 11 November [http://online.wsj.com/article/SB10001424052748704402404574527881984299454.html accessed 24 September 2013].

10. Fainaru-Wada, M. and Fainaru, S. (2013) *League of Denial: The NFL, Concussions and the Battle for Truth*, Crown Archetype.

11. In response to some of these concerns the NFL have increased the penalties for players that hit others helmet-to-helmet. But this has the potential to only shift, rather than eliminate, the risk. As Washington Redskins safety Brandon Meriweather realises, if the cost of hitting opponents high goes up, he will try to hit them low instead. But this transfers impact to the knee and increases the chance of causing damage to the anterior cruciate ligament (ACL), 'I guess I've just got to take people's knees out … You can't hit them high no more. You've just got to go low.' See Florio, M. (2013) Meriweather returns with a bang, *NBC Sports*, 28 October [http://profootballtalk.nbcsports.com/2013/10/28/meriweather-returns-with-a-bang/ accessed 17 November 2013]. Sure enough, on 8 December 2013 the Cleveland Browns safety T.J. Ward hit the knee of New England Patriot's star tight end Rob Gronkowski, resulting in a torn ACL. Like Meriweather, Ward recognised the perverse incentives that he faced, saying, 'If I would've hit him up high, there's a chance I was going to get a fine … It's kind of being caught between a rock and a hard place … When they set the rule, everyone knew what was going to happen.' See Smith, M.D. and Ward, T.J. (2013) If I hit Rob Gronkowski high, I would have been fined, *NBC Sports*, 9 December [http://profootballtalk.nbcsports.com/2013/12/09/t-j-ward-if-i-hit-rob-gronkowski-high-i-would-have-been-fined/, accessed 20 December 2013].

12. Becker, G.S. (1992) The economic way of looking at life, Nobel Lecture, [http://www.nobelprize.org/nobel_prizes/economic-sciences/laureates/1992/becker-lecture.pdf, accessed 24 September, 2013] (emphasis in original).

13. One example I like is when Nobel laureate Robert Solow explained why he was opposed to school vouchers. He said, 'It isn't for any economic reason; all the economic reasons favor school vouchers. It is because what made me an American is the United States Army and the public school system.' [See Klein, D.B. (2005) The People's Romance: Why People Love Government (as Much as They Do), *The Independent Review*, **10** (1), 5–37.] It's rare indeed for an economist to explicitly acknowledge that their wider opinions and beliefs conflict with their economic knowledge, and that they decide to follow the former. To be fair to Solow though, these are comments made during a Q&A so he wasn't attempting to influence public opinion.

14. Consider also how focusing on individuals is not about selfishness. In fact it forces you to see things from the perspective of other people.

15. I take this phrase from Alex Tabarrok paraphrasing Ludwig von Mises, see Tabarrok, A. (2011) Rewarding altruism: blood for money, *Marginal Revolution*, 7 December [http://marginalrevolution.com/marginalrevolution/2011/12/rewarding-altruism-blood-for-money.html accessed 24 September 2013].

16. The claim that people donate less blood if they get paid is typically attributed to Richard Titmuss, see 'Looking good by doing good', *The Economist*, 17 January 2009.

17. Winter, E. (2007) Incentive Reversal, The Center for the Study of Rationality and the Economics Department, The Hebrew University of Jerusalem [http://www.dklevine.com/archive/refs4843644000000000241.pdf accessed September 2013].

18. Dohmen, T.J. (2008) Do professionals choke under pressure?, *Journal of Economic Behavior & Organization*, **65** (3–4), 636–653.

19. This treatment of how bonuses backfire is inspired by the thoughts of Chris Dillow, see Dillow, C. (2011) How bonuses backfire, *Stumbling and Mumbling*, 19 September and Dillow, C. (2011) How bonuses backfire, *Stumbling and Mumbling*, 1 March.

20. See 'Clock-watchers no more', *The Economist*, 16 May 2009.

21. Horwitz, S. (1990) A subjectivist approach to the demand for money, *Journal des Economistes et des Etudes Humaines*, **1** (4), 459–471, at 461.

22. This quote is cited in Maital, S. (2011) *Executive Economics: Ten Essential Tools for Managers*, Free Press, p. 112. See Forsyth, J.E., Gupta, A., Haldar, S. and Marn, M.V. (2000) Shedding the commodity mind-set, *McKinsey Quarterly*, **4**, 79–85.
23. The claim is that 'the consumer will maximise her satisfaction (total utility) by ensuring that the last dollar spent on each commodity purchase should provide the same marginal utility per dollar spent on it' Gwartney, J.D., Stroup, R.L., Sobel, R.S. and Macpherson, D.A. (2010) *Economics: Private and Public Choice*, Cengage Learning, p. 161.
24. Smith, A. (1776 [1976]) *An Inquiry into the Nature and Causes of the Wealth of Nations*, University of Chicago Press, p. 33.
25. Diamonds do have industrial uses as well, but so too does water.
26. Would You Give Up The Internet For 1 Million Dollars? TFAS Video, *You Tube*, [http://www.youtube.com/watch?v=0FB0EhPM_M4 accessed 24 September 2013].
27. 'Kerry Packer' *The Economist*, 5 January 2006.
28. Cowen, T. (2012) *An Economist Gets Lunch*, E.P. Dutton & Co.
29. For a critique of the concept of Giffen goods see Garrison, R.W. (1985) Predictable behaviour: Comment, *American Economic Review*, **75** (3), 76–78.
30. The Alchian-Allen effect originates from Alchian, A. and Allen, W.R. (1964) *University Economics*, Belmont. Their original example concerns the consumption of grapes, and how a per unit shipping cost will shift relative consumption towards higher quality. Let's consider two bottles of wine that are both produced by Freemark Abbey Winery, in Napa Valley. There is a 2011 Edelwein Gold Riesling that sells for $75 and a 2012 Viognier for $30. The Riesling is 2.5 times more expensive than the Viognier. Imagine that you live in the UK, and that there is a $15 shipping charge per bottle. Your choice is therefore between a $90 Riesling and a $45 Viognier. The Riesling has become relatively cheaper, because it only costs 2 times the Viognier. This is the Alchian-Allen effect. Tyler Cowen and Alex Tabarrok have an important critique that specifies a number of instances where the Alchian-Allen effect is erroneously invoked [Cowen, T. and Tabarrok, A. (1995) Good grapes and bad lobsters: Applying the Alchian and Allen Theorem, *Economic Inquiry*, **33**, 253–256]. Returning to our previous example, we can conclude that British consumers will consume relatively more expensive Californian wine than Californians (because they face a lower relative price). It is tempting to try to extend this analysis and claim that British tourists that visit Napa Valley will also find the high quality wine to be relatively cheaper than locals. After all, what is the difference between shipping the wine to customers, versus shipping the customer to the wine? As Cowen and Tabarrok point out, however, the cost of travelling to Napa is not a per unit levy, but is instead an 'entry fee'. It should therefore be considered as sunk, and irrelevant to the decision of what type of wine to consume. It introduces an income effect with the relative price effect. For this reason, we need to be careful about attributing statements such as 'employees will shift consumption to higher quality goods when they are travelling on business'. Cowen and Tabarrok point out that for the Alchian-Allen effect to hold when *people* are being transported, it requires several additional assumptions. These are: (i) that they are planning high quality and low quality trips in future; and (ii) that the high quality good is positively related to a high quality trip. In which case the theorem applies to the trip as a whole, rather than the particular good.

CHAPTER 2

Cost and Choice

'Costs cannot be realised. They must remain for ever in a world of projecting, fantasising or imagining.'

—Mario Rizzo and Gerald O'Driscoll[1]

One day an expensive lawyer was visiting the offices of oil conglomerate Koch Industries, at their headquarters in Wichita, Kansas. He needed to make some photocopies and sought out a secretary and asked for directions. She offered to take care of it for him; he said he was happy to do it. But she insisted. She knew how much he was being paid, and what the value of his time was. If he spent that time doing photocopies, he was wasting resources. The lawyer couldn't argue with that logic, and gratefully handed over the stack of paper. Several weeks later he was back. He went to the same secretary and mentioned that he had more photocopying. On this occasion, however, she refused. She was in the middle of writing up an important contract and was working to a strict deadline. At that point in time, her time was more valuable. What I like about this anecdote is how a consideration of the costs of an activity is so deeply embedded within the organisation. You can only tell if you're creating value if you understand the costs of an action. The fact that costs are so often hidden is all the more reason to go searching for them.

The purpose of this chapter is to help managers to internalise the concept of opportunity cost reasoning, and to see how the cost structure of a firm and industry matters. We will look at what 'costs' are and how they shape decisions. Over the shorter term the decision facing a manager is the utilisation of a plant. The question is 'how much output should I produce, given the size of the plant?' Over the longer term the question is 'what should the size of the plant be?' The emphasis will be on the types of costs faced by managers, but it should be realised that the foundations of cost theory remain in the realm of subjective, individual choice. It is a real shame that so many textbooks give the impression that demand and supply analysis is the combination of subjective value and objective costs. The concept of cost is every bit as subjective as value. This is a theoretical point, but with direct practical applications. Rather than cut costs, we need to confront them.

2.1   OPPORTUNITY COST

The most important thing to understand about costs is how to internalise and apply the notion of opportunity cost reasoning. This is where we detach 'costs' from the accounting treatment of monetary values, and take a more philosophical approach to what costs are. Imagine that you are given a choice between three banknotes:

- £50
- £20
- £10

What is the cost of choosing the £20 note?

This isn't as simple a question as it appears. The obvious answer is '0', since I'm offering you the choice for free. If you were writing up your accounts there would be no receipt, so no cost. But it should be obvious that the *economic* cost is above zero. In the act of making a choice you are giving up an alternative course of action, and to an economist *that* is the cost of your decision. To economists a cost is an *action*, not a *price*. There are really two stages to identifying costs:

1. What is your 'next best alternative' (NBA)?
2. What is the monetary value of your NBA?

Students are often quick to try to attach numerical values to cost, but it is the NBA itself that is the cost. George Shackle referred to costs as the 'skein of imagined alternatives' precisely because we never *see* costs. By definition costs relate to actions that we don't take, and we make a best attempt to place a monetary value on them. They're hard to measure, precisely because we never actually see them.

So what is the 'cost' of choosing £20? The NBA is the £50 note and it is easy to estimate how much this is worth to us: £50.

Sometimes we need to be explicit that we are talking about opportunity costs (also known as 'hidden' costs, or 'implicit' costs) rather than accounting costs, but a good economist will always define and use 'cost' as 'the next best alternative'. And this isn't mere semantics; understanding the difference between economic and accounting costs can be a major source of competitive advantage.

One way to implement opportunity cost reasoning within an organisation is the concept of 'Economic Value Added' (EVA), a registered trademark of Stern Stewart & Company. The role of an accountant is to value assets and protect bondholders from potential bankruptcy. But what about equity holders? Joel Stern developed EVA as a student at the University of Chicago, part of a tradition in corporate finance that aimed to measure the economic value of company's activities.[2] Put simply EVA is an attempt to make the hidden cost of capital more visible, allowing managers to monitor and reward genuine value creation.

To an accountant 'profit' simply means that revenue exceeds costs. But to be *economically* profitable you need to go beyond ensuring that revenues exceed costs; you must deliver a profit that outperforms the next best alternative of the resources you utilise. The interest rate paid on government bonds is often used as a point of comparison, but most companies should be generating higher returns than this. The *weighted average cost of capital* is one benchmark that can be used.[3] The bottom line is that if a company is making less profit than it could have made doing other activities, from an economic point of view it is making a *loss* – even if accounting profits are high. As Peter Drucker said,

> *Until a business returns a profit that is greater than its cost of capital, it operates at a loss. Never mind that it pays taxes as if it had a genuine profit. The enterprise still returns less to the economy than it devours in resources. It does not cover its full costs unless the reported profit exceeds the cost of capital. Until then, it does not create wealth; it destroys it.*[4]

EVA isn't perfect and as you get lower down an organisation it can become increasingly difficult to measure economic profit. This is mainly due to shared resources and transfer pricing. But the NBA to these sorts of measures is either arbitrary guesses, or nothing. We are always groping in the dark, but EVA is a flashlight.

When economists have a book manuscript that we are trying to get published, we tend to favour agreements that keep the price of the book reasonably low. For me personally a sales price of more than £30 can be a bit daunting. But to what extent does the sales price capture the cost of reading a book? The cost of you reading these words is *not* the amount of money you paid to buy it. Forget cash. The cost is what you would be doing, if not reading this book. As Steven Horwitz says, 'the cost of the road that is taken is the foregone expected utility of the road not taken.'[5]

My obligation as an author is to generate enough value to cover *that* cost, not how much you paid out of pocket.

As you might expect, if economists view costs in a different way to accountants, then their understanding of profit will be different as well. For example, I teach on several different MBA programmes. Let's imagine that the standard rate for a day's teaching is £1000, and the client pays for the airfare, accommodation and meals. At the end of a 3-day course I will have no receipts, but will take home a cheque for £3000. The question is how much profit have I made? To an accountant, it would be £3000. But recollect that this is the market rate. If I were not teaching for this school, I would do so for another. In this case my NBA is 'lecturing for another client' and this is worth £3000. Suddenly the economic 'profit' becomes zero! The artist Albrecht Durer realised this point when he said,

> *My picture ... is well finished and finely coloured ... [but] I have got ... little profit by it. I could have easily earned 200 ducats in the time.*[6]

This finding is important. If you think about it, it's simply saying that my chosen course of action is increasing social wealth by the same as my favoured alternative. Therefore there is no *profit* signal for me to do one above the other. Socially, it doesn't matter. If something changed, and the school began paying £2000 per day, then there would be a clear market signal. The economic profit of £4500 would be alerting me to the fact that one of my options increases social wealth by *more* than the other. Now, I may not be motivated solely by money, and there may be intangible aspects of other offers that I take into consideration. I may enjoy the company of the programme management, or the local nightlife in a particular city. Indeed the next best alternative may not be lecturing elsewhere, but staying at home with my family. But 'the market' is helping me to decide what to do. Economic profit is providing a meaningful signal.

The startling implication of this is that it is pretty rare to find economic profit. This is what some economies refer to as 'pure profit opportunities', and the essence of entrepreneurship is being alert to these opportunities as they're created and/or discovered. This also explains why economists assume that in equilibrium firms make zero profit. It doesn't mean that they are struggling to survive. It just means that all factors (i.e. labour and capital) are receiving their opportunity cost. In 2011 Marissa Mayer was working at Google and earning a high salary. Let's imagine that it was around $2m per year. In anyone's book, that's a lot. But was she making a profit? In July 2012 she become the President and CEO of Yahoo! and earned almost $6m in her first year.[7] The fact that she got such a large pay rise after moving jobs suggests that she was earning less than her market rate beforehand. Despite being very wealthy, she was probably making an economic *loss*.

There's a famous saying in economics: 'there's no such thing as a free lunch'. Given that action always takes place over time, there is always an alternative course of action that you forgo. Understanding cost means that you think about what it might be. Since time is scarce, everything has a cost.

We've defined 'cost' as *the next best alternative*, but the reason this chapter is called 'Cost and Choice' is because the two are inextricably linked. In a book by that very name James Buchanan defined cost as follows:

> *[The chooser's] own evaluation of the enjoyment or utility that he anticipates having to forego as a result of selection among alternative courses of action.*[8]

2.2 DIMINISHING MARGINAL RETURNS

We are going to use a very simple model that will apply both to the output of an individual firm and the output of the economy as a whole. We can use a restaurant as an example. Let's assume that output is a function of two factors of production: capital and labour.[9] In this example 'capital' means physical capital – plant, machinery and equipment. It's reasonable to believe that over the short run these factors are fairly stable, and independent of our day-to-day changes in output. But let's consider what happens if we vary our other factor input, i.e. labour. If we measure labour in terms of hours per week,[10] it should be obvious that when labour is zero, output is zero. As the firm increases the amount of labour hired, we'd expect output to rise. Dramatically at first, because they will find ways to specialise in different tasks, and organise as a team. *Many hands make light work*. But at some point, if capital is held fixed, these gains in output will begin to decline. There are limits to how much use they can get out of their equipment. It can become more complicated to work as a team as the team size increases. *Too many cooks spoil the broth*. At some point output will peak. Beyond this point, adding more factor inputs will actually lead to a reduction in output. At the extreme, you have so many people getting in each other's way, unable to share equipment, that output may fall back to zero.

This phenomenon is known as **the law of diminishing returns**, which states that as more and more units of a variable resource (in this case labour) are combined with a fixed number of another resource (capital), then using additional units of the variable resource will eventually increase output at a *decreasing rate*. At such a point (the point of diminishing returns) it takes successively larger amounts of the variable factor to expand output by one unit. Or, to put it more simply, as you expand output marginal productivity (the extra output that you get for extra input) will eventually decline.

This law is useful to understand how real wage rates are discovered. Instead of looking at the relationship between labour and total output, we can look at the marginal impact of additional units of labour. In other words if hiring the 10th person increases total output from 200 units to 240 units, we can say that the marginal product of the 10th person is 40 units. Diminishing returns will mean that there's a point at which an additional unit means the marginal product is at its peak, and beyond that a point at which marginal product is zero. Intuitively, it must be the case that total output peaks when marginal product is zero. Once marginal product becomes negative – and each individual worker is causing a reduction in output – total output must fall. If marginal product shows each additional worker's contribution to output, we can put a value on that by multiplying it by the price of the good being sold. This figure, the 'marginal revenue product', is the market value of the work being done by that worker. That's why economists claim that in equilibrium your wage should reflect your marginal productivity.

The returns to each of the factors of production refer to the production function of an organisation – of the relationship between inputs and outputs. The concept of DMR is important because it affects your costs. If your marginal productivity is falling this means that you need more inputs to produce extra units of output. This means that the cost of producing those extra units (i.e. the marginal cost) is rising.

If the marginal cost (MC) is lower than the average cost (AC) then AC must fall. If a student's grade is below their average then it brings the average down. Diminishing returns mean that eventually marginal costs will begin to rise, so eventually average costs will.

A 'fixed cost' is a cost that is fixed with respect to changes in output. By contrast, a 'variable cost' is one that varies with respect to output. When the writer Alan Bennett offered to make a cup of coffee for Miss Shepherd (a lady who lived in a car in his garden) she said 'I don't want to put you out, just half a cup'.[11] The reason I found that funny, is because the bulk of the costs of making coffee are fixed (i.e. boiling the kettle, spooning in the coffee granules, adding sugar, adding milk, stirring). Whether you're making a half a cup, or a full cup, doesn't matter much. The variable costs are pretty low, and so her offer to reduce them is comical.

The reason why it's so important to understand the difference between the two is because some types of cost are irrelevant for decision making. Consider a company that has two different business units, one generating a profit of £5000, and another of £40 000. Let's also consider that although these figures incorporate the costs that are specific to each unit, there's a further £20 000 of corporate overhead (for example rent, general and administrative expenses, joint marketing, etc.). Overall, the business is profitable (the combined profit of £45 000 comfortably exceeds the overhead costs). Imagine that your finance director decides to deal with these overhead costs by splitting them up between each business unit, 'charging' £10 000 to each. In this situation, it would appear as if the first unit is making a loss of £5000, and the second one a genuine profit of £30 000. You might be tempted to close the first. But both units have a positive marginal contribution. It might make sense to 'assign' fixed costs for reporting purposes, but economically they are completely irrelevant. In this example, they are sunk.[12] They shouldn't cloud your judgement, and both units should be kept open.[13]

Concorde is a classic example of the 'sunk cost fallacy'. The British and French governments committed over £1bn of public money to develop the planes. Ultimately only 14 were built for passenger use and operated at a significant loss.[14] Decision makers were faced with a difficult situation – acknowledge that the project was losing money and reallocate resources to ones that generated more economic value, or continue investing in the project in the hope that it would claw back the losses. Policymakers felt that it would be a waste to retire it, but by waiting they wasted even more resources. They should have cut their losses. It was only after the 2000 Air France crash and September 11th terrorist attacks that Concorde was sent to retire in 2003.[15] A sunk cost is incurred due to an irreversible decision that turns out to be a mistake. The challenge with sunk costs is that confronting them tends to mean that you're admitting to a previous error. Perhaps this is why the sunk cost fallacy is so pervasive – it's a lot easier to buy some time in the hope that they turn out not to be a mistake after all, rather than admit to them and move on.

If we treat fixed costs as being sunk (at least in the short term), it means that we should ignore them. If a cost is sunk, it has no opportunity cost, and is therefore irrelevant to decision making. If you can't affect something, and it will occur in any scenario, it can't help you choose between scenarios. Therefore it is variable costs that should be the focus of attention, or more accurately, the relationship between revenue and variable costs. The **shut down condition** refers to the claim that a business unit should be open provided it can cover its variable costs. According to the shut down condition fixed costs are not relevant to the decision about whether to be open for business or not. Ultimately, you need to cover total costs. And if you can't, you should sell up the business or liquidate the assets. But in the short run, when you are deciding about whether to open or not, the only hurdle you need to meet is variable costs. If you expect to generate enough revenue to cover those, you're in business.

Now, imagine that you have been hired to advise a local probation service on ways to reduce costs. Everyone knows that the public sector is very costly, and a private company wishes to be given the casework. You estimate that the service needs to deal with a certain number of cases a year, and have established that the average cost for the public sector is significantly higher, across all ranges of output, than the private sector. Does that mean the private sector is the cheaper option? Not necessarily. The reason their average costs are higher is because they have higher fixed costs. Although the public sector has a higher average cost, it could well have a lower marginal cost. They can complete any given case at a lower cost, but high fixed costs (irrelevant in this instance) inflate their average cost. Economic thinking is about making decisions at the margin. Rather than ask what total costs are when spread across all output, you should focus on additional benefits and additional costs from the spot where you stand *today*. Forgetting to focus on marginal analysis increases the chance of allowing irrelevant, sunk costs affecting decisions – look forward.

Prior to low-cost carriers such as easyJet, airlines would typically fill about 70% of seats per flight. But the marginal cost of a seat is 0, and so selling any unused seat for a price higher than zero contributes to profits.[16] The implication is to do exactly what the low-cost carriers did: drastically reduce prices.

Managers should also be constantly vigilant for **transferred costs**. Economists use the term 'externalities' to refer to situations where the decision maker doesn't bear the full cost of their actions. They are inevitable, but have the potential to create cross-subsidisation. If one department is generating costs that are inflicted on others, you get a faulty signal of value creation. We all have colleagues that impose costs on others, whether it's getting someone else to book their travel arrangements, or do their photocopying. An economist's typical solution is to attempt to internalise the externality, and make decision makers bear the costs of their actions wherever possible.

The purpose of covering all this theory is to understand the supply decision of a theoretical firm. It is easier to visualise with charts and examples, but an intuitive understanding of the concepts can help make those visualisations sink in. Imagine trying to plot what happens to average costs as you expand output. There are three key points to make:

- As output increases average fixed costs will fall (you are dividing a fixed numerator by a steadily increasing denominator).
- The variable input (in our case labour) will exhibit increasing returns to scale over a certain range of output, putting downward pressure on average costs.
- But at some point diminishing returns will kick in, putting upward pressure on average costs.

What this means is that an average cost curve will always be a 'U' shape. It may be shallow, it may be steep. It may bottom out at a low level of output, or a high level. But diminishing returns will mean that it will be a 'U' shape.

We've used the concept of diminishing returns to see why marginal costs increase as output does. But we can use another concept as well. Recollect that demand curves slope downwards because as we consume more, we place a lower value on consuming additional units. This is because we put them to satisfying less and less pressing needs. Conversely, marginal cost curves slope upwards because the more we produce the greater the opportunity costs of using the inputs for any specific use. It's not just that the more labour we use, the less productive it becomes when capital is fixed. It's that the more labour we use for one production plan, the more labour is being kept from other potential uses. Marginal value curves must slope downwards. And marginal cost curves must slope upwards.

This relationship between average and marginal costs helps us to understand how firms decide the level of output they need to produce. For consumer behaviour, people act whenever the expected marginal benefit exceeds the expected marginal cost. Similarly, if firms are making decisions *at the margin*, they will be weighing up their marginal revenue (the revenue they receive from selling one extra unit) and the marginal cost. For simplicity, let's assume that marginal revenue is the same regardless of how much you sell. This is simply the market price of the good you are selling.[17] If marginal revenue exceeds marginal cost, it means you are selling the final product for more than the cost of making it. You will boost profit if you sell more. If, however, marginal revenue is lower than marginal cost, it costs you more to create the product than you can sell it for. In this case you will decide to produce less. And doing so will lead you to more profit. In equilibrium, you maximise profit when *marginal revenue equals marginal cost*.

What we've tried to do in this section is view short-term output decisions as a two-step process. Firstly, we need to consider whether we want to be open for business or not. And the shut down condition states that provided revenue covers variable costs, we open. Secondly, if we're open, we need to decide how much output to produce. And we maximise profit when marginal revenue (i.e. price) equals marginal cost. When we put these two things together, we generate something of immense importance. If the marginal cost curve is telling us our optimal output response in relation to different possible prices, we realise that we've generated a supply curve. A supply curve is the part of the marginal cost curve that is (i) positive and (ii) allows you to cover your variable costs.

2.3   THE PLANNING HORIZON

In the short run, managers are making a highly constrained choice about the optimal use of their current resources. But if we lengthen our time horizons and relax those constraints (i.e. we drop the assumption that the factors of production are fixed), the key question becomes 'how does scale impact long run costs?' The 'planning horizon' is another way of conceptualising the 'long run', and simply means that all costs are variable and therefore vary with respect to output. It doesn't mean that fixed costs don't *exist*, but that you are able to decide which fixed costs to commit to. To understand the difference, think of the year 2013 and consider the contrasting coaching styles of Arsène Wenger, of Arsenal and Rafael Benitez, of Chelsea. Benitez joined Chelsea in November 2012 following the sacking of the previous coach. He was appointed as 'interim' manager and it was publicly stated that he would only have the position on a temporary basis. Knowing that he would be leaving at the end of the season, the question he was asking was 'what is the best use of my current resources?' With little influence on player transfers, and little incentive to care about the team's medium-term development, his task was a simple one. Win trophies with the resources you are given. He promptly won the 2013 Europa League.

Arsène Wenger, by contrast, was appointed Arsenal manager in 1996. Since then he has won the Premier League three times (including going a season unbeaten), the FA Cup four times and reached the Champions League final. His ability to sign players with raw potential and then sell them for high fees once they have peaked fit with a conservative business model employed by their owners. Despite not winning a trophy for several years his position is safe and he is able to plan for the long term. The question he is asking is 'what resources do I need?' Both managers saw success with their clubs, and it was due to adopting an appropriate time horizon.

As in the short run, the long run average cost curve will be a 'U' shape. As output increases AC will initially decline, because fixed costs can be spread over more units. This is known as 'economies of scale', and we can split them into two types:

- Internal economies of scale (where average costs depend on the size of the firm):
  - Technical (e.g. the use of waste products, or the specialisation of human capital)
  - Commercial – both in terms of buying (bulk discounts) and selling (advertising costs)
  - Financial – better access to finance
  - Managerial – can spread the costs of HR, legal etc.
  - Risk bearing – can afford to invest heavily in R&D, product diversification, etc.
- External economies of scale (where average costs depend on the size of the industry):
  - Political – the impact of lobbying
  - Infrastructure – benefiting from the same transport hubs and communication networks
  - Local reputation
  - Supply of skilled labour
  - Access to raw materials/supplies
  - Knowledge spillovers – such as publicly funded research.

Big box retailers, like Staples, and out of town supermarkets have successfully reaped the rewards of economies of scale. Exclusive arrangements with suppliers mean that firms compete intensely for the ability to supply products, reducing their costs. The retailer and supplier thus share in the profit from such economies of scale. The other element of the planning horizon is **economies of scope**. This occurs when the cost of producing two goods together is less than producing them separately and is another source of advantage for larger firms.[18]

We hear about economies of scale (and to a lesser extent economies of scope) a lot and many people are concerned about the potential for efficient firms to grow indefinitely. Some argue that capitalism leads to an increasing concentration of capital – i.e. that average cost curves slope downwards over the whole range of output. And indeed this would generate behemoths. But those concerns tend to ignore one important fact. This is impossible! At some point average costs *will* begin to rise, because marginal costs will be upward sloping and diminishing returns will come to dominate. Once a firm gets to this point, it will start to exhibit 'diseconomies of scale', which are driven by the following:

- Managerial costs involved in coordination, control and monitoring
- Local knowledge
- Innovation and creativity.

These aren't hypothetical. In July 2008 *The Economist* made an incredibly prescient point about the business models of big banks, saying, 'Some think that, like Citi, AIG has become too complex for anyone to run.'[19] When I tell managers of FTSE 100 companies that scale is supposed to be a cause of efficiency they laugh in my face. The optimal scale of a firm – and indeed an industry – is determined by the shape of the average cost curve. Anti-capitalists are right that sometimes the 'optimal scale' will be big, but this isn't inevitable. It will only tend to be the case where there are high fixed costs and low managerial costs.[20] Energy companies, telecommunication firms or fast food outlets may be an example, and indeed these tend to be large (there are very few boutique oil companies). But for many other industries the diseconomies of scale kick in a lot sooner and the optimal scale will be reasonably small. High quality restaurants, plumbers and estate agents all tend to be quite modest in terms of the output produced. Indeed we also see examples of industries where the long run average total cost curve is pretty flat, such that there's no real advantage to being either big or small. Consulting, for example, tends to see very large multinational companies such as Accenture competing on a fairly even cost basis with small partnerships that specialise in a particular area. In an advert for DHL the manager of an SME complains about how difficult it is to compete with larger rivals that have more market power, whilst a manager of a large company complains about how startups are so much more agile. Both of them view logistics as their secret weapon (as you may expect) but both demonstrate that there are advantages to being large and to being small.

Another interesting example of the tension between economies and diseconomies of scale is found in knowledge-intensive companies. Pharmaceutical companies are desperately looking for researchers who will discover the next blockbuster drug, giving rise to another source of economies of scale, those that seek to reap the benefits of 'economies of ideas'. The larger the scale, the more likely you'll get lucky and have hired the right person. But working with genius has drawbacks. As *The Economist* puts it, 'talent-driven firms can be torn apart by feuds or rendered dysfunctional by egocentric behaviour.'[21]

If we want goods and services to be made as efficiently as possible, the aim should be to let firms experiment with different scales, and discover what the optimal size is.

2.4 COST VS. WASTE

One of the most common sources of complaints I hear amongst managers is that they waste their time in too many meetings. One study found that the average office worker spends around 16 hours per week in meetings, and a quarter of that time is wasted. And for civil servants it's even worse. They spend 22 hours in meetings, with one-third a waste of time.[22] This could well be because meetings are such a big source of hidden costs. Let's say you get invited to a meeting with five other people and it's scheduled to last 1 hour. The first point to make is that this is in fact a 6-hour meeting. The second point is that in most cases the cost is barely acknowledged, let alone confronted. This is because there isn't a receipt. The person that calls the meeting can do so 'for free'. But of course nothing is free, and the cost will be what those six people could otherwise have been doing. It's hard to measure what the value of their time is, but their market wage is a reasonable approximation.[23]

Managers can 'internalise' opportunity cost reasoning in this way, and constantly ask themselves 'what's the next best alternative to this course of action?' 'What am I sacrificing?' 'Is this truly the best use of my time and resources?' Koch Materials Company (KMC) had a profitable asphalt plant in Iowa and there was no reason why they would want to move. But a sales representative that understood opportunity cost noticed a newspaper article about a casino trying to find land in the area. It became clear that the casino valued that land more highly than they did, so they sold.[24]

As we saw, EVA is a technique to help opportunity cost reasoning permeate the company. If managers had to cover the cost of people's time when they called a meeting, we'd probably have fewer meetings. We'd certainly have shorter, more productive ones. The point isn't to monetise everything, but to try to make hidden costs explicit. Companies are increasingly realising that there's an opportunity cost to utilising office space. In fact some of them – such as BT – charge managers for the desk space used by their team. Let's imagine that in their present location this amounts to £8000 per desk, per year. The fact that most companies don't charge managers for their desk space does not mean that there isn't a cost. It just means that it's a hidden one. If this team weren't using those resources, another team would be able to. So how do we know which team values it the most? Perhaps many of the current team spend a lot of time working remotely. So the manager cannot justify spending £8000 per person on desk space that is rarely used. To conserve budget, she is incentivised to look for cheaper locations. Maybe another location would only 'cost' £6000 per desk. This is win-win. The manager is happy to conserve resources for more important needs. And it frees up the office space for a team that *does* value it so highly. Resources get moved from low to high value uses, once costs become visible. The fact that markets are quite crude is a source of their strength. Once costs are visible, decision making becomes significantly easier.

A simple way to implement opportunity cost reasoning is to hold meetings standing up, which tend to be substantially quicker than sit down meetings and studies suggest that decision-making quality remains the same.[25] When I had a tour of Pelisor Castle in Sinaia, Romania I was taken by the desk of King Ferdinand I. It was at chest height and didn't have a chair. Not only did he work standing up, but more importantly it meant that all of his meetings were conducted on foot. This was his attempt at encouraging brevity. Some firms hold meetings just before lunch for similar reasons.

One final point to make is that costs in and of themselves aren't bad. They are the market's way of signalling resource scarcity. Managers should constantly be searching for hidden costs, and bringing them into the light. As we've seen, economic calculation helps us to do that. But because costs result from the use of factor inputs, they need to be *optimised*, not *minimised*. In other words there's a big difference between cutting costs and eliminating waste. When I mention this to managers, they tend to argue that when they say 'cost cutting' they mean 'eliminating waste'. But it's not uncommon to see firms make cuts across the board. There's no doubt that across-the-board cuts have benefits (for example they are quite low cost). But they reveal that you don't know where the waste is taking place. And it's a manager's job to understand their business well enough to ensure that across-the-board cuts aren't necessary. On top of this they can signal a lack of leadership. Across-the-board cuts mean that you can avoid having to make a claim about where you believe the waste is. This can be deemed 'fairer', because you're treating everyone equally. But it also shows a lack of courage. Don't cut costs. Eliminate waste.

NOTES

1. O'Driscoll, G. and Rizzo, M. (1985) *The Economics of Time and Ignorance*, Routledge, p. 48.
2. Ultimately EVA derives from Alfred Marshall's concept of 'residual income' which, as we shall see, is the foundation of how we view entrepreneurship.
3. We can see the importance of opportunity cost more clearly with an example.

Business unit	Annual budget	After-tax income (NOPAT)	Economic profit
A	£100 000	£14 000	£2000
B	£200 000	£20 000	−£4000
C	£20 000	£4500	£2100

Here we have three business units with B generating the most after-tax income. If you only looked at this figure, you would believe that B is performing better than A, and C is doing poorly. However we need to recognise the opportunity cost of each unit. They each require resources, and those resources could have been employed elsewhere. Let's assume that the firm's cost of capital is 12%. In other words, they expect to generate a 12% return on the next best alternative course of action. Instead of looking at the after-tax income, we need to subtract the cost of capital. If we do so, we see that unit C is in fact generating more economic value.

Firms that take EVA seriously will have a profit and loss statement that looks something like this:

Net sales	£300 000	
Operating expenses	£100 000	
Operating profit (EBIT)		£200 000
Taxes	£50 000	
Net operating profit after tax (NOPAT)		£150 000
Capital charges (invested capital X cost of capital)	£100 000	
Economic Value Added (EVA)		£50 000

The crucial line is the capital charges that attempt to incorporate the opportunity cost of the resources used. EVA is equal to NOPAT − capital charges.

4. Drucker, P. (1995) The Information Executives Truly Need, *Harvard Business Review*, **73** (1), 54–62.

5. Horwitz, S. (1990) A subjectivist approach to the demand for money, *Journal des Economistes et des Etudes Humaines*, **1** (4), 459–471, at 464.

6. 'Portrait of the artist as an entrepreneur', *The Economist*, 17 December 2011.

7. Ellis, B., 'Marissa Mayer's first-year pay: $6 million', *CNN Money*, 1 May 2013 [http://money.cnn.com/2013/04/30/technology/marissa-mayer-pay/ accessed 17 November 2013].

8. Buchanan, J. (1969) *Cost and Choice: An enquiry in economic theory*, University of Chicago Press, p. 43.

9. In formal terms the equation for the production function is $Q = f(K_0, L)$.

10. The way in which we measure labour hours is an important point and we will return to it later. One might think that we measure labour simply by counting the number of staff. But we also need to factor in the amount of time that is worked. If a factory currently hires two people that work 10 hours per week, and hires an additional person to work 10 hours per week, then 'labour' unambiguously increases. But what about if while hiring the additional worker they cut the hours of their existing ones? Or what if they go down to just one worker, but give him a full-time (i.e. 35-hour per week) contract?

11. Bennett, A. (1999) *The Lady in the Van*, Profile Books.

12. It's not necessarily true that fixed costs are always sunk. I once had 6 months remaining on a £40 per month mobile phone contract, and treated it as a fixed cost that was sunk. But when I called the provider they agreed to switch me to a £20 a month tariff immediately. Factory space is a fixed cost, but not necessarily sunk. It's only sunk if the opportunity cost is zero, which is rare. Therefore the idea that fixed costs are irrelevant for decision making doesn't mean that they should be ignored in the real world. In many cases it is possible to realise that what you consider to be a fixed cost is in fact a variable cost.

13. To prove this, compare the profit if both are open (£25 000) with the profit if only the second one is open (£20 000).

14. 'Is this the end of the Concorde dream?', *Daily Telegraph*, 16 August 2000.

15. I believe this is the conventional account of Concorde, but it may not stand up to scrutiny. One could argue that BA and Air France *were* ignoring the sunk costs, and continuing to operate because it was profitable at the margin. The fact that Airbus decided not to continue maintenance may support this. Indeed if Richard Branson's attempts to buy and run BA's fleet were genuine, this could mean it was a political, not an economic decision to shut it down.

16. Having said this, if the airline is attempting to minimise the amount of fuel it carries, an additional passenger may represent a large marginal cost because it requires them to recalculate how much fuel to buy. This is why airlines may offer cheaper fares for advanced bookings (because it helps them to forecast passenger numbers), rather than for last minute ones.

17. In other words we assume that the market is perfectly competitive, and the firm has no ability to influence the market price. This is reasonable if it's a small firm, operating in a highly competitive market. We will relax this assumption when we look at competition theory.

18. More formally, Cost (Q1+Q2) < Cost (Q1) + Cost (Q2). Froeb, L.M. and McCann, B.T. (2008) *Managerial Economics*, Cengage learning (1st edition), p. 91.

19. 'Enter the quiet giant', *The Economist*, 19 June 2008.

20. Chapter 5 will consider the social costs of 'natural monopolies' which occur when the optimal size of a single firm coincides with the demand curve for the industry as a whole.

21. 'Of businessmen and ballerinas', *The Economist*, 9 February 2013.

22. Burn-Callander, R. (2013) UK workers waste a year of their lives in useless meetings, *Management Today*, 18 March. The argument in favour of meetings is that if it were easy to assess the activity of employees through arm's length measures then it could be outsourced. The purpose of the firm is to deal with the fact that some activities are hard to observe and quantify the value of (see Chapter 5 of Fisman, R. and Sullivan, T. (2013) *The Org. The Underlying Logic of the Office*, Twelve Books). In this sense meetings are a crucial tool of management, 'they're watching over and coordinating the hard work the market couldn't handle' (p. 151).

This is a valid point, but is a defence of meetings generally, and doesn't mean that all meetings create value. The challenge for management is to ascertain when the information exchanged in meetings might be conveyed in more efficient ways, and when to rely on the bureaucrat's tools of memos, meetings and reports. An understanding of cost can help with this.

23. There is an iPhone application called 'Meeter' and it is a way to help create more productive meetings. At the onset, you pass it around the table and everyone enters their salary. You then press 'start' and it keeps a running count of the hidden cost of the meeting. This isn't to say that *all* meetings are a waste of time. It's just that we can't *tell* if they're a waste of time unless we know how much they cost. It's only if you know the cost of something, that you have a realistic way of knowing if the benefits are greater.

24. Koch, C.G. (2006) *The Science of Success*, John Wiley & Sons, p. 110.

25. Silverman, R.E. (2012) No more angling for the best seat; more meetings are stand up jobs, *Wall Street Journal*, 2 February.

CHAPTER 3

Market Exchange

'The market is a democratic institution aggregating the decisions of whoever participates in it. When all is said and done, complaints about the market are nothing but complaints about the people themselves.'

—Paul Piccone[1]

In 2010 there were around 7000 people in the UK who needed a kidney transplant. Given that healthy adults only require one functioning kidney, this means that the potential supply is almost 38 million.[2] And yet less than 3000 operations were performed. This shortage means that around 1 in 10 of those needing a kidney will die before they get one. For those who need any organ transplant, three people die every day. To an economist the answer is simple: have a market. For many people, the idea is repugnant. But at what cost? How many lives are you willing to sacrifice to avoid feeling icky? Maybe it isn't a coincidence that the only country in the world to have a legalised market in kidney transplants is also the only country in the world that doesn't have a shortage?

Having discussed the concepts of demand and supply, the purpose of this chapter is to see how markets can bring them together. A 'market' as an institution through which buyers and sellers meet to trade goods and services. Historically, a market would be a physical place – usually close to ports or other transport hubs. This explains why geography has played an important role in how trade routes have developed. But markets can also be a virtual place, as modern technology allows us to trade with people remotely. Newspapers, telephone lines and the internet are all examples of how communication channels drive the scope of the market, and connect consumers and producers. Economists like to study markets to see how they coordinate resources at a social level. Managerial economists do so to find ways to implement them within the firm.

3.1 MARKET EQUILIBRIUM

Let's define some key terms. We define consumption as 'the realisation of want-satisfying capabilities', which means that when our pressing needs are being satisfied, we are consuming. But although it is consumption that we value, first we must produce. We define production as 'the creation of want-satisfying capabilities'. If we produce more than we currently plan to consume, we are 'saving'. For example if I like to consume two fish per day and today I catch three, I have savings of one fish. So far, there's no need for markets. But my consumption set is highly limited if it's constrained by things that I am able to produce myself. At some point I may decide that I wish to satisfy more of my pressing needs than I am able to do by myself, and so I choose to enter the market. As mentioned, if you produce more than you currently plan to consume, you are saving. But if you start to produce more than you *ever* plan to consume, you are doing something else. You are becoming a 'producer'. We call this 'specialisation'. By trading some of the good you have produced, you can access other goods (ones you cannot produce for yourself) that provide you with more utility. 'Exchange' is simply the transfer of a property right. And when exchange occurs between two people voluntarily, both must believe they are being made better off.

Let's take two consumers, Anne and Bert, and think about the marginal value they place on the same good (e.g. eggs). If we draw this on a graph, we can say a few things about it:

- It will be downward sloping (due to diminishing marginal utility)
- The height will depend on their wealth
- Since their tastes differ, their marginal value curves will be unique.

The reason markets exist is to allow trade, and the reason we trade is because we have different marginal valuations of scarce goods. We could show these two marginal value curves on the same graph by drawing Anne's stock of eggs running from left to right, and Bert's from right to left.[3] This allows us to compare their marginal value on the same scale and establish who places the highest marginal value for a given amount. Assume there are 40 eggs in total and both start off with 20 eggs each. Because tastes differ they *must* place a different marginal value on the 20th egg. Imagine Anne values it at 12p and Bert at 6p. It should be obvious that there is an opportunity for gains from trade – Bert should sell his 20th egg to Anne. As long as the price is between 6p and 12p both will be made better off.

Notice what's happened here – we start with two demand curves and because they are different we end up with a mutually beneficial exchange. Indeed a 'supply' curve is really an inverted demand curve!

Anne and Bert will continue to exchange eggs up until the point where their marginal values are the same. Let's assume that Anne values her 24th egg at 8p, and Bert values his 16th egg the same. In this instance they move from an initial endowment of (20,20) to one of (24,16) (i.e. a movement down Anne's marginal value curve, and a movement *up* Bert's). At this point we are in equilibrium (i.e. the marginal value curves cross), with a price equal to 8p.

Assuming they trade all eggs at 8p we can calculate the gains from trade. Recollect that Anne valued her 20th egg at 12p, whilst Bert values his 20th egg at 6p. If they trade at 8p they both make a profit of 4p. As they trade more eggs, their profit per transaction falls until they've fully exploited all gains from trade. We can call Anne's profit 'consumer surplus', which is the difference between her marginal value and the price. We'll call Bert's profit 'producer surplus', which is the difference between his marginal value curve and the price.[4]

So much for equilibrium in theory – what about in practice?

In the real world it is unlikely that Anne and Bert can fully exploit the gains from trade. We're assuming that they know each other and that they are in the same location. **Transaction costs** are the costs involved in using the price mechanism. They could be something as simple as the petrol it costs to get to the market, or as abstract as the knowledge required to find other sides of the market. The presence of transaction costs (and they are ubiquitous) will mean that Anne and Bert won't reach the equilibrium outcome of (24,16). After all, Anne will not be willing to pay 8p for the 24th egg if it costs her 1p to get to the market. So the consumer and producer surplus falls compared to our hypothetical, ideal state.

But imagine that there's a third party – a middleman. The middleman specialises in reducing transaction costs, for example by buying from Bert and selling to Anne with fewer transaction costs than if they did this directly. Let's say it only costs Anne 0.5p to deal with the middleman, as opposed to the 1p it costs to deal directly with Bert. In this case she would be willing to trade more units, and output moves closer to the equilibrium level. The impact of the middleman is that Anne's consumer surplus rises, Bert's 'producer' surplus rises, and the middleman earns a profit. This is possible because the middleman has converted **dead weight loss** (potentially efficient trades that aren't being made) into the realm of profit.

This doesn't mean that middlemen will always make consumers and producers better off. But it's the purpose of the market to balance out the costs of trading directly versus the costs of trading indirectly. Think about how we buy eggs in real life. We *could* buy directly from farmers, and the purchase price would be cheaper than in a supermarket. But think of the transaction costs involved in finding where your local farm is and taking time out of your day for a special trip just to buy eggs. Generally speaking, supermarkets act as a mutually beneficial middleman between the individual egg farmer and the consumer; all sides receive higher profit and the market moves closer to equilibrium. Middlemen are like bridges – they increase value by linking traders together. In a competitive market they are optional, and therefore we will only use them if they make our lives easier.

This argument is controversial, because it's common practice to view middlemen as a source of additional costs. But that's only if you're comparing them to the hypothetical idealised state where transaction costs are zero. In the real world they are likely to *reduce* the costs of exchange. Next time you're in a supermarket and think 'these eggs would be cheaper if I bought them from the farm' remember that *you're not at the farm*! Think of middlemen as being like postmen. Compared to a science fiction world where we can instantaneously and costlessly transport resources from one place to another, postmen raise the costs of exchange. Compared to a more realistic alternative, such as you having to deliver it yourself, they reduce costs. It's true that when we reduce transaction costs we have more efficient outcomes. But that is precisely the role that middlemen play. It's the competition between middlemen that reduces transaction costs, and converts dead weight loss into utility.

Indeed this is one of the main problems with taxes. The reason most people dislike taxes is because they raise the price of the goods that we buy. In this sense they reduce consumer surplus. If I believe that an inelastic jumper is worth £23 and its price is £20, I gain a surplus of £3. If there is a 10% tax imposed, and it means that the jumper now costs £22, then my surplus falls to £1. The difference of £2 is what the government collects. For most people this is annoying, because they would rather have the £2 for themselves. But given that we all utilise the services that governments provide, you may think this is somewhat selfish. But this isn't the reason economists worry so much about high taxes. Consider what happens if the tax is doubled, to 20%. Now the jumper costs £24, which is less than the value I place on it. In this case I no longer buy it. My consumer surplus falls to zero, and *so does the tax revenue*. Therefore taxation can generate dead weight loss. There are potentially beneficial trades that are no longer being made. Whilst middlemen – and the market process more generally – is constantly seeking to reduce such dead weight loss, taxation introduces it.

3.2   COMPARATIVE STATICS

Demand curves and supply curves both show the relationship between changes in price and changes in quantity. When combined onto the same diagram, they reveal the equilibrium price and quantity that deliver the largest amount of consumer and producer surplus. Their explanatory power comes from understanding how various shocks will affect those curves, generating a new equilibrium. Despite being an abstract, theoretical model, the demand and supply diagram is immensely useful. It's the basic lens through which economists view the world, and make sense of complex interaction. **Comparative statics** is the use of the demand and supply diagram to see what will happen to price and quantity following changes in the underlying economic conditions. It seems intuitively obvious that an increase in population will cause house prices to rise. But comparative statics helps us to clarify this. It does so by viewing the economic shock (the increase in population) in two ways. Firstly, we can see that it affects the demand curve (and not the supply curve). Secondly, it will cause an *increase* in demand (and not a decrease). By 'shifting' the demand curve outwards, we see that the equilibrium price and quantity will both be higher than previously. Ceteris paribus, an increase in population increases house prices.

Identifying a shock as primarily affecting demand or supply is pretty intuitive. Factors that influence demand include:

- Consumer tastes
- Price of substitute goods
- Income
- Buyers' expectations
- The number of consumers.

The list could go on, but it should be reasonably clear why these are primarily affecting the marginal value of the consumers. By contrast, the factors that influence supply are those that affect the costs structure facing producers. For example:

- Technological change
- Prices of factor inputs (e.g. land, labour, capital)
- Number of suppliers
- Supplier's expectations
- Prices of all other goods.

To engage in comparative statics you need to identify the source of change, and then ask yourself two questions:

1. Does it affect demand or supply?
2. Does it cause an increase or a decrease?

Comparative statics can be as complicated as you wish to make it. And in the real world multiple shocks will take place simultaneously, which means there's a limit to how much we can observe these effects. But it's precisely because the real world is complex, that we need a clear theoretical lens. If planning restrictions are lifted at the same time as population rises, the positive shift in the demand curve (upward pressure on prices) will coincide with a positive shift in the supply curve (downward pressure on prices). In the real world we can't hold all other variables constant, so the predictive power is severely curtailed. But there is use in knowing that a rise in population will mean that prices are higher than they otherwise would be. And indeed since both shocks imply an increase in quantity, comparative statics can still help us form a vision of the future.

The key reason why the market 'finds' a new equilibrium following a shock is because the price system adjusts to the new economic reality. Provided the price can reflect the underlying demand and supply curves, we expect to reach equilibrium, for the gains from trade to be fully exploited and for markets to 'clear'. It's the price system that does the remarkable job of converting our subjective value into terms that can be compared with other people. There is a certain beauty in the way this occurs, and Alexis Kirke and Greg Davies actually used the noise of an open outcry trading floor as the basis for an opera.[5] As George Shackle elucidated, prices allow our subjective values to find a type of social harmony:

> *Though valuation is in origin the personal and private act of the individual mind, yet it becomes through the device of the market a public and objective fact upon which every individual, at least in regard to goods for immediate consumption, agrees ... Prices, given this public authority and validity, enable collections of the most diverse objects to be measured in a single dimension ... economics might almost be defined as the act of reducing incommensurables to common terms.*[6]

As you might expect, if prices are prevented from functioning in this way markets will be less able to bridge buyers and sellers. Therefore price controls (laws that 'set' prices at certain levels) will be highly disruptive. There are two types of price control – ones that set prices above their equilibrium/market-clearing rate, and those that set prices below it. When prices are kept below their market-clearing rate, we call it a price 'ceiling'. This is because policymakers are trying to prevent it from rising upwards towards equilibrium. If prices are kept *above* their market-clearing rate, it's a 'floor'. Policymakers are trying to keep them artificially high.

A classic example of a price ceiling is rent control. It may be the case that the market generates an equilibrium price that is considered too high, and housing becomes unaffordable to low income people. With the best possible intentions, policymakers may attempt to resolve this problem by setting a maximum amount of rent that landlords can charge. The problem here is that although you can mask the underlying demand and supply curves that generated the original rental rates, you cannot escape them. The economic truth is that if people are compelled to trade at a price lower than the equilibrium price, there will be an excess of demand over supply. If the equilibrium weekly rent is £400 and rent control of £350 is adopted, there will be an increase in the quantity demanded, but a decrease in the quantity supplied. The result is a shortage. Markets are merely a way of allocating resources based on willingness to pay. If you remove the price system, there will be another way of allocating, such as willingness to wait. It may be willingness to bribe. Unless you want it to be entirely random, it *must* be willingness to do something. So economic theory tells us that shortages will occur. We can also speculate about what this might lead to:

- Black markets where buyers and sellers trade at prices closer to the market equilibrium
- Reduction in the future supply (due to potential supply being substituted into more profitable ventures)
- Fall in quality (landlords will have less pressure to maintain the quality because they are in a stronger bargaining position)

- Long waiting lists
- Bribery of those with discretionary ability to allocate resources (in the case of housing this may be city officials; it could just be a university housing officer)
- Inefficient use of existing supply (you might have a small family in a large apartment, and large families in small apartments because neither want to give them up)
- Reduction in the mobility of incumbents (if people are enjoying subsidised housing they'll be less likely to move).

We find evidence of all of the above when rent controls are adopted. When I walk around Berlin I can often tell whether I'm in a rent control neighbourhood just by observing the quality of the housing. After all, the equilibrium price is for a given level of quality. Buyers and sellers can negotiate based on price, but also based on quality. If sellers want to raise the real price of a good or service, they have two options: they can raise the nominal price and keep quality the same. Or they can keep the nominal price constant and lower the quality. If you remove their ability to raise prices, you're ensuring that quality will fall. As Assar Lindbeck famously said, 'in many cases rent control appears to be the most efficient technique presently known to destroy a city – except for bombing.'

Economic theory tells us that rent control is a bad idea, and over 75% of economists agree with the statement, 'a ceiling on rents reduced the quality and quantity of housing available'.[7] But the only reason I called it 'bad' is because I want a housing system that maximises social wealth. If you're someone that is unable to find a house due to rent control, you'll also probably say that it's a bad policy. But not everyone will agree. If you are one of the lucky ones to have a rent-controlled apartment, you'll love it! If you're a landlord specialising in low quality housing, you'll like it as well. Some economists do support rent control, but this may be because it's a disguised wealth redistribution. Whether it is 'good' or 'bad' depends on your goals. But it also depends on your understanding of the effects of price controls.

An even starker example of the disjoint between economic thinking and public under-standing is minimum wage legislation. A minimum wage is a price floor that is imposed on the labour market. As before, it is often the result of a well-intended desire to raise the wage rate of low paid workers. If the market rate is considered too low, policymakers can pass a law that makes it illegal to offer a wage below a designated amount. What's not to like? The problem is that arbitrary price floors do not change the economic reality. Imagine that the equilibrium wage rate for low skilled labour is £5 per hour. We may agree that this is very low, and mandate that firms can pay no less than £6 per hour. The simple economic truth is that when prices go up – ceteris paribus – *more* people are willing to supply the good but *less* people will demand it. The difference between high supply and low demand is a glut. And a glut in the labour market is called unemployment.

As before, negotiation is based on price and quality. Unless a worker's productivity has changed, the marginal value they create will be the same as before the minimum wage. Therefore their real wage should stay the same. If the nominal wage goes up, this simply means that the *quality* of the job will go down. Indeed we can predict several negative consequences of a minimum wage:

- A reduction in the number of hours worked
- Workers are required to cover more of their employment costs than before (for example they have to pay for their own uniform)

- Companies substitute capital for labour (capital has become relatively cheaper, so firms automate services that would have been provided by workers, or simply dispense with those services all together. For example petrol pump attendants, movie theatre ushers, etc.)
- Training becomes harder to receive (firms are unable to offer training to those workers willing to accept lower wages)
- Employed workers become less mobile (because they're less likely to find a job if they move location).

There's evidence to suggest that all of the above have followed minimum wages but it's important to remember the ceteris paribus condition. Minimum wages don't always lead to an increase in unemployment. If the minimum wage is set at a wage above the equilibrium rate, it shouldn't have an effect (in this instance it would be 'non-binding'). If the equilibrium rate rises over time due to increased labour productivity, this will mitigate the negative effects of a minimum wage. In a famous 1996 study conducted by David Card and Alan Krueger, an empirical claim was made that the introduction of a minimum wage in New Jersey did not reduce unemployment.[8] Since that controversial finding, the study was replicated and it's become known that the original survey asked the wrong question (they asked how many jobs had been lost, rather than how many hours had been reduced). Despite their popularity as a means to help the poor, *no replicated study has disproved the basic economic analysis that minimum wages harm low skilled labour.*[9]

So why are they so popular? One reason is ignorance. The discussion above is somewhat counterintuitive, and if you haven't studied economics you may not consider what the unintended consequences will be. It seems obvious that minimum wages *help* low skilled workers, because by definition wages will be higher. *But only for those with a job*! It is less obvious, but just as important, to also consider the low skilled workers who have now been priced out of the market, or the subtle ways in which existing jobs have become less desirable. The main reason why minimum wages are popular is because they benefit *some* low skilled workers at the expense of others. For those workers who retain their job at higher wages, minimum wages are good. They provide an effective barrier to entry that prevents other workers from competing for your job. Indeed the original reason minimum wages were advocated was to explicitly keep low skilled people *out* of the labour market.

In America, the Progressive movement that campaigned for minimum wage laws wanted them 'for women and women only'. They understood that this would make it harder for women to find jobs, but that was the whole point. They felt that women's place was in the home, and they didn't want them entering the labour market and undercutting men.[10] In South Africa minimum wages were one of a number of pieces of legislation adopted to deliberately keep low skilled black people out of the labour market. They were a racist policy explicitly designed to entrench and protect white workers.[11] It's rare to see minimum wages advocated on racist grounds these days, but it is common to hear thinly veiled concerns about 'immigrants taking our jobs'. If your concern is for minority groups, for low skilled people, or those currently out of the labour market, minimum wage laws are harmful. They are the equivalent of removing the first rungs on the ladder to prosperity.

Another important example of a price control is **anti-price gouging laws**. These are designed to prevent prices from spiking following natural disasters, and are intended to protect consumers from exploitation. It is typically seen as 'unfair' if producers profit from an emergency. But consider the consequences of keeping prices at pre-emergency levels.[12] Firstly, it creates an incentive for consumers to hoard. Given that people's willingness to pay has risen due to the emergency, they will receive even more consumer surplus at the original price. This will result in a shortage, and give an advantage to those who are first in line, at the expense of those who arrive later. Secondly, it will reduce the incentive for suppliers to respond. In an emergency costs are likely to rise, and if the price remains the same profit will fall. Both of these factors will reduce the availability of goods. Encouraging non-essential purchases to be made, and reducing the incentives for potential supplies, is the opposite of what is needed to coordinate resources. In December 2013 the BBC reported that bread prices had risen by 500% in parts of Syria.[13] But this isn't an example of the market failing. Expensive bread isn't the cause of the problem. It is a consequence. And the fact that the BBC used this data point as evidence for the breakdown of social coordination in Syria demonstrates their usefulness. Price spikes are signs that the market is working. They are an important signal.

Markets are an important way to allocate resources, but are not the only way. When governments want to allocate cell phone licences they have utilised lotteries. These have the advantage of being somewhat random, but they are also arbitrary. When some dentists from Cape Cod bid for a licence in 1989 they promptly won, and then sold it on for $41m.[14] A more conventional mechanism is a **beauty contest**, where policymakers receive bids and make a judgment about which is best. This has the advantage of allowing them to promote specific targets (such as increasing jobs or protecting the environment). When FIFA awarded the 2022 World Cup to Qatar it was on the grounds that it would help promote soccer in a new region. A beauty contest allows policymakers to use their discretion. The problem is that discretion generates scope for corruption. Beauty contests tend to be opaque and slow. But there's a bigger problem. The challenge isn't merely one of deciding how to allocate the resource. There is also the issue about discovering what the value of the resource actually is. For example, when 3G licences were being allocated in the UK people thought they were worth about £2bn.[15] These estimates were crude because no one knew what the value of the technology was. When it came to 2G licences the government sold them for just £40,000 per licence. The people with perhaps the best understanding of how much they're worth – the companies entering the beauty contest – have an incentive to understate the value. The economist's solution is to create a particular type of market. An auction.

There are two main kinds of auction. The first is a private value one, where the valuation of the asset being auctioned is deemed to vary from person to person. In this case the marginal values will be relatively independent. Many of the things we bid for on eBay are private value, since we only care about what it is worth to *us*. The second kind is a common value. Here, the marginal values are deemed to be reasonably equal. In this case, other people's bids may affect your own bid because they reveal information about how much you think it is worth. Rights to dig an oil reserve are common value because the underlying resource is worth the same to all bidders. The problem is that there's uncertainty regarding how much it is worth.

For a single asset, there are two ways of conducting the auction. One way is through 'open outcry', which means that each participant can see (and hear) what the other is doing. An English auction is a particular type of open outcry. The auctioneer will start off with a low amount, and bidders will attempt to outbid each other, up to a limit of their own marginal value. Note that the winner only needs to pay slightly higher than the value of the second highest marginal value. If you think of eBay, you may decide that you are willing to pay £40 for a first edition book. But if the next highest bid is £20 you will only have to pay £20.01. This means that you receive consumer surplus. By contrast, a Dutch auction is one that descends. Here, the auctioneer starts off with a high amount and gradually reduces it until someone makes a bid. The winner in this case will pay their own marginal value. In the book example they would pay £40. The advantage of a Dutch auction is that it is over quite quickly, and therefore may be more common for perishable items like fish, or flowers. The downside is that it's not as exciting. There's less participation than in an ascending auction, where everyone starts off bidding and people gradually get eliminated. Indeed some auction houses will rely on the fact that in an ascending auction bidders may get carried away and increase their willingness to pay purely because of the thrill of the auction.

The other way of conducting a single asset auction is 'sealed bid'. Participants will write down their bid and these will not be known to other participants. One type of sealed bid auction is a 'first price' one, where the winning bidder will pay the amount they bid. However if they believe that others are bidding lower than them, they may shade their bid. A 'second price' sealed bid auction means that the winning bidder only pays the amount bid by the second highest bidder. This is also known as a 'Vickrey' auction and has the benefit of being compatible with people's true preferences. It is the only auction where it is rational to bid your true value. This is because if you bid any less than your marginal value you may lose the auction even though you wanted to win. And if you bid more than your marginal value you may win when you wanted to lose. Thus the best strategy is to bid your marginal value. It is intuitively reasonable, and theoretically provable, that the results of an English auction will be the same as a second price sealed bid. And a Dutch auction will mimic a first price sealed bid.

The above holds for single asset auctions. If there are multiple assets being auctioned there is a choice between being a uniform price (i.e. winners all pay the same amount), or price discrimination (i.e. winners pay different amounts). Auction theory is popular because it demonstrates how blackboard theory can translate into real world outcomes. When the UK government wanted to auction off 3G licences they turned to a group of academic economists. By understanding auction theory, and testing it in a classroom with students, Ken Binmore and Paul Klemperer made their recommendations. The results were astounding. It raised £22.5bn, which equates to around 2.5% of GNP.[16] Markets are a discovery mechanism as much as an allocation one.

3.3 INFORMATION ECONOMICS

This may all work in theory, but how do markets function in practice? Even if prices are allowed to adjust, are markets perfect? Although it's true that economists tend to put a lot of trust in the ability of markets to find equilibrium, economists also spend a lot of time considering instances where they fail. There are a number of examples of 'market failure', one of which is the concept of **asymmetric information**. This occurs when actors on one side of the market have better quality information than those on the other. If we're buying and selling eggs, information is reasonably symmetrical. An egg is an egg. But in some situations it's hard to know the exact characteristics. Imagine a company that offered to pay £200 to anyone that had a skiing accident. Here the information is highly asymmetric, because you are likely to know whether you're a safe or reckless skier. But this isn't obvious to the company. You have better quality information than they do. We can see two implications of asymmetric information.

1. Adverse selection

    In our example, the skiers most likely to buy the product are the most accident-prone. If the odds of an accident are calculated across all skiers, the company will suffer from a selection bias. The insurance is attracting the 'wrong' kind of person.

2. Moral hazard

Even if the skier is a reasonably safe one, if they buy the insurance it will affect their incentive to ski safely. At the margin the insurance will encourage them to be more risky, and therefore make it more likely that they have an accident. It's a bit like wearing a helmet – the insurance changes people's incentives and therefore changes behaviour.

One way to view the difference between adverse selection and moral hazard is in terms of timing. Adverse selection relates to the type of people who will make the agreement. Moral hazard relates to people's behaviour once they've made the agreement. Both of them cause problems. For this reason we wouldn't expect to find a market in skiing insurance.

In 2001 three economists shared the Nobel Prize for their work on asymmetric information.

- George Akerlof demonstrated the problem of adverse selection with a model of the second hand car market. He argued that owners of cars will know whether they own a high quality car, or a low quality one (a 'lemon'). However potential buyers will only know the range of cars across the market as a whole. They will not know if any individual car is a lemon or not. This being the case, buyers will be willing to pay the average value of a used car. But this creates a problem for sellers. Some sellers (the ones with lemons) will be delighted by this, since the true value of their car is less than the market average. But the owners of high quality cars will be unhappy. In fact, they will refuse to sell their cars for the average price of all cars. But if high quality cars are withdrawn from the market, the average value of remaining cars will fall. Therefore buyers will revise down their offers, and once again anyone owning a car worth more than this will withdraw it. Ultimately the whole market unravels until there are only lemons left. Therein lies the market failure.
- Michael Spence shared the prize for his work on signalling. Signalling occurs when the better informed person takes costly actions to transmit information to the poorly informed. In the used car market this could be that the seller offers a warranty.
- Joseph Stiglitz was awarded the prize for his work on screening. Screening occurs when the poorly informed elicit the well informed to reveal their characteristics. For example the buyer could ask the seller to offer a warranty.

Signalling and screening can seem very similar, and they merely depend on who's making the move – the person with the information advantage (signalling) or the person with the disadvantage (screening). Spence and Stiglitz were particularly interested in human capital, and the way in which firms solve the information asymmetry in terms of a potential employee. They assumed that the employee knows whether they are high productivity or low productivity, but the firm does not know. Employees therefore engage in signalling (such as receiving an education), and firms engage in screening (job interviews).

The field of information economics had a large impact on the economics profession. Following the concepts and models developed by Akerlof, Spence and Stiglitz, it became difficult to simply assume that markets cleared. They cast real doubts on whether perfectly functioning markets should be considered the norm. On the contrary, because information is almost always imperfect the models of market failure should be considered the norm.

Most economics textbooks do a two-step treatment of information economics. They start off by explaining how markets work perfectly in theory, and then introduce real world frictions such as asymmetric information. This implies that there's a role for government intervention to 'correct' the market failure. But this approach is inadequate for two reasons. Firstly, it ignores government failure. The fact that markets fail is a necessary but not sufficient reason to argue that governments should intervene. You also need to demonstrate that market failure is larger than potential government failure. For example regulation can deter innovation and exclude new entrants. In the same way that adverse selection can cause the quality to be lower than what would occur with perfect information, regulatory attempts to improve it – such as quality standards – can mean that it's too high. If we passed a law to say that everyone should do their grocery shopping at Waitrose, you would solve the information asymmetry and guarantee that everyone was buying high quality products. But in doing so you'd price a lot of poor people out of the market. Regulation suffers from a knowledge problem (regulators do not know the marginal values of the buyers, or the opportunity costs of the sellers) and an incentive problem (regulators are prone to being lobbied, and pass laws that help the producer rather than consumer). Perhaps government isn't necessary.

Ultimately the second reason the two-step treatment is inadequate is because it ignores a third step, which is how markets respond to market failures. A close reading of Akerlof's famous article on lemons demonstrates this. After showing how, in theory, adverse selection can cause markets to unravel, he discussed how, in practice, firms respond. Interestingly, signalling and screening aren't necessarily signs of market inefficiency, but ways in which markets generate efficiency. We do see a functioning market in second hand cars in the real world, so firms clearly are able to find ways to circumvent the information asymmetry. They offer warranties. They invest resources in building a reputation for being trustworthy.

Indeed there are so many solutions to information asymmetries, that it can be hard to know which side of the exchange is supposed to have the superior information. Some textbooks use medical insurance as an example of asymmetric information, because we know whether we are healthy or not, but the insurance company doesn't. Having worked for a health insurance company, I can tell you that is a myth! They have access to all sorts of statistical analysis that makes them far more aware of your health risks than you do.

To sum up, information economics typically says:

1. Markets work in theory
2. The real world has frictions.
   But this isn't the end of the story. We need to add:
3. Solutions to market failure.

Or, as Arnold Kling puts it, there are three schools of thought. To Chicago economists 'markets work, use markets'. To Keynesian economists 'markets fail, use government'. But to Austrian economists 'markets fail, use markets'.[17] If there's inefficiency, then there is waste. And all waste is a profit opportunity. It is precisely because markets fail that there's an incentive for entrepreneurs to find new ways to do business. The identification of friction does not cast doubt on the ability of markets to serve as a coordination device. As my professor Peter Boettke would say, if it wasn't for real world friction we'd fall over whenever we tried to put one foot in front of the other. The 'information economists' are right – friction is the norm. But this isn't necessarily a bad thing. After all, try to imagine a world of perfect information. In the movie 'What Women Want', Mel Gibson had the power of understanding exactly what women were thinking. There was less of an information asymmetry. But even if such a world were possible, it wouldn't necessarily be desirable.

NOTES

1. Piccone, P. (1994) From the New Left to the New Populism, *Telos*, **101**, 173–208, at 202.
2. The actual figure is 37 723 700 and is using the number of persons aged 20–64 from Population Estimates for UK, England and Wales, Scotland and Northern Ireland, Office for National Statistics, 8 August 2013.
3. In other words as we move along the x axis Anne is gaining eggs and Bert is losing them. If we move in the other direction, from right to left, Bert is gaining eggs and Anne is losing them.
4. At this point it's worth recognising that in our story eggs have taken on an interesting characteristic. Initially the marginal value of an egg is its 'use value', which relates to the extent to which it satisfies the pressing needs of the consumer. Now that eggs are being exchanged it develops an 'exchange value', in addition. It may be that Bert originally had the following preference ordering:

   Apple
   Cake
   Lemonade
   Eggs

   If he's given a choice between eggs or lemonade, he'll choose lemonade. But let's say that Anne has some cake, and the following preference ordering:

   Eggs
   Cake
   Apple
   Lemonade

   In isolation, Bert would choose lemonade over eggs. But if he has an opportunity to exchange some eggs for Anne's cake, this will make him better off. The exchange value of eggs will mean it rises up his preference ordering (and therefore other goods will fall down). See Mises, L.v. (1912[1981]) *The Theory of Money and Credit*, Liberty Fund, p. 183.
5. 'Composer and behavioural finance expert create "reality" opera based on open outcry stock trading floor', 6 December 2012 [http://www.multivu.com/mnr/58659-barclays-opera, accessed 17 September 2013].
6. Shackle, G.L.S. (1992) *Epistemics and Economics*, Transaction, p. 9.
7. Rockoff, H. (2007) Price Controls. *Concise Encyclopaedia of Economics* (2nd edition) [http://www.econlib.org/library/Enc/PriceControls.html, accessed 17 September 2013].
8. Card, D. and Krueger, A.B. (1994) *Myth and Measurement: The new economics of the minimum wage*, Princeton University Press.
9. A thorough review of the literature on minimum wages was conducted by David Neumark and William Wascher in their book *Minimum Wages*. They found that 'minimum wages reduce employment opportunities for less-skilled workers, especially those who are most directly affected by the minimum wage' (p. 6). Neumark, D. and Wascher, W.L. (2008) *Minimum Wages*, MIT Press.
10. For more on the legislation that sought to keep women in the home see Leonard, T. (2005) Protecting family and race: The Progressive case for regulating women's work, *American Journal of Economics and Sociology*, **64** (3), 757–791. David Henderson has done historical work to demonstrate that progressive policymakers in the 1960s were explicit about their motivations for advocating minimum wages: 'the politicians who pushed for the increased minimum wage did not hide their motives. Nor, in an era of state-sanctioned segregation, did they feel the need to hide their knowledge of who the intended victims of minimum-wage legislation would be.' Minimum wages were implemented to prevent low-skilled black workers from competing with white people. See Henderson, D. (2001) *The Joy of Freedom*, Prentice Hall.
11. For some evidence of the way in which progressive regulations were specifically aimed at helping apartheid policies, see Williams, W.E. (1989) *South Africa's War Against Capitalism*, Praeger.

Although it is somewhat counterintuitive, free markets tend to be incompatible with discrimination generally. This is because discrimination is costly to the discriminator. My former Professor Walter E. Williams liked to question why American universities tended to have relatively more black students in athletic departments rather than the humanities. His argument was that college sports are more lucrative to a university than the quality of the humanities students, and therefore it is more costly to discriminate. Since a university will generate significant income from the results of their sports teams, they simply cannot afford to exercise discrimination. Indeed it is not a profitable strategy to discriminate against any group. If a company refuses to employ disabled people, for example (assuming that the disability is unrelated to their ability to perform the job), then this creates a profit opportunity for rival firms. Indeed Rich Donovan analysed companies in the S&P 500 index and created an index of the 100 companies that 'deal best' with disabled people. He found that 'over the past five years it has outperformed the broader stockmarket', and in 2012 Bloomberg decided to include it in their terminals. 'The new green', *The Economist*, 8 September 2012. Although it would be churlish to pretend that discrimination doesn't take place, the point is that it is unlikely to be in the financial interests of the discriminator to do it.

12. See Mohammed, R. (2003) The Problem with Price Gouging Laws, *HBR Blog Network*, 23 July.
13. Doucet, L. (2013) Syria's battle for bread, *BBC News*, 16 December [http://www.bbc.co.uk/news/world-middle-east-25397140, accessed 20 December 2013].
14. See Snider, J.H. (2007) The Art of Spectrum Lobbying, *New America Foundation*, August.
15. Binmore, K. and Klemperer, P. (2001) The biggest auction ever: the sale of British 3G telecom licenses [http://papers.ssrn.com/sol3/papers.cfm?abstract_id=297879, accessed 30 September 2013].
16. Binmore and Klemperer, The biggest auction ever (n 15).
17. Kling attributes the last school to 'Masonomics', for example see Kling, A. (2009) What Makes Health Care Different? *EconLog*, 22 July 2009 [http://econlog.econlib.org/archives/2009/07/what_makes_heal.html, accessed 17 November 2013].

CHAPTER 4

Prices and Economic Calculation

'The rain starts coming down harder. You wonder if you own an umbrella. You've left so many in taxis. Usually, by the time the first raindrop hits the street, there are men on every corner selling umbrellas. Where do they come from, you have often wondered, and where do they go when it's not raining? You imagine these umbrella peddlers huddled around powerful radios waiting for the very latest from the National Weather Service, or maybe sleeping in dingy hotel rooms with their arms hanging out the windows, ready to wake at the first touch of precipitation. Maybe they have a deal with the taxi companies, you think, to pick up all the left-behind umbrellas for next to nothing. The city's economy is made up of strange, subterranean circuits that are as mysterious to you as the grids of wire and pipe under the streets.'

—Jay McInerney[1]

You may have skim read the opening quote to this chapter, but I implore you to slow down and read it again. The purpose of this chapter is to illuminate those circuits that ensure that umbrella sellers appear when the rain starts to fall. When we use comparative statics we see how a change in economic conditions will cause a movement from one equilibrium to another. However the really interesting question is not whether we get from point A to point B, but *how*?

Comparative statics also imply that demand and supply curves exist independent of the institutions of market exchange. Indeed in many economics courses you will be 'given' a demand and supply curve and asked to calculate the equilibrium price and quantity. But in the real world these curves are *never* known; they are held subjectively and tacitly (i.e. it's unarticulated). Consequently the problem isn't a mere technical exercise about 'finding' prices, but a complex, social task to 'discover' them. Prices can only emerge through a market process – they don't exist independently. In markets prices are the communication devices that generate and disseminate knowledge.

Lots of companies are famous for having an entrepreneurial mindset, and this chapter will explain what entrepreneurship is, and how it can be harnessed within an organisation. We will look at concrete examples of how companies use price discrimination techniques, and we will see how the knowledge problem – knowing when umbrellas are needed, and where – is just as rife within firms as in society at large.

This chapter intends to move us away from viewing markets in static, equilibrium terms, and towards seeing markets as a dynamic process of price discovery. And the missing link is the prime mover of progress – the entrepreneur.

4.1 ENTREPRENEURSHIP

It is relatively recently that the concept of entrepreneurship has begun to feature in standard economic textbooks, and there are two main reasons. One is theoretical – entrepreneurship is not all that compatible with mainstream, 'neoclassical' economic theory. In standard models an 'auctioneer' is assumed to make the market clear prior to any trading taking place. But this begs the question about how, in the real world, resources get allocated in a market economy. The second reason is more practical – the 'supply side' revolution of the 1980s synonymous with Ronald Reagan and Margaret Thatcher reduced barriers to starting a business and championed wealth creation and enterprise. This led to a rise in the study of the macroeconomic effects of entrepreneurship, and the policy proposals relating to how to encourage it. It is telling that much of this attention has been led by academics within business schools, as opposed to economics departments. The study of entrepreneurship is seen to have direct policy relevance, and focuses on practitioners. But although the theoretical foundations of entrepreneurship have been neglected, they weren't ignored entirely. In particular, the Austrian school of economics has a long established theory of entrepreneurship. The term is so prevalent it can be quite confusing, so what we shall do is talk about what entrepreneurship *is*, but also what it is *not*.

When people talk about government policies to help entrepreneurship they tend to focus on start-ups, and the environment for small and medium-sized enterprises (SMEs). Whilst these are of undoubted importance, entrepreneurship is a far broader phenomenon. Small businesses (under 50 employees) constitute more than 99% of the number of UK companies, but less than half of employees and around a third of revenues. By contrast, even though just 0.2% of UK companies are 'large' (more than 250 employees) they employ around 40% of workers and generate almost half of all revenues.[2] If you want to boost jobs, boosting SMEs is an inefficient way to go about it. And not only are SMEs a small part of the UK economy, they are a very volatile one. The 'failure rate' of new businesses is around 30%, but of the 70% that typically survive after 36 months, only about 10% enjoy growth rates of more than 30% per year.[3] If entrepreneurship were only about the tiny proportion of small firms that actually grow, it would not play a crucial role in the economy. We need to take a broader view as to what constitutes entrepreneurship.

One of the most famous economists to write about entrepreneurship was Joseph Schumpeter. He was an eccentric, brilliant man who boasted that his ambition was to become the world's greatest horseman, dresser and lover. He later remarked that he only achieved two of those goals, adding that he never got on well with horses! It is telling that one of Schumpeter's most important books is called *The Theory of Economic Development*, because he identified the entrepreneur as the critical catalyst for change. He used the phrase 'new combinations' as being the essence of entrepreneurship, as entrepreneurs were those who discovered new ways to combine the factors of production. He offers a thrilling account of capitalism:

> *The fundamental impulse that sets and keeps the capitalist engine in motion comes from the new consumers' goods, the new methods of production or transportation, the new markets, the new forms of industrial organization that capitalist enterprise creates.*[4]

But note that it isn't only new *products* that are the impulse. Indeed he identified five separate types of 'new combination':

1. New products: this might be something that consumers aren't familiar with, or an improvement in the quality of an existing product.
2. New production methods: can be a technological improvement to reduce costs, or a new way of handling a product commercially.
3. New markets: either by creating a new market, or selling the product in an existing market where it wasn't previously sold.
4. New sources of materials: either newly created or simply applied from other sectors, they might be raw materials or half-manufactured.
5. New organisation of industry: such as increased market power, or more competition.

Indeed focusing on products misses the point completely. It encourages you to think of the good itself as the breakthrough, rather than the manner in which it is made available to consumers. Schumpeter later used the term 'innovation' to refer to the discovery of new combinations, and was at pains to distinguish this from the concept of 'invention', because, 'as long as they are not carried into practice, inventions are economically irrelevant'.[5] Entrepreneurship goes beyond having good ideas, 'It consists in getting things done'.[6] This is relevant whenever you hear people scorn the likes of Bill Gates, who 'merely' brought to market products that had been developed by other people. Schumpeter would argue that those products have no economic value *unless they're brought to market*, and it is this function that exemplifies genuine entrepreneurship. As *The Economist* says,

> *The technology industry likes to sneer at Microsoft as a follower ... That very first PC operating system was based on someone else's code. But Mr Gates's invention was as a businessman. His genius was to understand what he needed and work out how to obtain it, however long it took.*[7]

Schumpeter's emphasis on new combinations has an implication in terms of the type of firms that will carry them out. This is where start-ups do matter. He points out that innovation is more likely to come from new firms rather than old ones – 'it is not the owner of a stage coach who builds railways'.[8] He uses the phrase 'perennial gale of creative destruction' to refer to the manner in which innovation disrupts existing ways of doing things. It's not so much that this is desirable; rather it's an unavoidable part of progress. Innovation is ubiquitous and disruptive.

Another pioneer of entrepreneurship theory was an entrepreneur in practice. Richard Cantillon was born in Ireland and became one of the foremost political economists of the eighteenth century. His definition of an entrepreneur can be loosely translated as 'the undertaker of business ventures', and his genius was in viewing this as a process that took place over time. He pointed out that entrepreneurs tend to know the price of their inputs when they are bought. However they do not know the price at which they will be able to sell their output. It is the fact that entrepreneurs saddle the known prices of the present, and the unknown prices of the future, that generates their importance. Entrepreneurs are exposed to risk.

Well, not quite. Rather entrepreneurs are exposed to *uncertainty*, which is distinct from risk. In a seminal book called *Risk, Uncertainty and Profit*, American economist Frank Knight said:

> *An uncertainty which can by any method be reduced to an objective, quantitatively determinate probability, can be reduced to complete certainty by grouping cases. The business world has evolved several organization devices for effectuating this consolidation, with the result that when the technique of business organization is fairly developed, measurable uncertainties do not introduce into business any uncertainty whatever.*[9]

One way to think of this is the game of roulette. The ball will come to rest in one of 38 pockets. We don't know which one, but given that we know there's a 1/38 chance of it being in each, it isn't uncertain. It's a game of risk, not uncertainty. Uncertainty would be if the croupier dropped the ball, or a seagull flew across the table and stole it. Risk can be classified, and therefore be represented in a probability distribution. For uncertain situations, by contrast, there's no prior information. Measurement is impossible. We can view insurance companies, and financial markets more generally, as means of converting uncertainty into risk. We can insure against risk. But it isn't risk that gives us sleepless nights.

Although this view of uncertainty is synonymous with the Austrian school, many heterodox economists share it. Indeed Keynes captured the basic point:

> *By 'uncertain' knowledge, let me explain, I do not mean merely to distinguish what is known for certain from what is only probable. The game of roulette is not subject, in this sense, to uncertainty ... The sense in which I am using the term is that in which the prospect of a European war is uncertain, or the price of copper and the rate of interest twenty years hence ... About these matters there is no scientific basis on which to form any calculable probability whatever. We simply do not know.*[10]

Knight's contribution to entrepreneurship theory is by identifying this exposure to uncertainty as being the source of entrepreneurial profit. The entrepreneur is a speculator, in the sense that he is the residual claimant of an enterprise. Profit is defined as the 'residual earnings after all contractual claims (incurred for the use of resources) have been met', and therefore profit is the reward (but not the return) for entrepreneurship.[11]

But profit isn't solely a reward for entrepreneurial discovery. It is also a signal for resource mobilisation. It helps make value creation more tangible. Consider the act of making a sandwich. Let's say you add together bread, cheese, cucumber and vegemite. The final result tastes nicer than each component does separately (trust me). The value of the completed sandwich is higher than the value of the component parts. Maybe we put together bread, meatballs, cheese and white chocolate cookies. In this case the end result will taste disgusting. The value of the final good is less than the sum of the inputs.[12] The first sandwich is profitable, because it's worth more than the sum of its parts. The second is unprofitable, signalling that we're wasting resources. When Hurricane Katrina hit the Gulf Coast an entrepreneur called John Shepperson packed a truck with 19 generators and drove 600 miles. According to John Stossel and Gena Binkley he 'thought he could help and make some money'.[13] Maybe you find this a selfish thing to do, and wish for a world where wanting to help was enough motivation to act. But the 'reward for entrepreneurial discovery' is only one of the functions of profit. The other is a 'signal for resource mobilisation'. It's possible that Shepperson was only aware of the need for generators *because* there was money to be made.[14]

As important as Schumpeter and Knight are to the theory of entrepreneurship, we also need to introduce Israel Kirzner. He attempted to bring entrepreneurs inside the framework of standard economics, and made some simplifying assumptions. He assumed that there is a single commodity (i.e. no innovation) and a single time period (no uncertainty). He posited that entrepreneurs exploit profit opportunities via riskless arbitrage. He said, 'I view the entrepreneur not as a source of innovative ideas ex nihilo, but as being alert to the opportunities that exist already.'[15] And he defined 'alertness' as 'costless discovery'. It isn't about investing in entrepreneurial activity, but simply in noticing those opportunities that are all around us.

You could view this as merely a theory of 'luck' but it ties in with the concept of uncertainty. It is really a theory of 'surprise'. One of the most infamous examples of Knightian uncertainty was provided by Donald Rumsfeld, when he said:

> *Reports that say that something hasn't happened are always interesting to me, because as we know, there are known knowns; there are things we know we know. We also know there are known unknowns; that is to say we know there are some things we do not know. But there are also unknown unknowns – the ones we don't know we don't know.*[16]

If we don't know we don't know about something we can't look for it. However we *can* act upon it once we notice it. It's common to view the Schumpeter and Kirzner views as polar opposites, and Kirzner himself recognises this,

> *For Schumpeter the entrepreneur is the disruptive, disequilibrating force that dislodges the market from the somnolence of equilibrium; for us the entrepreneur is the equilibrating force whose activity responds to the existing tensions and provides those corrections for which the unexploited opportunities have been crying out.*[17]

But we can reconcile the two. It's not that the Schumpeter view takes an existing equilibrium and disrupts it, but that it reveals that the status quo wasn't really an equilibrium at all. It wasn't that the advent of the motorcar 'disrupted' the buggy industry, but that it revealed the prior inefficiencies. It moves us closer to a world where consumer desires are being met by how entrepreneurs steer the means of production. We are always in disequilibrium, but entrepreneurship moves us closer to plan coordination. Similarly we can consider the Kirzner view over a longer time horizon.

Let's say you get off the tube, it is raining, and you see an umbrella selling for £5. We'll invoke an assumption of zero transaction costs, and imagine that you *know* there are commuters 1 mile away who place a marginal value of £8 on the same umbrella. Note that this is an opportunity for arbitrage, and in a world of zero transaction costs it is completely riskless. Provided you buy low (at £5) and sell high (at £8) you will make a profit. The essence of entrepreneurship is exploiting arbitrage opportunities. Since action takes place over time, economic conditions may change. Maybe the person 1 mile away *doesn't* value the umbrella at £8. Maybe it will stop raining. But we only need to make a minor modification to our assumptions above – it's not that an entrepreneur arbitrages between two known prices, but that they arbitrage between present data and their *expectation* about future data.

> *The entrepreneur … deals with uncertain conditions of the future. His success or failure depends on the correctness of his anticipation of uncertain events … the only source from which an entrepreneur's profit stems is his ability to anticipate better than other people the future demand of the consumers.*[18]

And it goes beyond this. Entrepreneurship is not just anticipating demand, but anticipating unarticulated demand. Consumers don't directly tell entrepreneurs what it is that they want to buy because they may not know this themselves. Entrepreneurs need to understand how to satisfy our pressing needs better than we do; as Jonathan Margolis says, 'the beauty of inventions such as Walkman, iPod, iPad, and so on was that they came from the minds of visionary geniuses who could foresee a desire we didn't know we had'.[19] Indeed the key to innovation is thinking in terms of satisfying consumer needs, rather than making modifications and improvements to existing products.

The act of entrepreneurship is the 'best guess'/informed (delete as appropriate) judgement of those best able to anticipate what will be of value to customers. An 'entrepreneur' is someone that is performing that function. Entrepreneurship involves the twin acts of (i) noticing a profit opportunity; and (ii) mobilising the resources required to realise it. A nice definition is as follows:

> *Entrepreneurship is the pursuit of opportunity without regard to resources currently controlled.*[20]

I like reminding my students (especially French ones) of the time when George W. Bush was reported to have criticised the French for not having a word for 'entrepreneur', when of course the word comes from the French verb 'entreprendre', meaning 'to undertake'. The simplest definition of entrepreneurship is 'the undertaking of business ventures'.

4.2   THE FIRM

Most business ventures take place within firms. There are three main types. A proprietorship is an organisation in which the owner is the residual claimant. She has the rights to any profits, but the obligation of any debts. A second type is a partnership, where two or more individuals have ownership rights. A third type is a corporation. With limited liability laws individuals are able to buy a stake in a company that represents an upper limit on any potential losses they may incur. This makes ownership rights far more transferable and expands the pool of investors.

Economists only really began to study firms and organisations in the 1970s. Prior to that there had been lengthy and profound debates about rival economic systems, between capitalism and socialism. There was an established literature on why the decentralised nature of markets was superior to the hierarchical structure of planning. But economists had neglected the existence of the hierarchies that existed within capitalism.

We're going to make an assumption that the institutions that exist at the social level have parallels with those at the firm level. So an understanding of how the economy functions is of direct relevance to an understanding of how a firm does. And indeed theories of corporate management have been used as a basis for national planning. 'Taylorism', or 'Scientific management', assumes that order and coordination are the deliberate products of a planner's design. It therefore sought to replace tradition with objectively derived procedures. This in fact influenced the Soviet Union as they attempted to increase productive efficiency. As Joseph Stalin said,

The combination of the Russian revolutionary sweep with American efficiency is the essence of Leninism.[21]

The person who did most to stimulate interest in why firms exist was Ronald Coase. Coase was a remarkable economist, because although his insights were based on intuition and simple reasoning, his theory of the firm stemmed from his observation of real firms. In 1931 he was awarded a scholarship to visit the United States. As he says, he spent the time 'studying the structure of American industries, with the aim of discovering why industries were organized in different ways'.[22] His conclusions were written up as 'The Nature of the Firm', one of the most important economics articles ever published.[23] He identified that using the market was costly, and labelled these 'transaction costs'. He argued that firms weigh up the costs of producing things internally, versus using the market. Oliver Williamson added more detail to the manner in which transaction costs mattered.[24] Imagine that Audi buy the radios that they fit into their new cars from Panasonic, and that these radios have to be built to a certain specification. Once the contract has been signed both parties have an incentive to renege. Panasonic may attempt to raise the price of the parts, knowing that a new car without a radio will struggle to sell. Audi may call their bluff, figuring that it would be too hard for Panasonic to sell them elsewhere. Rather than spend money writing and enforcing contracts to mediate such market transactions, it may be cheaper for Audi to produce the radios themselves. They may buy Panasonic. This will give them the managerial tools of reward and punishment that are lacking in open market arrangements. This is known as the hold-up problem, and is a main reason why firms engage in vertical integration.

The transaction cost framework defines a firm as the centralised contractual agent in a team production process. Thinking of firms as teams is another important aspect, because teams utilise joint inputs and it can be hard to detect individual value contribution. A firm is essentially a way to pool individual talent and offer collective rewards. This is in contrast to hiring lots of freelance workers, and paying them market rates for the specific tasks that they perform. To paraphrase Chris Dillow, sometimes it's easier for managers to bang heads together, than haggle over contracts.[25] An extension of the transaction cost framework is known as a 'nexus of contracts' and views the firm as a focal point of a web of contractual arrangements. The bottom line is that the boundaries of a firm are determined by a search to reduce transaction costs.

The 'Coase theorem' is the idea that when transaction costs are zero, the allocation of property rights will be the same regardless of initial endowments. In other words, it doesn't matter to whom a government grants a radio licence, whichever company values it the most will end up owning it. It stems from a 1960 article by Coase called 'The Myth of Social Cost', and has been used as a rationale for introducing property rights regimes to common pool resources. Tradable pollution permits originate with Coase. Provided property rights are well defined and transaction costs are low, the socially optimal outcome will result. But this gives a somewhat misleading account of history. The 'theorem' was attributed to Coase by his colleague at the University of Chicago, George Stigler. Coase was only considering a zero transaction cost environment to emphasise the importance of transaction costs in the real world. It's a bit like a physicist saying, 'imagine a world without gravity; there would be no friction; thus gravity is important', and his mate summarising it as 'we live in a world without gravity'. Although it is possible to improve market efficiency by reducing transaction costs, they can never be eliminated.

The Coase theorem remains a contested and important contribution to economics, law, environmental studies and much else besides. Despite many efforts to contradict it, or downplay it, it occupies a central place in the toolkit of economists. Coase and Stigler also had Warren Nutter and Milton Friedman as colleagues, and during this time Nutter was intending to present a talk in Rochester called 'The Fallacy of the Coase Theorem'. As Stigler recounts,

> He [Nutter] made the mistake of taking a plane from Charlottesville and sitting next to Friedman and when he got to Rochester the paper was retitled 'A New Proof of the Coase Theorem' [laughter].[26]

An alternative way to look at the firm was pioneered by Edith Penrose in 1959.[27] She introduced the concept of 'capabilities', which are defined as the knowledge base of a firm. Building on this, Richard Nelson and Sidney Winter treat capabilities as the local and tacit knowledge that resides within companies.[28] The firm is seen as a local learning system that coordinates the knowledge possessed by employees. Whilst transaction cost approaches tend to be a more mechanical look at how firms respond to changes in relative prices, the capabilities approach takes a softer look at the internal routines of the organisation. Both are important components of how we understand the firm.

4.3   PRICE DISCRIMINATION

I remember when Apple launched the $399 iPod, in 2001, and thinking how expensive it was compared to the market average of $150. Analysts were quick to point out that it had less functionality than its rivals, it was entering a highly competitive market, and the technology industry was in a slump following the dot com crash. It seemed like wishful thinking to charge so much, and people began to make jokes that the name stood for 'idiots price our devices'.[29] But guess what – Apple were right. The pricing strategy was spot on, and they sold 236,000 within 6 months. I also remember following a live stream when the iPhone was announced, and once again analysts queued up to criticise Apple for pricing too high. And the same thing happened with the iPad. On each occasion Apple's sales exceeded expectations. Apple have a remarkable success rate at pricing new products and it's because they have understood value creation.

Prices are the outcome of the interaction between demand and supply, and as we've seen this means that a price will be below the marginal value of the buyer and above the opportunity cost of the seller. If we draw an equilateral triangle with the base along the bottom, the left corner will be the cost and the right corner will be the value. The relative bargaining power of the consumer and the producer will determine how the price falls in between, and who gets the greater share of the gains from trade.

When companies think about pricing strategy they often forget that this triangle exists, paying too much attention to the cost end, and not enough attention to the value. As we've already seen, a company wouldn't bother selling any units unless the marginal revenue (i.e. the price) exceeds their variable costs (this is the shutdown condition). Imagine that a company was launching a new product and set a price that was too high. The result would be that they wouldn't sell much, and they would have to respond by cutting prices. This isn't ideal, but it's doable. Imagine instead that they start off with a price that's too low. Now, they would want to raise the price, but it is a lot more difficult to do this once you've launched.[30] You would think that this fact – that it's harder to raise prices than to reduce them – would mean that firms err on the side of pricing too high. But on the contrary, according to an article in the *McKinsey Quarterly*,

> In our experience, 80 to 90 percent of all poorly chosen prices are too low ... Companies consistently undercharge for products despite spending millions or even billions of dollars to develop or acquire them.[31]

One explanation for this is that they're pricing based on cost, and neglecting value. Apple's success, by contrast, stems from pricing based on value, not cost. As Apple executive Schiller recognises, 'Apple's products aren't priced high – they're priced on the value of what we build into them.'[32] Let's look at this in more detail.

Since value is subjectively determined, it is impossible that potential customers will all have the same demand curves. The definition of price discrimination is charging *different* customers *different* prices for the *same* product. Instead of pricing based on cost differences, it's based on different customers' willingness to pay.

We need to be careful here, because as previously discussed costs are every bit as subjective as demand. Therefore it's difficult to determine whether costs are ever the same. A classic example of price discrimination is the fact that women's dry cleaning tends to be higher priced than men's.[33] But if the costs aren't the same, it isn't price discrimination.

There are three main forms of price discrimination

1. Perfect

   This is where the price reflects the unique marginal value of each customer and captures all consumer surplus. As you might expect this can be quite costly to engage in, so it's more common when the sales price is high (for example estate agents will try to sell highly similar houses for different amounts depending on the maximum willingness to pay of the customers).[34] An interesting example occurred when Radiohead allowed fans to choose the amount of money they paid in order to download their 2007 album, *In Rainbows*. If everyone were totally honest, and paid the amount they believed it was worth, this would be perfect price discrimination. Because the scheme was voluntary, however, at least one person (ahem) obtained some consumer surplus. Although the 'name your own price' model seems rife for abuse, it's employed with success in many industries. In situations where people's decisions are reasonably public (e.g. restaurants), evidence suggests that this is a viable strategy.

2. Direct

   Given that it can be costly to negotiate with each individual customer, some businesses may realise that they don't need to. Even though everyone's demand curve is unique, it may be the case that there are certain groups of people that all have a similar demand curve. For example students tend to have less disposable income than other people, so it might make sense for firms to have one price for students, and one for everyone else. The key issues that need to be addressed are (i) How do you identify the groups? (ii) How do you prevent arbitrage? In order for this strategy to work, it must be reasonably easy to know which group any individual belongs to, and you must be able to prevent those who receive the good for less to sell it on to those who have to pay more.

Many commentators believed that the launch of generic drugs would severely hurt the big pharmaceutical companies, but direct price discrimination segments customers into two groups: for those with an inelastic demand (i.e. not very responsive to price changes) you charge a high price. For those with elastic demand (i.e. very responsive to price changes) you charge a low price. Let's imagine that you have OAPs that are willing to pay a maximum of £2 for a drug, but the market as a whole will pay £8. If you could only charge one price (let's take the average price of £5) it will mean that OAPs can't afford it and also that you're forgoing £3 of potential revenue from everyone else. Direct price discrimination allows you to split the market in two and raise total revenue. It has the additional effect of lowering prices for the most price sensitive groups.

3. Indirect

In some cases it is impossible to categorise customers based on group characteristics, and/or prevent secondary markets from developing. Maybe the OAPs stockpile their cheap drugs and sell them on to the open market to make a profit. Maybe teenagers don a disguise and pose as OAPs. But price discrimination is still possible. Here, you accept that customers with a high willingness to pay *could* get away with pretending that they had a low willingness to pay, but you use a hurdle to discourage them from doing so. This is where generic drugs became so important. On the surface the ability to make very cheap versions of established brands seems to be harmful to the pharmaceutical companies. But branding is all part of the service being provided. If you're not price sensitive, you will want the drugs to have brand name recognition and a nicely designed box. If you are price sensitive then that doesn't matter so much. The two groups will end up paying different prices for the same product, even though both have the option to buy the cheaper one. Therefore the rise of generics allowed pharmaceutical companies to price discriminate, split their market in two and raise revenues. Other examples of indirect price discrimination strategies include:

- Quantity discounts – a single man won't buy a multipack of baked beans, but price conscious people will.
- Coupons – inelastic consumers won't be bothered to cut them out of a magazine and remember to bring them to the shop. But those like Jordon Cox, who stockpiled enough coupons to be able to buy an entire Christmas dinner for just 10p, will.[35]
- Performance-based – inelastic consumers will go for the 8GB iPhone even if they probably don't need the capacity, whilst elastic ones will go for the cheaper, 4GB one.
- Purchase/usage restrictions – rich people can get discounts from making advanced bookings if they want to, but the value of their time means they're willing to pay the full price.
- Paywalls – some newspapers use paywalls as an attempt to prevent non-subscribers from accessing their content, but many paywalls are easy to infiltrate. According to Felix Salmon it is precisely the weakness of the *New York Times*' paywall (all you need to do is alter the URL of the article to see it for free) that makes it work. Ultimately, the *New York Times* wants as large a readership as possible, but they know that some

of their readers either can't be bothered amending the address bar for every article they read, or enjoy the content and are happy about paying for it. The loose paywall helps separate customers into the price sensitive and price insensitive, and gives free content to the former and paid content to the latter.[36]

- Drop out discount – a former student sent me an email he'd received from a company that specialises in securing National Insurance numbers for foreign students. It requires you to register before showing the prices, at which point he decided that they were too expensive. A few minutes later, he received an email offering a 10% discount. Because he'd not completed the order straight away, he'd signalled his price sensitivity, and so the company reduced the price.[37]

- Knowledge-based – the so-called 'secret menus' of various fast food restaurants are becoming increasingly well known, but my favourite example is a sign in the reception of a hotel that reads: 'Ask us about our special offers!' The idea is that inelastic consumers are willing to pay the full rate anyway, and so they do not bother asking. But the price sensitive consumer will notice the sign and ask about the offers. In doing so they reveal themselves as being price sensitive and the hotel will offer a discount. The discount is available to anyone that asks, but the hotel assumes that only the price sensitive will do so! This is even more powerful when you realise that *they don't even need to have a sign*. They may just assume that price sensitive customers will ask for a discount anyway. There is a whole hidden world of price discrimination and so if you pay the full price for something you must clearly not be price sensitive. It's not so much that 'only a fool pays retail', but that only price insensitive people do.

Note that it can be hard to treat all of these as price discrimination, because you could argue that a 4GB and an 8GB are fundamentally different products. But there's an element of price discrimination to such product offerings. Another issue is that price discrimination isn't popular. Websites that ask for a discount coupon at the end of an order journey tend to find that click-through rates *decline*, since people realise that others are getting it more cheaply.[38] But we should embrace price discrimination!

By segmenting business (price inelastic) and leisure travellers (price elastic) airlines offer cheap tickets that *otherwise wouldn't exist*. Price discrimination allows rich people to subsidise poor people. Therefore if you're reasonably savvy, you can profit at the expense of the ignorant, lazy, rich people. For example in a world without price discrimination hotel rooms would reflect the cost of you staying there. But hotels can make a lot of money from additional services such as the mini bar, laundry and entertainment. You may look at the price of a bottle of Heineken and shudder, but price inelastic guests tend to buy it. And it's because the hotel suspect that you might buy it that they subsidise the cost of the room. It's because the minibar is so expensive that you can afford to stay there![39]

And don't forget that price discrimination only applies if it's the same good. However a cold bottle of Heineken in your hotel room is *not* the same good as a warm one on a supermarket shelf several miles away. When you use a mini bar you aren't paying for the drink, you're paying for the service it provides, which includes the convenience. Before the beer can be consumed it must be transported to where the consumer is. It is only 'ready for consumption' when it is in the mini bar, not when it is in the shop.[40] Compared to your next best alternative it is often pretty cheap.

Ultimately trade is a positive-sum game, and both you and the hotel benefit from the minibar. Perhaps it costs more than you'd like, and the hotel extracts a lot of consumer surplus.

But as long as the price is lower than your marginal value, and you're gaining *some* consumer surplus, just enjoy it!

4.4 THE KNOWLEDGE PROBLEM

Adam Smith talked about a model of society where man is governed by self-interest. This strikes many as either inaccurate, or regrettable. Wouldn't we all like to live in a society where this wasn't the case? The ideologists of the Russian Communist Party sought to eradicate cultural diversity by inducing a change in the character of the citizens of the Soviet Union. 'New Soviet man' would demonstrate selfless collectivism and enthusiastically spread the socialist Revolution. In doing so communism would solve the incentive problem, since people would instinctively act in accordance with the greater good. This is why propaganda was such an important tool in the efforts to change the nature of man – and indeed why so many middle managers like to use 'motivational' posters. The response by Ludwig von Mises was to give his intellectual opponents the benefit of the doubt. He granted them the assumption that the incentive problem was solved. But he pointed out that *even if* there's a transformation in human nature, this doesn't solve the economic problem of knowing how to allocate scarce resources.

People now define socialism to mean a myriad of different things, such as the advance of material equality, social 'fairness', etc. However in the context of the times socialism was defined as abolishing private property in the means of production to advance material prosperity. It is important to emphasise that socialism was advocated not on grounds of equality or fairness, but because it would deliver more wealth than capitalism. The stated goals of socialism were:

- Increased prosperity
- Efficient use of resources
- Elimination of business cycles
- Elimination of monopoly power
- Equitable distribution of wealth.

In response to this Mises argued that socialist planning was impossible. His argument was based on the following lines of reasoning:

1. Without private property there is no exchange.
2. Without exchange there are no prices.
3. Without prices there is no information.

He didn't doubt whether socialism could exist, but he demonstrated why it couldn't deliver its promises to generate wealth. By eliminating private property in the means of production you lose the information that only market exchange can generate. In fact it meant that socialism was impossible:

> *Once society abandons free pricing of production goods rational production becomes impossible. Every step that leads away from private ownership of the means of production and the use of money is a step away from rational economic activity.*[41]

He wasn't arguing that socialism was undesirable (although he believed this to be the case), he was arguing that it was inconsistent with its stated aims. Socialism cannot deliver on its promises because 'socialism is the abolition of rational economy'. [42]

The advocates of socialism read Mises' work, but they didn't understand it. Rather than retain private property rights as the foundation of a rational economic order, they tried to come up with ways to generate prices without having to rely on trading. The pioneer of 'market socialism' was Oskar Lange, who asked 'what if central planners *simulate* market competition, and use computers to solve the simultaneous equations?' In other words is resource allocation merely an accounting problem that can be overcome through better technologies?[43] He even talked about placing a statue of Mises in the central planning office, for helping them to improve on their efforts to plan. But he missed the key point: even if the planners have perfect *technical* knowledge, only the institutions of a market process can reveal the knowledge required to assess the alternative uses of the scarce factors of production. As Peter Boettke says,

> [i]n the absence of markets, how do planners know which goods to produce and what production techniques are economically feasible?[44]

The seminal article to address this point is F.A. Hayek's, 'The Use of Knowledge in Society'.[45] In it, he makes a distinction between 'scientific knowledge', which is 'knowledge of general rules', and 'the knowledge of time and place', which is 'special knowledge of circumstances of the fleeting moment not known to others'. You can see how this relates to the notion of entrepreneurship, because although scientific knowledge may be transferable to central authority, the knowledge of time and place is not. It can only be acted upon by an entrepreneur. As Hayek explains,

> the practical problem ... arises precisely because these facts are never so given to a single mind, and because, in consequence, it is necessary that in the solution of the problem knowledge should be used that is dispersed among many people.[46]

We can refer to this challenge as the Hayekian Knowledge Problem: the issue is not deciding upon the allocation of *known* resources, but rather the conditions for the discovery and assimilation of dispersed knowledge to actually *create* new knowledge. Hayek identifies the price system as the communication device that allows this knowledge to be captured. The price system is being used as **a surrogate for knowledge** and it performs three distinct roles:

1. Ex-ante – to forecast the profitability of future projects
2. Ex-post – to show us the profitability of past projects
3. Discovery – to alert entrepreneurs to possible projects.[47]

This is why rational economic calculation requires markets. In the words of Tyler Cowen,

> Without having access to market prices to evaluate the opportunity costs of resource use, socialist planners could not tell which outputs should be produced or how to produce them. When it comes to economic value, the socialist planner is literally like the blind man groping in the dark.[48]

Note that Hayek is praising the price system, as opposed to individual prices. He's not saying that all prices will be perfect, or at their equilibrium values. But according to Ludwig Lachmann 'equilibrium ... prices reflect nothing but the daily balance of expectation'.[49] Therefore they will always be in flux, and never stable. But it's precisely because they are in flux that they are an effective communication device.

This approach turns many textbooks on their head. Instead of viewing capitalism and socialism as different economic systems, there is only a continuum between rational calculation at one end, and arbitrary political discretion at the other. Indeed the Soviet Union was *not* a fundamentally different type of economy to the USA, it was actually a heavily regulated market economy stifled by monopoly production, rent-seeking and arbitrary intervention.[50]

Another way to look at this is to discard the conventional distinction between a 'market' economy and a 'planned' economy. As F.A. Hayek said,

> *This is not a dispute about whether planning is to be done or not. It is a dispute about whether planning is to be done centrally, by one authority for the whole economic system, or is to be divided among many individuals.*[51]

The ends of the continuum are plans by the many, versus plans by the few. Decentralised planning or central planning. Markets or hierarchy.

4.5   INTERNAL MARKETS

My favourite example of the extent of the incoherency of Soviet planning was a memo signed by Joseph Stalin that said,

> *Transfer the sewing machine belonging to the tailor's shop number 1 to factory number 7.*[52]

It seems ludicrous that a leader would have sufficient knowledge to know the most efficient location for a particular sewing machine, and we would all expect a system like this to result in chaos and arbitrariness. But many corporate leaders engage in just as farcical micro management. Indeed the point of this section is not to provide an ideological defence of capitalism, but to say that (i) economic calculation is the foundation of a successful economy; (ii) it is just as relevant within a firm. We do need to be careful once we start talking about firms because there are important differences. The main one is that in a market assets are *alienable*, but in a firm they're not. By 'alienable' we mean two things – 'control rights' (you can sell it), and 'cash flow rights' (you can keep the proceeds). By definition assets within a company are not alienable. If you don't believe me try to sell 'your' laptop and see what happens! It's a bit like the following joke,

> *My neighbour went on holiday recently and I offered to look after his house. 'Treat it as if it's your own' he said before he left, so I sold it.*[53]

By definition there is no ownership within a firm. If you own the tools that you use you are an independent contractor, not an employee. But we can use 'decision rights' as a means to replicate the alienability of assets within a firm, which basically means that managers control their own budget. Not that it belongs to them, but that they control it within certain specified limits. To understand the importance of decision rights think about the 'tragedy of the commons'. The basic lesson is that if nobody owns something, nobody looks after it. If someone owns it, somebody looks after it. If everyone owns it, then nobody looks after it. Decision rights need to be clearly defined such that we avoid the perils and paradox of 'common' ownership. Ownership leads to authority, accountability and responsibility.

The seminal account of this is by Michael Jensen and William Meckling and they argue that you need a control system with effective:

1. Measures (i.e. knowledge flows)
2. Incentives (such as decision rights).[54]

In Chapter 1 we discussed incentives at length, and the purpose of this chapter is to focus on measures. Koch Industries define a 'knowledge process' as 'methods by which we develop, supplant, share and apply knowledge to create value'.[55] Firms can and do use a price system, either via internal markets or shadow markets. If this isn't appropriate, metrics can be employed to replicate the knowledge generated by markets. One way of utilising suitable measures is benchmarking, although this can be criticised for restricting the ambition of a company. It can be very hard to outperform a benchmark, therefore to some extent benchmarking puts a constraint on firm growth. But when Southwest Airlines were the industry leader in on-time arrivals, they were still able to use benchmarking. They just had to take a broad view as to what services they provided, and ended up trying to emulate things they observed in Nascar.

Knowledge processes are about more than just measuring things. At an individual level our knowledge is limited by our technical feasibility and bounded rationality. Once management attempt to articulate local/tacit knowledge it becomes scientific knowledge and requires (i) interpretation; and (ii) argumentation. Sharing knowledge isn't a passive transfer, it's an active process that gives rise to criticism. For this to function we need open minds, tolerance and free speech – in Polanyi's terms a 'Republic of the Firm'. The implications for managers are as follows:

1. Ensure that knowledge is effectively acquired
2. Measure productivity where possible
3. Share knowledge with peers through constructive dialogue.

If a company is doing a decent job solving their internal knowledge problems, we should find evidence of the following:

- Sunk costs are ignored
- Profit centres clearly measure value creation
- Resources are transferred within the firm at opportunity cost
- Departments are not cross-subsidising
- An open minded approach to benchmarking
- Employees challenge procedures regardless of hierarchy.

The problem with using metrics is that these can only ever be a proxy for the things that you really care about – the creation of economic value. Therefore if the metrics are mis-specified you will end up with bad outcomes. Here are some famous examples:

- A Soviet nail factory measured the total weight of nails being produced. The outcome was a one ton nail.[56]

- The FBI measured performance based on the number of policy reports being produced. The outcome was a lot of reports that no one read.[57]
- A computer manufacturer wanted to improve the time it took to fix bugs, so they identified the number of fixes as a key measure and incentivised developers to improve on it. The result was that developers began writing sloppy code that would be easy to fix later on.[58]
- Charles Dickens' publisher paid him based on the number of words written. That's why his books are so long.

These all exhibit the **Heisenberg Principle** of incentive design: 'a performance metric is useful as a performance metric only as long as it isn't used as a performance metric.'[59] Which begs the question – why not measure *value* directly? Why not bring markets inside the firm? Why not 'markets not targets'?

Knowledge tends to exist in a dispersed and fragmented form throughout an organisation. By contrast decision rights tend to be concentrated within senior management. If an employee notices a particular issue they are supposed to bring it to the attention of their line manager. In other words information is supposed to flow up the chain of command to someone in a position of authority who will decide what to do. We can call this the 'hierarchical' system and when initiated in society at large it is socialism. Alternatively, you could have a regime where decision rights flow down an organisation to the person with access to the information. This is how markets function.

In a traditional American motor car assembly line, if you noticed a fault you were supposed to notify your manager. This is 'hierarchy', and seems to be common sense. But Toyota turned this upside down. The Toyota plants had a number of cords that dangle at various points along the assembly line. If an employee spots a problem rather than communicate to a superior (who would then decide what action to take) the employee can shut down production themselves. Whilst American and European assembly plants would require 25% of their floor space to correct faulty vehicles that came off the production line, Toyota had significantly fewer cars needing repair.[60] Sometimes people respond by saying that such a policy requires a well-educated labour force, or that this is OK generally but you need to switch to centralised command during a crisis. But think about the procedures if you notice a fire. What are you supposed to do? Inform a line manager? Or sound the alarm? In a crisis it's all the more important to rely on decentralised decision making that has access to the knowledge of time and place.

The infamous statistician Francis Galton noticed something fascinating about the fete game 'Guess the Weight of an Ox'. He found that the average guess tended to beat the most accurate individual guess. The idea that the aggregated information of the crowd can beat expert judgment is known as the 'wisdom of crowds'.[61] The simple way to put this is that 'the quant may be smarter than any other person in the room, but he's not smarter than the room as a whole'.[62] Or, as my Montenegrin students tell me, 'a man and a donkey are smarter than a man'. This phenomenon is deep and widespread. There is even evidence that it operates over time – multiple guesses made by the same person in different time periods are better than a single guess.[63] Markets are an institutional mechanism to draw upon the wisdom of crowds.

An internal market can be defined as 'an institution through which members of the same company buy and sell goods using a price mechanism', and they are becoming increasingly popular. In the 1990s BP Amoco used internal markets to try to reduce their Greenhouse gas emissions. They hit reduction targets nine years ahead of schedule.[64] Hewlett Packard used internal markets to let different departments buy and sell rights to computing power.[65]

And NASA's Cassini mission to Saturn managed to come in under budget after employing an internal market.[66] At a social level, we've seen how powerful markets are at allocating resources. There's no reason why they cannot be utilised within a firm. Instead of giving the head of IT discretion over who should get a new computer, and when, give employees a budget and let them decide what resources they need.

But markets aren't just about deciding who gets what. Markets also uncover information that wouldn't otherwise exist. HP gave salespeople shares to trade futures contracts on printer sales, and this market beat official forecasts.[67] In an internal market at Eli Lilly and Co employees bid up the value of drugs that became the most popular on the market. Google use internal markets extensively.[68] When the future is uncertain markets can help convert some of it into risk, and deliver real time probability estimates of various events. If this sounds like gambling, that's because it is. When internal markets are devoted to people's expectations about future events, we refer to it as a **prediction market**.

The advantage of prediction markets over experts is the wisdom of crowds. The advantage of prediction markets over surveys is the use of incentives. In a market there is a benefit to being right, and a cost in being wrong. If it's an internal one it may not be wise to trade with hard cash. But even if employees do not have real money on the line, you are creating incentives to be sincere. Whilst opinion polls ask 'would you buy?' a prediction market asks 'how many do you think we'll sell?' You should not be surprised that they generate different outcomes. And evidence suggests prediction markets are worth taking seriously. When it comes to US Presidential elections markets are closer than polls at predicting the winner 74% of the time.[69] One way to internalise this is to bet on your beliefs. If people disagree about something try to understand the intensity of the disagreement. We're used to democratic situations where one man gets one vote. But offices are political enough. In markets strength of preference wins out. If you're not willing to bet on what you claim, it implies you don't hold that belief very strongly. It helps to reveal information. According to Betsey Stevenson and Justin Wolfers,

> *The success of prediction markets and expectation polls tells us something truly humbling – that knowledge doesn't just reside in the executive suit or in the quantitative model. For executives nimble and humble enough to accept this, it presents a great opportunity.*[70]

NOTES

1. McInerney, J. (1984) *Bright Lights, Big City*, Vintage, p. 86.
2. Evans, A.J., Sola, D. and Poenaru, A. (2008) Enterprising Britain: Building the enterprise capital of the world, independent report for the Conservative Party.
3. Evans, Sola and Poenaru, Enterprising Britain (n 2).
4. Schumpeter, J.A. (1942[1950]) *Capitalism, Socialism, and Democracy*, Harper and Brothers, p. 83.
5. Schumpeter, J.A. (1934) *The Theory of Economic Development*, Transaction, [first published in 1911 as Theorie der wirtschaftlichen Entwicklung].
6. Schumpeter, *Capitalism, Socialism, and Democracy* (n 4), p. 132.
7. 'The meaning of Bill Gates', *The Economist*, 26 June 2008.
8. Schumpeter, *The Theory of Economic Development* (n 5).
9. Knight, F. (1921[2006]) *Risk, Uncertainty and Profit*, Dover, pp. 231–232.
10. Keynes, J.M. (1937) The General Theory of Employment, *The Quarterly Journal of Economics*, **51** (2), 209–223.

11. In their book *Organizing Entrepreneurial Judgment*, Nikolai Foss and Peter Klein view entrepreneurship as decision making under conditions of uncertainty, and provide an excellent contribution to the theory of the firm. Foss, N.J. and Klein, P.G. (2012) *Organizing Entrepreneurial Judgment*, Cambridge University Press.

12. I've used the vegemite sandwich as an example because it is my own favourite sandwich, and because I wanted to make a point about how preferences are subjective. The white chocolate cookie sandwich is the result of a Reddit strand asking Subway employees what the most disgusting sandwich they've ever been asked to make was. [http://www.reddit.com/r/AskReddit/comments/1a5rkq/subway_employees_of_reddit_whats_the_most/, accessed September 2013].

13. Stossel, J. and Binkley, G. (2006) MYTH: Price-Gouging is Bad, *ABC News*, 12 May [http://abcnews.go.com/2020/Stossel/story?id=1954352, accessed 17 November 2013].

14. A glib response to this is that it is obvious that generators would be needed. But Shepperson only has limited space in his truck. Why take generators, and not blankets, or water or medical supplies?

15. Kirzner, I.M. (1973) *Competition and Entrepreneurship*, University of Chicago Press.

16. The 'known and unknown' comment was made by Donald Rumsfeld at a press conference on 12 February 2002. He provides further discussion of the point he was making in his memoirs, Rumsfeld, D. (2010) *Known and Unknown*, Penguin, pp. xiii–xvi.

17. Kirzner, *Competition and Entrepreneurship* (n 15).

18. Mises, L.v. (1949[1996]) *Human Action: A Treatise on Economics*, Fox & Wiles, p. 290.

19. Margolis, J. (2011) So what's new? *Business life*, [BA in-flight magazine], March, p. 16.

20. Source: Schurenberg, E. (2012) What's an entrepreneur? The best answer ever, *Inc.Com*, 9 January [http://www.inc.com/eric-schurenberg/the-best-definition-of-entepreneurship.html, accessed 19 September 2013]. A detailed definition of entrepreneurship is that it is 'the manifest ability and willingness of individuals, on their own, within and outside existing organisations, to perceive and create new economic opportunities … and introduce their ideas in the market, in the face of uncertainty and other obstacles, by making decisions on location, form and the use of resources and institutions' (see Wennekers, S. and Thurik, R. (1999) Linking entrepreneurship and economic growth, *Small Business Economics*, **13** (1), 27–55, at 46–47).

21. See Hughes, T.P. (2004) *American Genesis: A Century of Invention and Technological Enthusiasm, 1870–1970*, University of Chicago Press, p. 251.

22. Coase, R.H., 'Biographical', NobelPrize.org [http://www.nobelprize.org/nobel_prizes/economic-sciences/laureates/1991/coase-bio.html, accessed 7 October 2013].

23. Coase, R.H. (1937) The Nature of the Firm, *Economica*, **4** (16), 386–405.

24. Williamson, O.E. (1979) Transaction-Cost Economics: The governance of contractual relations, *Journal of Law and Economics*, **22** (2), 233–262.

25. Dillow, C. (2007) Splitting the home office and transaction costs, *Stumbling and Mumbling*, 24 January [http://stumblingandmumbling.typepad.com/stumbling_and_mumbling/2007/01/splitting_the_h.html, accessed 7 October 2013].

26. Kitch, E.W. (1983) The fire of truth: a remembrance of law and economics at Chicago, 1932–1970, *Journal of Law and Economics*, **26** (1),163–234, at 227.

27. Penrose, E.T. (1959) *The Theory of the Growth of the Firm*, John Wiley & Sons.

28. Nelson, R.R. and Winter, S.G. (1982) *An Evolutionary Theory of Economic Change*, Harvard University Press.

29. See 'The meaning of iPod', *The Economist*, 10 June 2004.

30. One option might be to quickly release a 'new' version that has minor modifications.

31. Marn, M.V., Roegner, E.V. and Zawada, C.C. (2003) Pricing new products, *The McKinsey Quarterly*, **3**.

32. McCracken, H. (2012) Apple's Phil Schiller on the State of the Mac, Time's Technologizer blog, 26 October.

33. Landsburg, S.E. (1998) Taken to the Cleaners? *Slate.com*, 3 July. [http://www.slate.com/articles/arts/everyday_economics/1998/07/taken_to_the_cleaners.html, accessed 19 September 2013].

34. Having said this, in some cultures individual negotiating is used for small value items, such as food in a Moroccan souk.
35. Wallop, H. (2013) 'Extreme couponing': How I did whole Christmas shop for 4p, *Daily Telegraph*, 20 December.
36. Salmon, F. (2011) How the New York Times Paywall is Working, *Wired.com*, 14 August.
37. I am grateful to Bastien Hagen for sending me this example.
38. Oliver, R. and Shor, M. (2003) Digital Redemption of Coupons: Satisfying and Dissatisfying Effects on Promotion Codes, *Journal of Product and Brand Management*, **12** (2), 121–134.
39. Harford, T. (2007) Minibar Economics: Why you should stay at hotels that overcharge for drinks and Wi-Fi access, *Slate*, 17 February, [http://www.slate.com/articles/arts/the_undercover_economist/2007/02/minibar_economics.html, accessed 19 September 2013].
40. Mises, L.v. (1912[1981]) *The Theory of Money and Credit*, Liberty Fund, p. 196.
41. Mises, L.v. (1936[1981]) *Socialism*, Liberty Fund, p. 102.
42. Mises, L.v. (1920[1990]) *Economic Calculation in the Socialist Commonwealth*, Ludwig von Mises Institute, p. 26.
43. This is part of the reason for the rise of linear programming, and to some extent constitutes the advent of quantitative macroeconomics.
44. Boettke, P.J. (1989) Austrian Institutionalism: A Reply, *Research in the History of Economic Thought and Methodology*, **6**, 181–202, at 191.
45. Hayek, F.A. (1945) The Use of Knowledge in Society, *American Economic Review*, **35** (4), 519–530.
46. Hayek, The Use of Knowledge in Society (n 45), 530.
47. Boettke, P.J. (1990) *The Political Economy of Soviet Socialism: The Formative Years, 1918–1928*, Kluwer, pp. 130–131.
48. Cowen, T. (1995) A Review of G.C. Archibald's Information, Incentives, and the Economics of Control, *Journal of International and Comparative Economics*, **4**, 243–249.
49. Lachmann, L. (1976) From Mises to Shackle: An Essay on Austrian Economics and the Kaleidic Society, *Journal of Economic Literature*, **14** (1), 54–62.
50. See Boettke, P.J. (1993) *Why Perestroika Failed: The Politics and Economics of Socialist Transformation*, Routledge, p. 59.
51. Hayek, The Use of Knowledge in Society (n 45), 520–521.
52. Kapuscinski, R. (1994) *Imperium*, Granta (English translation). According to Kapuscinski, 'the system depended on that kind of punctiliousness, on a psychotic control of every detail, an obsessive desire to rule over everything'.
53. I recollect this joke appearing in a list of the best jokes from the Edinburgh festival, but I'm unable to find the source.
54. Jensen, M.C. and Meckling, W.H. (1976) Theory of the firm: managerial behaviour, agency costs and ownership structure, *Journal of Financial Economics*, **3** (4), 305–360.
55. Koch, C.G. (2006) *The Science of Success*, John Wiley & Sons, p. 101.
56. See Chapter 12 for more detail.
57. Fisman, R. and Sullivan, T. (2013) *The Org. The Underlying Logic of the Office*, Twelve Books, p. 231.
58. Adams, S. (1995) The Dilbert Principle, *Wall Street Journal*, 22 May [http://voxmagister.ifsociety.org/dilbert_principle.htm, accessed 17 December 2013].
59. Fisman and Sullivan, *The Org* (n 57), p. 231.
60. Womack, J.P., Jones, D.T. and Roos, D. (1990) *The Machine that Changed the World*, Harper Perennial.
61. Surowiecki, J. (2004) *The Wisdom of Crowds*, Doubleday.
62. Stevenson, B. and Wolfers, J. (2012) Crowds are this election's real winners, *Bloomberg*, 19 November.
63. 'The crowd within', *The Economist*, 28 June 2008.
64. Malone, T.W. (2004) Bringing the market inside, *Harvard Business Review*, April.

65. Malone, Bringing the market inside (n 64).

66. Wessin, R.R. and Porter, D. (2007) The Cassini Resource Exchange, *Ask Magazine*, **16**, 14–18.

67. Malone, Bringing the market inside (n 64).

68. Coles, P., Lakhani, K. and McAfee, A. (2007) Prediction Markets at Google, Harvard Business School Case No. 9-607-088, 20 August.

69. Berg, J.E., Nelson, F.D.,and Rietz, T.A. (2008) Prediction market accuracy in the long run, *International Journal of Forecasting*, **24** (2), 285–300.

70. Stevenson, B. and Wolfers, J. (2012) Crowds are this election's real winners, *Bloomberg*, 19 November.

CHAPTER 5

Competition and the Market Process

'Only through the principle of competition has political economy any pretension to the character of a science.'

—John Stuart Mill[1]

Despite its importance the term 'competition' had been used by economists up until the twentieth century with barely a thought – it meant the same as it did in common discourse. It was shared by both the classical economists and managers, and meant 'trying to outdo your rivals'. Whether in sport or in business 'competition' was a *verb*. As we shall see, however, an alternative view of competition began to dominate. Some economists treated 'competition' as an *adjective* with which to label various types of theoretical market. And policymakers used this as a basis to regulate. In this chapter we will look at the theoretical reasons why this came about, but also acknowledge a trend away from it. Increasingly the discipline is returning to the pre-twentieth century attention to processes, evolution and spontaneous order. This is good, because economic theory should reflect business reality. The key issue is whether we view markets as a dynamic process or as a static state.

There is a famous quote from Keynes,

The ideas of economists and political philosophers, both when they are right and when they are wrong, are more powerful than is commonly understood. Indeed the world is ruled by little else. Practical men, who believe themselves to be quite exempt from any intellectual influence, are usually the slaves of some defunct economist.[2]

This is especially true when it comes to competition theory. Even those who disparage and discount the advice of economists rely almost entirely on economic theories to make their arguments. Understanding the basis for regulation, and the role that collusion and monopolies play in a market economy, is a crucial part of the competitive landscape.

5.1 MARKET CONCENTRATION

Think of an archetypal market – a place where buyers and sellers meet to trade. It's probably noisy, chaotic and exciting. In the hustle and bustle of a Moroccan souk it's impossible to pass by a stall without entering into a frenzied negotiation. In some ways this embodies what economists have in mind when they talk about 'perfect competition'. Textbook models will make several assumptions, which come close to holding in places like Agadir. For example:

- A homogenous commodity (i.e. no product differentiation)
- A large number of relatively small buyers and sellers
- Free entry and exit into and out of the market
- Perfect information
- Perfect factor mobility
- Zero transaction costs.

These assumptions are important, because they generate some important implications. *If* the above assumptions hold, we can say that the market will exhibit two forms of efficiency:

1. Allocative efficiency

    If goods are homogenous then there will be a wide availability of substitutes. This will bid down the market-clearing price until price (P) equals marginal cost (MC). This implies that the value that consumers place on the good is equal to the cost of the resources used to produce it. In other words, resources are allocated such that the best value comes from their use.

2. Productive efficiency

    Free entry means that if firms are making profit (AR>AC) there will be new entrants, which raises AC for all firms, and competes away the profit. Similarly any losses (AR<AC) will result in firms leaving the industry, reducing AC.[3] In equilibrium firms make zero profit (AR=AC) and will end up producing at the minimum of the average cost curve. This occurs when goods are made at lowest possible cost. This puts the economy on the outer limit of what is known as the **'production possibility frontier'** (PPF).

If the assumptions of perfect competition fail to hold – if information is imperfect (i.e. asymmetric), if the factors of production are immobile, if there are significant transaction costs – then we are in the realm of 'imperfect' competition. Indeed let's imagine the polar opposite of some of the assumptions that we made:

- A clearly defined heterogeneous product with no close substitutes
- A single seller
- Prohibitive barriers to entry and exit.

All three of these serve as useful definitions of a 'monopoly' and generate important concerns. If perfect competition doesn't hold, we won't have allocative and productive efficiency. In particular, absent market competition firms may restrict output and increase prices so that they divert consumer surplus into profit. At this point it is important to stress that our definition of perfect competition and monopoly are imaginary constructs. They are hypothetical tools that economists use to benchmark reality. They are not literal descriptions of reality. However that didn't stop economists and policymakers from using this framework as a means to regulate real markets. To do so they attempted to measure the extent to which a market approximates a monopoly. The problem with identifying monopolies is that if you have a narrow definition (e.g. a single seller) then there are no monopolies, but if you have a broad definition (e.g. the seller of a heterogeneous product) then *every* good would count. We should also remember that substitutes are a subjective phenomenon and so there's no unambiguous way to define a substitute let alone 'close' ones. This didn't stop economists from using a vague definition, and generally speaking, if an individual firm has more than 25% market share it tends to be considered a monopoly. More formally, a 'Herfindahl Index' can be computed which sums together the squared market share of all of the firms in an industry. A perfectly competitive industry would have a Herfindahl index of 0, and a monopoly would be 1. The higher the number, the more concentrated the market. Notice that competition is being defined as *market concentration*.

The concept of **'natural monopoly'** refers to a situation where the economies of scale are so large that the optimal number of firms in the market is one. As we shall see, even in natural monopoly situations this doesn't mean that competition cannot occur. The water industry may be considered a natural monopoly, but it must still compete with other firms to acquire the scarce resources that they need. The copper used in pipes has multiple uses. Indeed the claim that 'we can't rely on competition because it is a natural monopoly' is flawed because we cannot tell if it is a natural monopoly unless we see how competitive it is.[4] In addition, we will look at how in some cases apparently 'natural' monopolies rely on barriers to entry (and *not* economies of scale), and how in other cases natural monopolies are beneficial for consumers.

5.2 COLLUSION

Focusing solely on perfect competition and monopoly therefore deprives you of any real world application. It's boring as well, because neither have scope for strategy. In the case of perfect competition firms are simply choosing a level of output in response to the given market price (over which they have no influence). In a monopoly the firm is making a pricing decision immune from the threat of competition. The concept of **'oligopoly'** is an attempt to make things more realistic, by introducing a degree of market power. It can be defined as a small number of sellers dominating the vast majority of a market. In contrast to perfect competition or monopoly, oligopolies give rise to strategic interaction, because your competitors' decisions will have a direct impact on what happens to you. There are three forms of oligopoly model that are interesting to understand:

1. Cournot competition
    This is where firms simultaneously choose a level of output. They would both like to split the market in two (i.e. act as a shared monopoly) but this isn't a stable outcome since both firms have an incentive to produce slightly more than the other in order to boost their own profit.
2. Stackelberg competition
    Where firms can make a sequential choice and first mover advantage means that whichever firm moves first can enjoy higher profits.
3. Bertrand competition
    Where firms simultaneously choose a level of price. Similar to Cournot competition, they would like to charge high prices and act like monopolists. But they both have an incentive to undercut the other and capture the entire market. At the extreme Bertrand competition demonstrates how you can end up with the perfectly competitive outcome (i.e. P=MC) with just two (non-collusive) firms competing. You can think of Unilever

and Procter & Gamble as an example of two firms that dominate a market (in this case consumer goods) and yet still compete such that prices are close to marginal cost. Indeed in some situations you don't even need a second firm, simply the *threat* of entry is sufficient to ensure the monopolist doesn't abuse their position. One Time Warner customer in Kansas City was very pleased to receive an increase in the speed of their internet service (from 10mbps to 15mbps) in addition to a cut in the price (from around $40 per month to $25). The reason for this was the potential entry of Google Fiber.[5]

Interest in oligopoly emerged not only because it seemed a way of utilising economic theory for policy prescriptions, but also because it allowed economists to utilise game theory. To an economist game theory *is* strategy, and it has become a highly popular way to understand decision making.

The reason regulators are particularly keen on oligopoly theory is because strategic interaction generates the possibility of collusion. The concern is that oligopolistic firms operate as a shared monopoly – i.e. a cartel. A cartel is an organisation of sellers designed to coordinate supply decisions so that the joint profits of the members will be maximised. But how worried should we be? It's a remarkable fact that even successful collusive behaviour fails to last over time. For example, in 1973 OPEC reduced oil production by 12% almost overnight. As you might expect, the price of a barrel of oil went from $9 before the hike to $50 by 1980. *This* is why regulators fear cartels. But in 1988 it was back down to just $15. What happened? Here's a clue: in 1973 50% of global oil was produced though OPEC. In 2006 it was 35%. High oil prices were a signal that incentivised several entrepreneurial responses:

- People conserve existing oil – people stop using oil for their less pressing needs.
- Suppliers search for new oil – oil companies won't be investing billions of dollars searching for oil in Nigeria when it sells for $9 a barrel, but at $50 a barrel it may become profitable.
- Buyers find substitutes for oil – remember that there are substitutes for everything. You may think that there are no substitutes for oil, but we always have a choice. If not oil, then gas or batteries. At the extreme consumers are able to abstain. In the book *Engleby* a vegetarian saw 'a single dish of sweaty dumpling and gravy' and complained to a steward that there was no option available. The unhelpful yet accurate response was, 'Of course there's an option, miss. You can either 'ave it, or not 'ave it.'[6]

As a result the effect of OPEC's supply side shock is that within 15 years prices had *halved*, and the world became less reliant on OPEC. According to *The Economist*, 'oil shocks do not hurt as much because oil is used less intensively than before, because the economy is more flexible and because central banks are better at controlling inflation.'[7] You could argue that cartels have immense power to inflict damage on consumers, but they only have a limited ability to follow through with this. The more they abuse their cartel position, the less stable it becomes. I'm not trying to trivialise what was an incredibly important period. But I am using a 'worst case scenario': this is an oligopoly that is actually run as a cartel in one of the most important global industries that is deliberately trying to screw customers ... and yet their power was significantly diminished.

But even if we agree that restricting supply makes customers worse off, don't producers have the right to choose their own level of output? The Trappist Abbey of St Sixtus of

Westvleteren will only sell two cases of their famous dark ale to each customer, who must have previously made an appointment to visit the Abbey. In November 2011 the monks released a batch of 93 000 six-packs, but only decided to sell 70 000 of them in the whole of 2012.[8] Should they be compelled to sell more? Most people would probably say no, and that the only times when restrictions of supply should be prevented are when they are done in concert with other 'competitors'. But collusion is inherently unstable. Experimental evidence reveals a number of factors that undermine attempts to collude:

- Number of firms – the bigger the cartel, the harder it is to maintain agreement.
- Detection of price cuts – it's often difficult to tell if members are cheating.
- Low entry barriers – it's not easy to prevent non-cartel members from competing.
- Unstable demand conditions – firms may have different outlooks for future demand, and disagree on how they should respond.
- Difference in costs – if some firms are more efficient than others they would prefer to capture more market share.

This takes us back to the Keynes quote. You often encounter non-economists who argue that certain forms of market are conducive to collusion and that this leads to inefficient outcomes. They are correct. But economists devote a lot of time to the study of collusion and the basic conclusion is that it's hard to see it work in theory, and rare to see it work in practice. But even if it does occur in practice, this doesn't necessarily mean that the benefits of trying to prevent it outweigh the costs. In Chapter 12 we will see that even if there are costs of market failure, this isn't sufficient to declare that government intervention is desirable. Even if market competition leads to 'inefficient' outcomes, what about the political costs involved in trying to correct them? In many cases collusion breaks down naturally, and competition can act as a swifter regulatory device than government intervention. Even if markets generate outcomes that are deemed inferior to a hypothetical alternative, attempts to correct it through regulatory intervention will take time and be costly. For example Fred Foldvary and Daniel Klein show how technology changes can often solve market failure quicker than government.[9] And regulating through competition avoids the danger that the regulatory agency gets captured by the industry, and ends up protecting *competitors*, as opposed to *competition*.

Perhaps the biggest downside of regulation is that it has what Jeffrey Friedman refers to as 'a homogenising effect on market behaviour overall'.[10] It is in the nature of markets for firms to compete on different margins and to experiment. This is how we discover what works, and what does not. By definition, regulation imposes a single opinion on all participants. It forces everyone to act in the same way. This creates systemic risk, because if that way turns out to be misguided, we have no alternative.

In the UK the regulatory body is the Competition Commission (CC), which describes itself as 'an independent public body that conducts in-depth inquiries into mergers, markets and the regulation of the major regulated industries, ensuring healthy competition between companies in the UK for the benefit of companies, customers and the economy'.[11] It will investigate mergers when the business being taken over has a turnover in the UK of at least £70 million; or the combined businesses supply (or acquire) at least 25% of a particular product or service in the UK (or in a substantial part of the UK), and the merger results in an increase in the share of supply or consumption. In order to do this they firstly define the market, then calculate the market concentration, and then make recommendations. These could include price ceilings, the forced sale of business units, or forced joint ventures. But are they necessary? Just because a firm has more than 25% market share doesn't mean that we automatically get bad outcomes associated with 'monopolies'.

5.3 MARKET CONTESTABILITY

The main insight from the static approach is that in perfect competition price should equal marginal cost. But if costs are subjective, how can we know what they are? Indeed in some situations the P=MC framework breaks down completely. Credit card companies operate in what is known as a **two sided industry** because they need to attract businesses that accept their use, as well as customers to carry them.[12] Their pricing strategy will be different from 'one sided' firms, because if their user base increases, it will increase demand for their product. Therefore it might be profit maximising to charge prices that bear little relation to their costs. They might give away free card readers to restaurants, to generate a large network effect. Nightclubs know that if they discount the entry for women, they can charge higher prices to men. Entrepreneurs are constantly generating pricing strategies that pour scorn on the neatness of textbook theory.

Recollect that in equilibrium perfectly competitive firms make zero profit. If this is true, then if you observe profit in the real world it implies that the market is not perfectly competitive. This is a problem, because the allocative and productive efficiency conditions fail to hold, and so we have the standard justification for competition regulation: the market is inefficient. But let's read that statement again. In *equilibrium* perfectly competitive firms make zero profit. The existence of profit could also imply that the market is in disequilibrium. We have a choice to make here. Do we view profit as a sign of inefficiency, or do we view it as a sign that we're not in equilibrium? The static approach is to assume we're in equilibrium, and therefore we view profit as a sign of inefficiency. The dynamic approach is to conclude that the market is simply in disequilibrium. And when you look at the absurdity of some of the assumptions we made at the beginning, this shouldn't be inconceivable. According to F.A. Hayek,

> [in competitive equilibrium] it is assumed that the data for the different individuals are fully adjusted to each other, while the problem that requires explanation is the nature of the process by which the data are thus adjusted.[13]

It's not surprising that profit seems an anomaly when you've already assumed that markets clear. In the real world, it's profit that ensures that they do.[14] But they are temporary phenomena:

> Pure profit opportunities emerge continually as errors are made by market partici-pants in a changing world. The inevitably fleeting character of these opportunities arises from the powerful market tendency for entrepreneurs to notice, exploit, and then eliminate these pure price differentials.[15]

Profits are not only temporary, according to this view, but also perhaps illusionary. Lipset and Schneider find that the public have a tendency to overestimate how much profit firms make.[16] There is often public support for taxes on the windfall profits of oil and gas companies, but in 2013 the profit margin for 'major integrated oil and gas' firms was just 6.1%.[17] But even if our understanding were accurate, a firm's accounting profit will overstate its real (or 'economic') profit. That isn't to say that firms don't make profit. But we need to carefully understand the social importance of profit.

In January 2008 Exxon Mobil announced record profits of $40bn. Most of us recoil at the largesse and think of things such as greed and desert. But profit serves two functions:

1. Profit provides an incentive – a reward for entrepreneurial discovery
2. Profit provides knowledge – a signal to mobilise resources.

One of the most important lessons of economics is seeing beyond the incentive function (and the issue of motivation) to consider the knowledge function (and the issue of calculation). Profit isn't merely a return on investment; it's the signal that allows entrepreneurs to navigate the market. Recollect that profit derives from an entrepreneurial exposure to uncertainty. It can be defined as 'residual earnings after all contractual claims (incurred for the use of resources) have been met.'[18] This is taking a dynamic view of markets. By contrast the static view defines profit as 'passive or accidental earnings as a consequence of deviations from perfect competition'. Sometimes these are referred to as 'rents', and imply that profits are regrettable and the only thing they signal is inefficiency and waste.

We can see this distinction between the dynamic and static view more sharply when we look at the implications for advertising. According to the static view, espoused by the likes of J.K. Galbraith, brands are a socially wasteful attempt to either signal wealth or capture rents. But advertising is only seen as inefficient 'rent' if you believe that the conditions of perfect competition already hold. According to the dynamic view, put forward by the likes of F.A. Hayek, advertising (i.e. the diffusion of information relating to products) is the means to generate the type of knowledge that perfect competition pre-supposes! Brands have important information content, and if we didn't have them where else would tastes come from?

Thus far we've contrasted the static and dynamic view of markets and suggested that by defining competition based on *concentration*, regulators misunderstand the nature of the market process. So what's the alternative? For a start, we need to consider what the appropriate benchmark should be.

- Not vs. historical state – if it's in the past, the data has changed.
- Not vs. hypothetical ideal state – perfect competition is a useful thought experiment to compare with the real world, but it's misleading to see it as an attainable goal. In 2007 the only two US satellite radio stations on the market – Sirius and XM – wanted to merge. Regulators objected on the grounds that moving from two firms to one reduced competition. And indeed in terms of market concentration, this is correct. But as Steve Chapman pointed out, 'the alternative to one (merged) satellite radio company may not be two companies but none'.[19] The main reason they wanted to merge was because they were losing money.

Rather, we might compare to what happens if only people licensed by authority can operate, or if prices are fixed by government planners.[20] In other words we're going to see how regulatory agencies can be a *source* of anticompetitive behaviour, as opposed to the *solution*.

Let us define a competitive market not as containing perfect competition characteristics (i.e. by market concentration), but one that is **contestable.** In other words, providing new entrants are able to challenge for the profits being generated by incumbents, the market is competitive. If we define a monopoly as 'an enforceable property right in a product or market share'[21] then we see that it's an extra-market phenomenon. Monopolies can only persist if legally protected. Since the *barriers* to entry and exit are due to government regulations, their only responsibility in providing a 'competitive market' is refraining from restrictions on businesses. Remarkably, according to this view, regulation and competition policy are not ways to control monopolies – they're the reason monopolies exist! In fact regulations can be counterproductive since they raise the cost of doing business, offering an advantage to existing firms, or larger ones who can afford legal advice and regulatory expertise. When entry is free we get the good results regardless of the situation with market share.

It's important to make a clear distinction here between barriers to entry and costs of entry. In particular:

- Costs of entry are an important part of the market process. Since they reflect real scarcities they provide a market test for potential entrepreneurs and in doing so prevent resources being wasted. They are an unavoidable *constraint*.
- Barriers to entry are imposed upon a market process. Because they are a political phenomenon they are unrelated to the cost (in terms of resources used) of a particular product. Unlike costs of entry, barriers can prevent value-added enterprises from satisfying unmet needs. They are an unnecessary *obstacle*.

In the UK more than 90% of motorway service stations are operated by just four companies – Extra, Moto, Roadchef and Welcome Break. But this lack of competition is the result of barriers to entry. It is very hard to get planning permission to build new ones, and they cannot be made into a destination in their own right.[22]

Another type of barrier to entry is government licensing. Many people would argue that professions such as doctors or lawyers should require a government approved licence to operate, but even interior designers need one these days. According to *The Economist*, 'Florida will not let you work as an interior designer unless you complete a four-year university degree and a two-year apprenticeship and pass a two-day examination.'[23] They claim that the number of workers that need a licence has risen from under 5% in the 1950s, to around 30% now. To see how this harms labour mobility they present the following example,

> *Jestina Clayton is an African hair-braider with 23 years of experience. But the Utah Barber, Cosmetologist/Barber, Electrologist and Nail Technician Licensing Board told her that she cannot practise her craft unless she first obtains a license – which means spending up to $18,000 on 2,000 hours of study,* none of it devoted to African hair-braiding.[24]

You don't need to be a conspiracy theorist to wonder whether these regulations are designed to help protect consumers, or to help protect the interests of rivals.

Although barriers to entry play a critical role in harming the market process, there is a tendency for people to use the term 'barrier' too loosely. Based on the definitions above, things like economies of scale, product differentiation, advertising or network effects are in fact *costs* of entry, not barriers. Often they are real scarcities (e.g. advertising costs), or costs already incurred (e.g. start-up costs). If a potential competitor cannot cover these costs, then it is not a profitable venture and it is not a market failure if they are unable to gain command of scarce resources. After all *constraints* play an important role in assuring the efficient allocation of scarce capital – it's only *obstacles* that undermine this process. A dynamic view of markets sees temporary profit as a sign of the market functioning well, and sees little harm in sustained profits provided they're based on superior efficiency.[25] It's quite possible that a small number of firms have long run average total cost curves such that they can produce goods at a cheaper per unit price than their rivals. In this situation they may well generate a large market share and prices will be higher, and output lower, than it would be in a theoretical economist's unobtainable imagination. But as F.A. Hayek said,

> *A monopoly based on superior efficiency, on the other hand, does comparatively little harm as long as it is assured that it will disappear as soon as anyone else becomes more efficient in providing satisfaction to the consumers.*[26]

To justify the claim that 'monopolies' that are based on superior efficiency may not be so bad, consider three examples of some particularly unpopular ones: Walmart, Starbucks and McDonalds. Instead of viewing them as socially harmful monopolies (the static view), we will look at the case for them being socially beneficial and highly competitive (the dynamic view).

■ Walmart

Walmart is one of the chief examples of how big box retail generate economies of scale that they can pass on to consumers through lower prices. Whatever your thoughts on the aesthetics of Walmart, don't underestimate the savings it has generated for ordinary consumers. Attempts to measure this vary, but according to one study 'the presence of Wal-Mart translates directly into consumer savings amounting to $287 billion in 2006 – $957 per person and $2,500 per household.'[27] And note that you don't even have to shop at Walmart to enjoy this because their presence lowers prices in *all* supermarkets.

It is common to lament the fact that such savings come at the expense of community, but there are two alternative points to consider. Firstly, 'community' may not be to everyone's taste. When Lidl opened a store in Baltimore, Ireland there was a local boycott because it threatened the existence of the existing independently run shop. But before long people began to see how much cheaper it was, and wondered why they'd been paying so much for so long. The owners of the original shop ended up selling it because of the backlash.[28] Beneath the tired clichés about how 'women like to shop' there is an important point about the coincidence of retail and women's liberation.[29] The fact that supermarkets are 'anonymous' is one of the reasons why people – women in particular – may prefer them. When the Universities of Surrey and Exeter did a project on shopping in post-war Britain they found some fascinating examples, including how it wasn't just their convenience that attracted young and working class women,

> *A retired secretary recalled, as a young bride, asking the butcher for a tiny amount of mince. 'Oh having a dinner party, madam?' he sneered. A woman who bought anything expensive or unusual risked disapproving gossip, spread by shop assistants. The project found press advertisements promoting the anonymity of supermarkets.*[30]

Supermarkets have had a phenomenal impact on affordability, quality and variety of food consumed. Thanks to supermarkets the price of groceries fell by a third from 1975 to 1997 (in real terms), and there was more than a tenfold increase in the range of products.[31] We have economies of scale to thank for that.

But this doesn't mean that supermarkets ignore community altogether. My favourite example of this occurred when Hurricane Katrina struck the Gulf Coast of America in 2006. There is an iconic photograph of a convoy of Walmart lorries attempting to deliver products to Louisiana, parked on the freeway because they didn't have authorisation to enter. Whilst the government bureaucrats dithered, commercial enterprises like Walmart had plans to serve their customers. Steven Horwitz has documented the lengths that Walmart went to, and even sheds light on the motivations that lay behind them.[32] In the middle of the crisis the CEO sent the following private memo to employees:

A lot of you are going to have to make decisions above your level. Make the best decision that you can with the information that's available to you at the time, and, above all, do the right thing.[33]

- Starbucks

    Traditionally, competition policy is supposed to protect consumers from the special interests of producer groups. But some people argue that although some monopolies can benefit consumers, they have a negative impact on their rival producers. Aside from the fact that this is what is supposed to happen in a competitive system, it's not necessarily true. Starbucks are routinely accused of putting small independent coffee shops out of business. But they don't! During Starbucks' high growth phase of 2000–2005 the number of small independent coffee houses in America increased by 40%. A Slate article points out that when Starbucks opened six new stores in Omaha in 2002, business at *all* coffeehouses rose by almost 25%.[34] Partly this is because Starbucks are good at predicting areas of high-income growth. But partly it's because Starbucks have increased the demand for coffee, and this spills over into the entire industry.

- McDonalds

    Finally, let's not forget the employees of these monopolists. In April 2011 despite rising food prices and an economic downturn, McDonalds created 50000 new jobs.[35] Even more incredibly, in a *Washington Post* article George Will points out that McDonalds operates a franchise business model, which means that running a McDonalds is an opportunity for entrepreneurs to access their economies of scale and run a successful business. He claims 'McDonald's has made more millionaires, and especially black and Hispanic millionaires, than any other economic entity ever, anywhere.'[36] Thus far I've not been able to find a counterexample that disproves this stunning claim.

Some people have argued that large employers such as Walmart, Starbucks and McDonalds exploit their employees by paying them a wage that is below a 'living wage'. But these companies are not monopolies in the sense that their employees don't have a choice. If someone voluntarily chooses to take a low paid job it is because they deem it the best option available to them. It seems odd to denigrate the employer – the organisation providing them with the main share of any 'living wage' – for not doing more. Surely the firms that provide jobs to poor people are part of the solution, not the problem?[37]

5.4 MONOPOLY POWER

When we talk about 'dynamic' competition timescale becomes very important. And no one would argue that the profits of Walmart, Starbucks and McDonald's are 'fleeting'. But it's surprising just how quickly large businesses can feel the forces of competitive pressure. Although they have a strong incentive to prevent competition, it is incredibly difficult to maintain a monopoly position over time. There is a perennial battle for the consumer's money, meaning that competition is always and everywhere a part of human action. Even though the railroad companies were big and powerful, they couldn't prevent the emergence of cars and planes. Long run average costs will always slope upward at some point, and a natural monopoly can only exist for as long as it retains its efficiency. As Ludwig von Mises said,

> *What a newcomer who wants to defy the vested interests of the old established firms needs most is brains and ideas. If his project is fit to fill the most urgent of the unsatisfied needs of the consumers or to purvey them at a cheaper price than their old purveyors, he will succeed in spite of the much talked about bigness and power of the old firms.*[38]

Empirical evidence – over a reasonable time horizon – backs this up. If you looked at the Forbes 100 list of the biggest companies in the US in 1917, and compared it to 1987, you'd find the following:

- 61 of the firms no longer existed
- 21 of them still existed, but had fallen out of the top 100
- 18 of them were still in the top 100.

Of those 18, 16 fell behind the market average, meaning that just 2% of the 100 biggest firms in 1917 outperformed the market over the next 70 years. They were General Electric and Kodak (who have since gone bankrupt). Indeed Kodak provides a fascinating case study because for a long time it seemed like a behemoth. Even though it pioneered the first digital cameras in the 1970s, most of its profits came from processing film. Ultimately it was unable to manage this transition and was defeated by its rival's aptitude at embracing technological change. Bigness does not seem to beget bigness.

If you want to look at a more recent study over a shorter period of time, we can compare the Euro Stoxx Index 50 from 1987 to 2005. Then only 10 out of 50 survived. If you look at the 500 biggest US companies in 1980, less than half of them still existed in 2000.[39] Another interesting finding is looking at the fate of the 172 companies that comprised the Fortune 50 from 1955 to 1995. There, of the firms that fell to or below the GNP growth rate (i.e. of the firms that stopped outgrowing the economy as a whole), just 4% managed to get back to above 1% GNP growth. The bottom line is that it is incredibly hard to sustain competitive advantage over a reasonable period of time. And it seems that this process of creative destruction is increasing. According to *The Economist*, 'In 1980 a corporation in the top fifth of its industry had only a 10% chance of falling out of that tier in five years. Eighteen years later that chance had risen to 25%.'[40] The more you look at the data, the more it seems that profits are indeed fleeting.

Different fields within economics approach competition in slightly different ways. The **Industrial Organisation** (IO) approach is to say that competition depends on industry characteristics such as high barriers to entry, low buyer power, low supplier power, low threat from substitutes and low levels of firm rivalry. The **resource-based view** (RBV) says that competition depends on having superior resources (which are heterogeneous and immobile), for example technology, physical capital, intellectual assets, human capital, financial resources and organisational excellence. Therefore the advice to practitioners is to reduce costs, increase value (e.g. through product differentiation) and reduce competitive intensity. But why bother doing any of this if profits are a sign of uncompetitiveness? In order for companies to have space for wealth creation there needs to be a regulatory environment conducive to entrepreneurship. Ultimately that means the removal of government-spawned barriers. Anti-monopoly policy is remarkably simple. In the words of the anarcho-capitalist Murray Rothbard,

> *Opinion has been traditionally "antimonopoly." Yet it is clearly not only pointless but deeply ironic to call upon government to "pursue a positive antimonopoly policy." Evidently, all that is necessary to abolish monopoly is that the government abolish its own creations.*[41]

The idea that capitalism generates an increasing concentration of capital is a compelling and deep rooted one. But it is theoretically unsound (due to increasing costs of management); and empirically invalid (industry concentration has fallen considerably since the 1950s).[42] It stems from the mistaken view that since perfect competition delivers efficiency, anything other than perfect competition is inefficient. But if we view the market as a dynamic process it is contestability not concentration that matters. We can finish with a lengthy, but highly prescient quote from John Mathews:

> *The idea of* perfectly competitive equilibrium *has become so central, so axiomatic, that its absence is now referred to as a case of market imperfection, or market failure, or information asymmetry, and so on – all terms connoting a departure from the ideal. Yet there is a marked cognitive dissonance between the perfect equilibrium of these economics models and the day-to-day business reality that real firms face – one where prices have to be discovered, where competitors' innovations can take away your market, where competitive intelligence has to be paid for (as opposed to the assumption securing PCE that information is costless and instantaneously transferred), and so on. Disequilibrium by contrast evokes chaos, unpredictability, messiness, risk, and uncertainty. It is uncharted territory.*[43]

As Hayek said, 'the argument in favour of competition does not rest on the conditions that would exist if it were perfect.'[44]

NOTES

1. Mill, J.S. (1848) *Principles of Political Economy, with Some of Their Applications to Social Philosophy*, London; Longmans, Green and Co.
2. Keynes, J.M. (1936[1973]) *The General Theory of Employment, Interest and Money*, Cambridge University Press, p. 383.

3. I've made an assumption that the industry for the inputs is not perfectly competitive and so the costs are bid up due to new entrants. If the industry for inputs is PC the existence of profit will entice new firms to enter, and we can show this as a positive shift in the supply curve. This will result in the equilibrium price returning to the original level.
4. See Mark Pennington's effective critique of Joseph Stiglitz's arguments about natural monopoly, in Pennington, M. (2011) *Robust Political Economy*, Edward Elgar, p. 31.
5. Northrup, L. (2013) Time Warner boosts my speed, cuts my bill: I just happen to live near Google Fiber, *Consumerist.com*, 30 January.
6. Faulks, S. (2007) *Engleby*, Hutchinson.
7. 'Shock treatment', *The Economist*, 15 November 2007.
8. 'Brewed force', *The Economist*, 17 December 2011.
9. Foldvary, F.E. and Klein, D.B. (2003) *The Half Life of Policy Rationales*, New York University Press.
10. Friedman, J. (2010) Capitalism and the crisis, in Friedman, J. (ed.), *What Caused the Financial Crisis?* University of Pennsylvania Press, p. 45.
11. http://www.competition-commission.org.uk/about_us/, accessed 21 September 2013.
12. 'Matchmakers and trustbusters', *The Economist*, 8 December 2005.
13. Hayek, F.A. (1948[1980]) The Meaning of Competition, in *Individualism and Economic Order*, University of Chicago Press, p. 94. Indeed, we need to choose between a static and a dynamic approach. As Kenneth Boulding put it, 'We are not simply acquiring knowledge about a static system which stays put, but acquiring knowledge about a whole dynamic process in which the acquisition of knowledge is itself a part of the process.' Boulding, K. (1966) The economics of knowledge and the knowledge of economics, *American Economic Review, Papers and Proceedings*, **56**, 1–13, at 9.
14. It's important to remember that we're talking about economic profit here, not accounting profit. In many cases what people observe as profit is in fact a loss, once opportunity costs are factored in.
15. Kirzner, I.M. (1982) Competition, Regulation, and the Market Process: An 'Austrian' Perspective, *Cato Policy Analysis* **18**.
16. Lipset, S.M. and Schneider, W. (1987) *The Confidence Gap: Business, labour and government in the public mind*, Johns Hopkins University Press, pp. 176–178.
17. Using http://biz.yahoo.com/p/sum_qpmd.html [accessed 4 October 2013]. The most profitable industry on the list was 'Broadcasting – TV', but we tend not to hear much about that.
18. Knight, F. (1921[2006]) *Risk, Uncertainty and Profit*, Dover.
19. Chapman, S. (2007) In a world of options for consumers, fear of mergers is misplaced, *Baltimore Sun*, 26 June.
20. Hayek, The Meaning of Competition (n 13), p. 100.
21. O'Driscoll, G.P. and Rizzo, M.J. (1985) *The Economics of Time and Ignorance*, Routledge, p. 149.
22. As anyone who has chauffeured a group of drinking Bayern Munich fans around the M25 will attest there are not enough service stations to provide adequate toilet facilities on Britain's busiest motorway. And yet when Cobham services opened in 2012 it came after 19 years of planning. It is also one of the few service stations in the UK to have an 'El Mexicana' canteen, meaning that for me at least it constitutes a destination in its own right. 'Serviceable', *The Economist*, 5 January 2013.
23. 'Rules for fools', *The Economist*, 14 May 2011.
24. 'Rules for fools' (n 23) [emphasis added].
25. If you think that big firms can exploit customers consider the following. Pharmaceutical companies have a drug that reduces the chance of dying from cancer by 20%. And yet you can buy a 100-day supply for under $1. (See 'Wonder drug', *The Economist*, 11 December 2010.)
26. Hayek, The Meaning of Competition (n 13), p. 105.
27. 'The Price Impact of Wal-Mart: An Update Through 2006', *Global Insight*.
28. My knowledge of this story from Ireland comes from family and friends that live in the town.

29. Zola, E. (1883 [2008]) *The Ladies Paradise* (originally published as *Au Bonheur des Dames*), Oxford University Press.
30. 'A nation of shoppers', *The Economist*, 21 May 2011 (emphasis added).
31. 'One to ten', *The Economist*, 7 July 2012.
32. Horwitz, S. (2009) Wal-Mart to the rescue: Private enterprise's response to Hurricane Katrina, *The Independent Review*, **13** (4), 511–528.
33. Rosegrant, S. (2007) Wal-Mart's Response to Hurricane Katrina: Striving for a Public Private Partnership. Kennedy School of Government Case Program C16-07-1876.0, Case Studies in Public Policy and Management. Cambridge, MA: Kennedy School of Government (p. 5). Cited in Horwitz, S. (n 32), p. 516.
34. Clark, T. (2007) Don't Fear Starbucks, *Slate.com*, 28 December.
35. 'The bottom of the pyramid', *The Economist*, 25 June 2011.
36. Will, G. (2007) Lovin' It All Over, *Washington Post*, 27 December.
37. The same logic regarding the menu of choices applies to sweatshops. To outside eyes they may seem like exploitation, but if you believe in the autonomy and dignity of those who voluntarily want the jobs, you have to conclude that they do so because their realistic alternatives are even worse. Closing sweatshops may seem a worthy goal, but what if their now unemployed workers become beggars or prostitutes? We all rank order our preferences and commit our resources to achieving the top of the list. We help those less fortunate by expanding their menu of choices, not by removing the top of their list. See Powell, B. and Skarbek, D. (2006) Sweatshops and third-world living standards: are the jobs worth the sweat?, *Journal of Labor Research*, **17** (2), 263–274, Powell, B. and Zwolinski, M. (2012) The Ethical and Economic Case Against Sweatshop Labor: A Critical Assessment, *Journal of Business Ethics*, **107** (4), 449–472 and Powell, B. (2014) *Out of Poverty: Sweatshops in the Global Economy*, University of Cambridge Press.
38. Mises, L.v. (1949[1996]) *Human Action: A Treatise on Economics*, Fox & Wiles, p. 276.
39. 'The silence of Mammon', *The Economist*, 19 December 2009.
40. 'The transience of power', *The Economist*, 16 March 2013.
41. Rothbard, M.N. (1970[2009]) Power and Market, in *Man, Economy and State with Power and Market*, Ludwig von Mises Institute, p. 1143.
42. Ghemawat, P. (2011) *World 3.0: Global Prosperity and How to Achieve It*, Harvard Business School Press.
43. Mathews, J. (2006) *Strategising Disequilibrium and Profit*, Stanford Business Books, p. 3.
44. Hayek, The Meaning of Competition (n 13), p. 104.

CHAPTER 6

Capital Theory and Recalculation

'The generic concept of capital without which economists cannot do their work has no measurable counterpart among material objects; it reflects the entrepreneurial appraisal of such objects.'

—Ludwig Lachmann[1]

Nokia was founded in 1865 as a wood-pulp mill in southern Finland. Around 30 years later a rubber company was set up in the same town (which had become known as Nokia), and 20 years after that a cable company was created. In 1967 these three companies merged and the modern company was born.[2] Up until 1980 around 90% of their sales were in 'rubber, cable, and other basic products', and almost half of their customers were within Finland.[3] When Jorma Ollila took over as President and CEO in 1992 the company was in a mess. They were an inward looking conglomerate without strategic focus. The collapse of the USSR dented a major trading partner and losses were mounting. But they had a plan. Nokia decided to focus on telecommunications and mobile phones (with a particular emphasis on the GSM digital standard), and over a few years sold off all other product lines.[4] When they released the Nokia 2100 in 1994 they were hoping to sell 400 000. They sold 20 million.[5]

Not all stories of entrepreneurship have such stunning results, but they all share similar themes. The focus of a company often shifts over time, as product innovation and changing demand lead to new opportunities. Macroeconomic factors can cause disruptions, and attempts to deal with them can be costly. The resources that are required to produce one plan may become redundant. But another entrepreneur, with another plan, may see something of value. The traditional factors of production are land, labour and capital. Some textbooks add 'entrepreneurship' to that list but to me this is a disservice. Entrepreneurship is the meta-factor of production – it determines how other factors of production are mixed together and to what purpose they are utilised. This chapter looks at how this entrepreneurial process is influenced by wider economic activity. It is about the adjustment process of markets, and the bridge between microeconomic behaviour and macroeconomic outcomes. It is through their command of capital – 'the physical production structure of an economy, including machinery, buildings, raw materials, and human capital'[6] – that entrepreneurs act. We will look at three different aspects of this:

1. We should make a distinction between the conditions facing individual businesses and the wider economy – managers should pay attention to their microclimate.
2. Labour market adjustments and the phenomenon of unemployment are an important part of how markets adjust.
3. If previous business errors are revealed, or if economic conditions change, entrepreneurs need to recalculate. Because capital is heterogeneous this process will be costly and take time.

Economists tend to focus on the labour market as the key market during periods of economic change. But we will look at human capital (i.e. skills) as a form of capital more generally.[7] As Michael Spence said, 'the fact that it takes time to learn an individual's productive capabilities means that hiring is an investment decision.'[8]

6.1 MICROCLIMATE

I was once teaching in the Black Sea resort of Mamaia and some students wanted to take me to visit the archaeological site of Histria. Founded in the seventh century BC, it is a well-preserved hamlet on the banks of the coast allowing a tranquil wander through marble columns and clay tiles of an unfathomable age. But after a long day teaching, a game of beach volleyball and a swim were more appealing. 'Don't worry – it's going to rain this afternoon' they said, 'you can go to the beach tomorrow.' I decided to get in the car, but after an hour sitting there in the sweltering heat I began thinking about macroeconomics. In particular, how easy it is to be misled by looking at the wrong data. When we met for class the next day, I asked why the weather forecast was inaccurate. It turned out that the students had been looking at a map of Romania, which was supposed to be overcast and cool. And indeed it was. But if they'd have looked at the specific part of the country where we were, it was 30 degrees and sunny. I tried to use it as a teaching moment. The climate is important because it determines general trends. But your situation may be part of a microclimate. When businesses focus on macroeconomic indicators, there's a danger of getting swept up in the big picture and losing sight of the more crucial local issues.

No businesses experience a 'recession', because 'recessions' are a general trend that affects the economy as a whole. If we wish to understand how declining aggregate incomes affect an individual business, we need more information. It depends on the type of business, and indeed the quality of management. Even during the depths of the financial crisis, many US financial institutions were looking healthy. As Jeffrey Friedman has pointed out, Wells Fargo had to be forced to take bailout money, and regional banks such as BB&T didn't want or need support. In early 2009 the Beal Bank of Plano launched a major expansion plan, buying up almost $30 billion of assets from banks that were failing.[9]

A recession is a great excuse for poorly run businesses, because you're expected to endure a difficult time. But this isn't inevitable. For a well-run business a recession is actually an opportunity. Your competitors are more likely to be going out of business, putting downwards pressure on your input costs. In Ireland office rents fell by 50% from 2008 to 2010 and labour costs by 10%.[10] Firms that anticipate a downturn and diversify into inferior products (i.e.

those that have negative income elasticity) will actually prosper. For example, the following newspaper reports show that 2009 was a good time for some companies:

- 'The German discount supermarket chain Aldi has given the green light to a multimillion-dollar refurbishment and upgrade for 150 of its stores nationwide ... The push is in line with evidence that consumers are preferring to patronise discount department stores and supermarkets.'[11]
- 'The tough economy appears to be helping fast food conglomerate Restaurant Brands ... it expects to announce an annual profit of about $11 million next month. Again its KFC business is driving growth, where same store sales were up 5.5 per cent on the equivalent quarter last year.'[12]

The Economist points out that referring to recessions as 'slowdowns' is misleading, because this is when the dynamic nature of an economy comes to the fore: 'distressed assets can be bought for a song, talented people hired cheaply and new ideas given an airing.'[13] Their columnist, Schumpeter, suggests three types of firms that prosper in a recession. Firstly, 'established giants'. These are the 'the market leaders that entered the recession with cash in their pockets and sound management systems under their belts'.[14] Secondly, innovators. They use DuPont as the classic example of a company that utilised the conditions during the Great Depression to invest in R&D and recruit unemployed scientists. Nylon was just one of the inventions they soon brought to market.[15] As Jeff Stibel, the Chairman and CEO of Dun & Bradstreet Credibility Corp, urges 'don't divest just because the economy is rotten.'[16] The third type of firm is those who seek to reposition themselves. They use Nokia as an example of a company that reacted to the post-communist turmoil by abandoning the vast majority of their business lines and concentrating on the fast expanding market for mobile phones. These companies all saw through the headlines of doom and became the forces of (as opposed to victims of) creative destruction. Survey data from the 1990–91 recession in the UK found that the fall in profits and employment was concentrated in a relatively small section of the economy:[17]

- 10% of companies accounted for 83% of the gross fall in profits and 85% of the gross fall in employment.
- 40% of firms saw their profits rise.
- 50% raised employment.

In a survey of 300 companies conducted between December 2008 and February 2009 (i.e. during a recession):[18]

- 21% planned to expand abroad.
- 38% expected to make an acquisition.
- 35% expected to launch a joint venture with a former competitor.

It is a surprising yet common finding that the microclimates can vary dramatically from the general climate. The aggregate indicators mask a wide variety of experiences, and paint a distorted view of what the average situation is like. Remarkably, over the course of the 1991 recession more than half of British households saw income rise.[19] In 2012 Sky News even did a feature called 'The Lopsided Recovery'. They found that although Britain as whole suffered from recessions in 2009 and 2012, this was not experienced across the island. London, for example, didn't have a recession in 2012.[20] Nominal GDP in East London actually increased in 2008 and 2009. London as a whole avoided recession in 2012. Whilst by contrast the North East ended 2012 still 5% below its level in 2008.[21] As Tim Harford says,

> *the variability in individual experience completely drowned out the distinction between growth and stagnation in the underlying economy.*[22]

6.2 UNEMPLOYMENT

Although some people prosper in a recession, it also generates hardship, and unemployment is a particularly damaging weather front for many of those who experience it. In Chapter 7 we shall look in more detail at the relationship between unemployment and output, but for now we are still viewing the labour market as an essentially microeconomic concept. In the UK the labour force is split up in the following way:

- Household population (age 16+) =
  - Full-time employment (age 16+)
  - Part-time employment (age 16+)
  - Unemployment (age 16+)
  - Economically inactive (age 16–64)
  - Economically inactive (age 65+)

This shows that employment and unemployment are not simply two ends of a pole. The unemployed are the part of the labour force that don't have a job. But there is a danger that focusing too narrowly on unemployment means we ignore those who become so pessimistic about finding a job that they become 'economically inactive'. Chris Dillow points out that in the first quarter of 2012 UK 'employment' fell by 902 000, but only 443 000 became unemployed. The rest gave up looking for work. Therefore we should be careful about focusing on the unemployment rate as the signal of the jobs market.[23] But this doesn't mean that there was no job creation. At the same time 530 000 people moved from unemployment to work, which constitutes around 20% of the total amount of unemployed people. And a further 342 000 moved from economic inactivity to work. As Dillow says, we should view unemployment as a fast moving river, rather than a pool.[24]

But even in fast moving rivers, there is a risk of stasis. The concept of **hysteresis** refers to lengthy periods of unemployment where human capital depreciates to such an extent that a new job is impossible. This is incredibly harmful for the individual concerned, and indeed for the economy as a whole. Economists like to think that the unemployment rate fluctuates around a 'natural' rate. But hysteresis means that temporary changes in unemployment become permanent. The more time people find themselves out of the labour market, the harder it may be to re-enter. Therefore the costs of adjustment get magnified because rather than just see people spend time unemployed whilst they look for work, they can get caught in a vicious cycle of unemployability.

We can categorise three ways to think about unemployment:

1. Frictional

This is the type of temporary unemployment that workers voluntarily take. Perhaps you're moving house and decide to leave your job and find a new one elsewhere. Maybe you just decide you want a new career and quit your old job in order to devote time to looking for a better one.

2. **Structural**

This occurs when workers' skills and available jobs become incompatible due to economic change. For example when the UK began trading more with Europe the shipping trade moved from the North West to the South coast. The skills of Liverpool dockers became less valuable and unemployment occurred as they retrained.

3. **Cyclical**

Unlike the frictional and structural unemployment, there is the potential that workers are willing to work at the current market wage rate but simply can't find a job. This category is sometimes referred to as 'involuntary' and was originally invoked to explain the occurrence of lengthy unemployment such as that experienced during the Great Depression.

When Andy Gray lost his job as a football commentator for Sky Television he had a decision to make. Should he look for other channels that would be willing to hire him, or should he consider a different career? If he held out for a rival broadcaster to match his previous salary he would be frictionally unemployed. Eventually he became a radio show host for Talk Sport. The fact that this requires different (but related) skills implies that he was temporarily structurally unemployed.[25] But these categories are never given. They're a function of the prevailing wage offer.

So what causes unemployment? To classical economists, in a flexible economy all unemployment is voluntary and temporary. Ultimately the economy will be in equilibrium with real wages being driven by real productivity, operating at full employment.[26] If a worker has a marginal product that is less than the prevailing wage rate, they will be unable to find a job. The appropriate policy response to frictional and structural unemployment is mainly supply side reforms to improve the general functioning of the labour market. The 'cause' of unemployment is simply policies that prevent real wages from adjusting to new economic conditions. For example:

- Trade union pressure to preserve jobs
- Worker resistance to pay cuts
- Minimum wages
- Government licensing
- Excessive tax rates.

A common explanation for the sort of persistent high unemployment we see in various European economies is the concept of a **dual labour market**.[27] The idea is that the labour force is split into workers with permanent jobs who are costly to fire (i.e. 'insiders'), and temporary workers that are easy to fire ('outsiders').[28] Typically it is low skilled groups, such as young people who are outsiders. When there is a fall in demand, firms will tend to let go of outsiders, but find it hard to resist pressure from insiders to increase wages.[29] There is also potential for insiders to engage in collective bargaining at the expense of outsiders. A minimum wage is a classic example, because it can raise the wages of those with jobs, whilst pricing outsiders out of the labour market. Alternatively, if outsiders commit their resources to trying to become insiders, rather than to reregulate the labour market, this will lead to a further increase in labour costs.

To classical economists all unemployment is voluntary. There may be policies that are hampering the market, but provided workers have realistic wage demands they will find a job. Or, as Serbian actor Lazar Ristovski puts it, 'when there is no work, I come up with some'.[30] However, cyclical unemployment suggests that even if the supply side is doing well unemployment can exist if there is a shortfall of aggregate demand. In this case the appropriate policy response is monetary or fiscal policy, and we will look into this in more detail in later chapters. For now, a suitable definition of unemployment is the following: 'a person who lacks a job is unemployed if he or she wants work, has suitable skills, and has realistic expectations about compensation.' It comes from Warren Gibson, who goes on to point out that 'these are vague terms; they make unemployment a murky concept'.[31] I also like Floyd Arthur 'Baldy' Harper's definition: 'involuntary leisure of a person who is willing to work at the free market price'.[32]

But we should also consider the possibility that private, optimising behaviour generates unemployment even when aggregate demand is strong. This happens if firms pay their employees more than the market-clearing level. We refer to these as 'efficiency wages', but why would they do this? Some reasons include:

1. Nutrition

    Workers need energy in order to work, so a firm may decide that providing a decent wage will be in their own interest. In poorer countries firms might need to pay a wage high enough to allow workers to sustain themselves and not fall ill.

2. Absenteeism

    It is costly to train new workers and so firms want to encourage a low staff turnover. In 1915 Henry Ford increased wages to $5 a day to compensate workers for the monotony of the job (i.e. new assembly lines). This increased productivity and improved retention rates.[33]

3. Selection problem

    It may be the case that good workers are unwilling to take low paying jobs because they signal low productivity to potential future employees.

4. Shirking model

    If everyone is paid their market rate and there is no unemployment, people will be indifferent to being fired. Given that it's costly to monitor employees, one way to ensure that they work hard (i.e. don't 'shirk') is to pay them an above market rate. In this case the cost of being fired is significant. If it's hard to increase the probability of catching shirkers, raising the cost of shirking is one alternative.

Therefore equilibrium unemployment can be seen as a discipline device, and efficiency wages are a way to monitor workers and reduce moral hazard. For senior managers it is relatively easy to monitor their behaviour, since their output is more visible. Consequently owners tend to use performance related pay for managers, and efficiency wages for other employees. But don't forget that the goal of managers should be to understand the unique value creation of each employee. In other words if you resort to efficiency wages it's a sign that you're not doing your job as manager.[34]

Perhaps one reason why there's such public hostility towards bonuses is because they're typically used as a tool to reward senior managers. Usually the only experience that regular employees have of them is as an arbitrary way to share some common bonus pool. The problem therefore isn't bonuses per se, but the way they are applied. If managers were doing their job all employees – not just senior managers – would have compensation tied to clearly communicated and agreed upon goals.

As important as understanding the causes of unemployment is, it's also important to understand what *doesn't* cause unemployment. Or at least factors that may appear to cause unemployment, but ultimately are not responsible for the unemployment we see around us. They all rest on what is known as the 'lump of labour fallacy' which is the notion that there are a fixed number of jobs. As we will see, the labour market is a complex, dynamic process that is continually adapting to new economic conditions.

1. Immigration

It may seem obvious that when foreign people come into a country they 'take' the jobs of the indigenous population. But often immigrant labour ends up doing jobs that local workers simply do not want to do (or at least aren't willing to do at the market wage). As A.A. Gill says,

> the Chinese moved into every town and village in the country, opening Pagoda and Lotus takeaways in foul-mouthed, soot-black angry, stupid back-to-back streets. Whenever I came across them in the grim North, I wondered at their fortitude, the inner resolve and the flickering comfort of some grand dream that sustained them in these grassless, thankless, vicious places. Putting up with drunken vileness, thick-tongued racism, uncaring slurping, the insistence on chips and forks and ketchup. The tiny margins made on using cuts of pig, lamb, and chicken the English didn't deign to bother with. The tedious, relentless jokes about cats and Alsatians. And the grinding, chilly, thankless loneliness of it. There should be a huge statue on the M1, like the Angel of the North; it should be the unknown Chinaman, the silent, uncomplaining brigade of foodie missionaries.[35]

In doing so, immigrants actually create new jobs by contributing to economic growth. But the main insight from economics is that immigration, and even mass immigration, does not cause a reduction in local wages. Even in extreme cases such as the influx of immigration to Israel, when it rose by 12% from 1990–94, there was 'no adverse impact of immigration on native outcomes'.[36] It is commonly believed that when the UK allowed the new Central and Eastern European members of the EU free access to the labour market in 2004, this harmed the employment figures for domestic workers. But it's a myth. A paper from the Institute for the Study of Labour showed no impact on employment (even for youth and low skilled), and no significant impact on wages.[37] A UCL study found that new migrants have a positive impact on public finances.[38] But looking at these specific instances and the immediate impact underestimates the dynamic benefits of immigration. As Jonathan Portes points out 'the benefits are not just that we get cheap and willing Eastern European workers, but that we get students, some of whom will stay and set up businesses; researchers who will both collaborate and compete with natives; refugees whose children will invent things that none of us have thought of; and so on.'[39]

2. Technology

Again, it seems intuitively correct that technological improvements reduce jobs but in fact they change the type of jobs on offer. It's not as if computers have replaced humans – they have become a tool with which humans boost their productivity. Automation allows us to produce goods and services at lower cost that we otherwise could. Ed Herr, a potato chip manufacturer, reckons that if he made them the old fashioned way they'd cost up to $25 per bag.[40] This increased efficiency leads to greater social wealth, and should be embraced. There's an old story about two men watching some construction work, at the centre of which a mechanical digger shifts vast amounts of rubble onto the back of waiting dump trucks. One man laments, 'if they didn't have the digger there'd be 10 men doing that work with spades'. The other responds, 'and if they didn't have spades there'd be 100 men doing it with spoons'.[41] This is the problem when governments attempt to 'make work' – shouldn't the aim be to create enough prosperity to allow us to enjoy more *leisure*? Economic growth results from doing more with fewer inputs. Provided we're getting richer, job destruction is *good*. As Adam Gurri says, 'If someone finds a way to provide value to hundreds of millions of people and it requires no more effort from them than batting their eyelashes, that would be a win.'[42] Create value, not jobs.

3. Loss of manufacturing

As countries get richer you tend to see a decline in the amount of manufacturing, and this generates a public desire to 'make things'. Part of the concern about outsourcing and offshoring is that manufacturing jobs are seen as being more conducive to growth than service ones. In terms of nominal value added, Britain has fallen from 5th largest manufacturer in the world in 2002 to 9th in 2012. Manufacturing accounts for just 10% of GDP. But this says more about the rise of services than the decline of manufacturing. In absolute terms the UK makes twice as much stuff as it did in the 1950s[43] and is still one of the largest manufacturers in the world.[44] It is a sign of progress that you can produce more with fewer workers. It means that productivity has increased.

For people that pine for times past it's useful to think about some of the jobs that no longer exist, precisely because we are wealthier.[45]

- Elevator operators: because an elevator would only make one journey at a time it was inefficient so operators were used to ensure it'd stop on the floors people needed. As this became automated they were no longer required.[46]
- Pinsetters: would work in a bowling alley clearing up knocked over pins and setting them up for the next bowler.
- Rover drivers: would ride on the back of felled trees as they were floated downstream to be cut. This was an incredibly dangerous job in uncomfortable conditions.
- Icemen: prior to domestic refrigerators icemen would have to deliver 25–100 pound blocks of ice.
- Lamplighters: would carry heavy ladders down public highways and be responsible for lighting up to 300 gas lanterns per hour.
- Knocker-uppers: would use a long stick to tap on the bedroom window of clients, and make sure they were on time for work.[47]

In the same way that recessions can have a microclimate, there is a microclimate of unemployment. The labour market is always in a state of flux. In the US around 65% of new jobs tend to be 'churn', which is when workers move from one job to another.[48] According to research by the University of Nottingham, from 1997–2005 (i.e. before the financial crisis) around 2.65m private sector jobs were lost every year in the UK. The reason this wasn't leading to mass protests and social breakdown was because even more – around 2.76m – were being created.

What this shows is a dramatic job churn of around 50 000 per week. Recessions tend to be when the pace of new job creation falls below the rate of job losses, but this doesn't hold across all industries. In the UK between 2011 and 2013 the number of paramedics doubled, whilst graphic designers and company secretaries grew by almost 50%.[49] There's job growth during downturns and there are job losses during booms. People are being made unemployed, and choosing to become unemployed, all the time. Even when the economy is doing well around one in seven private sector jobs are lost each year in the UK.[50] It can be very dangerous to intervene, and attempt to try to centrally plan this process of creative destruction.

The biggest problem is knowing whether jobs are being lost for frictional, structural or cyclical reasons. In theory, the main role for government in remedying structural unemployment is by creating a competitive economy. This means allowing workers to adjust their skills to meet changes in the economy. Although it may be well intended to want to help people who lose their jobs, it is counterproductive if efforts to do so hamper the functioning of the labour market. After many years of bailouts and government support the MG Rover factory in Longbridge closed in 2005. Although 6000 people lost their jobs, around 80% were back in work within a year.[51] More importantly,

> The collapse of MG Rover may even prove to be a boon to the region. Some think that loss-making Rover held back the local economy. It also tied up skilled workers who might have been more valuable elsewhere.[52]

The difficulty is in knowing where the highest value uses of labour are. The danger is that a skills mismatch develops where workers develop expertise in tasks that don't generate economic value. One example of a skills mismatch has been raised by Alex Tabarrok. He has made the claim that 'American students are not studying the fields with greatest economic potential', and highlights the case of Joe Therrien. Having graduated as a drama teacher Joe became disillusioned, and decided to retrain by getting a degree in puppetry. He spent three years, and $35 000, but has been unable to find a job since. He ended up back as a drama teacher.[53]

It is tempting to gloss over this coordination failure, and consider that the worker has a high marginal productivity, it's just that prevailing economic conditions prevent firms from employing them at their market wage. This type of cyclical unemployment is the rationale for government assistance, but attempts to slow down the dynamic nature of markets can have negative unintended consequences. As Martti Vihanto says,

> If the government makes a mistake and gives money to workers who are unemployed because of primary changes or who are soon able to discover profitable employment in the open market, the process of coordination is hampered.[54]

Falling real wages, like any other price, are an important signal for entrepreneurs to understand the best use of resources. In the Keynesian view unemployment constitutes 'idle resources' and this implies that any job is better than no job. But even 'idle' resources play an important function in the economy. We cannot know which industries have underemployment outside the market process.

It is easy for tenured academics to advocate creative destruction, and I want to express empathy with those who lose their jobs from it. But part of the argument is a belief in the potential of workers to create economic value. In his classic book *The Fifth Discipline*, Peter Singe highlights the fact that many employees take the view 'I am my job'. Perhaps it is our tendency to identify with the tasks that we perform, rather than the capabilities we possess, that creates resistance to creative destruction.[55]

Ultimately, wages are the price of labour. Therefore for labour markets to adjust to new economic conditions, the wage rate should change. All economists would agree that if nominal wages were perfectly flexible then the labour market would clear, and there would be no unemployment. However we need to be careful because in the real world prices aren't perfectly flexible. They're 'sticky'. And wages are especially sticky.[56] In his book *Why Wages Don't Fall During a Recession,* Truman Bewley provides ethnographic evidence to help explain why the labour market doesn't clear.[57] The basic argument is as follows:[58]

- Although inflation means that real wages will fall during a recession, nominal wages are a lot stickier.
- Although workers may see their nominal wage fall if they switch jobs, for a given worker in a given job nominal wage cuts are very rare.
- The reason for this is because nominal wage cuts are very bad for morale, and this has a negative impact on productivity.
- The reason firms don't just reduce the nominal wage offered to new hires is because once those new hires settle in, and realise they are doing the same jobs as the existing workers, this will damage their morale – and the morale of the existing workers.
- On the rare occasions where firms do cut nominal wages, this should be clearly explained to workers to mitigate the impact on morale.
- Firms should also recognise that nominal wage cuts will result in their most productive workers wanting to leave.
- By contrast, layoffs mean that their least productive workers would leave.
- Layoffs are best managed as quickly as possible, with credible assurances of job security to those who remain.

Also, employees tend to have contracts with a fixed salary. The reason people aren't paid with stock options and bonuses contingent on company performance is because we offload some of that risk onto the firm. By their very nature wages are sticky. That's the whole point. We want some certainty. For the economy as a whole, if all firms introduce moderate wage cuts there will be no unemployment. But the best option for any individual firm is to lay off workers. And that is how wage rigidities can result in unemployment effects.

6.3 RECALCULATION

Although the labour market is typically seen as the crucial market for economic adjustments, let's also consider the role of the market for capital goods. To some extent this has been neglected by economists, and we can see why when we think about how we understand capital.

There was a 1980s children's TV show in England called 'Bertha'. It was an animated programme set on the shop floor of a factory. The title character was a large machine with googly eyes, whizzing arms and a conveyor belt tongue. Each episode would involve her making a different product. To some extent economic models assume that all factories contain a Bertha, and that switching between one product and another is no more complicated than reprogramming a machine. Perhaps with the advent of 3D printing, this won't seem quite so ludicrous. But it *is* ludicrous. Machines may be versatile, but they have limited uses. In economic terms, capital goods are heterogeneous.

Recollect that what we ultimately care about is utility, which is enjoyed in the act of consuming. The only reason we produce, therefore, is in order to be able to consume. And whilst consumer goods are those that directly satisfy us, producer or 'capital' goods are those that we use in order to create them. And there are two different ways we think about capital goods.[59]

1. Capital is like Play-Doh

 Play-Doh is a homogenous substance that is easy to alter. Different units of Play-Doh are almost perfectly substitutable for each other.
2. Capital is like Lego

 Lego bricks are heterogeneous and impossible to alter. Different units can only fit together with certain others, therefore the complementarity of bricks is very important.

This 'Lego' view of capital is exemplified in the work of Ludwig Lachmann, and Peter Lewin.[60] They point out that capital goods are heterogeneous and have two key properties. Firstly they are **asset specific**. This means that they can only be used for a limited number of purposes. At any given moment capital goods will be devoted to their most profitable use. But often these could be different uses to those originally planned. The second property is that they're **complementary**. They must be used jointly, but not in any combination. Entrepreneurs therefore need to find the optimal combinations of capital goods. Economic change will disintegrate existing combinations and force entrepreneurs to find new ones.[61]

This has important implications, because if capital goods are heterogeneous there is no natural unit of measurement. Economists try to get round this by using market prices as a guide, but this only makes sense if they are equilibrium prices. This also runs the risk of conflating capital with money. 'Capital value' is defined as the *perceived* value of a particular production plan. We're talking about the process of how capital valuations function within a market rather than the size of the capital stock. Ultimately we cannot measure the capital stock: we can only talk about the structure of capital.

The implication for management is that we view firms as collections of capital resources, and the growth of a firm as capital accumulation. A firm's survival depends on its ability to readjust its capital structure in response to changes in market conditions, and balance the need for diversification with the vulnerability of having a complex capital structure. If economic calculation provides the crucial means for entrepreneurs to navigate their commercial activity, then recalculation is what happens when those original plans get disrupted. Calculation comes prior to allocation, and recalculation comes prior to reallocation. Arnold Kling coined the term 'recalculation', and our definition is 'to calculate again, either to correct previous errors or to incorporate new economic conditions'.[62]

One example is the Millennium Dome. It was built on the Prime Meridian in Greenwich to serve as a focal point for the UK's New Year celebrations on 31 December 1999. It then opened to the public with a range of exhibitions, but after only attracting half the forecast visitors it closed on 31 December 2000. According to the National Audit Office in 1997 it was forecast to cost £758m and generate a lifetime income of £359m. In actual fact it cost £789m and only generated £189m.[63] Just because this error was made, doesn't mean the resources were totally wasted. In 2005 the site was sold to Anschutz Entertainment Group and the shell of the dome was used to house a 20 000 seat entertainment centre branded as the O_2 arena. They even managed to recover £4.5m from the sale of the assets – art galleries bought some of the installations, and waste bins found themselves at various theme parks. But this was for significantly less than they were 'worth' as part of the Dome. Other assets, such as staff uniforms, had no other uses and represented a pure waste of scarce resources.[64] Ultimately switching the use of the Dome took time and was costly.

There are industries that attempt to salvage value from failed entrepreneurial endeavours. They essentially split assets into two categories: waste (which end up in a landfill) and those that can be put to different uses. All inefficiency is a profit opportunity, and declining industries have potentially valuable capital goods assigned to low value uses. Entrepreneurship is the creative pulse that creates new capital structures out of old ones. Marc de Beyer is a German who noticed the decline of local churches, and saw the liquidation process as an opportunity to arbitrage. He sells 3.6 metre long church pews for €40 and 6m ones for €60. He says,

> *Altars often find new places in Eastern Europe … There's a big demand there because new churches are always being built.*[65]

In November 2011 St Joseph's Church Arnheim, which had been empty for five years, reopened as a profitable skate park.[66] In March 2013 the Premier League football team West Ham United announced that it would be utilising the Olympic stadium from London 2012 as their new home. But even sports stadiums are heterogeneous. It is estimated to cost £190m to convert the facility into something suitable for football matches. Retractable seats will cover the running track to ensure fans are close to the action, and the capacity will be reduced from 80 000 to under 60 000 seats.[67] When put in these terms it doesn't seem anything extraordinary. This is what the market looks like. But we need to recognise two things: (i) the creative ways in which capital goods are reallocated; and (ii) the waste of resources that occurs when errors are made. The former can reduce the latter, but not eliminate them. Given that economic conditions are in continual flux, there will always be recalculation and both human and physical capital will be reallocated to different uses. This is why you need to be very careful about looking at the book value of company's assets. All you see is the capital value in its present use. But the amount that it is worth depends on how it fits into the production plan of a potential buyer. When using Lego the key isn't to use up as many bricks as possible, but to build something coherent. A 2x2 red block can be incredibly important if you're building a fire engine and don't have enough. But if you're making a castle it could be worthless. The art of crisis management is an understanding of salvage value. According to David James, 'in creating a special-purpose asset like a factory, you must build in flexibility so you can get out of it if you need to.'[68] But if this doesn't happen, it's possible that 'there was little scope for creating more value by converting the assets to some other purpose'.[69]

When economists talk about **zero marginal product workers** this isn't a judgment about their intrinsic worth as individuals. It's saying that they're in the wrong job and that their talents lie elsewhere. Millennium Dome branded uniforms have no value in their intended use and no value in alternative uses. Their employees have no value in their intended use, but plenty of value in alternative uses. A ZMP worker is someone that is in the wrong job. It is a sign of coordination failure, not market failure. Markets, and the system of economic calculation, are a way of helping them find out what that is.

When companies go bankrupt it's important to realise that the waste of resources occurs when the decisions are made, not when the bankruptcy occurs. Similarly a recession is not when errors are made, but when they are revealed. A recession is a cluster of entrepreneurial errors, and therefore a recession requires a lot of recalculation. The recalculation is the confrontation of those past errors. It is tempting for policymakers to try to mask those errors, and stimulating aggregate demand is a little like trying to freeze the economy. It gives the appearance that everything is OK, but only because nothing is able to move. The alternative is to allow the economy to thaw, and encourage a quick period of recalculation and reallocation. The aim of macroeconomic policy shouldn't be to avoid recessions, but to avoid making the mistakes that make a recession inevitable. For this we turn to macroeconomic policy.

NOTES

1. Lachmann, L.M. (1956 [1978]) *Capital and its Structure*, Sheed Andrews and McMeel, p. xv.
2. Doornik, K. and Roberts, J. (2011) Nokia corporation: Innovation and efficiency in a high-growth global firm, Stanford University Graduate School of Business, Case No. S-IB-23, February 2011, p. 2.
3. Doornik and Roberts, Nokia corporation (n 2), p. 2.
4. Doornik and Roberts, Nokia corporation (n 2), pp. 4–5.
5. Doornik and Roberts, Nokia corporation (n 2), p. 7.
6. Lewin, P. (2012) Austrian capital theory: why it matters, *The Freeman*, 30 May [http://www.fee.org/the_freeman/detail/austrian-capital-theory-why-it-matters, accessed 26 November 2013].
7. It is common for economists to treat capital as fixed in the short run, and in the long run treat it under the guise of growth theory. As this chapter will argue, this is unsatisfactory.
8. Spence, M. (1973) Job market signalling, *The Quarterly Journal of Economics*, **87** (3), 355–374.
9. Friedman, J. (2010) Capitalism and the crisis, in Friedman, J. (ed.), *What Caused the Financial Crisis?*, University of Pennsylvania Press, p. 45.
10. 'Riding the tiger', *The Economist*, 9 October 2010.
11. 'Aldi splashes out $1b on upgrade', *Sydney Morning Herald*, 14 March 2009.
12. 'KFC revamp and promotions help Restaurant Brands dish up rise in sales', *New Zealand Herald*, 3 March 2009.
13. 'Thriving on adversity', *The Economist*, 3 October 2009.
14. 'Thriving on adversity' (n 13).
15. 'Thriving on adversity' (n 13).
16. Stibel, J. (2012) Don't divest just because the economy is rotten, *HBR Blog Network*, 18 February [http://blogs.hbr.org/2011/02/dont-divest-just-because-the-e/, accessed September 2013].
17. Geroski, P. and Gregg, P.A. (1997) *Coping with Recession*, Cambridge University Press. Cited by Dillow, C. (2005) Geroski on recession, *Stumbling and Mumbling*, 31 August [http://stumbling andmumbling.typepad.com/stumbling_and_mumbling/2005/08/geroski_on_rece.html, accessed 23 September 2013].
18. Survey by Baker Tilly, cited in 'Recession puts groups in mood to expand', *Financial Times*, 15 June 2009.
19. Flanders, S. (2009) It might not be you, *Stephanomics Blog*, 23 February.
20. The study was using an early estimate of GDP and subsequent data revisions suggest that the UK as a whole did not suffer from a recession in 2012.
21. Conway, E. (2013) Making sense of Britain's lopsided recovery, *Sky News*, [http://news.sky.com/story/1018975/making-sense-of-britains-lopsided-recovery, accessed 23 September 2013].
22. Harford, T. (2009) Some recession experiences are more equal than others, *Financial Times*, 21 February.
23. Dillow, C. (2012) Unemployment: a river not a pool, *Stumbling and Mumbling*, 16 May [http://stumblingandmumbling.typepad.com/stumbling_and_mumbling/2012/05/unemployment-a-river-not-a-pool.html, accessed 23 September 2013].
24. Dillow, Unemployment (n 23).

25. Gray was sacked for making insensitive comments to a female colleague and has a reputation for being something of an anachronism. As a player he was aggressive and 'old fashioned', and as a pundit he is enthusiastic and passionate. At a similar time broadcasters were bringing in analysts that looked more deeply at the technical and tactical side of the game. This is my attempt to portray a structural element to the example.

26. **Total factor productivity** refers to the efficiency with which an economy transforms raw inputs into final goods.

27. Bentolila, S., Dolado, J. and Jimeno, J.F. (2012) The Spanish labour market: A very costly insider-outsider divide, *VoxEU.org*, 20 January [http://www.voxeu.org/article/jobless-spain-what-can-be-done-about-insider-outsider-divide, accessed 3 October 2013].

28. Blanchard, O.J. and Summers, L.H. (1987) Hysteresis in unemployment, *European Economic Review*, **31** (1–2), 288–295.

29. 'The reform club', *The Economist*, 22 September 2012.

30. Panic, I.K. (2013) Talent is a gift from god (an interview with Lazar Ristovski), *Air Serbia Review*, December.

31. Gibson, Warren C. (2011) Unemployment: What is it?, *The Freeman*, November.

32. Harper, F.A. (1957) *Why Wages Rise*, Foundation for Economic Education, p.102.

33. See Henry Ford's $5-a-Day Revolution, Ford News Center, [http://corporate.ford.com/news-center/press-releases-detail/677-5-dollar-a-day, accessed 22 November 2013]. According to Daniel Raff the compensation policy was adopted in 1914 and was primarily to avert the threat of collective action. See Raff, D. (1988) Wage determination theory and the five-dollar day at Ford, *Journal of Economic History*, **48** (02), 387–399.

34. Imagine that you have 10 workers and estimate that their average productivity is £10 per hour. In the real world we never see uniform distributions, and it is a safe bet that some of those workers will have a marginal productivity above £10, and some below. Whilst it is hard to know exactly what the marginal productivity for any given worker is, we need to think about it carefully. In the scenario above think about who has good job satisfaction. Who will be telling his friends what a great company it is to work for? The person who gets paid £10 to create £8 of value. By contrast, the disgruntled employee will be the one who generates £12 of value, but is subsidising the less productive worker. The high productivity employee has the comfort of knowing that they're unlikely to lose their job, but they are a constant flight risk. Another firm would be willing to pay them a higher wage. The secret of remaining employed is to ensure that your marginal productivity is always higher than your wage. But this is the problem with 'horizontal pay equity norms'. A good manager should understand the unique value creation of their team, and pay in accordance with that.

35. This quote appeared in the print edition of A.A. Gill's column in *The Sunday Times*.

36. Friedberg, R.M. (2001) The impact of mass migration on the Israeli labour market, *Quarterly Journal of Economics*, **1116** (4), 1373–1408.

37. Lemos, S. and Portes, J. (2008) New Labour? The Impact of Migration from Central and Eastern European Countries on the UK Labour Market, IZA Discussion Paper No. 3756, October.

38. Dustmann, C., Frattini, T. and Halls, C. (2009) Assessing the fiscal costs and benefits of A8 migration to the UK, Centre for Research and Analysis of Migration, Discussion Paper 18/09, July.

39. Portes, J. (2012) Why Ed Miliband shouldn't apologise for making the right decision on Eastern European migration, National Institute of Economic and Social Research blog, 22 June [http://niesr.ac.uk/blog/why-ed-miliband-shouldnt-apologise-making-right-decision-eastern-european-migration#.UkNmXGRAR9Y, accessed 22 September 2013].

40. See 'Secrets from the potato chip factory', http://vimeo.com/62709769.

41. Pirie, M. (2012) *Economics Made Simple: How Money, Trade and Markets Really Work*, Harriman, p. 47.

42. Gurri, A. (2011) Create value not jobs, 4 December [http://adamgurri.com/?p=78, accessed 23 September 2013]. Or, as Fisman and Sullivan put it, 'No one wants to *work*. That's why it's called

work', in Fisman, R. and Sullivan, T. (2013) *The Org. The Underlying Logic of the Office*, Twelve Books.

43. The average value in the Index of Production for the 1950s was 46.48 and it was 96.4 in 2012 (2010=100).

44. 'UK falls behind Brazil in manufacturing', *Financial Times*, 21 March 2011.

45. The Jobs of Yesteryear: Obsolete Occupations, *NPR*, 5 March 2010 [http://www.npr.org/templates/story/story.php?storyId=124251060, accessed 23 September 2013].

46. Note that one of the reasons why they were automated was because of minimum wage laws.

47. '7 ways people woke up, pre-alarm clock', *Mental Floss*, [http://mentalfloss.com/article/24117/7-ways-people-woke-pre-alarm-clock, accessed 23 September 2013].

48. 'Go for the churn', *The Economist*, 11 February 2012.

49. 'Britain's fastest growing jobs', *Daily Telegraph*, [http://www.telegraph.co.uk/finance/jobs/10307542/Britains-fastest-growing-jobs.html?frame=2670830, accessed 23 September 2013].

50. Hijzen, A., Upward, R. and Wright, P. (2007) Job Creation, Job Destruction and the Role of Small Firms: Firm-Level Evidence for the UK, Globalisation and Economic Policy Research Centre, University of Nottingham, February 2007.

51. 'Soft landing at Longbridge', *The Economist*, 10 March 2006.

52. 'Soft landing at Longbridge' (n 51).

53. Tabarrok, A. (2011) Not from the onion, *Marginal Revolution*, 5 November. Note that Tabarrok is clear that he is not mocking Joe for training in what could be considered a trivial profession. Tabarrok's point is that there are millions of unemployed Americans, desperate for work, and yet the case of Joe has been used by this particular newspaper as an example of a problem with the jobs market: 'even in a wealthy society it's a privilege to have the kind of job that Kim [Executive Editor of The Nation] thinks are the entitlement of the middle class.'

54. Vihanto, M. (1992) Competition between local governments as a discovery procedure, *Journal of Institutional and Theoretical Economics*, **148**, 411–436.

55. Senge, P.M. (1990) *The Fifth Discipline*, Doubleday/Currency.

56. Note that the whole point of minimum wages is to prevent nominal wages from adjusting. See Caplan, B. (2013) The myopic empiricism of the minimum wage, *EconLog*, 12 March [http://econlog.econlib.org/archives/2013/03/the_vice_of_sel.html, accessed 3 October 2013].

57. Bewley, T.F. (2002) *Why Wages Don't Fall During a Recession*, Harvard University Press.

58. This summary closely follows Caplan, B. (2013) Why Don't Wages Fall During a Recession?: Q&A With Me Channeling Truman Bewley, *EconLog*, 23 September [http://econlog.econlib.org/archives/2013/09/why_dont_wages.html. accessed 23 September 2013].

59. The capital as Play-Doh vs. capital as Lego analogy originates with Peter Boettke.

60. Lachmann, *Capital and its Structure* (n 1) and Lewin, P. (1999) *Capital in Disequilibrium*, Routledge.

61. Lachmann (n 60).

62. According to Kling, recalculation is an 'Austro-Keynesian' model. It is 'Austrian' in the sense that 'it emphasizes the role of markets in processing information. During a Recalculation, there is too much information to be processed in too little time.' And it is Keynesian in the sense that 'during the Recalculation there are multiplier effects. Unemployed people cut back on their spending, and that in turn requires further adjustment, including more temporary unemployment.' Kling, A. (2009) The recalculation model, simplified, *EconLog*, 6 September [http://econlog.econlib.org/archives/2009/09/the_recalculati.html, accessed 23 September 2013]. We can also think of it as an Austro-Austro model in the sense that the 'multiplier' effects can also be seen as the fact that heterogeneous capital means recessions will take time and be costly. I understand this to be similar to the Wicksellian 'cumulative rot' which is perfectly consistent with an Austrian view.

63. 'Winding-up The New Millennium Experience Company Limited', Report by the comptroller and auditor general, 17 April 2002. [http://www.nao.org.uk/wp-content/uploads/2002/04/0102749.pdf, accessed 23 September 2013].

64. See the 'Millennium Dome Collection' website, http://www.dome2000.com, accessed 23 September 2013.
65. 'Dutchman Helps to Liquidate Dying Churches', *Der Spiegel*, 22 December 2011.
66. 'Dutchman Helps to Liquidate Dying Churches' (n 65).
67. 'West Ham Olympic Stadium move "a mistake" Richard Caborn', *BBC Sport*, 22 March 2013 [http://www.bbc.co.uk/sport/0/football/21897902, accessed 23 September 2013].
68. James, D.N. (2002) The Trouble I've Seen, *Harvard Business Review* 42–49.
69. James, The Trouble I've Seen (n 68).

CHAPTER 7

Public Finance

'(If you drive a car), I'll tax the street,
(If you try to sit), I'll tax your seat,
(If you get too cold), I'll tax the heat,
(If you take a walk), I'll tax your feet.'
—'Taxman', The Beatles[1]

S tudying 'public finance' helps us to understand the role of the government within an economy. It looks at how they raise the money required to pay for public spending, and gets at the heart of the relationship between ordinary people and the state – we can define the state as that organisation said to have a legitimate monopoly on force (and sidestep the tricky issue of what constitutes legitimacy).

Public finance is important for managers because all companies have tax obligations. These obligations change over time and can be hard to anticipate. Understanding the objectives of policymakers can help with this. Not all government spending is funded through current taxation, and we will look at how the bond market developed as a means to finance spending. All companies utilise bond markets, not only to borrow money, but also to accumulate information about future inflation and sovereign default risk. We will also look at the history of banking, and assess some of the key strengths and weaknesses of the present monetary system. As we move into macroeconomic concepts we will start outlining the models and schools of thought that help us to illuminate the complexity of modern economic activity.

7.1 TAXATION

Arguably the most important function of government is the protection of private property – both domestically (in terms of the police force and judicial system) and internationally (i.e. basic national defence). However these are relatively cheap to provide. For example, in the UK less than 10% of public spending is for the Home Office, Department of Justice, Foreign Office and Ministry of Defence combined.[2] In 1820 the government only accounted for around 5–10% of total economic activity.[3] Since then it has grown dramatically, funding services such as social protection, health and education. In 2011–12 these constituted 30%, 19% and 13% of total government spending respectively.[4] In an influential study Vito Tanzi and Ludgar Schuknecht found that the maximum justifiable size of the state was 30–35% of GDP.[5] According to Tanzi,

> *All the theoretical reasons advanced by economists to justify the role of the state in the economy, including the need to assist the poor, could be satisfied with a much smaller share of spending in GDP ... if the governments could be efficient and more focused.*[6]

Where does the money come to pay for this? There are three main ways that a government can raise revenues:

1. Tax
2. Debt
3. Inflation.

Arguably a fourth category of 'net income from government assets' could also be included. This would include the money that governments make when they sell off assets, or income that they generate from the ownership of assets. In the nineteenth century various utility services such as water and gas works generated revenue for the UK government, and many countries around the world operate for-profit 'sovereign wealth funds'. The US Treasury believes that it will end up making a profit on the stakes it bought in some of the bank and auto bailout packages of 2008, prompting some to argue that this should become a genuine alternative to taxation. But if you take the combination of rent, interest and dividends received by the state it is only around 3.1% of total economic activity in the OECD area.[7]

Chapter 8 looks in more detail at how inflation serves as a type of tax, and Chapter 9 looks at the extent to which debt is merely deferred taxation. This chapter will focus on introducing some of the concepts needed to understand these various forms of taxation.

In the UK the largest share of government receipts is income tax (around 25%) followed by national insurance contributions (17%) and VAT (17%).[8] In my experience students are surprised at the extent to which the richest pay the largest proportion of income tax. For example, the richest 1% of taxpayers earn around 12.6% of all income, but contribute 27.7% of income tax receipts. The richest 1–5% take home 12.7% of income and pay 19.3% of income tax. The poorest 50% of the population earn 23.4% of income, but only cover 10.3% of the tax bill.[9]

Another area of public ignorance is the conflation of deficits with debts. Next time you run a bath think about public finance. There are two key aspects that you need to control – the flow of water (whether more is coming in from the tap than leaving by the drain), and the stock of water (how much is in the bath). The government budget is simply government receipts (T) less government spending (G). It shows the flow of government activity. If receipts are higher than spending there is a **budget surplus**, and the state is effectively saving money. If receipts are lower than spending there is a **budget deficit**, which tends to be funded through additional borrowing. A deficit essentially means that there is more water entering the bath from the taps, than is leaving through the drain. In which case, the water level (i.e. public debt burden) will be rising. In order for the debt level to fall, there needs to be a surplus (more water being drained away than is being added). The confusion comes when governments attempt to have a balanced budget, and people confuse this with having no debt. In fact, all it means is that the debt level is unchanged. You would need sustained budget surpluses to bring down that total amount. It's no surprise that the general public confuses the two, given that even the Deputy Prime Minister mixes them up. In a speech in 2012 Nick Clegg said,

> *We have set out a plan – it lasts about six or seven years – to wipe the slate clean to rid people of the deadweight of debt that has been built up over time.*[10]

What he was alluding to were the plans to reduce the size of the budget deficit, ignoring the fact that *any* budget deficit is still *increasing* the amount of public debt. We should also make a distinction between the total deficit and the **structural deficit**. The latter is the fiscal position once the short-term impact that a recession has on spending and taxes has been taken out. For example during a recession the unemployment rate tends to increase and thus tax revenues fall and benefit payments increase. The structural deficit would be the budget position *if* those cyclically unemployed people were back in work.

One of the key aspects of tax reform is incidence (who pays it), and in particular the difference between statutory incidence (the legal assignment) and the actual incidence (the person who ends up paying). Indeed the burden of tax is independent of whether it is imposed on buyers or sellers in a market, because it depends on the relative elasticities of demand and supply. For a good like cigarettes which have a highly inelastic demand curve it doesn't matter that HMRC collect the tax from sellers – most of it is passed on to consumers through higher prices. The person that writes the cheque is not always the one who pays the bill.

Until 1987 all dogs in the UK required a licence that cost around 37p. We can think of this as a tax on dogs. But of course it wasn't the dogs that paid the tax. Televisions don't pay the licence fee, and houses don't pay stamp duty. Only people can pay tax. Consider corporation tax. In the same way that dogs, TVs and houses aren't economic agents, neither are corporations. As Peter Drucker said, 'The legal entity, the company, is a reality for shareholders, for creditors, for employees, and for tax collectors. But *economically,* it is fiction.'[11] Indeed corporation tax can only be paid by a combination of the following:

- Shareholders (through lower dividends)
- Employees (through lower wages)
- Customers (through higher prices).

Plenty of studies have been undertaken to establish the relative split, and much of the evidence points to workers taking the hit. A CBO study argues that around 70% of the burden of corporate income tax is paid for by domestic labour, whilst another study found that a 1% increase in corporation tax cut wages by 0.8% over the next five years.[12]

In his famous book *The Wealth of Nations*, Adam Smith argued that the tax system should have four maxims.[13] The first is proportionality – the burden of tax should fall on those most able to shoulder it, given that they have more resources that require the protection of the state. The second is certainty – people should know in advance how much tax they need to pay, and when they need to pay it, so that the tax collector has no discretion. The third is convenience – tax should be paid at a time and in a manner that is convenient. And the fourth is economical – as much as possible of the revenue gained should actually reach the treasury. Although these are all important, there are additional considerations that contemporary tax proposals tend to value. We can present a fuller set of maxims, as follows:[14]

1. Efficiency – taxes should be low enough to incentivise work and investment and minimise distortions.

2. Fairness – the burden should fall on those who can bear it the most, it should be legitimate, and it should be neutral with regard to economic decisions.
3. Simplicity – it should be easy to collect and easy to understand.
4. Predictability – it should enable planning by having minimal revisions.

It is commonly accepted from empirical studies that high taxes harm growth. Christina and David Romer found that 'tax increases appear to have a very large, sustained, and highly significant negative impact on output'.[15] Fabio Padovano and Emma Galli found that effective marginal income tax rates were 'negatively correlated with economic growth'.[16] Horst Feldman found that 'high top marginal income tax rates and low income threshold levels at which they apply are particularly detrimental',[17] and Andreas Bergh and Martin Karlsson found that 'government size (measured both by taxes and spending relative to GDP) is negatively related to economic growth'.[18]

To understand what causes these unfavourable results of high taxation, consider the concept of the Laffer curve. This curve was first presented by American economist Arthur Laffer on the back of a napkin in a restaurant. He wanted to show that if there were no taxes there would be no tax revenue. But he also pointed out that if tax rates were at 100% there would be no incentive to work and therefore tax revenue would also be zero. By drawing a simple diagram with tax rates on the horizontal axis and tax revenue on the vertical, he established that revenues must be maximised at some rate between 0 and 100.[19]

What he was getting at is the distinction between static and dynamic effects. If you earn a bonus of £1000 and the tax rate is 40% then the tax revenue would be £400. If you raise the rate to 50% then you might predict that revenue increases to £500. But this analysis is static, because it assumes that the change in revenue has no effect on behaviour. In reality higher taxes reduce the incentives for working, and at some point we would expect people to alter their behaviour. It may be that you do not consider this additional work worthwhile unless you receive at least £550. In this case the tax rise would cause you not to bother doing the work and therefore tax revenues would be zero. After all, 40% of *something* is higher than 50% of *nothing*. The problem is that the static and dynamic effects work in opposite directions. As Laffer himself said, 'the consequences of the change in tax rates on total tax revenues are no longer quite so obvious.'[20]

When John F. Kennedy became president in 1961 the highest rate of tax in the US was 91%. *91%!* When he decided to cut this to 70% he relied on a Laffer curve argument:

> *It is a paradoxical truth that tax rates are too high today and tax revenues are too low and the soundest way to raise the revenues in the long run is to cut tax rates.*[21]

One example of how people respond to tax changes is what happened following the increase in the top level of income tax in the UK to 50%, in March 2010. The Exchequer earned £1bn less than they expected because high income individuals shifted around £16bn of income that would have been taxed in the future to 2009/10. In doing so they benefited from the previous 40% rate. What is remarkable is not so much that people would do this, but that (according to HM Treasury) it 'was not factored into the Budget costing at all'.[22] Therefore 'it illustrates how willing and able high-income individuals are to adjust their behaviour in response to changes in tax rates.'[23]

Things look static in the short run, so it may be possible for the Treasury to do a one-off tax grab. But people are forward looking and are constantly trying to anticipate policy. It's therefore very naïve to treat economic activity independently of the tax regime. Some of the dynamic effects include:

- Tax evasion – these are illegal efforts to not pay tax that is due on current activity.
- Tax avoidance – this is often defined as legal efforts to minimise tax obligations on current activity, but I prefer to split it into two distinct things:
  - Tax *planning*, which is using the tax code as it is intended
  - Tax *gaming*, which is exploiting loopholes within the tax code in ways that policymakers had not intended.[24]
- Emigrating – making current activity non-taxable (or at least taxable in another jurisdiction).
- Working less – reducing current activity.

Advocates of lower taxes often stress the third point, and indeed there's lots of survey evidence that suggests high net worth individuals and global companies consider moving abroad if tax obligations become too high. But this can be overblown. After all directors are obliged to routinely assess their place of domicile, and consider alternatives. Many of the 'threats' are hollow. The far greater risks of high taxes are the unseen effects – the difference between the amount of activity taking place currently, versus how much would take place in an alternative tax regime. The easiest way to avoid tax is simply by avoiding work.

The Laffer curve is a brilliantly simple way to conceptualise tax rates, but it has two major downsides. The first is that we never know whereabouts on the curve we are. All it tells us is that it's conceivable that lower taxes would boost revenues. Some policymakers seem to believe that the Laffer curve shows that lower taxes will always boost revenues, but this isn't the case. If it's possible to draw general conclusions then 40% certainly seems to be an upper limit, but every tax, in every country – and indeed faced by every individual – will have its own unique Laffer curve.[25] The second problem is that it shows the tax rate associated with maximum tax revenues. Indeed it's almost taken as given that the goal is to generate as much revenue as possible. But this ignores the deeper issue of what the optimal size of the state should be. Depending on what the government spends money on, it can't be taken for granted that higher revenues are desirable.

7.2　BONDS

Understanding the bond market is crucial to understand how government participates in the monetary system, since it is the ability to issue bonds that provides an incentive for inflation. It also provides a way of seeing how interest rates serve as important signals in an economy.

A bond is a debt security – it is the promise to pay a certain amount of money at specified points in the future (usually this will be an annual return). If you buy a bond then you are effectively lending money to the seller. The supply of bonds is therefore the equivalent of the demand for **loanable funds**. Let's look at the loanable funds market in more detail.

£1000 today is not the same thing as £1000 in a year. This isn't just because of the effects of inflation, because a car today is not the same thing as a car in a year. It is because economic goods are always more valuable the closer in time they are to us. This is why we are constantly choosing between consumption today and *more* consumption tomorrow. All else being equal we would want to consume today, therefore the only reason we'd be willing to wait is if that patience is rewarded. The concept of 'interest' provides this reward – it compensates people for giving up their ownership of resources for a period of time. Interest rates play a crucial role in helping us make tradeoffs between different time periods. Many textbooks define interest as the 'price of money', but this is untrue. The interest rate is the ratio of money in the present with money in the future. It is the price of *time*.

The balance between consumption and investment is determined in the market for loanable funds. Some people are patient, have money to spare and are willing to exchange present goods for even greater future goods (savers). Other people want to bring forward their future income and spend it today (borrowers). The supply and demand for loanable funds operate like any market and generate an equilibrium quantity (i.e. the amount of lending) and equilibrium 'price' (the interest rate). Interest rates are neutral if they reflect the balance between supply and demand. But like other markets, it can be manipulated by policy to drive the market rate away from the neutral rate. Generally speaking, the market rate of interest is the opportunity cost of capital, and is a proxy for time preference.

Bonds were pioneered in Renaissance Italy as a way for government to finance war. If governments are spending more than they are able to raise in tax then they can borrow money from investors by selling bonds. Since government has the power of taxation such bonds will often be considered lower risk than those issued by private companies. And therefore the ability to repay ultimately rests on the tax base – government bonds are future taxes.

In the UK government issued bonds are referred to as gilt-edged securities, or 'gilts'. They can be issued in £100 units and promise to pay a fixed income over a pre-specified term. Consider the following issue from 2008:[26]

£100 nominal of 4.75pc Treasury Stock 2010

It contains several pieces of information, including:

- The **principal** that is returned when the bond expires (also known as the 'face' or 'par' value).
- The **coupon**, which is used to calculate the amount the bondholder receives. This is usually paid every six months and the bond itself used to have detachable 'coupons' that would be presented for redemption when the interest was due.
- The **name** of the gilt.
- The **maturity** – the date on which you receive the principal.

In this case you will have received £4.75 income a year until 2010 (typically split into two payments of $(100*0.0475)/2 = £2.375$ each), and then receive the return of the £100 principal. Note that there's a really important piece of information that isn't contained above: *the price*. This is because the price is set by the interaction of demand and supply. It depends on how much people are willing to pay for this asset.

We can list three main determinants of bond prices:

1. Inflation expectations
    Inflation erodes the value of future payments, so reduces people's desire to purchase future income streams. To protect against this you can buy an index-linked gilt, where the coupon and final redemption payment are tracked to movements in the Retail Price Index

(RPI). In the UK around 25% of gilts are index linked, which is quite a lot compared to other countries.

2. Interest rate expectations

There is an inverse relationship between interest rates and the price of gilts. If interest rates are 3% then the return of 4.75% looks good and people will bid up the price to above the nominal value of £100. By contrast, if interest rates were above the coupon, the gilt would be less attractive and the price would fall below the principal.[27]

3. Economic confidence

Government's ability to repay debt depends on their future tax revenues, therefore people may be less inclined to buy gilts if there's a slowdown.

The role of credit ratings agencies is to provide investors with guidance on the quality of various bonds. Although they have a bad reputation amongst the public this information helps to reduce borrowing costs.

Imagine that it is 2009 and our gilt is currently trading at a price of £110.

The **current yield** is the interest rate based on the buying price as opposed to the nominal value. It shows us the return that the bondholder would get if they held it for a certain period of time, and can be calculated as the coupon divided by the market price, or in our case $4.75/110 = 4.3\%$. Hence if prices fall the yield will rise (there is an inverse relationship).[28] This situation was evident when the Bank of England increased its holdings of gilts in 2009:

With £75 billion to spend in the next three months and the majority of the money earmarked for gilts, the Bank of England's presence as a buyer in the market has sent gilt prices rocketing and yields plummeting.[29]

The **yield to maturity** (YTM) helps us to see what return the bondholder might expect, since it incorporates an assumption that coupons are reinvested, and that the bond will be held until it matures. It gives you the discount rate such that the sum of all future cash flows (i.e. coupons and principal) is equal to the price.

The **yield curve** is the relation between the interest rate (or cost of government borrowing) and the time to maturity. As previously discussed we would expect an increasing function over time due to time preference. The longer the time period the greater the interest rate needs to be to compensate lenders.

An **inverted yield curve** occurs when long-term yields fall *below* short-term yields. Under unusual circumstances, long-term investors will settle for lower yields now if they think the economy will slow or even decline in the future. It means that the asset is deemed riskier next year than in several years hence – i.e. things are coming to a head. Therefore an inverted yield curve might be viewed as a predictor of recessions.[30]

Bond markets can be a valuable source of information because they combine a number of different forms of expectation. In particular we can use bond markets to infer two key indicators:

1. Using bond markets to estimate **inflation expectations.**

Real interest rates are simply the nominal interest rate minus inflation. Therefore we can rearrange this equation and see that an implicit inflation expectation is contained within the spread between the yields of nominal and index-linked bonds. For example, on 2 November 2010 the yield on a US Treasury bond was 1.25%, whilst the yield on an index-linked bond of the same maturity was -0.55%. This implies that the market's inflation expectations were 1.8%.[31]

2. Using bond markets to estimate **sovereign default risk.**

As previously discussed sovereign debt is often referred to as 'risk free' on account of the government ability to tax. But governments can and do default on their debt. From 1800 to 2006 there were 250 defaults on external debt and 68 defaults on domestic debt.[32] One way of approximating the riskiness of a particular country's debt is to see the premium it trades at over a benchmark country. If, for example, German bonds are assumed to be the safest the spread between the yield on Greek and German debt provides an indication of the relative riskiness.[33]

7.3   BANKING

A large difficulty with trade is that we don't always have what other people want. For example, I specialise in producing economics articles. But these are of little use to me when I need to ride on the bus. For some strange reason, few bus drivers are willing to accept a copy of my latest academic article in exchange for a single fare. One option is that I restrict my trading partners to only those who actually want economics articles. But – unfortunately – this would consign me to a lonely life of poverty. Alternatively, I could be slightly less selfish and consider what the bus driver may want to have, rather than what I'd like to offer. For him, a chicken may be more useful than an economics article, so I may attempt to exchange an article for a chicken with someone else, and then use the chicken to pay for my bus ride. Chickens may prove to be a more marketable commodity (and thus more likely to be wanted by the bus driver) than economics articles. But chickens are cumbersome.

As a society we have tried using different commodities as a medium of exchange. There are certain qualities that we can say are especially desirable – it should be easy to transport, hardwearing, divisible and relatively scarce. But there's no inherent property that tells us whether something is well suited to being used as a means of payment. Indeed the main quality we need in money is a reasonable expectation that *other people* will accept it. But when something *is* used as a medium of exchange it becomes money. The important thing to realise is that money originates as an actual commodity, and then strong network effects mean that once something starts to be commonly accepted it makes sense for *everyone* to use the same thing. Historically this has tended to be precious metals such as gold, silver or copper. But there's nothing special about gold. People only used it as money because there was a reasonable expectation that other people would accept it in exchange. The more commonly used it was, the more generally accepted it became. But this is a voluntary, organic process.

In this regard money is a spontaneous order, and very similar to others like the English language or the law. Modern coins may be stamped with the image of a King or Queen, but as Carl Menger said 'in its origin it is a social, and not a state institution.'[34]

Economic trade can occur without money, but money makes it significantly easier. It allows us to move from a barter economy to a monetary economy; from direct exchange to indirect exchange. It brings people closer together.

The establishment of a monetary economy does create complications. The classical school (i.e. economists of the eighteenth and nineteenth centuries) held that real variables (things measured in physical quantities) can be analysed separately from nominal variables (things measured in currency). The **classical dichotomy** (as shown in Table 7.1) is the idea that

TABLE 7.1 The classical dichotomy

Real variables	Nominal variables
Quantities and relative prices	Expressed in money terms
• Real GDP	• Money supply
• Capital stock	• Price level
• Real wages	• Inflation
• Real interest rate	• Wages
	• Nominal GDP

real factors only affect real variables, and nominal factors affect nominal variables. We can understand things like GDP without needing to know about inflation (P) or the money supply (M), which only affect other nominal variables. If this is the case money is said to be **neutral**.

Most people get paid a nominal salary. Your real wage is when inflation is taken into consideration. The difference between real and nominal is therefore money. The simplest way to understand whether something is real or nominal is to ask whether it would exist in a barter economy. If it could, then it's a real factor. If it can only exist with money, then it's nominal.

The emergence of commodity money was therefore a major breakthrough in human history, but even though precious metals such as gold satisfy the basic criteria for money, it is inconvenient to carry them about with you. And it is dangerous, since you may become a target for thieves and robbers. There have been three main evolutions in the history of money and banking:

1. Banks emerged to issue **certificates of deposit**. They significantly reduce the cost of carrying gold because instead of paying for something with the actual gold, you simply transfer a claim to that gold. Instead of giving you 1 pound of gold, I can simply give you a certificate that allows you to withdraw 1 pound of my gold from my bank. Soon these notes begin to circulate so widely that people simply stop carrying gold.
2. If people routinely accept the notes as a medium of exchange, then what is the point of having all that gold sitting in the vaults? Since gold is a valuable commodity this places a large opportunity cost on the monetary system. If banks only hold **fractional reserves** (i.e. only retain a portion of their customers' deposit available for immediate redemption) this will free up resources for other uses. This is where we have two conflicting stories about what happened next. Some economic historians claim that bankers spotted a sly opportunity – they could issue additional certificates of deposit and simply cross their fingers that no one would notice. Of course if for some reason lots of people with bank notes all came to redeem 'their' gold the bank would be unable to pay out, but this was a risk worth taking for the ability to create new money.[35] The other claim is that depositors were aware of this innovation, and saw how it benefited them. By lending out a fraction of the gold being held the bank would be able to generate interest, and they could pass some of this on to the depositors themselves. Depositors were willing to treat the bank note as an IOU rather than a receipt, because the interest they received compensated them for the slightly increased risk of a bank run.[36]

   Many people still believe that their bank deposits are 'theirs', and are merely being stored by their bank.[37] But regardless of public opinion, bank notes operate as a debt instrument and not a bailment. This means that when you deposit money in the bank it ceases to be your property, and from a legal perspective becomes a loan to the bank. Their obligation is to give it back to you when you demand it, and most of the time they are able to do so. Indeed rather than being the weakness of the banking system, the threat of a bank run is a source of strength. It can serve as a conditioning device to ensure that banks are cautious and responsible.

For a number of reasons, however, it became a widely held opinion that banks were inherently prone to runs and that their own private insurance arrangements were insufficient to prevent systemic crises. This resulted in the emergence of **central banks**. The original role of the central bank was to prevent bank runs from spreading through the entire system, by doing two things:

a. Offering lines of credit to sound banks that cannot find credit by other means;

b. Closing down unsound banks in an orderly manner.

During the financial crisis *The Economist* said 'support was supposed to be short-term, not continuous: a central bank should be an emergency room, not a hospice.'[38] But as the two original roles make clear, central banks should be both ERs and hospices. The difficulty is knowing when to act as a hospice (i.e. allow insolvent banks to go bust with dignity) and when to act as an ER (i.e. save illiquid ones).

The key to accomplishing the latter is to send credible signals that they are willing and able to support banks that are suffering from blind panics, and their ability to do this depends on the **volume of reserves** at their disposal. The godfather of central banking was Walter Bagehot (also the first editor of *The Economist* magazine). He wrote the central bankers' bible, called *Lombard Street* which included the famous 'Bagehot Rule':[39]

Lend freely, but at a penalty rate.

The aim was to avoid moral hazard by punishing banks that required emergency provisions (and thus ensure that only solvent ones would be able to afford it), but to maintain liquidity by ensuring that there was an unlimited ability to lend. But there is only a finite amount of gold. This brings us to the third main evolution in money:

3. Break the link between money and the underlying commodity. If there is no obligation to convert money into something like gold (i.e. you have eliminated the liability of paper money) then there is no limit to the amount of money you can create. Such **fiat money** allows central banks to literally provide unlimited resources to the banking system. But in doing so you generate a very important power. The creation of fiat money thus coincides with the nationalisation of the ability to print money with the creation of a government monopoly.

Modern technology means that we rarely use bank notes for transactions. Modern bank accounts come with payment mechanisms that allow us to transfer money directly from one account to another. But this doesn't change the economics. It just means that bank accounts with debit cards also constitute money, and that private banks also contribute to the money supply.[40] Some people claim that banks have too much power, and that only the government should be allowed to create new money. But the foundation of the banking system is the central bank. In many ways private banks are mere tentacles of a centrally planned banking system.

7.4 SAVING

Imagine that you are stranded on a desert island. Your immediate priority is to find food, and being close to the ocean you venture out to catch some fish. Without tools this will be a long and arduous task. Maybe you can catch a few with your bare hands, or perhaps forage for some crabs. But what you really need is some equipment, for example a spear. What resources do you need to make a spear? You might look for a stick, and either a rock or piece of flint with a sharp point. You would need some vines to bind them together. The realisation that these resources can be utilised as tools is an example of entrepreneurial discovery.[41] It also shows that there's no such thing as a 'natural' resource. The sticks and vines only have value because they fit into your entrepreneurial plan. There is a problem though. The time you spend making the spear is time that you do not spend fishing. Indeed the only way you can make the spear is if you have enough fish to eat whilst you work. In economic terms the fish is a *consumer* good because it directly generates utility. But foraging is highly unproductive. What you want are *capital* goods such as spears that allow you to create such consumer goods. These do not directly increase utility, but are a crucial way to increase the amount you can consume over time.

It is this span of time that is important. If you can catch four fish per day with your bare hands, and need to eat two per day to survive, it is possible to 'save' two fish per day. Savings are simply income that isn't consumed. But before you can start making capital goods you need to have an entrepreneurial plan – a vision of how long it will take you to make the spear, and whether you have enough fish to survive that long. Let's assume your plan works, and your new spear allows you to catch eight fish per day. You now have plenty of fish to consume. But you are still spending time fishing, when you could be engaged in leisure. It would be far quicker (and more pleasant) if you had even better capital equipment. For example, if you can upgrade from a spear to a boat. So what resources do you need to build a boat? You need wood, more vines, etc. But the critical resource is *fish*. There is no point spending 10 days building a boat and then dying of hunger. You need a stockpile of resources in order to devote time to the production of capital goods. In short, you need to save before you can invest.

If your judgment is accurate, and your capital goods are produced and ready to use before you've depleted your savings, then you are a successful entrepreneur. Indeed this process, in a nutshell, is economic growth. It occurs when people look to the future. When they divert resources from the immediate satisfaction of their desires (consumption) to the production of capital goods (investment). As the stock of capital goods rises, we become more productive, and wealthier. It also means that our time horizons are expanding.

Remember in 2010 when 33 Chilean miners were trapped underground for over two months.[42] Think about the decision to begin exploration for copper, and how distant any returns would be on such an investment. A main source of growth is when people are willing to make those short-term sacrifices in favour of long-term rewards. Prosperity stems from a steadily increasing capital stock, brought about by higher savings. Many people seem to believe that the Industrial Revolution was some kind of miracle. But it was just one stage in this process.[43]

We've already seen how firms combine factors of production (such as labour and capital) to generate goods and services. We can use this to build a very crude model of the whole economy. We add 'land' as the third factor of production, and use 'entrepreneurs' to refer to those who direct the use of those resources. As we've seen, people have a choice to make with the income (Y) they receive. They can either consume it, or save it. Most economics textbooks explain this process in a slightly different way. They rely on the 'circular flow of income' to show how goods and money move between firms and households and vice versa. The model

I'm using is different, and focuses more on a time structure of production. But I think it makes more sense for two reasons. Firstly, the circular flow suggests that once goods are consumed the economic process has finished, but consumption is only meaningful in that it generates utility, and thus satisfies the pressing needs of consumers. Secondly, savings should not 'leak' out of the model (as they do in the circular flow), because they are the foundation of economic growth. When people decide to save, those resources aren't dormant. If you only decide to spend half of your paycheck, the remainder doesn't just sit in a shoebox.

The act of saving is also the act of investment – this 'pool of savings' is what allows productivity to increase. The role of financial intermediation is to allow entrepreneurs to invest without having to save their *own* resources first. But this can only occur because someone *else* has done the saving. This process of investment will make the factors of production more efficient – either by improving land, educating or training labour, or providing better quality machines and other capital goods. With the expanded and more efficient factors of production we can produce even more goods and services. And again people choose whether to consume now or improve productivity further. Too much consumption and we don't have a future. Too much investment and we don't enjoy the present. The economy is comprised of millions of people making a decision about trading off immediate consumption versus future, and even greater consumption. We can represent this in a simple equation, which we will use to build a model of the entire output of an economy:

$$Y = C + I$$

But this will create a tension. As we've defined it the economy should be viewed as a structure of production that takes place over time, rather than a circular flow where everything is instantaneous. We will return to this later.

7.5   REAL BUSINESS CYCLES

In an agricultural economy one might expect business cycles to be driven largely by natural phenomena, such as weather patterns or population changes. And indeed over the longer term it is the productivity of land, labour and capital that will determine a country's growth potential. A **business cycle** is a periodic fluctuation in economic activity, relative to a long run trend. According to Arthur Burns and Wesley Mitchell,

> *A cycle consists of expansions occurring at about the same time in many economic activities, followed by similar general recessions, contractions, and revivals which merge into the expansion phase of the next cycle; this sequence of changes is recurrent but not periodic, in duration business cycles vary from more than one year to ten or twelve years.*[44]

The key thing about this definition is that it involves a comovement of economic indicators. There are always entrepreneurial errors occurring in a market economy. Sometimes, however, there are clusters of errors. In other words, periods of systematic expansion and contraction.

It is common for people to resort to psychological explanations for economic activity, such as the notion that entrepreneurs get 'swept up' in waves of optimism, or widespread panic during a downturn. Whilst not denying that things like confidence play a role, it's telling that these theories are so vague. For one thing 'greed' is an entirely unsatisfactory explanation for economic booms. This isn't to say that greed doesn't exist, but that it's more of a constant than a variable. It could even be the *key* factor in a stock market bubble, but I'm not aware of a convincing explanation for how *changes* in greed drive markets. I prefer to view greed in the same way that we view gravity when it comes to plane crashes. It is trivially true that plane crashes are 'caused' by gravity, but it's not a satisfactory explanation. It begs the question – why are crashes the exception, given that gravity is always there? Similarly when markets are working fine it's not as if there's no 'greed'. What we need is an *economic* explanation for the root cause of booms and busts.

Firstly, consider the economy in its natural state. Here, business cycles are caused by random productivity shocks. The 'cycle' would just be a continually efficient response to external shocks, and therefore the economy is technically always in equilibrium. This explanation of business cycles, known as 'real business cycle theory' rests on several assumptions:[45]

- Agents have rational expectations.
- Markets clear (we are always in equilibrium).
- The economy follows a random walk, so there *is* no underlying trend.[46]
- The intertemporal substitution of labour (i.e. people make voluntary choices to substitute between labour and leisure depending on the wage rate offered).[47]
- Money is neutral (it doesn't affect real variables), therefore monetary policy plays no role (which is why it is called a *real* business cycle).
- Fluctuations in output are fluctuations in the natural rate of output.

If this holds true the cause of economic fluctuations is all about supply side (i.e. 'real') shocks. Some examples of possible shocks:

- Environment (earthquakes, droughts, floods)
- Price of energy (OPEC, Iraq war)
- War/civil unrest (general strikes)
- Government regulation (e.g. import quotas)
- Productivity shocks (technological changes such as the internet).

Real business cycle theory championed the use of what are called **dynamic, stochastic general equilibrium models** and heralded a new era in macroeconomic technique. But the essence is very simple – perceived instability is just an efficient response to new conditions. Indeed one can question whether governments should even attempt to manipulate the economy by moderating booms and busts – by interfering with the efficient response to new conditions they only make things worse. If you think about a heart rate monitor peaks and troughs occur naturally, and are a sign of health. If a doctor tried to create a flat rate the patient would die.

7.6 NATIONAL INCOME ACCOUNTING

A typical way to split up the subject matter of economics is to make a clear distinction between micro- and macroeconomics. Microeconomics is typically defined as the study of individual consumers, households, firms or industries. The basic demand and supply diagram is the bedrock of microeconomic analysis, and the main application is things like competition policy.

By contrast macroeconomics looks at the national or international area, or the aggregated sum of the economy as a whole. The problem with this distinction is that it can be somewhat arbitrary and it generates inconsistencies.

Indeed it's a shame that economists specialise so much, to the extent that it's rare to contribute to both micro- and macroeconomic theory. In most universities they are taught as separate courses, and often in separate semesters. But from the 1970s onwards there was a backlash against this separation, as many economists sought to provide 'microfoundations' for macroeconomics. The aim was to make sure that macroeconomic models were compatible with the assumptions made about economic agents in micro. However the success of this endeavour is still being debated. One problem is that many economists treat macro as merely being a bigger version of micro. Whilst microeconomics is about supply and demand, macroeconomics is simply *aggregate* supply and *aggregate* demand. We use lower case notation for a market (e.g. q) but upper case for a country (Q). But all this aggregation has problems. What does it mean to say that the GDP of Finland is similar to the GDP of Portugal? These are very different economies, and the composition of GDP is important. We might find that Mike Tyson weighs the same as Kirstie Alley, but this tells us little about their respective physiques.

The classical school of economics is a broad term that applies to most economists from 1776 (the publication of Adam Smith's *The Wealth of Nations*) to 1936 (Keynes's *General Theory*). The main points of the classical school are the following:

- Output and employment are determined by the interaction between the labour market and an aggregate production function.
- There are only temporary, voluntary deviations from full employment.
- Long run supply is constrained by factors of production.
- The economy is self-regulating, therefore government intervention is disruptive: the optimal policy is laissez-faire.

GDP stand for 'Gross domestic product' and is the cash value of final goods and services produced within a given time period. There are three ways in which it is calculated and in theory they should all be equal. The first is the **output approach**, which looks at the final value of goods and services traded. The second is the **income approach**, which measures the total amount of income earned (such as rent, wages and profit). Finally the **expenditure approach** is the total amount of money spent. We usually use 'Q' to refer to output, and 'Y' to refer to income, but since these should be equal we can represent GDP as the sum of consumption and investment:[48]

$$Y = C + I$$

In Chapter 9 we will introduce government spending to the model, and in Chapter 10 foreign trade. For now we are taking a simplified view that only focuses on the domestic private sector. We can go into more detail, and you will often see references to 'Gross *national* product' (GNP) instead. For a country like Ireland, where there's a big difference between the output produced within its borders (GDP) as opposed to by its citizens (GNP) – due to the amount of foreign firms that are based there – we need to be careful about which figure we look at. Indeed some statistical agencies report 'Net national product' (NNP) or 'Gross national income' (GNI). There are lots of combinations of G's and N's, and D's and N's, and

P's and I's. But they are basically the same, and for our purposes let's treat them as being equivalent. GDP is our measure of output.

We need to be very careful about attributing too much to GDP figures. For a start, a lot of changes are random. Or to put this more accurately, a lot of the changes in GDP are so small they are indistinguishable from being random. Chances are that any news item about the latest figures is just showing the ebbs and flows around a general trend. In addition to this it is subject to revision. In the UK the Office for National Statistics releases three separate estimates, each a month apart and utilising more information. As you might expect, the third release is the most accurate, but the first release is the one that gets most attention. The headline figure is the least reliable.[49]

Economists are often accused of knowing the price of everything but the value of nothing. But national income accounts demonstrate where there's a real disjoint between what economists understand, and how that gets translated into the policy and public realm. David Henderson uses the term 'GDP fetishism' for when people judge a policy based only on whether it increases GDP, without considering how it impacts living standards.[50] We can list several reasons why GDP diverges from living standards, and is therefore a bad measure to target:[51]

1. **Non traded labour**

   GDP only measures output that is traded, but not all 'work' ends up on the market. In 2013 former Oasis front man Liam Gallagher split from his wife and began dating his personal assistant. If they got married, ceteris paribus, GDP would fall.[52] This is because as his employee the value of her labour is counted in GDP figures. But were they to marry, and have a different contractual arrangement for their relationship, presumably she would stop receiving a wage. Previously traded labour would become untraded. The same amount of work is being done, but GDP falls.

2. **Under appreciation of leisure**

   When slaves were emancipated in the US South they reduced the amount of labour they supplied by one third. This meant that GDP fell, but only because they valued their leisure by more. The measured value of their production fell, but their wellbeing was higher.[53]

3. **Government services measured at cost**

   Because they don't sell goods and services on the open market we can't measure the value created by government. But it is plausible that at least some government production is worth less than it costs. In Turkmenistan there is a large monument with a 39-foot gold plated statue of former leader Saparmurat Niyazov that rotates throughout the day so that he's always facing the sun.[54] These types of project have little economic value, in which case measured GDP overestimates wellbeing.

4. **Ignores opportunity cost**

   There is a great joke that when an earthquake hit Blackpool, on the north west coast of England, it caused £500 000 worth of improvements. Ordinarily though when a natural disaster strikes welfare unambiguously falls. But this isn't captured in GDP figures. However the costs of rebuilding will be part of measured output. If a hurricane destroys a pier, and it later gets rebuilt, you're back to where you started. You aren't any better off. In fact you're worse off, because you had to commit scarce resources to rebuilding the pier, rather than investing in other projects. However GDP figures will treat this as a gain.

The neglect of opportunity costs is known as the 'Broken Window Fallacy', which originates from Frederic Bastiat.[56] He tells a parable of a boy who breaks his father's shop window, and receives a scolding. However a crowd forms and someone asks what would become of the glaziers if no windows were ever broken? The problem, as Bastiat points out, is that the gain to the glazier is only the *seen* effect. To an untrained eye it may look as though the creation of work is a good thing, and indeed GDP figures would support this view. But we should also consider the *unseen*. Namely the goods that the shopkeeper would have bought, if he hadn't needed to spend it on his window. The reduced income of the tailor (from whom he would otherwise have bought a suit) is less tangible, but just as important, as the increased income of the glazier. The common sense view that damage is bad is correct. It has the potential to increase measured output, but by less than would have happened were it not for the damage.

5. Short time horizon

If you chop down some trees and sell them for paper, this will help to boost economic activity. But once all the trees are gone, you're out of resources. In many environmental situations, bad institutions mean that there's an incentive to deplete resources at the expense of the long run. This is encouraged by the fact that GDP figures will be presenting such depletion as 'growth'.

In the same way that the production function of a firm considers output to be a function of labour and capital, the same goes for the economy-wide aggregate production function. And since capital is assumed to be reasonably fixed (at least in the short term) national output is simply the result of the equilibrium level of employment combined with the current capital stock.

But as the pioneer of national income accounting, Simon Kuznets, famously said, 'the welfare of a nation can scarcely be inferred from a measure of national income.'[57] In the classical model the level of output for the economy stems from the smooth functioning (or otherwise) of the labour market. If we assume that the labour market is reasonably free and flexible then it will be in equilibrium with a given level of employment and a market wage rate. Since there are no gluts or shortages in equilibrium, by definition there is no unemployment. Or, any unemployment that exists will be a result of temporary factors such as people voluntarily deciding to look for a new job or companies relocating. Employment will be at its 'natural' rate, and output will be at its potential.

NOTES

1. *Revolver*, Parlophone Records, 1966. "Taxman" words and music by George Harrison © 1966, Reproduced by permission of Sony/ATV Music Publishing LLC., London W1F 9LD.
2. Budget 2011, HM Treasury, pp. 47–48. This is especially true for countries that free ride on US military spending, although there is a legitimate debate as to whether this constitutes a public 'good' or public 'bad'.
3. See Gross Public Income – United Kingdom 1801–1980, in Mitchel, B.R. (1988) *British Historical Statistics,* Cambridge University Press.
4. Budget 2011, HM Treasury (n 2).
5. Tanzi, V. and Schuknecht, L., 2000 *Public Spending in the 20th Century*, Cambridge University Press.
6. Tanzi, V. (2005) The economic role of the state in the 21st century, *Cato Journal*, **25** (3), 617–638.

7. *The Single Income Tax*, 2020 Tax Commission, May 2012.
8. Budget 2011, HM Treasury (n 2).
9. There is a nice graphic to show this at Sinclair, M. (2012) The rich, the poor and the middle pay a lot of tax. *Tax Payers' Alliance Blog*, 16 April [http://www.taxpayersalliance.com/economics/2012/04/rich-poor-middle-pay-lot-tax.html, accessed 26 September 2013].
10. See Curtis, P. (2010) How Nick Clegg got it wrong on debt, *The Guardian Politics Blog*, 9 May [http://www.theguardian.com/politics/reality-check-with-polly-curtis/2012/may/09/nickclegg-davidcameron, accessed 26 September 2013].
11. Drucker, P. (1995) The Information Executives Truly Need, *Harvard Business Review*, **73** (1), 54–62.
12. Mankiw, N.G. (2006) Who pays the corporate income tax? *Greg Mankiw's Blog*, 24 August and 'A toll on the common man', *The Economist*, 1 July 2006.
13. These four canons stem from Smith, A. (1776[1976]) *An Inquiry into the Nature and Causes of the Wealth of Nations*, University of Chicago Press. See Pirie, M. (2012) *Economics Made Simple: How Money, Trade and Markets Really Work*, Harriman; and Rhoads, J. (2010) Adam Smith's four principles of taxation, *Greater Boston Tea Party Blog*, 10 April [http://greaterbostonteaparty.com/?p=220, accessed 26 September 2013].
14. See Tax Matters: Reforming the Tax System, The Report of the Tax Reform Commission, October 2006.
15. Romer, C. and Romer, D.H. (2010) The macroeconomic effects of tax changes: estimates based on a new measure of fiscal shocks, *American Economic Review*, **100**, 763–801.
16. Padovano, F. and Galli, E. (2001) Tax rates and economic growth in the OECD countries (1950–1990), *Economic Enquiry*, **39** (1), 44–57.
17. Feldmann, H. (2010) Government size and unemployment: Evidence from industrial countries, *Public Choice*, **127** (3-4), 451–467.
18. Bergh, A. and Karlsson, M. (2010) Government size and growth: Accounting for economic freedom and globalization, *Public Choice*, **142** (1-2), 195–213.
19. As with many 'discoveries', Arthur Laffer was hardly the first economist to make this point. But he did a lot to popularise the concept.
20. Laffer, A. (2004) The Laffer curve: past present and future, *Heritage Backgrounder*, 1 June.
21. Address and Question and Answer Period at the Economic Club of New York, 14 December 1962.
22. Budget 2011, HM Treasury (n 2).
23. Budget 2011, HM Treasury (n 2).
24. This helps demonstrate that there is an important difference between, for example, married couples that receive tax credits versus comedians setting up offshore companies to transfer income into loans. At the moment they would both be referred to as tax avoidance.
25. Saez, Slemrod and Giertz find that the revenue maximising rate for the US is just over 55%, which is only slightly higher than the actual tax burden that Americans faced as of 2008 (note that this is a combination of things like Federal and State income tax, Medicare, and various sales taxes). Saez, E., Slemrod, J.B. and Giertz, S.H. (2012) The Elasticity of Taxable Income with Respect to Marginal Tax Rates: A Critical Review, *Journal of Economic Literature*, **50** (1), 3–50.
26. This example is taken from Farrow, P. (2008) Interest rates: How do gilts work and where can I buy them? *The Daily Telegraph*, 7 November.
27. Farrow, Interest rates (n 26).
28. The yield to maturity (YTM) is the anticipated return if you hold until maturity (assuming that all coupons are reinvested). It's the typical way to compare all components of a bond.
29. Grote, D. (2009) Gilt yields plunge as Bank of England prepares to splurge 'new' cash, *City Wire*, 10 March.
30. Harvey, C.R. (1986) Recovering Expectations of Consumption Growth from an Equilibrium Model of the Term Structure of Interest Rates, University of Chicago Dissertation. [http://faculty.fuqua.duke.edu/~charvey/Research/Thesis/Thesis.htm, accessed 26 September 2013].

31. 'Accentuate the negative', *The Economist*, 4 November 2010.

32. Reinhart, C.M. and Rogoff, K.S. (2011) The forgotten history of domestic debt, *Economic Journal*, **121** (552), 319–350.

33. For some charts that use bond yields as a gauge for sovereign default see 'A contagious Irish disease?', *The Economist*, 25 November 2010 and 'European bond spreads', *The Economist*, 27 March 2010.

34. Menger, C. (1892) On the Origins of Money, *Economic Journal*, **2**, 239–255.

35. See Rothbard, M.N. (1963[2005]) *What Has Government Done to our Money?* Mises Institute.

36. See Selgin, G. (2013) Those dishonest goldsmiths, *Financial History Review*, **19** (3), 269–288.

37. In a survey for the Cobden Centre 74% of the general public believed that they were the legal owner of the money in their current account, rather than treating it as a loan to the bank. See 'Public Attitudes to Banking' The Cobden Centre, June 2010.

38. 'In a spin', *The Economist*, 29 December 2010.

39. Although *Lombard Street* is often seen as a sort of rulebook, it is not clear whether Bagehot endorsed that system. George Selgin uses the analogy that having a central bank is like having a lion in the living room – it's not a good idea. A lion tamer can give you some advice about what you should or shouldn't do if you find yourself in this situation, but such advice shouldn't be seen as an endorsement of your predicament. Even if you have very *good* advice, you should still do your best to avoid being in a situation where you need to use it.

40. We will define and discuss the money supply in more detail in Chapter 8.

41. Sautet, F. (2010) The competitive market is a process of entrepreneurial discovery, in Boettke, P.J. (ed.), *Handbook on Contemporary Austrian Economics*, Edward Elgar.

42. 'Chile mining accident (2010)', *New York Times*, 12 October 2011 [http://topics.nytimes.com/top/reference/timestopics/subjects/c/chile_mining_accident_2010/, accessed 25 November 2013].

43. The Industrial Revolution got its name because British economist Arnold Toynbee was giving a talk on economic history and wanted to generate a large crowd. To jazz it up he called it the 'Industrial Revolution' and it stuck. But it wasn't a real revolution. It wasn't a moment in history. Yes, economic growth has been exponential since that point, but it began a lot earlier and has simply compounded.

44. Burns, A.F., and Mitchell, W.C. (1946) *Measuring Business Cycles*, National Bureau of Economic Research.

45. Kydland, F.E. and Prescott, C. (1982) Time to build and aggregate fluctuations, *Econometrics*, **50**, 1345–1370.

46. Nelson, C.R. and Plosser, C.I. (1982) Trends and random walks in macroeconomic time series. Some evidence and implications, *Journal of Monetary Economics*, **10**, 139–162.

47. One of the reasons why non economists find these sorts of models implausible is because the intertemporal substitution of labour implies that the Great Depression might also be considered the Great Vacation, since it was a time when many people opted to sit out of the labour market and enjoy some time at home.

48. Note that we define investment as the purchase of new capital goods. In this sense buying shares is not investment; it's merely a transfer of ownership rights.

49. In October 2013 the *Financial Times* published an interview with the CEO of Lloyds Banking Group, Antonio Horta-Osorio, and quoted him as saying: 'To be able to start paying taxpayers' money back in two-and-a-half years is significantly better than I thought, especially after the sovereign debt contagion and the double-dip recession' [Goff, S. and Jenkins, P. (2013) Job half done for Lloyds' chief António Horta-Osório, *Financial Times*, 13 October 2013].

   The problem with this is that in June 2013 the growth figure for 2012 Q1 was revised from 0.1% to 0%, which meant that there was no recession in 2012, and therefore no 'double dip' recession at all.

50. Henderson, D.R. (2010) GDP fetishism, *Library of Economics and Liberty*, 1 March.

51. See Henderson, GDP fetishism (n 50).

52. This example is based on Paul Samuelson's famous quip that if a man marries his maid it would cause GDP to fall.
53. Hummel, J.R. (1996) *Emancipating Slaves, Enslaving Free Men*, Open Court. Taken from Henderson, GDP fetishism (n 50).
54. Orange, R. (2011) Turkmenistan rebuilds giant rotating golden statue, *Daily Telegraph*, 24 May.
55. Henderson is open to the possibility that the Transportation Security Administration (TSA) does in fact create value by reducing the chances that people's planes will be hijacked. But he makes the following claim. Some people will be willing to pay money to avoid using the TSA line, and for them the TSA reduces their utility. Some people are happy to incur additional costs in the perceived security vs. liberty trade off. Henderson claims – and I agree – that the former will exceed the latter. It certainly won't be $6.3bn *lower*.
56. Bastiat, F. (1850) *That Which Is Seen, and That Which Is Not Seen*, Impr. de F. Pérez.
57. Kuznets, S. (1934) National Income, 1929–1932. 73rd US Congress, 2d session, Senate document no. 124, p. 7.

Monetary Theory

'Inflation is always and everywhere a monetary phenomenon.'

—Milton Friedman[1]

One of the chief worries of any monetary system is that one arm of the state ends up financing the other. When Robert Mugabe's government became involved in the second Congo War they resorted to the printing press to fund their spending. Endemic corruption and a lack of faith in the value of the currency led to one of the greatest hyperinflations of all time. At the peak, in November 2008, prices were doubling every day.[2] And by 2010 Zimbabwean dollars were so worthless there were signs asking people not to use them as toilet paper.

By contrast, from 1991 to 2009 Somalia did not have a central bank, and since then efforts to launch one have been difficult. Whilst US dollars have been the currency of choice for large payments, the Somali shilling continues to circulate. The 1000 shilling note is worth about the same as the ink and paper required to make it, and therefore the incentives for forgery are minimal. It operates as a commodity currency, where the supply is determined by the costs of production, rather than government edict. Despite this – or perhaps even because of this – there was price stability.[3] Indeed the payment system in Somalia is relatively advanced due to the emergence of private money transfer operators and other types of informal banking networks. In 2006 over half a billion dollars a year was being sent as remittances, with commission rates of just 5%.[4]

The aim of this chapter is to present a contemporary and easy to understand version of **the quantity theory of money**. I will explain how it provides a simple explanation of how and why inflation occurs, and the ways in which monetary policy is used to influence the economy. You may hear in the news that 'the Bank of England has cut interest rates' – this chapter will help you understand the models and assumptions that guide their decisions. You can consider this chapter to be a basic training guide for central bankers. But it will also try to set these debates in the broader context of whether the costs of trying to conduct complicated monetary policy outweigh the benefits. In doing so, it highlights some of the ways in which inflation can generate false signals that can induce managerial errors. Whilst it is impossible to fully distinguish between false and true signals, an awareness of the difference can be a major source of competitive advantage.

8.1   INFLATION

'Inflation' can be used by economists to mean different things, so it is important to be clear about what is being 'inflated'. Most economists are referring to the 'general price level', which is a vague term that attempts to capture an overall trend in prices throughout the entire economy. In practice this is impossible to gauge, and so various price indices are used as a proxy.[5]

The most important is the **consumer price index** (CPI), which is the official measure within the Eurozone to assess inflation rates across countries. It tracks changes in the prices of consumer goods and services that are bought by households. In the UK it is compiled by the Office for National Statistics, and they simply have a list of items that constitute a 'typical' basket of goods. They track any changes in the price of those goods and use this to construct an index. But there are several dangers of this method:

1. Consumption patterns change over time

    There is a large amount of discretion that goes into choosing what constitutes a 'typical' basket of consumer goods, especially since people's tastes change and technology alters what people buy. In 2010 for example lipstick was replaced by lip-gloss, to reflect its rising popularity. Also in 2010 BluRay disc players replaced disposable cameras, demonstrating the impact of technological improvements. In 2011 smartphone apps replaced mobile phone ringtones, and oven-ready joints replaced pork shoulders.[6] Does it make sense to compare price changes when the products are changing? Some economists would say that if you want to measure inflation it is unavoidable. Others would say that this is why attempting to measure it is dangerous.

2. Habits respond to price changes

    Another problem with price baskets is that people don't passively respond to changing prices. If the price of something goes up they are likely to substitute it with something that is cheaper. This suggests that CPI might *overstate* the prices that people face, since it lags behind actual consumption choices.

    On the other hand, if people are not able to substitute away from high inflation items, but they still get removed from the basket, this will mean that the CPI *underestimates* inflation.

3. Quality isn't constant

    It might make sense to use changes in the price of a pencil to make an inference about the value of money, but this assumes that the good is identical in two different time periods. For many goods, the quality will change. Standard manual toothbrushes now often have a pressure-sensitive head, and more durable bristles. If the price remains the same, but product quality improves, this will mean that the CPI overestimates inflation.

4. Quantity isn't constant

    Some firms will avoid changing the price they charge by changing how much of the good they provide. In 2009 Skippy peanut butter added a small indentation to the bottom of their plastic jars. This reduced the volume from 18 ounces to 16.3, but since they still cost $3.39 the 'price rise' isn't obvious.[7] Similarly, in Kibera people drink an alcoholic drink called busaa from half litre tin cans. When the price of raw materials rises, instead of raising prices bar owners just cut a strip of tin around the top of the can. According to *The Economist*, 'the punters prefer that to higher prices'.[8]

5. Mistakes are costly

If price indices were merely academic attempts to understand the world the above wouldn't matter greatly. But as we shall see CPI has become an important policy target, and therefore if mistakes are made it will have large ramifications. For example, from 1997–2009 it emerged that the ONS were only surveying some clothing prices during sales.[9] This underrepresented the actual prices that were being paid, perhaps by as much as 0.3 percentage points.

6. Open to corruption

When an economic indicator becomes an important policy target there is an incentive for figures to be manipulated. One of the ways Argentina's statistics institute suppressed the high inflation that occurred during the Nestor and Cristina Kirchner Presidencies, was by omitting quantities after decimal points, rather than rounding them. Therefore a rate of 2.75% would, for example, be officially recorded as just 2%.[10]

Partly because of some of the problems with the CPI there are other prices indices that economists look at. One is the **retail price index** (RPI), which is the traditional measure that was used for policy decisions. It is a slightly broader measure than CPI because it includes retail as well as consumer items, typically relating to housing costs. You may also hear of RPIX, which is the RPI excluding mortgage payments. It is popular because interest changes have direct effects on mortgage rates, and if you include mortgage payments in your measure of inflation you can get perverse results when interest rates are cut to raise inflation.

Another measure of inflation is the **producer price index** (PPI), which is also known as 'factory gate' inflation and looks at the prices paid by firms as opposed to households. If PPI is running higher than CPI it suggests that firms are being squeezed in having to pay higher prices for their raw materials than they are able to charge for their final products. Indeed this demonstrates that 'inflation' isn't a uniform experience. Different companies, households and indeed individuals will face different rates of inflation. During the 2000s it was likely that younger people faced lower rates of inflation than the elderly, because the types of goods they bought (such as clothing and computers) were rising at a lower rate, and in many cases falling. Several websites offer 'personal inflation calculators' so that you can pierce the aggregation of the 'typical' consumer and see the impact of inflation on *you*.

As with many economic variables, the impact of inflation is ambiguous. We will come on to the purported benefits of inflation later, but for now let's focus on the costs. **Hyperinflation** occurs when prices are rising by more than 50% per month and can completely destroy an economy. Prices cease to function as a communication device. People devote resources to protecting themselves from the harm of inflation, by cashing payslips as soon as they're received, and doing their shopping before prices have a chance to rise even further. In Germany in 1923 people would burn money because it was cheaper than using it to buy wood. In Zimbabwe in the 2000s people were using dollars as toilet paper.

We might agree that hyperinflations destroy an economy, but there's a danger that we make too artificial a distinction between inflation and hyperinflation – they're only a difference of scale not scope. You don't need hyperinflation to cause widespread damage to the economy, and indeed society. Keynes' main worry about inflation was not the impact on output, but on the social fabric.[11] Remember that the price system is a communication network that permits economic calculation. In the words of Steven Horwitz,

The greatest damage done by inflation is precisely the separation of the induced variable of price from the underlying variables of tastes, technologies and resources.[12]

He goes on to specify the main costs of inflation, which we can split into two categories.

1. Costs of a rise in the price level
   a. Perhaps the most obvious cost of inflation is that it **reduces the value of money** (in other words it acts as a tax on money balances). Therefore those who hold a large part of their wealth in financial assets (such as pensions) can suffer greatly from the declining value of money. In extreme instances people can see their entire life savings wiped out.
   b. Some economists might say that this is not really a cost because other groups will gain from inflation. Indeed it is not automatically the case that society as a whole is worse off if there's **a redistribution of wealth from savers to debtors**. However this takes a purely static view, because if people are being penalised for saving then this will reduce the supply of credit, which is socially costly.
   c. Economists also refer to the **menu costs** of price changes. The simplest example is the costs that businesses incur in terms of updating their menus whenever inflation goes up. This can seem trivial, and indeed firms find ways to minimise these costs. On Brittany Ferries the prices are given electronically, so they can be changed with a few taps of a keyboard. This is why restaurants use chalkboards for their daily specials – it would be too expensive to print new menus to keep up with fluctuating prices. In some cases the 'fish of the day' won't even be listed.[13]

      But there's a deeper issue here. Scott Sumner gives the example of his father, who was a real estate broker from 1965–85. In his early years he would be able to provide a decent estimate of the value of a property, using previous sale prices for similar houses as a reasonable guide. But subsequent inflation meant this eventually became impossible. The only way to know the value is to remember some form of price index and also the specific dates at which each house was sold in order to compare everything on the same scale. As Sumner says, 'this store of human capital rapidly depreciated'.[14] It's common for older people to think that cars are expensive now, because in their day a good car was a lot cheaper. Inflation is the reason why they're wrong (the real price of cars has fallen), but the *costs* of inflation are the fact that people act in accordance with this. Inflation disrupts the cognitive act of comparing the value of economic goods.

      When Argentina endured hyperinflation in the 1980s people went out of business because they simply couldn't estimate the replacement cost of their goods being sold. There was a total breakdown of economic calculation. By contrast, in his excellent account of the period *And the Money Kept Rolling In (and Out)* journalist Paul Blustein noticed that when inflation was brought back under control taxi drivers no longer needed to use special conversion tables to work out the fare. They could calculate in their heads again.[15]

2. Costs of a change in the composition of the price level
      Since inflation is a rise in the *general* price level, many textbooks only focus on the costs of a rise in *all* prices. But inflation doesn't occur in a uniform manner. Prices don't all rise by the same amount. Indeed the real costs of inflation are down to the change in composition of the price level. Think of the price system as a constellation of

objects. Inflation isn't just that on average they are rising, it is that within that general movement there is a lot of change. This will create resource misallocations and a reduction in coordination. We can split these into two main types.

a. **Cantillon effects** – if you think about *how* new money enters the economy it should be obvious that it will not dissipate in a uniform way. It is injected through specific sectors, and the effects will take time to pass through the economy. If you pour honey onto a plate it will build up at the point it lands, and only gradually disperse around it.

A 'helicopter drop' is a thought experiment by which new money is printed and then literally dropped from the sky by a helicopter. This would certainly get new money in the hands of the people, and has the additional benefit of being hard to reverse.[16] In reality (and we will look at this 'transmission mechanism' in more detail later), new money comes into the economy through the banking system. Therefore we might expect, for example, the wages of people within the banking system to rise before the general price level does. Therefore they may benefit from inflation. However other people may be further away from the source of money creation, and only see their wages rise following an increase in the prices of goods that they consume. This suggests that people will compete to get as close to the source of new money as possible. We therefore might expect to see bubbles develop wherever new money enters the system.

b. **Signal extraction problems** – entrepreneurs are constantly using the price system to make forecasts, and to assess previous decisions. If they see the prices of their product rising, then this suggests that it is in high demand and therefore they should expand their production. But the price rises could simply be a consequence of inflation. If this is the case, expanding production would be a bad idea because the relative demand for those products hasn't changed. As a concrete example imagine that someone buys a house for £200 000, spends £10 000 on improvements and then sells it a few years later for £220 000. You would conclude that they've made £10 000 profit, and they might use this as affirmation that they are savvy entrepreneurs and should reinvest the money in another project. But house prices may have risen during this period anyway. Indeed if the house would have been worth £220 000 regardless of any modifications they haven't made a profit at all. They've made a *loss* of £10 000. They are confusing profit as a reward for entrepreneurial endeavour, with the arbitrary gains of inflation. It is impossible for entrepreneurs to fully distinguish their 'market' profits (the reward for entrepreneurial action) from the arbitrary effects of inflation.

Tyler Cowen lists three different kinds of signal extraction problem:[17]

▪ Entrepreneurs confuse real and nominal price changes.
▪ Interest rates provide entrepreneurs with misleading information about their forthcoming expenditure streams.
▪ Entrepreneurs incorrectly estimate the permanence of any observed changes to prices and interest rates.

The first kind is perhaps the best known, and it is also referred to as 'money illusion'. But all three introduce important sources of discoordination to the economy. Inflation is costly because it sends false signals. In particular, when there is a divergence between expected and unexpected inflation we can see clusters of entrepreneurial errors.

Now that we've discussed the rate of inflation (P) and GDP growth (Y) we can start to see how macroeconomic variables relate to each other. The quantity theory is one of the most important tools for economists as it is a simple way to capture the primary cause of inflation: too much money.

The quantity theory can be written as follows:[18]

$$M + V = P + Y$$

'M' represents changes in the money supply, which requires a little explanation. It is important to be careful whenever an economist talks about 'the money supply' because in fact there are several ways to measure it and it depends on what you define as 'money'.

You may have heard the money supply referred to as M0, M1, M2, M3 or M4. These are successively broader measures, with M0 only including things like cash, whilst M4 includes a large number of different financial assets. Economists like to look at a narrow and broad measure because of the way in which the central bank relates to commercial banks. A narrow measure is limited to the parts of the money supply that are controlled directly by the central bank. More formally, the 'monetary base' is equal to: (i) the reserve accounts held by commercial banks at the central bank; and (ii) currency (which includes notes and coin). This is also known as 'central bank' money, and the central bank can decide to make this whatever it wishes, either by minting coins, printing notes, or crediting reserve accounts.

But commercial banks can also 'create' money in the sense that deposit accounts can be used as a form of payment. Therefore a slightly broader measure of the money supply will include not only the monetary base but also some kinds of deposit accounts. The **money multiplier** shows the change in the number of deposits for a given monetary base, and indicates the effectiveness of the bridge of intermediation.

Indeed a broader measure still might include some kinds of savings accounts, because even though they don't serve as money they are a very close substitute. Ultimately there is a spectrum of liquidity with narrow money at one end and broad money at the other. The broader the measure the greater the role of the banking system, relative to the central bank, in determining the money supply.[19]

Ordinarily we would expect increases in the monetary base to get amplified by the banking system into broader money. However when the banking system is in distress the central bank may find that this channel fails to work properly, and that increases in the monetary base get offset by contractions in the credit being extended by commercial banks, such that the broad money supply falls.

Different countries focus on different measures. The 'narrow' money supply in the UK is called 'Notes and Coin' and the 'broad' money supply is M4ex (which is simply M4 excluding some kinds of building society accounts). Measuring the money supply is relatively easy, once you've decided on which definition to use. Central and commercial banks keep track of how much money is in circulation. For the 'notes and coin' measure you literally add up the number of £5, £10, £20 notes etc. and multiply by the face value.

The other variables in the quantity theory take less explanation. 'V' stands for 'velocity of circulation', and there are two ways to think of this. One is that it is an indicator of the speed at which money passes through the economy. Imagine that everyone writes their name on a banknote whenever they receive one. At the end of the year you simply look at the number of names and use this as a measure of how often money changes hands. The other way to view 'V' is as an indication of the demand to hold money. It may seem that the demand to hold money is infinite, but we're not talking about 'how much money people would like'. After all, the demand for Ferraris isn't 'how many Ferraris people wish to buy', it is 'how much people are willing to pay for Ferraris'. In the case of money, this means the proportion of your wealth you wish to hold as cash. This cannot be infinite, because (i) people don't want to hold their entire wealth as money; (ii) the amount of money you are able to demand is constrained by your finite wealth. If the demand for money rises it means that people wish to hold more of their wealth as money, and therefore they look to sell goods and services in exchange for money. An increase in the demand for money is the equivalent of a fall in the velocity of circulation, since people will also choose to hold onto the money in their possession. When we say that 'V' is falling we are effectively saying that people's demand for money is rising.

The right hand side of the quantity theory is more familiar. As we've already seen 'P' is the rate of inflation and 'Y' is the growth rate of GDP. Note that 'Y' is *real* GDP and 'P + Y' is *nominal* GDP.

So far I have been slightly misleading. $M + V = P + Y$ is not really a theory; it's an identity. Based on the above analysis it is true by definition. It simply says that *changes in the amount of money spent (M + V) are always equal to changes in the price of all things bought (P + Y)*. But the quantity theory goes beyond stating this identity to make three important claims:[20]

1. Causation is seen to run from left to right, i.e. that changes in $M + V$ cause changes in $P + Y$.
2. V is reasonably stable and is independent of M.
3. In the long run Y is caused by real factors (i.e. land, labour and capital) and is also independent of M.

This is convenient, because *if* V and Y are fairly constant and *if* causation runs from left to right then we have a very clear explanation for inflation. Any rise in P *must* be down to a rise in M! This is the core insight of the quantity theory – if you want to understand what is happening to inflation, you need to look at the money supply.

Some economists speak as if changes in M will lead to a proportional and uniform change in P. For example if the money supply grows at 5% then *all* prices will immediately rise by 5%. Obviously this is unrealistic, since the entire price constellation will be disrupted. However the quantity theory does make an important point: the absolute amount of money in circulation doesn't matter. Indeed it's only by realising this that we can focus on the damage caused by *changes* in the money supply (be it inflation or deflation). In July 2005 Romania dropped four zeros from their currency. Literally overnight goods that cost 3 776 000 leu became 377.60 leu. Provided this happens to all prices, at the same time (and remember that wages are a price), then the impact on the economy is essentially zero. The problem is that actual inflation will always affect the price constellation because prices adjust over time.[21]

In the same way that an imbalance between the demand for and supply of money can cause prices to drive up, an imbalance between the demand for and supply of goods and services can impact inflation. This is because an excess demand for money is the same thing as an excess supply of goods, and an excess supply of money is the same as an excess demand for goods. Indeed there are three 'types' of inflation that commentators often refer to.

1. Cost-push inflation
    If there are forces restricting aggregate supply, bidding up the prices of inputs, this could lead to inflation. This can explain how prices spike following natural disasters, since the supply side of an economy gets wiped out. The implied policy goal would be to engage in supply side reforms that improve the resilience and flexibility of the economy.

2. Demand-pull inflation

This is where high rates of total spending bid up prices because the economy is operating close to full capacity. Policymakers will focus on trying to reduce aggregate demand, either by fiscal policy (i.e. increasing taxes or reducing government spending), or monetary policy (i.e. raising interest rates). The **output gap** refers to the differences between actual GDP growth and potential growth. The idea is that if there's a big difference inflation will be low. But when growth is at potential it will put upward pressure on prices.

3. Built in inflation

This is what policymakers fear the most: it occurs when workers adapt to past inflation by demanding higher wages, which are then passed on to consumers through higher prices. You can see how this creates a 'wage-price spiral' and becomes counterproductive. When the government negotiates pay deals with unions they often invoke this danger, saying that there is no point granting hefty pay increases if this generates inflation. The problem with this argument is that for any individual union they want pay hikes for their members but not for others. The aim of unions is to maximise the returns to their members, not the smooth functioning of the economy as a whole. But if wages automatically increase in response to inflation this can create a vicious circle.

The problem with viewing inflation through the lens of aggregate demand and aggregate supply is that you can lose sight of the core truth that inflation is a monetary phenomenon. For example many policymakers blame inflation on things like high gas prices. But often the price rises we witness are a *consequence* of inflation, not a *cause*. Oil shocks don't cause *all* prices to increase, just those closely linked to the use of oil. Therefore it's still possible to substitute away from the price rise. For example, consider what Joe Chaib, the owner of a Shell station in Houston, told a reporter,

> *'The people will only spend so much money on gas, so they drive less,' he told me. His customers now are filling their tanks halfway. They are buying fewer bags of chips, fewer drinks, even fewer packs of cigarettes these days. Some people have even begun to join carpools.*[22]

If the price of some goods rises, and the money supply is stable,[23] then people compensate for the higher prices by reducing their spending on other goods and services. We can respond to higher gas prices in two main ways. Firstly, **we find substitutes for gas**. The extent to which we can do so depends on the price elasticity of gas (as we discussed in Chapter 1), and we would expect the elasticity to increase over time. But there are some immediate ways in which we can reduce our gas consumption, such as eliminating unnecessary journeys. The second way we respond is by **cutting down on other purchases**, for example chips, drinks and cigarettes. But see how the increase in gas prices is offset by a decrease in the prices of those goods. It isn't a rise in general prices, but a change in relative prices. Oil prices aren't necessarily the *cause* of inflation, they *are* inflation!

When hyperinflations occur, such as the one in Germany in the 1920s, or in Zimbabwe in the 2000s, they are often presented as being 'uncontrollable'. But the quantity theory gives us a solution. There is a famous story about Austrian finance officials going to the office of Ludwig von Mises, at the University of Vienna, asking him how to stop the hyperinflation. He replied by saying, 'meet me at midnight'. And at midnight they came back and Mises asked them to follow him outside. They strolled through the moonlit streets of Vienna and eventually they arrived at the central bank. Mises put his fingers to his lips and asked them to be quiet. All they could hear in the dead of night was the sound of the printing press churning out more currency. His advice was simple: 'Turn it off'!

So if inflation is costly, and we understand the main cause, then why does it occur? In short, because it's a form of taxation. As Keynes said,

> *A government can live for a long time … by printing paper money … It is the form of taxation which the public finds hardest to evade and even the weakest governments can enforce, when it can enforce nothing else.*[24]

We can look in detail at the main reasons why inflation is encouraged by the government.

1. Seignorage

    This is the difference between the 'use value' and the 'exchange value' of money, in other words the 'profit' that can be gleaned from producing it. When the predominant form of money was gold coins seignorage was highly important. When the supply of coins is monopolised this can become quite lucrative, and the classic example is 'clipping'. This occurs when the monetary authority reduces the gold content of a coin but mandates that it must still purchase the same amount of goods and services. In other words it is 'worth' 1 pound but has less than a pound's worth of gold in it. If the market were competitive, you might expect people to refuse currency that is debased in such a way, but money is often controlled by the state. Therefore legal tender laws and other restrictions on trade can ensure that debased currency still circulates.

    The fact that so much of the present money supply is electronically generated means there's little scope for seignorage profits. For example the Royal Mint made a profit of just £3.6m in 2010–11.[25] Some of this is by selling commemorative coins to the public for more than they cost to make. They can also earn profit on the circulating coins that they produce, but in many cases this is negligible. The metal content alone of a 10p coin costs 4.5p, and this is why in 2012 the Royal Mint introduced new ones (with steel, rather than a mixture of copper and nickel).[26] In a modern economy seignorage gains are relatively low.

    In January 2011 a blogger called 'Beowolf' came up with an ingenious way to 'solve' the US debt crisis based on seignorage.[27] The Treasury Secretary could commission a platinum coin that is given the entirely arbitrary face value of $5tn, and use it to 'pay off' the national debt. It is intriguing because it is legally and economically possible. But there are other ways in which inflation helps governments deal with debt.

2. Monetise debt

    Inflation is bad for savers, because it erodes the value of their money. But it is good for debtors – it means that the money they pay back is worth less than what they borrowed. And the government is one of the biggest debtors in the economy. One of the main causes of economic crises is when indebted governments resort to the printing press. In the words of Ben Bernanke,

    > *[P]eople know that inflation erodes the real value of the government's debt and, therefore, that it is in the interest of the government to create some inflation.*[28]

    Obviously people are less likely to lend money if inflation is likely to occur, and they will seek some form of premium. Inflation only monetises nominal debt, and therefore one option is to buy index-linked investments. These are tied to the inflation rate so that the principal rises with inflation. The UK government is one of the biggest issuers of index-linked bonds, and these comprise about 25% of all of the gilts that they issue. But this still leaves 75% of UK government debt that can be eroded through inflation.

3. Bracket creep

In 1997 around 2 million people in the UK were 'top rate' income tax payers, paying a marginal rate of 40%. These were supposed to be right at the top end of the income spectrum. However the threshold of £26 100 was a nominal figure. Therefore inflation meant that people's earnings were rising but if the threshold remains the same (or rises at a slower rate) more people get pushed into the higher tax bracket.[29] By 2004 an additional 1.5 million people were top rate taxpayers.[30] According to Philip Booth, from 1979 to 2012, 'the higher rate tax band has dropped relative to wages by nearly 40%.'[31]

Bracket creep (also known as **fiscal drag**) is a reason for the middle classes to be careful about voting for taxes on the 'super rich', because over time inflation makes us all 'super rich' in nominal terms, even though our relative wealth may be unchanged.

4. Real wage adjustments

The above reasons can sound a little like conspiracy theories – that the reason inflation exists is because the government benefits from it. But there is another important reason though, and it's an economic one. Recollect that many economists treat the labour market as the key to the flexibility of the economy. In other words the duration of a recession is a function of how quickly wages adjust. In theory a decline in aggregate demand shouldn't cause a recession, provided all prices (including wages) respond quickly. And if all prices are falling by 2%, a 2% nominal wage cut doesn't mean that you're any worse off.

However many economists believe that the public suffer from 'money illusion', which is when they confuse nominal with real variables.

A 5% pay rise sounds good, but if inflation is 10% then you are worse off. Indeed in this situation you have suffered a 5% wage *cut*. In theory, people should treat a 5% pay rise in a world of 10% inflation exactly the same as they would a 5% pay cut with zero inflation. In both cases, your 'purchasing power' has fallen by 5%. However there is evidence to suggest that people are more resistant to nominal wage cuts than real wage cuts. If this is the case, recovery will be slower than it otherwise would be. Therefore whilst economists all recognise the dangers of high inflation, many think a positive, moderate rate (such as 2%) can help 'grease the wheels' of the economy by allowing real wage cuts to take place without people resisting so much.

Consider the following test of whether you suffer from money illusion:

a. You receive a 1% pay rise and CPI is at 2%.

b. There is no inflation and you receive a 1% cut in your take home pay.

You should realise that the two are the same, but think about how you would feel under each scenario. The Bank of England are essentially doing the dirty work of your boss.

8.2 MONETARY POLICY

Most members of the OECD opt for independent central banks as their monetary regime, and therefore monetary 'policy' becomes a political tool. Monetary policy is the process by

TABLE 8.1   Monetary policy

Tools	Targets
Interest rates	Inflation
Monetary base	GDP
Reserve requirements	Unemployment
Expectations	Exchange rate

which the monetary authority manages the money supply, and the chief mechanism is through interest rates. The main aims tend to be 'monetary stability', which is often defined as (i) low inflation; and (ii) confidence in the currency. The macroeconomy is a complex system with many interrelated variables. Indeed the reason many students get confused by macroeconomics is because they cannot 'see' how those variables interact. Attempting to do so is a pointless task though; it is far too complex to comprehend. The goal of macroeconomics can never be to truly 'understand' the economy. To try to simplify things, Table 8.1 shows a list of economic variables split into whether they are a 'tool' that the monetary authority can attempt to use, or a 'target' that they may wish to control.

We will look later on in more detail at monetary policy tools, but times were when the monetary authority would attempt to deliver numerous objectives and be given a fairly large amount of scope in terms of how they went about doing so. But there is a dismal track record of failure. Generally speaking the use of 'discretion' became superseded by the adherence to publicly known 'rules'. Since we do not have confidence in policymakers' ability to fine-tune the economy we only grant them the ability to act within the constraints of clear frameworks. Also, such rules reduce uncertainty about what actions central bankers may take, and therefore help manage expectations. We can list some of the more famous monetary policy rules:

- Friedman rule

  This is named after Milton Friedman, the father of modern monetarism, and it is simply the logical application of the quantity theory. If inflation is caused by increases in the money supply, and you want low and moderate growth in output, increase the monetary base by a low and moderate amount. Friedman suggested 2% per year. That's it. No policy committees, no discussions, no judgement. You could even programme a computer to ensure that the monetary base grew at 2% per year and this would deliver as close to monetary stability as we can hope for:

$$M = 2\%$$

- McCallum rule

  The main problem with the Friedman rule is that it assumes that the velocity of circulation is reasonably constant. Bennett McCallum advocated a rule that was slightly more complicated and provided a target for changes in the monetary base:

$$M = Y^* - V - 0.5(Y - Y^*)$$

  As before M refers to the monetary base, but there are other elements of the equation of exchange included. Y is the actual growth of nominal GDP, Y* is the target growth of nominal GDP, and V is a 4-year average of the velocity of the monetary base. This provides a rule for what to do with the monetary base based on the deviation of NGDP from target.

▪ Taylor rule

Instead of using the monetary base as the tool of monetary policy, some economists advocate the use of interest rates. John B. Taylor pioneered a rule that allows policy-makers to plug in real data and see what the optimum interest rate should be.[32] A simple version is:[33]

$$i = 1.5(P) + 0.5(Y - Y^*) + 1$$

We are using 'i' to refer to the policy interest rate, but most of the other variables are the same as above. P is actual inflation (over the last 4 quarters), Y is actual GDP and Y^* is 'potential' GDP.[34]

▪ NGDP target

Imagine that the economy is growing at 3%, and there is an inflation target of 2%. We can use the quantity theory to show that the equivalent NGDP target would be 5%. One advantage that NGDP targets have over an inflation target is that this allows productivity improvements to manifest themselves as lower prices. Another advantage is that it allows prices to rise when there is a negative real shock. If there is a natural disaster, for example, prices *should* rise because they *should* reflect real scarcities.[35]

We often hear that central banks are 'independent', and whilst this is an important trend it is often overstated. In reality all major central banks are owned by the government and operated under licence. The government grants the central bank its powers – it decides what target they should hit and what tools they have at their disposal. Therefore it's important to stress that central banks only have *operational* independence. They only have the freedom to decide how best to hit their *assigned* target with the tools they've been *authorised* to use.[36]

Despite listing the above as rules there is a lot of discretion involved in how they are implemented. Ideally, a rule will be so clear that it doesn't matter who – if anyone – is implementing it. It used to be the case that central banks would try to influence a range of macroeconomic variables, but from the 1990s there was a trend to focus purely on price stability. This is partly as an attempt to limit the scope of what they're trying to accomplish (and thus make it more likely that they'll succeed), and partly because economists feel that if price stability occurs then the rest (strong GDP, low unemployment, stable value of the currency) will fall into place. As Ben Bernanke said in 2006,

> *The evidence of recent decades, both from the United States and other countries, supports the conclusion that an environment of price stability promotes maximum sustainable growth in employment and output and a more stable real economy.*[37]

The US Federal Reserve (or 'Fed') has a 'dual' mandate of delivering both low inflation and low unemployment. Indeed different central banks have slightly different goals. For simplicity I am going to explain the 'one target one tool' approach, which can be used as a basis for understanding more complicated policy. Quite simply, it means that the central bank is committed to using the interest rate to keep inflation within a publicly known range. In addition they are expected to release minutes and explain their decision making to the public in a transparent manner. In terms of Table 8.1, 'one target one tool' just focuses on the top row of the list. The target is inflation, and the tool is interest rates.

The main mechanism by which this is supposed to work stems from our formula for GDP:

$$Y = C + I$$

We can expand this by considering the impact that interest rates have on the two components. Changes in consumption and investment are both a function of changes in interest rates. We can use the term 'aggregate demand' to refer to the total spending in the economy, which, as the quantity theory shows, is the equivalent of the cash value of GDP (i.e. nominal GDP, or $P + Y$):

$$AD = C(i) + I(i)$$

If interest rates go up it becomes more attractive to save, mortgages become more costly, and therefore people will reduce their consumption. It also becomes harder for firms to finance their capital projects and so investment falls. Therefore there's a *negative* relationship between interest rates and aggregate demand. Similarly if interest rates are cut we would expect people to consume more (they will choose to save less) and businesses will borrow more for investment spending. Again, there's a negative relationship between interest rates and aggregate demand.

If the economy is reasonably close to full employment then increases in aggregate demand will bid up prices, whilst falls in aggregate demand will cause prices to fall. We therefore have a very crude framework for policy decisions:

- If inflation is >2% the economy is overheating so you increase interest rates and reduce aggregate demand.
- If inflation is <2% the economy is slowing down so you cut interest rates to boost aggregate demand.
- If inflation is =2% it is on target and interest rates are about right.

This sounds very simplistic, and you might expect that central bankers have complicated models to predict by exactly how much they need to change interest rates to get a given change in inflation. They do. But they don't work very well. Some people mock policymakers for looking at previous inflation as a guide to decision making, since this is like driving a car by looking in the rear view mirror. But economists are pretty bad at making forecasts, and therefore some prefer to rely on what we know about the past rather than what we don't know about the future.[38] In addition what we do know about the way interest rate changes feed through into the economy is that they have 'long and variable lags'. The rule of thumb is that any change in interest rates will show up in inflation and output around 18 months later. Therefore lots of tweaking and fine-tuning will create chaos. Policymakers often prefer to act cautiously and wait to see what the impact of a raise or cut is before acting further.

So far I have simply referred to 'the interest rate', as if there is only one. In reality there are multiple interest rates that are important and so it is worth clarifying exactly which one people refer to when they talk about monetary policy.

The main policy rate that central banks influence is a short-term risk free rate. The idea is that this acts a benchmark for other interest rates, and we can sketch out a rudimentary transmission mechanism:

1. Short-term risk free rate – i.e. a policy rate, or (central) Bank Rate, that bridges banks with the central bank

2. Money market rates – i.e. an interbank rate, such as LIBOR, that bridges banks with other banks
3. Rates on bank loans and deposits – i.e. a prime rate, or base rate, that bridges banks and their customers
4. Financial asset prices.

In the UK the main policy rate is 'Bank Rate' which is the interest rate it (i) charges commercial banks for some types of short-term lending; and (ii) pays on their (excess) reserve balances. All commercial banks are required to hold a reserve account with the Bank of England, which is supposed to act as a type of buffer. In some countries the central bank mandates the amount of reserves (usually as a fraction of deposits) that they are supposed to keep. A typical level is around 3%, but in the UK banks voluntarily set their own targets. Note that one form of monetary policy is to change this reserve requirement. If banks were required to keep more money on reserve then they would have less to lend out to their customers. Hence in February 2011 Beijing tightened monetary policy (in an effort to reduce inflation) by increasing reserve requirements. If you wanted to stimulate the economy, by contrast, you would reduce reserve requirements.

There are essentially two ways for the central bank to affect the short-term risk free rate.

The first way is to focus on supply. Recollect that the monetary base is comprised of (i) reserve balances and (ii) currency. The central bank can create as many bank reserves as it wishes, and thus hit any level of the monetary base it desires. Obviously the broader the measure of the money supply being used, the less control the central bank has. One of the lessons of the Great Depression is that it is possible for a central bank to attempt to increase the money supply (by increasing the monetary base), only for it to be offset (rather than amplified) by a contraction in bank lending and other components of the broad money supply. In other words, the bridge of intermediation can collapse.

Central banks alter the amount of reserves through the process of **open market operations** (OMO). This involves the buying of securities or the lending against collateral using newly created money. If the central bank wishes to increase the monetary base by £10bn they simply buy £10bn worth of financial assets (such as government bonds) and credit the accounts of the purchaser. The recipient of the money will then spend it and it works its way through the financial system. If the central bank wishes to decrease the monetary base they can sell off some of their existing assets and retire the money they receive. Some people find it odd to imagine a central bank destroying money, but every day there are new bank notes being printed to replace old ones. All they need to do is ensure that slightly fewer new ones are released. When it comes to electronic accounts it is even easier.

The second way to conduct monetary policy is by focusing on demand. Here the aim is not really to hit a particular *quantity* of reserves, but to focus on *price*. And in this context the 'price' of reserves is the short-term risk free interest rate. Central banks influence the demand for reserves through **operational standing facilities**, which are not as complicated as they sound. Here's how it has traditionally worked in the UK:

- Commercial banks choose a target amount of reserves that they wish to hold.
- They receive Bank Rate on those reserves.
- If they have *more* reserves they can use a deposit facility within the Bank of England, which earns a rate *below* Bank Rate.

TABLE 8.2   Policy rates

	Bank of England	**European Central Bank**	**Federal Reserve**
Floor	Deposit facility rate	Deposit rate	Reserve rate
Policy rate	Bank Rate	Main refinancing operations	Federal funds rate
Ceiling	Lending facility rate	Marginal lending facility	Discount rate

■ If they have *less* reserves they can borrow from the Bank of England at a rate *above* Bank Rate (details of this are published a month later so that there's no negative publicity).

This creates a 'corridor' of interest rates that provides two main functions:

1. It acts as an arbitrage mechanism to keep money market rates close to Bank Rate.
2. It acts as a means to manage payment shocks.

When the Bank of England began paying interest on reserves in 2006 and the Federal Reserve in 2008 it was to introduce a corridor system. Unfortunately different central banks use slightly different terms, and the interest rates that act as ceiling and floor are slightly different. Table 8.2 tries to combine the usual treatments:

Imagine that you are in charge of a commercial bank, and you need to have a certain fraction of deposits in your account at the central bank by close of business that day. The deposit rate is how much you earn on any funds that you have in that account (in the UK it is paid on the amount in excess of your targeted reserves). Typically banks will try to minimise the amount of money in their reserve accounts because they can generate higher returns with other investments. But if they get this wrong they could find themselves short. In which case there are only two places to go to borrow the reserves required.

One is the central bank, who will charge the **discount rate** (the rate paid on overnight loans made by the central bank to commercial banks). The central bank can unilaterally set this because they are the final provider (in the UK this is slightly different to the discount 'window'). The other option is to borrow from other commercial banks, i.e. on the open market. This is **the interbank rate**, which is the rate that commercial banks charge each other on their reserves held at the central bank, and this provides the bulk of liquidity to the banking system. The London Interbank Offer Rate (LIBOR) is an interbank rate that reflects step 2 in our transmission mechanism.

In the US the Federal funds rate *is* an interbank rate, and the Fed uses open market operations to shift the supply of reserves up and down in order to hit a target nominal rate. As Gregory Mankiw explains, although newspapers report that the Fed 'sets' the interest rate they are really using their influence over the supply of reserves to hit a target price.

A newspaper might report, for instance, that 'the Fed has lowered interest rates.' To be more precise, we can translate this statement as meaning 'the Federal Open Market Committee has instructed the Fed bond traders to buy bonds in open-market operations so as to increase the money supply… and reduce the equilibrium interest rate to hit a new lower target'.[39]

David Moss uses a good analogy to show how interest rates are in fact a cover for changes in the money supply.[40] When you drive a car it is the flow of gas to the engine that generates movement, even though we look at the speedometer to see how fast we're going. Interest rates are just one indicator showing the effect of changes in the monetary footprint. We tend to look at interest rates for the signal, but it's the money supply doing the driving.

From around 1997 to 2007 the system of inflation targeting seemed to be working. CPI was being kept fairly close to target, GDP was growing and the currency was stable. And then the financial crisis occurred. According to Martin Wolf,

> *Most of us – I was one – thought we had at last found the holy grail. Now we know it was a mirage.*[41]

So far we've said that if the central bank wants to increase aggregate demand they will cut interest rates. But what if interest rates have been cut so much they can't go any lower? If policymakers try to make interest rates negative, depositors can simply switch to cash.[42] This is the conventional explanation for why fiscal policy is necessary, and we will look at this in the next chapter. But before we do, I want to stress that it is a myth that the short-term risk free rate is the only tool of monetary policy. If you look at the transmission mechanism mentioned previously, we can think of other ways for the central bank to influence the economy.

When interest rates hit the 'zero lower bound' you'd be forgiven for thinking that economists panic. This is when you start to hear exotic concepts such as quantitative easing being discussed. It seems as though economists are scrambling for something, anything to try. It is certainly the case that crises breed desperation. But let's try to understand the differences between zero lower bound policies and standard open market operations (which are occurring on a daily basis). Here's how OMO operate:

The central bank uses open market operations to buy and sell **government bonds** from **commercial banks** with newly created money to influence the interbank market and hit a target **short-term interest rate**.

Note that I have put four different terms in bold (counting 'short term' and 'interest rate' as two separate terms). This is because there are four main zero lower bound policies, and each one involves tweaking the statement above.

1. Qualitative easing – the central bank changes the *quality* of assets bought and engages in the purchase of assets other than government bonds. This could include private bonds or even junk bonds if they wish.
2. Credit easing – the central bank changes the list of institutions that they buy assets from. Instead of only dealing with a particular set of commercial banks they could buy assets direct from the non-bank commercial sector or even from specific businesses such as SMEs. The central bank essentially becomes an investment vehicle in private debt.
3. Operation twist – the central bank changes the maturity of the assets being bought, and tries to flatten the yield curve by purchasing longer term assets.
4. Quantitative easing – the central bank targets the *quantity* of assets bought rather than the *price* (i.e. the interest rate).

Quantitative easing is therefore seen as a form of open market operation that we have previously discussed. It is simply printing money to buy bonds. It wasn't invented in 2008; central banks use the basic principles all the time.

There are two main ways in which it is supposed to work. The first is the **liquidity channel**. If banks have more money they should increase their lending to consumers and this directly increases the broad money supply. The second is the **yield channel**. When the central bank buys assets this bids up their price and therefore reduces the yield. Sellers that receive the new money will substitute into other assets that have relatively higher yields (e.g. company shares or bonds). This bids up those prices as well reducing yields across the entire market. As we know there is an inverse relationship between interest rates and aggregate demand, so this should boost economic activity.[43] If the transmission mechanism breaks down, the central bank moves its focus from stage 1 to stages 3 and 4. Instead of looking at interest rates to see whether monetary policy is easy or not, you must also look at the size of the central bank balance sheet.[44]

In December 2012 the Federal Reserve adopted a policy of **forward guidance**. This can be viewed as an attempt to target expectations. They make a commitment to keep interest rates at a low level until a specified threshold is met. For example, until unemployment falls below 6.5%. One of the problems with this is that there are conceivable scenarios where you'd want to increase interest rates despite unemployment being above the threshold. In response to this the central bank will incorporate various 'knockouts'. For example forward guidance is abandoned if inflation rises above 2.5%, or financial market stability is threatened. But the fact that these can be somewhat ambiguous demonstrates that forward guidance is a discretionary (rather than rule bound) policy.

The reason quantitative easing is controversial is because the central bank is financing government debt. The reason they focus on government debt is because this is the 'risk free' benchmark, and relatively neutral. Imagine the controversy if the Bank of England directly facilitated the debt of individual firms. How would they choose which ones to buy without being accused of favouritism and corruption? But hyperinflation is always down to one arm of the government financing the debt of the other. In theory this isn't the case in the UK or US, because the central bank is not allowed to *directly* purchase government debt. But note the profit opportunity being presented to commercial banks. You know that the government is issuing lots of debt, and you know that the central bank is committed to purchasing lots of it. All you need to do is buy from one and sell to the other. Whether or not you use the proceeds to grant more loans to your customers, or whether you simply park it in your reserve account that generates a risk free return, is up to you. Nice work if you can get it.

8.3 MONETARY REGIMES

Everybody accepts that the government has an incentive to inflate, and therefore it is difficult for them to credibly commit not to do so. *If* the market expects low inflation, then a burst of inflation will temporarily boost employment (and indeed monetise debt). So policymakers are in a game – they have an incentive to renege on promises as soon as they are trusted, and this would prevent trust from developing in the first place. This is known as the **time inconsistency** problem. The key issue in monetary policy is how can governments credibly commit to a low inflation environment? There are three main ways that have been tried:

1. Independent central banks

    One option is to outsource monetary policy to a group of independent economists. In 1997 the then Chancellor Gordon Brown granted operational independence to the Bank

of England. This was a major policy to signal to markets that the Labour Party could
be trusted with the economy. Unlike politicians, the Bank of England's Monetary Policy
Committee (MPC) were less tied to short termism or populism. The problem with this is
that the scope of independence is relatively narrow, and when there is a lot of attention
on the central bank – for example during a financial crisis – it can become a politicised
institution. Ultimately if a country has a very low level of credibility then handing policy
decisions over to economists is unlikely to make much difference, and bigger steps are
required.

2. Fixed exchange rates

If a country has a major credibility problem it can outsource its monetary policy
to a different country, and peg their exchange rate. In this way they can piggyback on
the credibility of the country they fix their exchange rate to. If they fix to a number
of other currencies, this is called a **currency board**. This doesn't completely solve the
credibility problem because it's still possible for them to abandon the fix, but it may be
easier to commit to the fix than to low inflation. If they went even further, and merged
their monetary policy, this would be a **currency union**. Again, the credibility lies in the
expected permanence of the arrangement.

3. Commodity standard

Both of the above still rely on the government managing the money supply. Historically though this is a relatively new phenomenon. An alternative is to use some type
of commodity as money. In the nineteenth century there was a government administered
'gold standard' that tied the value of currency to the price of gold. But does government
need to be involved at all?

Most modern economies have a large amount of government intervention in the monetary
system. Consider the following barriers to competition:

- Legal tender laws
- Monopoly of base currency
- Government backed lender of last resort
- Deposit insurance
- Bank regulation.

Not all economists believe that central banks should conduct monetary policy, believing instead
that the market should set the supply of money. Free banking economists such as Kevin Dowd
question why the market principles that we rely on for other goods and services should not
also be utilised for money.[45] According to Lawrence White free banking is 'an obvious and
simple idea'.[46] It just means that banks are free to offer substitutes for money, and customers
are free to choose whether to use them as money. Kurt Schuler claims that a free bank is
characterised by having: (i) competitive note issue; (ii) low legal barriers to entry and (iii) no
central control of reserves.[47] And George Selgin points out that in a free banking regime the
banking system would ensure that the money supply automatically adjusts to offset changes
in the demand to hold it (velocity).[48] If this is the case, monetary policy would be completely
'neutral'. Relative prices would not be being distorted, and there would be a tendency for the
supply of money, and demand for money, to reach equilibrium. Furthermore, without policymakers setting interest rates based on policy considerations, they would be at their natural rate

(i.e. the balance between the demand for and supply of loanable funds). Curiously, a free banking system would deliver something that resembles an NGDP target of 0%.

8.4 MACROECONOMIC FLUCTUATIONS

In the previous chapter we saw how 'real business cycle' theory claims that what we observe as 'cycles' are in fact optimal responses to new conditions, and all shocks come from the supply side. For agricultural economies this is highly convincing, but they do not seem to be enough to explain contemporary periods of expansions and contractions. For example, in April 2011 Japan suffered the fourth most powerful earthquake since 1900,[49] around 40 miles off the coast of the Oshika Peninsula. This triggered a tsunami that reached 6 miles inland, causing extensive damage to infrastructure across the North East. Three nuclear reactors at the Fukushima power plant went into meltdown, leaving around 10% of households in the entire country without electricity, and all 50 of the country's nuclear reactors out of use.[50] As of September 2013 there were officially 15 883 people dead, 2654 missing, and 6146 injured.[51] It is hard to imagine a bigger, or more real shock. And sure enough the economy entered recession, with the Q1 GDP growth rate contracting 3.7% (compared to the same quarter of the previous year).[52] But the earthquake struck only in the last month of that quarter. And by Q3 Japan was out of recession and growing at 6% per annum.[53] The unemployment rate dipped somewhat in mid-2011, but is hard to distinguish from the general trend.[54] If the macroeconomic impact of something that colossal is so muted, there must be other causes of the business cycle.

The New Keynesian approach argues that it isn't shocks – be they demand side (i.e. nominal) or supply side (i.e. real) – that are the problem. Rather, the emphasis should be on the frictions (or market imperfections) that amplify those shocks into employment and output effects. Based on a Keynesian perspective, they are 'new' in the sense that they attempt to use models with microeconomic foundations.

They treat money as being non-neutral and show how this can generate macroeconomic fluctuations. New Keynesian models tend to emphasise the role of information asymmetries, and focus on the following market failures:

- Coordination failure
  It may be in everyone's common interest for prices to respond quickly to new conditions, but no single firm has an incentive to do so unilaterally. Therefore the costs of price adjustments can cause unwelcome swings in output.
- Financial market failure
  Ben Bernanke and Mark Gertler show how banks may use a firm's net worth as a way to lower monitoring costs. This will lead to increased investment during the upturn of a boom, but reduced investment in the downturn.[55]
- Labour market failure
  Issues such as hysteresis and dual labour markets show how initial deviations in the actual rate of unemployment can turn into changes in the natural rate.

Rather than assign blame to market failures, the Austrian theory of the business cycle focuses on how the central bank can cause massive disruptions to the process of economic calculation.[56] We can tell the following simple story. Imagine that you are a construction company, planning to build some new houses.[57] Let's consider how the economy should function. Imagine that the general public decide that they would like to forgo some present consumption, in order to have higher purchasing power in future. They have become more patient. This increase in the supply of loanable funds will push interest rates down. The signal being sent to the construction company is to borrow money, and build houses. Your business plan will look more profitable, and you start building. At some point in the future, you will complete the houses and put them up for sale. Consumers will use the interest earned on their higher savings to buy them. Everyone is happy.

Now we can contrast this with an alternative scenario, this time with no change in time preference.[58] Instead, assume that the central bank pursues an easy monetary policy. This will generate inflation, and push interest rates below their natural rate. Note that it provides the same signal as before. Construction companies will build houses. However the difference is that consumer preferences haven't changed. The lower interest rates are not a result of voluntary savings, but of **forced savings**. The reason people are forgoing consumption is not because they want to have more in future, but because their purchasing power is being diminished by higher inflation. The problem isn't that firms are investing too much (i.e. over investment), but that faulty signals are enticing them to invest in the wrong projects (i.e. malinvestment). Eventually the construction company will realise that their plans are wrong. Inflation is eating into their profit. Policymakers may respond to the rising inflation by increasing interest rates, and turn the boom into bust. The builder will not be able to afford the real resources required to complete the project. Once it becomes clear that people aren't as wealthy as they thought, projects get liquidated. But because capital goods are heterogeneous these entrepreneurial errors will take time and be costly to correct. A recession is the inevitable outcome of the boom, as entrepreneurs recalculate. As Niall Ferguson has said,

> *The key point is that without easy credit a true bubble cannot occur. That is why so many bubbles have their origins in the sins of omission and commission of central banks.*[59]

According to Charles Kindleberger's seminal account, the five stages of a bubble are as follows:[60]

1. Displacement – changes to profit opportunities
2. Euphoria – a feedback process where profits feed into high asset prices
3. Mania – the prospects of easy money induce novices to join in
4. Distress – insiders look for the exit door
5. Revolution – prices start to fall causing a stampede.

In conclusion there are some generally accepted points about monetary theory that are worth holding dear. Firstly, **inflation is a monetary phenomenon** – the root cause is excessive money creation. Secondly, **money is not neutral**; therefore monetary growth can affect real variables and cause misallocations of capital. Monetary stability is crucial for a prosperous society.

Money is unlike any other good in the economy because it is the only one that does not have its own market. If you think about it this makes sense – how much would £100 cost?

Who would exchange £100 for £100? It's bizarre. When people refer to 'the money market' or the 'price of money' they are actually referring to something else.

- Interest rates aren't the price of money – they are the ratio of money in one time period versus money in another. They are the price of money in relation to *time*.
- Exchange rates aren't the price of money – they are the price relative to a foreign currency.
- The price deflator isn't the price of money – it's the price relative to goods and services.

In each instance we are simply using money to measure the value of something else. Money doesn't have a 'price' of its own. As Leland Yeager says,

> *Because money is traded on all markets and on none specifically its own, and because it has no specific price of its own to come under specific pressure, an imbalance between its supply and demand has far-reaching consequences.*[61]

If there is a problem in the market for shoes then it is the price mechanism that will adjust to find equilibrium. It won't adjust immediately, and we would expect to see harmful spillovers into the market for leather, or shoe polish, etc. But it won't cause a system-wide problem. *Money* on the other hand is one half of all economic exchanges. If there is an imbalance between the demand for and supply of money there is no single market that can adjust. *Every* market in the economy will be affected. When central banks mismanage the money supply the entire economy suffers.

NOTES

1. This quote is often associated with Milton Friedman but it is quite hard to find an original source. I believe it is Friedman, M. (1963) *Inflation: Causes and Consequences*, but the earliest I am aware of is Friedman, M. (1970) The Counter-Revolution in Monetary Theory, IEA Occasional Paper, no. 33.
2. Hanke, S.H. (2009) R.I.P. Zimbabwean dollar, Cato Institute, 5 February [for a collection of articles in the Zimbabwe hyperinflation see http://www.cato.org/zimbabwe, accessed 25 November 2013].
3. Powell, B., Ford, R. and Nowrasteh, A. (2008) Somalia after state collapse: Chaos or improvement?, *Journal of Economic Behaviour & Organisation*, **67** (3-4), 657–670.
4. Coyne, C.J. (2006) Reconstructing Weak and Failed States: Foreign Intervention and the Nirvana Fallacy. *Foreign Policy Analysis*, **2**, 343–361.
5. As ever, we should exercise caution before attributing too much to a price index. As Ludwig von Mises pointed out, 'there are many ways of calculating purchasing power by means of index numbers, and every single one of them is right, from certain tenable points of view; but every single one of them is also wrong, from just as many equally tenable points of view' Mises, L.v. (1934[1981]) *The Theory of Money and Credit*, Liberty Fund, p. 26.
6. 'Smartphones enter the nation's basket', *Metro*, 16 March 2011.
7. See Poundstone, W. (2010) *Priceless: The hidden psychology of value*, Oneworld, pp. 4–5.
8. 'Upwardly mobile Africa', *The Economist*, 22 December 2012.
9. Harris, J. (2011) King lifts lid on inflation error, *City AM*, 17 February.
10. As *The Economist* says, this isn't trivial: 'a 1% monthly inflation works out at an annual 12.7%, whereas 1.9% monthly compounds to 25.3%'. 'The price of cooking the books', *The Economist*, 25 February 2012.

11. Keynes, J.M. (1924) *Tract on Monetary Reform*, Macmillan.
12. Horwitz, S. (2003) The Costs of Inflation Revisited, *Review of Austrian Economics*, **16** (1), 77–95.
13. David Kestenbaum provides a fascinating explanation for why a bottle of Coca-Cola cost 5c for over 70 years. One reason was that the president of Coca-Cola agreed to sell the syrup used for the drink at a fixed price, but sold control over the bottling. This meant that they wanted as many bottles to sell as possible, so they launched a marketing campaign that told customers a bottle of Coke would cost 5c. Although the bottler wanted to have a larger mark up, they were unable to increase the price above what the customers expected. Another reason for the duration of this price was technological. Vending machines were built to accept a 5c coin. It would be possible to accept a 10c coin, but this would require them to double the price of the drink. See Kestenbaum, D. (2012) Why coke cost a nickel for 70 years, *NPR*, 15 November [http://www.npr.org/blogs/money/2012/11/15/165143816/why-coke-cost-a-nickel-for-70-years, accessed 29 September 2013].
14. Sumner, S. (2008) Score-Keeping with Selgin, *Cato Unbound*, 28 September [http://www.cato-unbound.org/2009/09/28/scott-sumner/score-keeping-with-selgin/, accessed 29 September 2013].
15. Blustein, P. (2005) *And the Money Kept Rolling In*, Public Affairs.
16. As the *Financial Times* says, 'Demand stimulus by helicopter money need not be more inflationary than other types. It could be less so, since by definition it does not come with a built-in expectation of future reversal through tax rises (unlike public borrowing) or monetary tightening (unlike quantitative easing)', 'Helicopter money and supply siders', *Financial Times*, 6 February 2013. Note that a helicopter drop may be a way to generate a more uniform dispersal of new money, but it doesn't avoid the relative price effects or menu costs of inflation. I am also making an assumption that the helicopter drop is literal and that the wealth effects are completely random. This avoids the main argument against them, which is that policymakers would ensure the drop occurs over their own vested interests.
17. Cowen, T. (1997) *Risk and Business Cycles,* Routledge, p. 78.
18. We use the dynamic version of the quantity theory advocated by Cowen, T. and Tabarrok, A. (2012) *Modern Principles: Macroeconomics*, Worth (2nd edition).
19. Sometimes it can be confusing to see a chart of the 'Irish' money supply, for example, in comparison to the rest of the Eurozone. From 2006–07 the money supply in Ireland was growing at around 40%, and then turned negative in 2008. But isn't Ireland part of the Eurozone? If they share a currency how can their money supply deviate? The answer is because we tend to look at broader measures. The 'money supply' referred to above is M3, and cash is only a small component of that. The reason for looking at M3 is to see a broader reflection of the activity in the individual country's banking system.
20. Blaug, M. (1995) *The Quantity Theory of Money: From Locke to Keynes and Friedman,* Edward Elgar.
21. To be more precise, what happened in Romania is not a change in the money supply, but a change in the currency. It is impossible to change the money supply and have a proportional and uniform change on prices.
22. Krauss, C. (2011) Filling Stations Fret Over Price Creep, *New York Times*, 9 March [http://green.blogs.nytimes.com/2011/03/09/filling-stations-fret-over-price-creep, accessed 29 September 2013].
23. I am also assuming that all other variables remain unchanged. According to the quantity theory, it is possible that a change in M does *not* lead to a change in P, but only if V and/or Y changes.
24. Keynes, *Tract on Monetary Reform* (n 11), p. 46.
25. Royal Mint Annual Report, 2010–11. [http://www.royalmint.com/~/media/Files/AnnualReports/ar20102011.ashx, accessed, 29 September 2013].
26. Ellicott, C. (2012) Steel yourselves for the smaller new 5p and 10p that will save Treasury £8 million a year, *Daily Mail*, 23 January 2012.
27. Beowulf (2011) Coin Seigniorage and the Irrelevance of the Debt Limit, 3 January. [http://my.firedoglake.com/beowulf/2011/01/03/coin-seigniorage-and-the-irrelevance-of-the-debt-limit/, accessed 29 September 2013].

28. Bernanke, B. (2002) Deflation: Making sure 'it' doesn't happen here, Remarks at the National Economists Club, Washington DC, 21 November [http://www.federalreserve.gov/boarddocs/speeches/2002/20021121/, accessed September 2013].

29. For historical tax thresholds see http://www.rate.co.uk/tax/incometax9500.html, accessed 29 September 2013. For the figures used see http://www.tax-news.com/news/UK_Treasury_Set_To_Benefit_From_Bracket_Creep___15495.html, accessed 29 September 2013.

30. To be fair, the government were raising the thresholds based on inflation. But earnings were rising faster than inflation, so bracket creep still occurred.

31. Booth, P. (2012) Thirty years of fiscal drag, *Institute of Economic Affairs Blog*, 16 May [http://www.iea.org.uk/blog/thirty-years-of-fiscal-drag, accessed September 2013].

32. As Roger Garrison has argued the Taylor Rule is not really *prescriptive* but *descriptive*. What it does is formalise previous Federal Reserve policy decisions, therefore it's not so much a guide for policy as a tool that says 'if you want to continue making policy decisions in line with previous ones, here's what to do'.

33. See Arnold, R.A. (2013) *Macroeconomics*, Cengage (11th edition), p. 351.

34. The 'classic' version of the Taylor rule is more like the following:

$$i = r + P^T + a(P - P^T) + b(Y - Y^*)$$

It sets $P^T = 2\%$, $a = 1/2$ and $b = 1/2$. As with the 0.5 value in the McCallum rule (which is sometimes given as Φ) a and b are just parameters. Their values don't have any real economic significance, other than that they link the variables together in a way that fits with the historical evidence.

For another simple version see Tobin, J. (1998) Monetary policy: recent theory and practice, Cowles Foundation Discussion Paper No. 1187 [http://cowles.econ.yale.edu/P/cd/d11b/d1187.pdf, accessed 6 October 2013].

35. In this discussion of monetary policy rules we are merging, to some extent, rules and targets. We are also glossing over whether we should target growth rates or levels. For example, let's say we have an inflation target of 2%, and it turns out that this year inflation was 1%. A growth rate target would just reset, and intend to create 2% inflation for the next year. A level target would extrapolate a 2% growth path, and intend to catch up to it. Therefore in year 2 it would attempt to create an inflation rate above 2% to compensate for some of the missed inflation of the previous year.

36. Furthermore, according to Robert Shapiro, 'throughout the [Federal] Reserve's history, its formal independence was substantively compromised whenever it tried to resist specific directions from any administration' (quoted in Bartlett, B. (2000) Thank you Federal Reserve, *American Enterprise*, pp. 20–23).

37. Bernanke, B. (2006) Panel Discussion: Comments on the Outlook for the U.S. Economy and Monetary Policy, at the International Monetary Conference, Washington, DC, 5 June.

38. In fact a forecast that inflation will be the same in one year's time is more accurate than the Bank of England's forecasting model. See Heath, A. (2012) QE not the answer to UK's problems, *City AM*, 10 February 2012.

39. Mankiw, N.G. (2006) *Macroeconomics*, Worth Publishers (6th edition).

40. Moss, D.A. (2007) *A Concise Guide to Macroeconomics*, Harvard Business School Press.

41. Wolf, M. (2009) Central banks should target more than just inflation, *Financial Times*, 5 May.

42. Having said this, 'switching to cash' is costly, and therefore it is possible for depositors to tolerate negative interest rates provided they're mild and not expected to last long. It may seem odd to talk about negative interest rates, but recollect that there are multiple interest rates in an economy. It is possible to have a negative interest rate; it simply means that the customer is paying the bank. This is similar to having a fee for a deposit box. Indeed it is possible for central banks to charge commercial banks for their reserve balances. The Riksbank, in Sweden, charged interest on excess reserves, meaning that if commercial banks wanted to hold more reserves than necessary they would have to pay a fee. This is a way for central banks to get money into the real economy. By contrast, in 2008 the Fed started to pay interest on reserves, incentivising banks to restrict lending.

43. In addition if shares are part of income, and share prices rise, this should boost consumption as well. This is why it is odd if savers complain that quantitative easing is reducing yields, because it is also boosting equity prices.

44. The term **tapering** relates to the rate at which the central bank balance sheet changes. As *The Economist* says, according to some Fed officials 'slowing the pace at which that stock increases means monetary conditions loosen less quickly, but does not mean they tighten', 'How to taper safely', *The Economist*, 14 September 2013.

45. Dowd, K. (1989) *The State and the Monetary System*, Hemel Hempstead: Philip Allan, and New York: St Martin's Press.

46. White, L.H. (1989) *Competition and Currency*, New York University Press, p. 1.

47. Schuler, K. (1992) The world history of free banking: an overview, in Dowd, K. (ed.) *The Experience of Free Banking*, Routledge.

48. Selgin, G. (1988) *The Theory of Free Banking: Money Supply under Competitive Note Issue*, Rowman and Littlefield.

49. 'New USGS number puts Japan quake at 4th largest' *CBS News*, 14 March 2011. [http://www. webcitation.org/5xgjFTgf4, accessed 6 October 2013].

50. 'Japan Earthquake – Tsunami Fast Facts', *CNN*, 20 September 2013 [http://edition.cnn.com/ 2013/07/17/world/asia/japan-earthquake—tsunami-fast-facts/index.html, accessed 6 October 2013].

51. 'Damage Situation and Police Countermeasures associated with 2011 Tohoku district - off the Pacific Ocean Earthquake', *National Police Agency of Japan*, [http://www.npa.go.jp/archive/ keibi/biki/higaijokyo_e.pdf, accessed 6 October 2013].

52. Twaronite, L. and Kitchen, M. (2011) Japan's economy slips back into recession, *Market Watch* [http://www.marketwatch.com/story/japans-economy-shrinks-sharply-in-january-march-2011-05-18, accessed 6 October 2013].

53. 'Japan exits recession triggered by March earthquake', *Daily Telegraph*, 14 November 2011 [http://www.telegraph.co.uk/finance/economics/8887894/Japan-exits-recession-triggered-by-March-earthquake.html, accessed 6 October 2013].

54. Sumner, S. (2013) Money matters, *The Money Illusion*, 16 March [http://www.themoneyillusion. com/?p=20114, accessed 6 October 2013].

55. Bernanke, B. and Gertler, M. (1989) Agency costs, net worth, and business fluctuations, *American Economic Review,* **79** (1), 14–31.

56. Mises, L.v. (1912[1953]) *The Theory of Money and Credit*, Yale University Press; Hayek, F.A. (1931[2008]) *Prices and Production*, Mises Institute; Garrison, R. (2001) *Time and Money*, Routledge.

57. Mises, L.v. (1949[1996]) *Human Action*, Fox & Wilkes, p. 560.

58. This account is based mainly on Garrison, R.W. (1997) The Austrian theory of the business cycle, in Glasner, D. (ed.), *Business Cycles and Depressions*, Garland Publishing, pp. 23–27.

59. Ferguson, N. (2008) Wall Street Lays Another Egg, *Vanity Fair*, December.

60. Kindleberger, C.P. (1978) *Manias, Panics, and Crashes: A History of Financial Crises*, Macmillan.

61. Yeager, L.B. (1968) Essential properties of the medium of exchange, *Kyklos*, **21** (1), 45–69, at 64.

CHAPTER 9

Fiscal Policy

'The World is a very complex system. It is easy to have too simple a view of it, and it is easy to do harm and to make things worse under the impulse to do good and make things better.'

—Kenneth Boulding[1]

At the turn of the twentieth century the principles of a free society were under threat. Karl Marx presented two main critiques of capitalism. The first was that it creates increasing concentrations of capital (i.e. monopolies) and the second was that it generates systematic contractions (i.e. business cycles). Chapter 5 intended to challenge the first claim, and this chapter is focused on the second. We have already seen how central banks can generate booms and busts. We will now look at how decisions about taxing and spending can make things better, or possibly make them worse. Far from being inherent properties of capitalism, business cycles and economic crises are more often down to government policies that misunderstand how markets are supposed to work. Attempts to 'calm markets' and 'restore confidence' have the potential to backfire if people become uncertain about what actions government will take, and divert resources to trying to anticipate and protect themselves from policy errors. Managers are constantly trying to form expectations about the future, and fiscal policy should be a prominent consideration.

It is hard to underestimate the impact that both World Wars I and II had on the discipline of economics. During the 'progressive era' of 1900–14 the US economy was being increasingly centralised through legislation such as anti-trust, the Food and Drug Act and working conditions statutes. All of these sought to protect consumers against monopolies. But the key change came following World War I. The success of winning the war turned people's attention to the failures at home. Americans thought 'if the state can successfully organise society during a war, why not during the peace?' Wars are obviously times when government involvement in the economy increases, but the key thing is that once the war is over big government remains. Prior to World War I government income was under 10% of US GDP. During the war it spiked to over 25%, but once the war was over it only fell to 15–20%. Then there was World War II, and the size of government hit almost 35%. After the war it only fell back down to 20–30%. Each time it dropped back to a higher level than before. Wars aren't a temporary increase in the size and scope of the state; they tend to introduce a step change. Indeed this is one of the hidden costs of war.

The purpose of this chapter is to provide a more historical setting to the rise of government intervention in the economy. We will look at how economic theory provided a theoretical rationale for fiscal policy, and how this has been utilised by various governments as a means to tame business cycles. Over the course of the twentieth century economists went from being observers of the economy to its architects.

9.1   THE GREAT DEPRESSION

If ever there was a historical case that demonstrates the difference between the general public and the consensus of the economics profession it is the Great Depression. When I first began teaching in 2006 students would find it a little old fashioned to provide a brief overview of what happened in America in the 1930s. But the 2008 financial crisis demonstrated two things. Firstly, that we have not yet eradicated business cycles, and therefore there's value in studying historical cases. Secondly, many current economists learnt their trade by studying the Great Depression, and journalists and policymakers reflect those beliefs. Rightly or wrongly our views on this episode shape our entire understanding of the role of government in the economy. Therefore it's especially sad that the conventional wisdom is based on three myths.

Myth 1: Speculation and greedy bankers on Wall Street caused a bubble

In actual fact the main cause of the asset price bubble was loose monetary policy by the newly created Federal Reserve. It was created in 1913 to 'never allow another panic', but did just that.

Myth 2: The stock market crash caused a depression

There wasn't a clear link between a declining stock market and a declining economy. By Spring 1930 the Dow Jones had rebounded. The Wall Street crash corresponded with a fall from about 340 to 200. By April 1930 it was almost back up to 300. In fact 1933 and 1935 were two of the best years ever seen, and they occurred right in the middle of the Great Depression.[2] The real causes of the Depression were mistakes by the same organisation that caused the bubble: the Federal Reserve. The classic treatment of this was by Milton Friedman and Anna Schwartz.[3] A student of this was Ben Bernanke, who later went on to become the Chairman of the Federal Reserve. Here are what he identified as the four key errors, as pointed out by Friedman and Schwartz:[4]

1. In Spring 1928 monetary policy started to tighten and continued until the October 1929 Wall Street crash. This crash demonstrated that the Fed had the power to curtail what they deemed excessive exuberance, but at a high cost.
2. Once Great Britain left the gold standard in September 1931, speculators turned their attention to the US dollar. Private investors sought to convert dollars to gold, and in an effort to reduce the loss of gold reserves the Fed raised interest rates sharply. Their focus was more on maintaining the value of the dollar, than resolving the problems in the banking system.
3. The Depression was well under way by Spring 1932 and Congress wanted the Fed to loosen monetary policy. Eventually open market operations began in

April 1932 (reducing interest rates on government bonds and corporate debt) but Fed officials were not committed to monetary expansion.

4. From December 1930 to March 1933 President Roosevelt declared a 'banking holiday'. This led to around half of all US banks either closing or merging with other ones. Bank panics spread and even those that survived cut back on lending.

Myth 3: The New Deal and WW2 ended the Depression

In actual fact government policy turned a downturn into a depression. In December 1932 Herbert Hoover raised the top rate of income tax from 25% to 63% (and the lowest rate by *400%*) amongst a large range of policies that were New Deal in all but name; as one of President Roosevelt's advisors admitted, 'practically the whole New Deal was extrapolated from programs that Hoover started.'[5] The top rate of income tax eventually rose to 94%, which crippled the incentives for work.

In addition the Smoot-Hawley tariffs were imposed on imports, which led to retaliations that amplified the falling global trade. Did large scale public spending save America? In short, no. The economic recovery of the 1940s occurred after New Deal policies had been abandoned:

> *New Deal labor and industrial policies did not lift the economy out of the Depression as President Roosevelt had hoped ... The subsequent abandonment of these policies coincided with the strong economic recovery of the 1940s.*[6]

As Amity Shales said, 'What might have been an ordinary cyclical downturn was turned into a cataclysm by bad politics. The New Deal then made matters worse, prolonging the Depression.'[7] According to the Treasury Secretary Henry Morgenthau, 'We are spending more than we have ever spent before and it does not work ... I say, after eight years of this administration, we have just as much unemployment as when we started ... and an enormous debt to boot.'[8] You may suspect that I'm biased, but the generally accepted judgement amongst economists is that, 'an unexceptional downturn then was converted into the Great Depression by the actions of central banks and governments'.[9]

As for World War II, this did more to divert spending from consumer goods to military armament rather than boost growth. It certainly didn't improve living standards. After all, a military draft is a good way to reduce unemployment, but it hardly makes people better off. Prosperity only returned once the war was over.

> *The war itself did not get the economy out of the Depression. The economy produced neither a 'carnival of consumption' nor an investment boom, however successfully it overwhelmed the nation's enemies with bombs, shells, and bullets. But certain events of the war years – the buildup of financial wealth and especially the transformation of expectations – justify an interpretation that views the war as an event that recreated the possibility of genuine economic recovery. As the war ended, real prosperity returned.*[10]

But if the New Deal of World War II didn't end the Great Depression, what did? The most widely accepted explanation was provided by Christina Romer, who argued the recovery was due mainly to monetary expansion as opposed to fiscal stimulus.[11] Gold inflows increased the money supply and lowered real interest rates, thus stimulating investment spending. She also points out that self-correction played little role in the growth of real output 1933–42. Ultimately the main causes of the Great Depression were threefold:

1. The over-stimulated economic euphoria of the 1920s – not one caused by 'greed'.
2. The draconian monetary policy pursued by the Fed from 1930–33 – not the crash itself.
3. A rapid rise of protectionism that contributed to a collapse in global trade, and a punitive rise in income taxes in 1932 – these hindered recovery, they didn't promote it.

This really isn't controversial amongst economists. Blaming the Fed isn't a minority view; it's something that the Governor himself readily admits to. On the occasion of Milton Friedman's 90th birthday Ben Bernanke said the following:

Let me end my talk by abusing slightly my status as an official representative of the Federal Reserve. I would like to say to Milton and Anna: Regarding the Great Depression. You're right, we did it. We're very sorry. But thanks to you, we won't do it again.[12]

However the impact of the Great Depression was the destruction of the faith in markets of a generation of intellectuals. As Lord Skidelsky said, 'if the first world war left economic liberalism reeling, the Great Depression of the 1930s was virtually a knockout blow.'[13]

9.2 FISCAL STIMULUS

Let's assume that there's a recession and the demand for labour falls. What's supposed to happen? According to the classical view there are essentially five steps:

1. Recollect that over time output is determined by real factors (the long run aggregate supply curve).
2. But in the short run there may be deviations (the short run aggregate supply curve).
3. If there's a recession this means that aggregate demand has fallen.
4. Workers will revise down their wage demands, which shifts the short run aggregate supply curve to the right.
5. Output is restored at the full employment level, just at a lower price level.

The thing to note is that the adjustment is supposed to take place through the labour market, and depends on wage rates responding to the fact that there's a recession. (Remember that if *all* prices are falling this isn't necessarily making workers worse off because their real wages will be constant; it's just *nominal* wages that will fall.)

The problem with a falling price level though is that people have an incentive to defer spending. In the same way that inflation erodes the value of money, deflation increases it. But if people withhold consumption this will exacerbate the recession. We could even find ourselves in a self-fulfilling prophecy where people's expectation of a recession makes one occur. Policymakers may believe that there is nothing fundamentally wrong with the economy but simply a lack of aggregate demand is causing GDP to be below its potential. So what can they do? They can implore people to start spending money. But what if the people don't listen? They can cut interest rates to boost aggregate demand, but what if they hit the zero lower bound (ZLB)?

The essence of Keynesian policy is the combination of two things:

1. Some form of **price rigidity** (also known as 'stickiness') that prevents wages from adjusting and therefore markets don't clear quickly (certainly not instantaneously, which many models assume).[14]
2. The notion that increases in aggregate demand only generate inflation when you're at full employment, and that in a recession there is a gap in **effective demand** (i.e. an output gap) which means AD can be increased without being inflationary.

Keynes agreed that over time the market would adjust but this was of scant consolation to those suffering during the recession. He famously said,

> *In the long run we are all dead. Economists set themselves too easy, too useless a task if in tempestuous seasons they can only tell us that when the storm is long past the ocean is flat again.*[15]

But we need to be careful here. Although contemporary Keynesians can get this wrong, Keynes himself understood that 'the long run' does not refer to calendar time. On the contrary, as Mario Rizzo points out, economists tend to refer to 'the long run' to mean 'when all of the variable elements in a model are fully adjusted'.[16] There is nothing to say whether this will be lengthy or quite rapid. But even if this would take many years, as Hubert Lyautey said to his gardener, 'if a tree takes 150 years to mature, that's all the more reason to plant it as soon as possible'.[17]

So the policy question is, can government intervention speed up this process of adjustment? And here was Keynes' revolutionary innovation – our previous equation for aggregate demand is incomplete. In addition to consumption and investment we should also include government spending:

$$AD = C + I + G$$

If people won't spend money then the government can step in and spend it for them! It's obvious why this would appeal to politicians, since it gives them an economic rationale for spending money. Indeed they can spend money under the cover that it is in the public interest. How heroic!

My favourite example of a quasi-Keynesian public works programme actually pre-dates Keynes. Some time between 1805 and 1840 a businessman called Joseph Williamson began employing people to dig tunnels, under the Edge Hill part of Liverpool.[18] Very little is known about their purpose, and according to the *Liverpool Mercury* 'no earthly use can be assigned these tunnels'.[19] But according to historian Richard Whittington-Egan, Williamson's main motivation was 'the employment of the poor'. Unemployment was high following the end of the Napoleonic wars, and Williamson employed hundreds of returning soldiers. He lived near to the local Poor House and treated it with abhorrence.[20] He wanted them to have jobs, but since there weren't many available he made some up. Not only in the digging of redundant tunnels, but 'some of the labourers were carting piles of stones from one place to another, others were alternatively pumping water out of, and empting (sic) it back into, a well, while yet more were occupied in an aimless turning of grindstones'.[21] The apparent economic value of their efforts was zero, but this was deemed better for their dignity – 'all received a weekly wage and were thus enabled to enjoy the blessings of charity without the attendant curse of stifled self respect.'[22] Given that Williamson spent his own money, there was no burden on the taxpayer. But that sort of policy – putting job creation above value creation is the essence of a stimulus plan. Williamson has since been touted as a great public benefactor, but according to Claire Moorhead it was a very private 'public work'.[23]

Not all fiscal stimulus plans create zero value. Some positively destroy it. In the summer of 2013 a series of protests in Turkey criticised the government for pursuing costly and environmentally damaging infrastructure projects.[24] The Soviet Union was famous for putting jobs and short-term output boosts ahead of economically and ecologically sustainable development.[25]

The fiscal multiplier is the assumed relationship between changes in G and changes in GDP. According to Arnold Kling, it is the 'response of GDP to a given alternative path of government spending'.[26]

- A multiplier bigger than 1 implies that for every £1 increase in government spending, GDP will increase by more. This is the classic Keynesian rationale because it is supposed to kick start the rest of the economy.
- If the multiplier is less than 1 it means that some private sector spending is being 'crowded out' by the increased role of government.
- It's even conceivable that the multiplier is less than 0, i.e. that the stimulus ends up shrinking the economy by reducing C and I by more than G goes up.

Estimates of the fiscal multiplier are controversial. But two points need to be made. Firstly, we cannot ignore the hidden costs of a fiscal stimulus. There's a multiplier involved in private spending as well. Secondly, these are empirical assertions. We don't know whether the multiplier is high or low. Policymakers are wrong to assume that *any* increase in government spending will kick start the economy, and economists are wrong to claim that *any* increase will automatically be offset by lower consumption. But we should look at some famous cases, such as World War II. According to Robert Barro, rather than there being a multiplier, government spending actually *reduced* GDP:

> [T]he war raised real GDP by $430 billion per year in 1943–44. Thus, the multiplier was 0.8 (430/540). The other way to put this is that the war lowered components of GDP aside from military purchases ... Wartime production siphoned off resources from other economic uses.[27]

In a study of the entire twentieth century, Michael Owyang, Valerie Ramey and Sarah Zubairy found 'no evidence that multipliers are greater during periods of high unemployment in the U.S. In every case, the estimated multipliers are below unity.'[28]

Remember that there are only three forms of government finance: tax, debt and inflation. It would be unwise to fund an increase in government spending through higher taxes, because this would lead to a reduction in consumption. Therefore the Keynesian policy prescription is to increase G above the tax revenues being generated, funding it through borrowing and thus running a budget deficit. We will call a **'fiscal stimulus'** an increase in the budget deficit in order to boost aggregate demand.

Here's how it's supposed to work in theory – when the growth rate of the economy falls below potential the government boosts AD by a deficit-financed increase in spending. And once the economy recovers and tax revenues are high they run a budget surplus and use this to pay off the debt. Benevolent policymakers 'smooth the cycle' by increasing debt during a downturn and paying it back in the boom. Former Canadian Finance Minister Paul Martin summed it up well,

> *In the postwar years, many economists argued that you did not need to be in the black every year, as long as budgets were balanced over the course of the economic cycle, so that deficits during slumps would be paid off with surpluses in good years.*[29]

Sounds good in theory. But what about in practice?

> *[I]t didn't work in the real world of politicians … once governments find that they can get away with borrowing instead of taxing to pay the bills … it is almost impossibly tempting for politicians to do it again and again until the debt is out of control.*[30]

Gerald O'Driscoll has made an excellent point:

> *The more powerful one believes fiscal stimulus to be, the more adept the Keynesian policymaker must be. If the stimulus has powerful positive effects when added, it will have powerful negative effects when withdrawn. Hence, the application of stimulus and its withdrawal must be precisely timed.*[31]

He goes on to add that the withdrawal of the stimulus is not the only inevitable dampening effect. At some point the stimulus must be paid for, and this will also reduce output. Consequently any initial benefit from a stimulus must be weighed up against the retrenchment that comes when it is withdrawn, and then paid for. Ultimately it is a matter of time horizons.

The main issue here is the relationship between borrowing and taxes. After all, borrowing is not really an alternative to taxes, it's simply a way to defer them. If you care about your children, you will adjust your planning to take into account anticipated rises in taxation – families will be forward-looking. At the extreme this suggests that the present value of future liabilities will equal the present value of all assets (and therefore no net wealth has been created). According to Robert Barro,

> *in the case where the marginal net-wealth effect of government bonds is close to zero […] fiscal effects involving changes in the relative amounts of tax and debt finance for a given amount of public expenditure would have no effect on aggregate demand, interest rates, and capital formation.*[32]

Barro's claim that people respond to bond financed spending in the same way that they'd respond to tax financed spending rests on some important assumptions. For example that capital markets are perfect; that there's a fixed path of government expenditures; and that people have intergenerational concerns. If the economy was comprised of selfish people without children, they may well not care about future tax obligations, and treat deficit financed spending as an increase in net wealth.[33]

This issue stems from David Ricardo and is typically referred to as **Ricardian equivalence**. Although it's a source of much debate amongst economists it is ultimately an empirical issue. Whether or not people treat bonds as net wealth can depend on a multitude of factors. But here's the type of evidence you may look for:

> [O]ne study by Matthew Shapiro and Joel Slemrod concluded that most US citizens used a 2001 tax windfall to pay off their debts, leaving more money available to pay future taxes – Ricardian equivalence in action.[34]

Economists tend to agree that an effective fiscal stimulus requires three characteristics.

Firstly, it needs to be timely. It needs to begin whilst the economy is still in recession. Even Keynes agreed that the economy will self-correct 'in the long run', therefore the stimulus needs to kick in before this happens. If there's a delay in implementation you may as well wait for the natural correction. So resource mobilisation is key. But recollect from Chapter 6 the discussion of capital goods. Investment projects take time.

Secondly, it needs to be temporary. The Keynesian argument that boosting aggregate demand won't simply lead to inflation assumes that there's an output gap. Once the economy is back to its potential a stimulus would be inflationary. Therefore not only should the stimulus kick in when the economy is still in recession, it needs to be unwound as the economy recovers. This is where the politics comes in. Politicians like an excuse to spend money, since they can direct it towards their supporters. But the supporters want permanent, not temporary, spending plans. Therefore there's a danger that a stimulus is used as a vehicle to enact permanent spending commitments.

Thirdly, it needs to be targeted. The whole point is that the stimulus brings back on line the idle resources. If government projects use workers that would otherwise be employed in the private sector there's no point (and if the government projects are less value-creating than private sector projects, it would make things even worse). If the resources aren't idle, government spending 'crowds out' private spending (the rise in G is offset by a fall in C or I). But it is difficult to only target idle resources; therefore the marginal entrepreneur is now having to compete with the public sector. In addition 'idle' unemployment serves an important function in the economy – we need markets to adjust to changes in data. Even if there's a shortfall in AD policymakers lack the signals to know what type of projects would create economic value. It's easy to say 'build more houses', but there is also an obligation to know how many, what kind and where.

Keynes himself expressed doubts about the type of fiscal stimulus plans policymakers favour:

> Organized public works, at home and abroad, may be the right cure for a chronic tendency to a deficiency of effective demand. But they are not capable of sufficiently rapid organisation (and above all cannot be reversed or undone at a later date), to be the most serviceable instrument for the prevention of the trade cycle.[35]

In addition to the emphasis on price rigidities and effective demand, there was a third aspect to the Keynesian revolution that swept the discipline of economics. This was the rise of economics as a 'science'. It was down to Keynes that economists substituted tweed jackets with lab coats and began to consider their subject 'hard' science rather than social science. Before Keynes the discipline was more likely to be referred to as 'political economy', which sounds like sociology, philosophy or theology. But during the twentieth century there was a transformation of the discipline to a more quantitative, scientific approach. 'Economics' emerged, which sounds more like physics or mechanics. The reason for this is that the Keynesian policy prescription introduced aggregate variables, and these needed to be measured. Adam Smith had no idea what the GDP of Scotland was in 1766, but it didn't matter because he wasn't trying to 'boost' it. As soon as economic indicators became policy levers there was a rush for measurement. The field of national income accounting was born, and statistic agencies cropped up to provide data. The discipline was stepping into a new age of 'economist as saviour'.

A number of important trends in the twentieth century contributed to a rise in the planning mentality:

- Colonialism meant that governments wanted ways to organise the relations of other countries from afar.
- Municipal socialism responded to increased urbanisation with public works.
- A growing middle class was becoming agitated by 'poverty amidst plenty'.
- Development economics was emerging based on the pillars of (i) infant industry arguments,[36] and (ii) neo-Keynesian growth models.

Throughout all of this the USSR was seen as a viable alternative and the rich west followed suit. The US did not nationalise as many key industries as countries like the UK and France, but there is a fine line between heavy regulation and explicit nationalisation.

Although the wave of Keynesianism was strong there were a few important voices of dissent.

One voice was **Friedrich Hayek**, who pointed out that the Keynesian framework was built on the assumption that we are in a recession, and that there are idle resources. But how can you have a theory of depressions that starts off assuming that you're in one? Hayek's analysis began with the economy at full employment, and he then attempted to show how a recession can occur. At the time though, this was seen as abstract and fanciful. Keynes' work seemed to fit the times. But the first rule of economics is that we live in a world of scarcity. The assumption that some resources are 'idle' implies that their opportunity costs are zero. But this is not even economic analysis! Hayek had previously spent a lot of time critiquing Keynes' work on monetary theory, only for Keynes to change his mind and distance himself from his earlier claims. Hayek assumed that something similar would happen again, and didn't bother to engage with it. He doubted that anyone would take it seriously. Hayek saw the problem as a coordination one – how do we know where resources should be employed to create maximum value? He thought the price mechanism was the solution, and that government interventions disrupted these important signals. The rap videos created by John Papola and Russ Roberts do an excellent job of capturing the economic debate between Hayek and Keynes in a witty, enjoyable format.

Another voice of dissent was **Milton Friedman**, who tackled the Keynesian system on its own terms. In particular he challenged some of the assertions that the Keynesian system relied on.

- Keynes believed that people's consumption is proportional to their income (this is known as the 'consumption function'). For example, if the 'marginal propensity to consume' is 0.7 this means that for every £100 of additional income received, people will go out and spend £70. Keynes thought the problem with tax cuts was that a lot of the increase in income would be saved, rather than spent. If poorer people have a higher MPC then a fiscal stimulus should be targeted at them. But Friedman challenged this – theoretically and empirically. He argued that people don't simply spend a stable proportion of their income, but take a longer term view. He developed the **permanent income hypothesis**, which claims that people look at their expected lifetime income, and make spending decisions based on this.[37] This is why it makes sense for students to get into debt – there's a realistic expectation that future income will be high enough to pay for it. We make spending decisions based on this lifetime income, rather than our current income.

- Keynes also believed that the demand for money stemmed mainly from people's liquidity preference, and therefore the interest rate was a key determinant. Friedman provided evidence that it was due to less volatile factors such as incomes and habit.[38]
- Friedman also challenged Keynes' view of history, and his monetary history was primarily focused on correcting what he deemed to be myths about the monetary causes of the Great Depression.[39]

In many ways Friedman was simply restating the claims of the classical economists in the new language that Keynesian economics had ushered in.

Two other voices of dissent were **James Buchanan** and **Richard Wagner**, who looked at the political reality of Keynes' policy prescriptions. They argued that politicians would always be keen to borrow money during a recession to boost the economy. But they questioned whether there would be the same political incentives to use the boom times to pay off debt. Given that political cycles are reasonably short, why would politicians make tough decisions that will benefit future governments? They predicted that rather than benevolent politicians 'smoothing the cycle', we would see permanent budget deficits. And this is exactly what we saw. They warned that a permanent budget deficit means a steadily increasing public debt.[40]

One final voice of dissent was **Warren Nutter**, one of the very few economists of the time that challenged the empirical claims of Marxism and socialism. He showed that capitalism had not led to increasing concentrations of capital, and in fact socialist countries had *more* monopolies. He also queried the growth figures coming out of the USSR and claimed that it wasn't an economic powerhouse.[41] The argument was reasonably simple. There was initial growth but this was mainly because it started from a low base. Since it was purely technical growth, diminishing returns kicked in quite soon. By contrast, the US was engaged in genuine innovation, leading to endogenous growth. After all, rising living standards are about *consumption* not *production*. It was only when the Soviet system formally collapsed in 1991 that it became obvious how misleading their growth figures were. Nutter was vindicated.

9.3 EXPANSIONARY FISCAL CONTRACTIONS

It is tempting to believe that because G is a component of GDP, increases in G (holding T stable) will boost GDP by definition. But this may only hold over the short term, with an implicit assumption that you already have a reasonably balanced budget. But what if the government has already been running a budget deficit, such that public debt levels are high and there are genuine fears that they may not be able to afford to pay it off? It's conceivable that the boost to confidence caused by government stimulus is outweighed by the damage to confidence caused by even higher debt levels. In this situation it is possible that reductions in the budget deficit (i.e. a fiscal contraction, or 'adjustment') can do more for growth. As the European Central Bank have said, 'a fiscal contraction may turn out to be expansionary if the expectation channel becomes sufficiently strong.'[42] Indeed it is possible that moving towards a more balanced budget can be better for growth than more debt, even in the short run. According to a report from the ECB,

> *Many economists are convinced that longer-term benefits from fiscal consolidation are in a trade-off with short-term deceleration in output growth. However more recent research suggests that curbing fiscal imbalances contributes to faster growth already in the short run.*[43]

Essentially this means that governments may choose to focus on prioritising the confidence of the bond markets, rather than the confidence of domestic consumers and businesses. Having said this, it's rarely a case of one or the other. It may be that the public are as concerned by the amount of borrowing (i.e. deferred taxation) as the bond markets are. Journalists like to pretend that 'the markets' are separate from the public, but financial institutions are just intermediaries. In many cases it is the public who own the pension pots that have invested in government debt. What it comes down to is how people react, and we can't know this based on theory.

In the same way that there are pros and cons to a fiscal stimulus, we should also look at the alternative – a fiscal contraction. The question is, under what circumstances is it conceivable that a reduction in government deficits stimulates growth?

The first problem is defining the fiscal stance. There are typically two ways that economists do this. One focuses on the *effects* of the policy. In other words we can define a fiscal contraction as when the cyclically adjusted primary budget deficit falls by at least 1.5% of GDP. The alternative is to focus on the *intentions*, and just choose some absolute level independent of external shocks that may also affect the economy.

According to Alberto Alesina, 'not all fiscal adjustments cause recessions. Countries that have made spending adjustments to reduce their deficits have made large, credible and decisive cuts. Even in the very short run, many reductions of budget deficits, even sharp ones, have been followed immediately by sustained growth rather than recessions.'[44] There are examples of expansionary fiscal contractions, even in the short run:[45]

- In 1981 the UK was in recession and 364 economists wrote to Margaret Thatcher warning her not to cut government spending. She did so anyway, and the recovery began that very quarter.[46]
- Denmark in 1983–86 cut public spending and saw an increase in consumption.
- Ireland in 1987–89 saw the budget deficit decline at the same time as debt fell and growth increased.
- Canada in the 1990s cut government spending from 17.5% of GDP in 1992–93 to 11.3% in 2000–01.[47]
- In 2008 Latvia saw output fall by 10%, and in 2009 by 18%.[48] Following a loan from the IMF they maintained their currency peg (to the Euro) and sought to cut public spending and wages. This resulted in a fiscal contraction of around 14% of GDP.[49] Not only did it

have reasonable public support – the government was re-elected in 2010[50] – the economy also rebounded quickly.[51]

- In the US real current public expenditure fell by 1.5% from the middle of 2009 to the middle of 2011, and yet there were nine successive quarters of economic growth.[52]

It's important to look at some of the contributing factors for these success stories, however. Typically interest rates were high prior to the fiscal contraction, and therefore there was scope to cut them. In the case of Denmark the economy was in a reasonably strong position prior to the contraction (around 4% GDP growth). In some instances the currency was able to depreciate in order to boost net exports (and indeed this is one of the channels in which an expansionary fiscal contraction is supposed to work). In the case of Canada, its main trading partner, the US, was enjoying high growth that allowed Canadian exports to increase from 33% of GDP in 1994 to 45% in 2000.[53]

Following an analysis of six historical examples of fiscal contractions in the UK, a Policy Exchange report suggests that a successful fiscal contraction has the following general characteristics:[54]

- There are real cuts to spending (as opposed to relying on economic growth to reduce spending as a share of GDP).
- Although it is better to cut spending before there's a crisis, sometimes a crisis is required for cuts to be politically feasible.
- The contraction should be comprised of 80% spending cuts and 20% tax rises.

Goldman Sachs looked at every OECD fiscal contraction since 1975, and found that:

> *decisive budgetary adjustments that have focused on reducing government expenditure have (i) been successful in correcting fiscal imbalances; (ii) typically boosted growth; and (iii) resulted in significant bond and equity market outperformance. Tax-driven fiscal adjustments, by contrast, typically fail to correct fiscal imbalances and are damaging for growth.*[55]

But it's interesting to note that spending cuts are better than tax rises both in terms of their economic effects and also their popularity. According to Alberto Alesina and Silvia Ardagna 'those [fiscal adjustments] based upon spending cuts and no tax increases are more likely to reduce deficits and debt over GDP ratios than those based upon tax increases.'[56] And perhaps this is why they are more popular – governments who cut spending lost power 20% of the time, whilst those that raised taxes lost power 56% of the time.[57]

We previously saw how the 'core' functions of government account for less than 10% of their spending. One could argue that these are necessary functions of the state and help to generate the platform for economic growth.[58] Other economists might give wider scope to the growth-enhancing potential of government, and put this figure closer to 25%. But within this range government spending tends to work together with economic growth. As Andrew Lilico points out, however, 'once government spending rises above about 25 per cent of GDP for each additional percentage point of GDP the government spends, growth is around 0.1–0.15 per cent lower per year.'[59] He points out – quite rightly – that growth isn't the be all and end all, and if you doubt that private charities would care for the sick and needy you may be perfectly happy to sacrifice a little economic growth in order to fund such social provisions. But he also shows that once the government accounts for 35–60% of GDP the damage to wealth creation becomes significant.

9.4 CONFIDENCE

One complaint about the Keynesian framework is, in the words of Hayek, that 'Mr Keynes' aggregates conceal the most fundamental mechanisms of change'[60] – that the economist as engineer operates as if macroeconomic variables interact with each other like some sort of machine. But this mechanistic view neglects that all economic interactions come through people. Unlike physics, economics does not have any 'constants', therefore it's impossible to derive a set of laws that determine how changes in the money supply affect inflation, or how output impacts employment. Indeed it's how individuals react to policy that determines its impact. Robert Lucas uses a chess analogy, as if policymakers are engaged in an attempt to move pieces around the board to suit their desired outcome. In the economy, however, the pieces can move for themselves. Therefore a key channel is expectations. Scrap that – *the* key channel is expectations. Everything else depends on expectations. And since the height of the Keynesian revolution in the 1970s there has been a sustained movement away from a mechanistic view of the economy to focusing more on expectations.

One way to view the role of expectations is how policy changes affect confidence.

When the US Treasury Secretary Henry Paulson prepared to speak to the press on 29 September 2008, his communications advisor Michele Davis said, 'this is about market confidence. Don't talk about mechanics.'[61] In March 2009 UK Chancellor Alistair Darling said he would take 'whatever action is necessary' to deal with the ongoing financial crisis.[62] In May 2010 the President of the European Commission, Jose Manuel Barroso, said that the Eurozone would do 'whatever it takes' to save the Euro.[63] The reason they did so – I assume – is because they believed it would reassure people that they had things under control. This is possible. But it's also possible that it would scare people. When governments respond to crises by enacting new policies their aim is to make things better. But if those policies are going to have an impact people will need to devote time to understanding them.

The argument in favour of fiscal contractions is that when governments make credible efforts to live within their means, this increases confidence and leads to more investment immediately:

> *If the fiscal consolidation is read by the private sector as a signal that the share of government spending in GDP is being permanently reduced, households will revise upwards their estimate of their permanent income, and will raise current and planned consumption.*[64]

We can create two caricatures of how economists approach this issue:

1. Some say that the private sector take their cue from the government, and need to feel confident that there will be a recovery before they invest.
2. Some say that government interventions create uncertainty. If investors want certainty and stability then the threat of arbitrary and large scale intervention will reduce confidence.

The economist Robert Higgs coined the term **regime uncertainty** as an explanation for the duration of the Great Depression.[65] He argued that the scale of intervention was so high that the private sector became genuinely fearful that their investment plans would not be stable. Around 90% of the capital gains in the Dow Jones Industrial Average occur when Congress is out of session, implying that when it is in session there is additional uncertainty and entrepreneurs hold off.[66] According to the investor Lou Jiwei, 'right now we do not have the courage to invest in financial institutions because we do not know what problems they may have ... If it [regulation] is changing every week, how can you expect me to have confidence?'[67] In January 2009 the UK government announced a five-point plan that was intended to deal with the ongoing financial crisis. But as the Bank of England's Monetary Policy Committee pointed out, 'it initially had little impact on market sentiment'.[68] Their explanation was simple – 'financial market participants were waiting for more detail on the plan.'[69]

Ultimately this issue comes down to confidence. But does anyone know enough about confidence to be able to manage it? Who is to say whether more borrowing and spending will reassure markets and boost confidence? Or if, on the contrary, a higher debt burden will destroy it? As Gregory Mankiw says,

> *The sad truth is that we economists don't know very much about what drives the animal spirits of economic participants. Until we figure it out, it is best to be suspicious of any policy whose benefits are supposed to work through the amorphous channel of 'confidence.'*[70]

What do we know about the fiscal multiplier? Most economists would agree that when the economy is at full capacity the multiplier is zero. The only debate is what happens when there's spare capacity, but even then there are a number of factors that can dampen the strength of the multiplier. Generally speaking:[71]

- Tax cuts have lower multipliers the greater the propensity to save.
- Multipliers are low if the additional government borrowing causes interest rates to rise.
- Multipliers are lower for temporary tax cuts than they are for permanent ones.
- The more open the economy the lower the multiplier (because part of the stimulus spending will go on imports).
- Multipliers are lower in countries that have high debt levels (i.e. around 60% of GDP).
- Monetary policy needs to accommodate fiscal policy.

This can help us to create a rudimentary checklist to see if a fiscal stimulus is likely to work. First, we need to establish whether we have the right preconditions. Is the recession the result of a negative shock to AD (as opposed to productivity)?[72] Secondly, do we have the right appetite? Are we willing to sacrifice future growth for a present boost? If so, we can then ask whether the economy is in the right shape to respond well to a fiscal stimulus:

- Are savings rates low?
- Are interest rates low (and likely to stay low even with additional government borrowing)?
- Are proposed tax cuts permanent?
- Is the economy reasonably closed from foreign trade?
- Are debt levels low?
- Is monetary policy accommodating?

Finally, even if the above hold, we need to ask whether the stimulus is well crafted. Is it timely, temporary and targeted? Needless to say, this is a high bar to reach.

9.5 LAISSEZ-FAIRE

We can consider three different ways to respond to the business cycle. The first is regulation, and this is the prime rationale for central banks and state oversight. The majority of the economics profession would say that despite its track record of failure, government money is the best way to balance the gains from growth with the cost of periodic systemic crises. The second way pays attention to the role of demand deposits. Because banks keep fractional reserves, they are unable to redeem all deposits at any one time. Therefore even a threat of a bank run can be enough to cause one. Murray Rothbard said that banks should be mandated to keep 100% reserves for demand deposits.[73] Chicago economists such as Irving Fisher and Henry C. Simons have endorsed plans that raise reserve requirements for the narrowest forms of money. More recently, Laurence Kotlikoff's proposal for 'limited purpose banking' seeks to mitigate the effects of fractional reserve banking.[74] The third option is to have an entirely laissez-faire regime. Free bankers argue that the problem isn't fractional reserves per se, but how they combine with the policies of the central bank. Their solution, therefore, would be to abolish the central bank.

To the monetarist and Keynesian schools of thought the main cause of a recession is a deficiency of aggregate demand. Their debate is one about how best to stimulate it – whether by monetary policy, or fiscal policy. But they both accept that there is a vital role for government, and it is because consumers are not buying enough stuff. The Austrian school approach, by contrast, blames the recession on a breakdown of coordination. They argue that producers are producing the wrong kind of stuff. If this is the case, fiscal or monetary stimulus could make things worse because it preserves the existing capital structure, preventing it from being rearranged. In the words of an IMF report, the Austrian view claims that

> *[a]n economy in recession does not respond well to expansionary monetary and fiscal policies.*[75]

Roger Garrison explains that the distinction between the different schools of thought rests on the diagnosis of the problem. He asks the following question:

> *Did the collapse occur (a) in the midst of a period of healthy growth because of sheer ineptness of the central bank or (b) near the end of a policy-induced boom that was unsustainable in any event and in the midst of confusion about just what the problem was and how best to deal with it?*[76]

If your answer is (a) then you're a monetarist or Keynesian and the solution is either monetary or fiscal policy. Austrians, by contrast, would answer (b). For Austrians the recession is where the inevitable consequences of the boom reveal themselves. The economy just prior to the recession should be seen as the height of an artificial boom, and not something to return to.

You often hear that during a recession we have to 'do something'. But this instinct for *a policymaker* to act should be balanced by recognition that they may make things worse. Laissez-faire means 'let it be' and we should consider whether it is worth having on the table as a policy option.

The case for laissez-faire policy does not imply a laissez-faire attitude towards policy reform. There are plenty of important ways in which government could help a recovery, but these would focus more on the supply side. For example, allowing labour markets to adjust to the new conditions, by improving incentives for work and training, reducing barriers to labour mobility and reducing wage rigidities. Indeed the whole point of a recession is that it is a period of intense activity by entrepreneurs, and additional activity by policymakers can undermine that.

If your dog walks onto a frozen lake your instinct tells you to venture out and rescue it. But as many dog walkers learn to their cost each year, this urge should be resisted. The annual accounts of men (and it is always men) who lose their lives trying to save their dogs are tinged by the ironic fact that the dogs almost always survive. 'Don't just do something, stand there!' would be better advice.

To Austrians the main cause of a slow recovery is regime uncertainty, and failed attempts to stimulate demand. The proper role of monetary policy during a recession is a point of debate within the Austrian school. Those who advocate 100% reserves would argue that a contraction in the money supply is a necessary means to purge the excesses of the boom period. Those whom I've thus far labelled as 'free bankers' would make a distinction between the primary recession (caused by the structural imbalances built up during the boom phase) and a secondary recession (which results from a contraction in NGDP if the central bank allows the money supply to fall). The former would say that central banks should literally do nothing. The latter would say that they should try to balance the risks of too easy monetary policy with monetary policy that is too tight. In other words that the central bank should ensure that liquidity provisions are made to solvent banks.

As an example of how laissez-faire policy responses differ from what tends to happen, we can look at Japan in the 1990s. In the first few months of that decade Japan suffered a stock market crash followed by a recession. From 1993–2003 GDP grew on average by just 1%.[77] In fact by the end of 2003 the CPI was lower than where it was in 1997. According to John Greenwood, policymakers responded in several phases.[78] The first one was to launch a fiscal stimulus, which caused the government budget to go from a surplus of 2.1% in 1990, to a deficit of 7.9% by 2000. They also cut interest rates, and pioneered quantitative easing.[79] According to Ben Powell, Japan also tried direct lending and bailouts.[80] Policymakers threw the kitchen sink at the economy, and tried everything other than confronting the problems head on. Rather than needing to freeze the economy, perhaps it needed to thaw? The general lesson from Japan is that you cannot have a genuine and sustained recovery unless you solve the underlying causes of the crisis. In the case of Japan this was a huge real estate bubble. But instead of being closed down, troubled institutions were propped up. Balance sheets weren't restructured. Malinvestments weren't reallocated. As Martin Feckler said in the *New York Times*,

> In total, Japan spent $6.3 trillion on construction-related public investment between 1991 and September of last year [2009] … This has led many to conclude that spending did little more than sink Japan deeply into debt, leaving an enormous tax burden for future generations.[81]

9.6 THE PHILLIPS CURVE

The Phillips curve is named after William Phillips, a New-Zealander who spent most of his career at the LSE. He is known for two fascinating contributions to economics. The first is the creation, in 1949, of a computer designed to model the entire economy. The 'Monetary National Income Analogue Computer' (MONIAC) sounds ludicrous to recount now but should be seen as an important cultural artefact for the pretence of science. It was designed as a teaching device, to demonstrate how macroeconomic variables affect each other. Rather than use an electronic system the 'computer' used water, which represented money. As it flowed through the structure you could alter a series of taps and plugs to direct spending into certain parts of the economy. Economists lapped up this 'hydraulic' approach to modelling economic activity, and it was also used as a simulator. Modern, complex computer models are the descendants of this device, of which around a dozen were made and are housed in museums across the world.

His second major influence is the 'Phillips curve', one of the most hotly contested and well-known graphs in economics. It was presented in a 1958 paper and rests on a simple observation: an inverse relationship between unemployment and the rate of inflation.[82] This provided a major empirical boon to the developing Keynesian orthodoxy, since it suggests that there's a stable tradeoff between these two key indicators that policymakers can manipulate. The theoretical explanation for this rests on a wage bargaining model that says wages are a function of (i) inflation expectations; (ii) the rate of unemployment and (iii) everything else.[83] If inflation expectations are low, the claim is that low unemployment will lead to higher wages (workers' bargaining power is higher because there's not a large amount of potential workers to replace them). Since higher wages would be passed on through costs into higher prices, the 'cost' of lower unemployment is higher prices.

The implications of this were astounding – it suggests that the 'natural rate' of unemployment doesn't exist! That government can pick and choose between combinations of unemployment and inflation, and raise employment (and boost output) provided they could live with a little inflation. The policy conclusion is obvious – a steadily increasing money supply.

Since the model rests on inflation expectations, the assumptions were challenged on these grounds.

Milton Friedman responded by pointing out that we've been talking about *nominal wages*. If wages are rising and prices are rising then *real* wages are static. If workers have **adaptive expectations** they will base their decisions on what they've learnt from past time periods. In other words an initial bout of inflation might take people by surprise (and thus unemployment falls in the short run) but over time people will come to expect this and factor it into their wage demands. In short, the increase in expected inflation will cause the Phillips curve to shift outwards such that we're back at the 'natural rate'. Friedman argued that the purported tradeoff between inflation and unemployment is a myth, and that it's possible to have both. The fact that the US economy suffered from stagflation soon after he made this point made it even more compelling. The classical view was retained – that in the long run an increase in the money supply will create inflation without impacting employment or output. He said that inflation can only reduce unemployment under the natural rate if it is steadily increasing (and that this would ultimately lead to hyperinflation). Therefore he renamed the natural rate as the 'Non-Accelerating Inflation Rate of Unemployment' (NAIRU).

Friedman's colleague at the University of Chicago, Robert Lucas, went one step further and asked why should we only be concerned about historical information? Rather than adapting their expectations, he posits that workers have **rational expectations**, and use all publicly available information to form 'correct' judgements. If this is the case, workers would predict the outcome of any known monetary policy and adjust their behaviour. For example, if the government planned to increase inflation workers would anticipate this and negate any effect on employment (because nominal interest rates would rise when inflation is expected, not experienced). If this is the case, central bankers need to be very careful about what they say.

Indeed the only way a policy can be effective is if it is unanticipated and therefore random. This is what's known as the 'policy ineffectiveness proposition'.[84] A key outcome, that almost all economists are keen to stress, is that it is *unanticipated* changes in inflation that cause the damage.

According to Peter Boettke we can summarise the history of government intervention in the macroeconomy with a simple flow chart. It explains periods of hyperinflation and the causes of sovereign debt crises.[85] It is relevant for Weimar Germany, Mugabe's Zimbabwe and most of the Western world as of today. The 'old adage' of macroeconomics is as follows:

1. Governments run **permanent budget deficits**, which leads to a steadily increasing debt burden.
2. Unable to fund this through taxation or borrowing, ultimately the government seek to **monetise the debt**. The inflation that results creates an artificial boom, by pushing interest rates below their natural rate.
3. When the malinvestment made during the boom becomes evident, there is a bust and the economy enters a **recession**.

At this point, a recovery would involve sorting out the original problems that caused the mess. But given that recessions introduce their own debt, it is tempting for policymakers to just repeat the process for as long as possible. After all, it's not so much that 'in the long run we're all dead', but 'in the long run someone else will get the blame'.

NOTES

1. Boulding, K.E. (1986) Proceedings of the 7th Friends Association for Higher Education Conference, Malone College, p. 4.
2. 'The Big Bear', *The Economist*, 18 October 2008.
3. Friedman, M. and Schwartz, A.J. (1963) *A Monetary History of the United States*, Princeton University Press.
4. Bernanke, B. (2004) Money, Gold, and the Great Depression, H. Parker Willis Lecture in Economic Policy, Washington and Lee University, Lexington, Virginia, 2 March [http://www.federalreserve.gov/boarddocs/speeches/2004/200403022/, accessed 30 September 2013].
5. These comments were made by Rexford Guy Tugwell, quoted in Reed, L.W. (1998) Great myths of the great depression, *The Freeman*, 1 August. [http://www.fee.org/the_freeman/detail/great-myths-of-the-great-depression accessed 30 September 2013].
6. Cole, H.L. and Ohanian, L.E. (2004) New Deal Policies and the Persistence of the Great Depression: A General Equilibrium Analysis, *Journal of Political Economy*, **112**, 813.
7. 'Sticking pins into an icon', *The Economist*, 19 June 2007.
8. Shales, A. (2009) FDR Was a Great Leader, But His Economic Plan Isn't One to Follow, *The Washington Post*, 1 February.
9. 'Paper chains', *The Economist*, 19 August 2010.
10. Higgs, R. (1992) Wartime Prosperity? A Reassessment of the U.S. Economy in the 1940s, *The Journal of Economic History*, **52** (1), 41–60.
11. Romer, C.D. (1991) What Ended the Great Depression?, *The Journal of Economic History*, **52** (4), 757–784.
12. Bernanke, B. (2002) FRB Speech: Remarks by Governor Ben S. Bernanke, at the conference to honor Milton Friedman, University of Chicago, 8 November.

13. Skidelsky, R. (1997) *The Road from Serfdom*, Penguin.
14. The Federal Reserve Bank of Atlanta produce an index of sticky prices [https://www.frbatlanta .org/research/inflationproject/stickyprice/, accessed 30 September 2013].
15. Keynes, J.M. (1924) *Tract on Monetary Reform*, Macmillan.
16. Rizzo, M. (2010) 'In the long run, we are all dead': What did Keynes really mean?, *Think Markets*, 28 June [http://thinkmarkets.wordpress.com/2010/06/28/%E2%80%9Cin-the-long-run-we-are-all-dead%E2%80%9D-what-does-it-mean/, accessed 30 September 2013].
17. 'Wanted: chief firefighter', *The Economist*, 4 June 2011.
18. Williamson wasn't the only British eccentric with a penchant for tunnelling. The reclusive William Cavendish-Scott-Bentinck, 5th Duke of Portland, had a labyrinth of rooms built underneath his estate at Welbeck Abbey, in Nottinghamshire.
19. Whittington-Egan, R. (1985) *Liverpool Characters and Eccentrics*, The Galley Press.
20. Private correspondence with Claire Moorhead, Treasurer for The Friends of Williamson's Tunnels.
21. Whittington-Egan, *Liverpool Characters* (n 19).
22. Whittington-Egan, *Liverpool Characters* (n 19).
23. Private correspondence with Claire Moorhead (n 20).
24. 'The new young Turks', *The Economist*, 8 June 2013.
25. I have presented a fairly sceptical treatment of fiscal stimuli, but it is consistent with the broad consensus amongst economists. As John Cochrane has said, 'economics, as written in professional journals, taught to graduate students and summarized in their textbooks, abandoned fiscal stimulus long ago... [the fiscal stimulus is] taught only for its fallacies'. Cochrane, J.H. (2009) 'Fiscal Stimulus, Fiscal Inflation, or Fiscal Fallacies?' Unpublished manuscript, 27 February [http://faculty.chicagobooth.edu/john.cochrane/research/papers/fiscal2.htm, accessed 7 October 2013].
26. Kling, A. (2008) Lectures on macroeconomics [http://arnoldkling.com/econ/macrolectures.html, accessed 4 October 2013].
27. Barro, R. (2009) Government Spending is No Free Lunch, *Wall Street Journal*, 22 January.
28. Owyang, M.T., Ramey, V.A. and Zubairy, S. (2013) Are government spending multipliers greater during periods of slack? Evidence from 20th century historical data, NBER Working Paper No. 18769.
29. Henderson, D. (2010) Canada's budget triumph, Mercatus Center Working Paper, 30 September.
30. Henderson, Canada's budget triumph (n 29).
31. O'Driscoll, G. (2011) Keynesian death spiral, *Think Markets*, 4 August [http://thinkmarkets.wordpress.com/2011/08/04/%E2%80%9Ckeynesian-death-spiral%E2%80%9D/, accessed 30 September 2013].
32. Barro, R. (1974) Are Bonds Net Wealth?, *Journal of Political Economy*, **82** (6):1095–1117, at 1116.
33. The economic historian Niall Ferguson created a controversy by pointing out that Keynes' emphasis on shorter time horizons coincides with the fact that he was a childless homosexual. The basic idea is that he was less concerned about the future because he didn't have children of his own. And that he didn't have children because he was gay. As far as I'm aware this is a common and semi-serious point that many economists make. But it is grossly unfair. Keynes was known to have wanted children and it is generally understood that Keynes and his wife Lydia Lopokova suffered a miscarriage. Ferguson is aware of these facts, and his public apologies demonstrate a lot more sympathy and awareness than his original, off the cuff comments imply. See Ferguson, N. (2013) An unqualified apology, *NiallFerguson.com*, 5 April [http://www.niallferguson.com/blog/an-unqualified-apology, accessed 30 September 2013], and Ferguson, N. (2013) An open letter to the Harvard community, *The Harvard Crimson*, 7 May [http://www.thecrimson.com/article/2013/5/7/Ferguson-Apology-Keynes/, accessed 30 September 2013].
34. Harford, T. (2008) Why a tax cut just isn't fair on teenagers, *Financial Times*, 31 May.
35. Keynes, J.M. (1942) *Collected Writings*, vol. XXVII, p. 122.

36. Some people argue that in young (i.e. 'infant') industries private firms would not invest in the high fixed costs required to generate economies of scale. There is therefore a role for government to step in and cover the initial costs of production.

37. Friedman, M. (1957) *A Theory of the Consumption Function*, Princeton University Press. When I was a student I was walking with a friend and was approached by a homeless person asking for money. He pointed at my umbrella and implied that I was being tight. I glibly said that due to student debts I was probably poorer than him. But I was forgetting the permanent income hypothesis. My future income would probably be high, so I could afford to be generous today. It was a humbling lesson in economics for me.

38. Friedman, M. (ed.) (1956) *Studies in the Quantity Theory of Money*, The University of Chicago Press.

39. Friedman, M. and Schwartz, A.J. (1963) *A Monetary History of the United States*, Princeton University Press.

40. Buchanan, J. and Wagner, R.E. (1977) *Democracy in Deficit: The political legacy of Lord Keynes*, Academic Press Inc.

41. Nutter, G.W. (1962) *The Growth of Industrial Production in the Soviet Union*, Princeton University Press.

42. 'Cut or loose', *The Economist*, 16 July 2011.

43. Rzonca, A. and Cizkowicz, P. (2005) Non-Keynesian effects of fiscal contraction in new member states, European Central Bank Working Paper Series No. 519.

44. Alesina, A. (2010) Fiscal adjustments: What do we know and what are we doing?, Mercatus Center Working Paper No. 10-61.

45. See 'Cut or loose' (n 42) and Alesina, A. and Ardagna, S. (2010) Large changes in fiscal policy: taxes versus spending, *Tax Policy and the Economy*, Volume 24, The University of Chicago Press, pp. 35–68.

46. Booth, P. (ed.) (2006) Were 364 economists all wrong? Institute of Economic Affairs.

47. Henderson, Canada's budget triumph (n 29).

48. 'And for my next trick', *The Economist*, 6 November 2010.

49. 'Guts and glory', *The Economist*, 9 October 2010.

50. 'Guts and glory' (n 49).

51. Blanchard, O., Griffiths, M. and Gruss, B. (2013) Boom, Bust, Recovery Forensics of the Latvian Crisis, Fall 2013 Brookings Panel on Economic Activity, 19–20 September 2013.

52. Ormerod, P. (2011) 'Expansionary fiscal contraction' *IEA Blog*, 9 November [http://www.iea.org.uk/blog/expansionary-fiscal-contraction, accessed 30 September 2013].

53. 'Far from the meddling crowd', *The Economist*, 30 October 2010.

54. Lilico, A., Holmes, E. and Sameen, H. (2009) Controlling spending and government deficits, *Policy Exchange*, November.

55. Broadbent, B. and Daly, K. (2010) Limiting the Fall-Out from Fiscal Adjustment, Goldman Sachs Global Economics Paper No. 195, 14 April.

56. Alesina, A. and Ardagna, S. (2009) Large changes in fiscal policy: taxes versus spending, NBER Working Paper No. 15438, October.

57. Alesina, A., Carloni, D. and Lecce, G. (2011) The electoral consequences of large fiscal adjustments, NBER Working Paper No. 17655, December 2011.

58. Although there is an emerging research programme that looks at the desirability and feasibility of anarchy. See Stringham, E. (2006) *Anarchy, State and Public Choice*, Edward Elgar.

59. Lilico, A. (2012) Why does cutting government spending mean faster growth?, *The Daily Telegraph*, 29 April.

60. Hayek, F.A. (1931) Reflections on the Pure Theory of Money of Mr. J. M. Keynes, *Economica*, **33**, 270–295.

61. Paulson, H.M. (2010) *On the Brink*, Hachette, p. 319.

62. Moss, V. (2009) London Summit 2009: Alistair Darling vows to do whatever it takes to beat economic crisis, *Daily Mirror,* 15 March [http://www.mirror.co.uk/news/uk-news/london-summit-2009-alistair-darling-382642, accessed 30 September 2013].
63. 'Europe's three great delusions', *The Economist,* 22 May 2010.
64. Giavazzi, F. and Pagano, M. (1990) Can fiscal contractions be expansionary? Tales of two small European countries, NBER Working Paper 3372.
65. Higgs, R. (1997) Regime uncertainty: why the Great Depression lasted so long and why prosperity resumed after the war, *The Independent Review,* **1** (4), 561–590.
66. Ferguson, M.F. and Witte, H.D. (2006) Congress and the Stock Market (13 March). Available at SSRN: http://ssrn.com/abstract=687211.
67. Bradsher, K. (2008) China Shuns Investments in West's Finance Sector, *New York Times,* 3 December.
68. Minutes of the Monetary Policy Committee Meeting, 4 and 5 February 2009, 18 February 2009.
69. Minutes of the Monetary Policy Committee Meeting (n 68).
70. Mankiw, N.G. (2009) Shiller on animal spirits, *Greg Mankiw's Blog,* 27 January [http://gregmankiw.blogspot.com/2009/01/shiller-on-animal-spirits.html, accessed 30 September 2013].
71. 'Much ado about multipliers', *The Economist,* 24 September 2009.
72. Cowen, T. and Tabarrok, A. (2012) *Modern Principles: Macroeconomics,* Worth (2nd edition).
73. Rothbard, M.N. (1962) The Case for the 100 Percent Gold Dollar, in Yeager, L.B. (ed.), *In Search of a Monetary Constitution,* Harvard University Press.
74. Kotlikoff, L.J. (2010) *Jimmy Stewart Is Dead: Ending the World's Ongoing Financial Plague with Limited Purpose Banking,* John Wiley & Sons.
75. Oppers, S.E. (2002) The Austrian Theory of Business Cycles: Old Lessons for Modern Economic Policy? IMF Working Paper.
76. Garrison, R. (2001) *Time and Money,* Routledge.
77. Ito, T. and Mishkin, F. (2004) Two decades of Japanese monetary policy and the deflation problem, NBER Working Paper No. 10878.
78. Greenwood, J. (2006) Monetary policy and the Bank of Japan, in *Issues in Monetary Policy,* Booth, P. and Matthews, K. (eds) John Wiley & Sons.
79. Greenwood is quite convincing in his arguments that these monetary measures were modest in comparison to the fiscal efforts, and his conclusion is that the Bank of Japan should have been a lot more aggressive.
80. Powell, B. (2007) Japan, *The Concise Encyclopedia of Economics.*
81. Fackler, M. (2009) Japan's big-works stimulus is a lesson, *New York Times,* 5 February.
82. Phillips, A.W. (1958) The Relation between Unemployment and the Rate of Change of Money Wage Rates in the United Kingdom, 1861–1957, *Economica,* **25** (100), 283–299.
83. The algebraic form of this model is $W = P^e F(U, Z)$.
84. Lucas, R.E. (1976) Econometric Policy Evaluation: A Critique, *Carnegie-Rochester Conference Series on Public Policy,* **1**, 19–46; Sargent, T. and Wallace, N. (1976) Rational Expectations and the Theory of Economic Policy, *Journal of Monetary Economics,* **2** (2), 169–183.
85. As Peter Bernholz said, 'hyperinflations are always caused by public budget deficits which are largely financed by money creation'. Bernholz, P. (2006) *Monetary Regimes and Inflation: History, economics and political relationships,* Edward Elgar.

CHAPTER 10

International Economics

'Free trade will be the link to bind
Each nation to the other;
'Twill harmonize the rights of man
With every fellow brother.'
—Origin unknown[1]

Joško Joras lives near the Dragonja River, close to the border between Slovenia and Croatia. His mother was Slovenian and spent several years in a Nazi concentration camp during the occupation of Yugoslavia.[2] He has lived in the house for over 40 years, and considers it part of Slovenia. But one day he went to buy a washing machine, and became the centre of an international diplomatic stand-off.

According to Croatia, Joško's house is within their territory, and Croat customs officials wanted him to pay import duties. Joško refused. He decided to use a gravel track between the Slovenian and Croatian border to get home, until the Croatian border police tried to block it off. He responded by erecting a Slovenian flag from his balcony and a large sign that reads, 'This is Slovenia' on the side of his house.

Why does this all matter? How important are national borders? Few topics in economics create as much consternation and debate as trade theory. Whilst economists tend to view the globalisation of exchange as being essentially benign and welfare enhancing, the public often see it as a dangerous threat.[3] This is because from an economic point of view national borders are completely arbitrary. If prosperity stems from the extent of the market and the division of labour, you want it spread over as wide a geographical area as possible. If restrictions on trade (such as tariffs or quotas) make little sense when imposed between different cities, they make no more sense when imposed between different countries.

The aim of this chapter is to demystify some of the concepts relating to trade. We will look at how foreign exchange rates rest on basic demand and supply analysis, and how they affect a firm's performance. We'll also look at how different currency regimes can impact strategic planning, and present some of the key things economists know about financial crises.

10.1   GLOBALISATION AND TRADE THEORY

One day a stranger arrives in a town.[4] Amidst much fanfare he declares that he has made a discovery – a remarkable discovery – and that he can make televisions and mobile phones and refrigerators and cars and all sorts of other goods much more cheaply than existing companies. People are dubious, but watch as he buys up a large plot of remote, coastal land and erects a gigantic factory. He hires 5000 people, who all sign a contract to promise *never* to reveal his secret, and none of them do. Each day, they go through the gates in silence, and each day they go home again. Interested bystanders watch them, and try to talk to them, but nothing.

It isn't only people who turn up each morning, as trucks full of grain and coal also arrive. Then, one day, the mysterious entrepreneur announces that they're ready. And with that, truckloads of televisions, mobile phones, refrigerators, cars and all sorts of other goods start rolling out of the factory and into shops all over the country. People can't get enough – the products are better quality and cheaper than what they are used to, and everyone wants to know his secret. He is hailed as a hero, a modern Edison or Bell. His employees are well paid and content. His customers delighted. Investors rush to invest. Politicians court and praise him. But not everyone is happy: his competitors are livid, and go to extreme lengths to learn how he does it. They call him a 'monopolist' and lobby government to intervene. 'His technology is ruining us!' they claim. But their cries are exposed as the hollow whimper of special interests, unable to keep up with technological progress.

Then, a little while later, a journalist manages to get a job in the factory. He brings in a secret camera and sees something incredible. There are no machines! There is no factory! The property simply leads down to the seafront and a large dock. The grain and coal are being loaded up onto container ships that take them overseas. And from the other direction they arrive with televisions, mobile phones, refrigerators and cars. The entrepreneur doesn't produce anything at all. His discovery is *trade*.

The journalist exposes the secret and there is a public outcry. Politicians lament foreign competition and announce public spending to boost domestic manufacturing industry. Consumer groups boycott the products because of cheap foreign labour. The factory closes. The workers lose their jobs. Domestic prices go up. Quality goes down. And the entrepreneur is reviled.

When Adam Smith wrote the *Wealth of Nations* in 1776, one of his chief accomplishments was to critique the prevailing views about trade policy. The sixteenth century to late eighteenth century were dominated by **mercantilism** – the belief that national wealth is maximised by increasing exports and accumulating precious metals in return. This coincided with the emergence of nation-states and they competed for resources through trade policy. Smith provided a coherent and penetrating critique of mercantilism by arguing three main things:

1. Trade is positive sum. When two people exchange goods it is because they both believe they are being made better off, and whether they are in two different countries makes no difference.
2. Specialisation leads to growth. A division of labour means that we can concentrate on more efficient production, and allows us to trade for things we can't make for ourselves.
3. Laissez-faire policy is truly egalitarian. Mercantile trade policies help merchants by increasing the cost to consumers. An egalitarian trade policy would help consumers (by allowing cheap imports) rather than producers (who want to keep prices high).

At the time Smith's insights led to a revolution of thought away from mercantile protectionism and towards nineteenth-century free trade. However mercantilism struck back. The Great Depression saw the end of economic liberalism, and World War II unleashed a military-industrial complex that once again sought to dictate trade policy based on the special interests of producers.

But what are the arguments in favour of free trade? The main one is the concept of comparative advantage.

I enjoy mowing the lawn, and I'm pretty good at it. I don't just cut the grass; I pick out weeds, put down seed, tidy the edges and borders, and roll it into a nice striped pattern. I'll often split my weekends between writing articles and gardening. But on some occasions I have a deadline and my time becomes scarcer. My decision about what to do becomes an economic one, because there's an opportunity cost involved. Each hour in the garden is one less hour writing. I can't do both. So I prioritise whatever is most valuable to me, in this case writing. And I pay a neighbour's son, Rudyard, to mow the lawn. The cost of getting him to do it is lower than not having enough time to finish my writing.

So I settle down in my study and begin typing away, but after a while I decide to check up on him. It's frustrating to watch. He can't mow in a straight line, keeps having a break, and is taking far longer than I would. I'm tempted to say 'Forget it! I'll do it myself'. In economic terms we can say that I am the more productive gardener, *and* the more productive writer. I can mow more square feet per hour than him, and can write more pages per hour. I have an **absolute advantage** over him in both gardening and writing.

But this doesn't mean that I should do both. Even though I am *more* productive at both tasks, I'm not *as more* productive at both. If I do what I'm the 'most best' at, and he does what he's 'least worst' at, we can both benefit from cooperating!

This is the principle of **comparative advantage:** exchange is mutually beneficial if one produces that which he can do at *lowest opportunity cost*. Rudyard is able to mow the lawn at lower cost to me than if I did it myself, in precisely the same way that whenever we buy a good or service, it'll usually be far cheaper than if we gave up the time and resources necessary to make it ourselves.

If my writing takes off, and the demands on my time increase, Rudyard and I will probably adopt a routine. And the more time he spends mowing the lawn the better he will become. Even my frustration at having someone perform the task to a lower quality level than I can do it myself will help matters: I am richer as a result of the arrangement, and can provide capital equipment (such as a better lawnmower) to help him out. It is because of **specialisation** and investment that he may well become a better gardener than me. An absolute advantage is a function of our skills and expertise, and these are subject to change.

This is the process in which we have a **division of labour**, meaning that jobs tend to be tasks that are related to each other, but involve separate operations. Knowing where to specialise and how to divide up labour is the driving force behind the massive output and productivity of modern industry. The logic is pretty simple – if it's cheaper to buy something than it is to make it yourself, buy it. If it's cheaper to import something than it is to produce it yourself, import it.[5]

Although earlier writers had already alluded to the principle of comparative advantage, David Ricardo made the first systematic exposition in the early nineteenth century. He noted that different countries not only have different natural resources, but since labour and capital were (relatively) immobile they will have different cost advantages. In other words, some countries will be more efficient at producing certain goods than others.

He used the example of England and Portugal, both producing wine and cloth. Even though Portugal was *more* productive at both, it would not be *as more* productive at both. So if Portugal specialises in the product it is 'most best' at, and England specialises in what it is 'least worst' at, they can trade with each other for their mutual benefit. This is a phenomenal finding – that *all* countries can be made better off through trade.

We can therefore see the importance of comparative advantage:

- It is ubiquitous, since it exists wherever there are different skills and/or different resources.
- If we can't all do everything ourselves (i.e. if we face a constraint), it's a means to allocate production so that our total output increases.
- It is a signal that tells us about relative productivity, so that we know what is our lowest opportunity cost, and therefore what to specialise in.
- The more productive in society benefit from being able to concentrate on what they do the best, and can use their extra income to trade with those with lower opportunity costs.
- The less productive in society can utilise their low opportunity cost and find employment. If people specialise in what they have a comparative advantage in, they will become more productive.
- Absolute costs don't determine the gains from trade, *relative* costs do.
- Society in general benefits from the increase in incomes, output and productivity.
- The only way to have sustainable increases in real incomes is to have genuine increases in real productivity.

The implication for management is clear. Your *competitive* advantage lies in where you have a *comparative* advantage. The principle of comparative advantage is little more than the application of opportunity cost reasoning to trade theory. But it is the bedrock of many trade models, and we can see how a few of the most important ones build directly upon the version described above:

- Heckscher-Ohlin model[6]
    They consider multiple factors of production (land, labour and capital) and show how differences in factor endowments determine a country's comparative advantage. For example Australia produces more food than the UK because they have a greater endowment of land.
- Stolper-Samuelson theory[7]
    An increase in the relative price of a good increases the return to the factor that is used most intensively. If the price of wool jumpers increases, then there will be an increase in real wages to the (labour intensive) wool industry, but a decline in the real wages to those in capital intensive industries.
- Rybczynski theory[8]
    An increase in endowment will cause the output of the good that uses that factor more intensely to increase disproportionately. If there's increased migration to Australia, then production of labour intensive goods will increase, but production of capital intensive goods will decline.

As time has passed the mathematics within the models has become more complicated, and the nuances have been focused on. But the statements above are consistent with common sense – trade theory tells us that an economy will be relatively effective at producing goods that are intensive to the factors with which the country is relatively well endowed.

It would be an exaggeration to say that globalisation is entirely benign, and we will look in more detail at this in Chapter 12. But the reason trade models form such a central core of economic theory is because trade is seen as the way in which we increase our wealth. What is clear is that the absence of trade – autarky – is brutal. Fortunately, self-sufficiency is impossible. Next time you're sitting at a bar take a look at the bottles behind it. Vodka from Russia and Sweden; whisky from Scotland; red wine from Argentina, Chile and France; white wine from Australia and South Africa; gin from England; bitter from Ireland; lager from Belgium and Holland. Every bottle having touched innumerable hands on their respective journeys. One of the most quintessentially English products is Worcestershire sauce, but look at the list of ingredients. You don't find anchovies in Worcester![9]

Some of the most controversial debates focus on how corporations participate in international trade, but often this rests on a misunderstanding of certain key terms:

- Outsourcing: The delegation of activities to a specialist service provider
- Offshoring: The delegation of activities to a foreign location
- Foreign Direct Investment (FDI): The cross-border acquisition of physical capital.

Immediately we can see one source of popular confusion. 'Outsourcing' has nothing to do with international trade per se – if a company hires a private firm to clean their offices, then this is outsourcing. If we apply the concept of comparative advantage, it should be clear why outsourcing is important. However too much outsourcing is dangerous. Boeing outsourced a lot of the production of the 787 Dreamliner, but encountered major difficulties. They were unable to ensure that all of the component parts fitted together, or that the subcontractors completed the work on time. Ultimately they felt that they had to buy some of the subcontractors, so that they could exercise the managerial control they needed to complete the work.[10] Firms must weigh up the costs and benefits of too much outsourcing, relative to too little. Often times the press use outsourcing to refer to companies that move jobs overseas, but provided those jobs are still being done by the same company this is in fact 'offshoring'.

The main argument in favour of offshoring is that it can be a more efficient way of performing a task. Think of call centres as an example. Many UK firms have offshore call centres, in countries like India. (These would be owned by the firm, but based overseas. They are therefore also an example of FDI.) The main reason is cost – a significant part of the cost of a call centre is labour, and wage rates in India tend to be lower. It isn't just that costs are lower though. As more firms offshore it becomes an incentive to invest in complementary assets. Whether it's training of the workers, the infrastructure of the phone networks or the ease and convenience of travelling to the site, these are all positive spillover effects that increase the efficiency of the Indian call centre industry. In the UK a popular backlash began to develop, as Indian operators were seen to be less competent than those based in the UK. Stories about operators mispronouncing English words, or indeed being difficult to understand, meant that firms began to reassess their strategy. More recently, there has been a trend for 'onshoring', where operations return from overseas. An analyst sums it up:

> *Offshoring call centres has often resulted in reduced customer service quality, and latterly increased customer attrition as other providers now offer 'UK-only call centres'. This has become a real differentiator in the UK retail, banking and mobile telecoms sector.*[11]

So perhaps this is a nice example of consumer sovereignty. Since customers prefer UK-based call centres, firms respond to provide them. But if this was the case, why not just have premium rate phone numbers for mildly xenophobic customers? There may also be a cost explanation, because wage rates in India have been rising, reducing the cost advantage for offshoring. Ultimately managers must weigh up the costs of labour, with the costs of training, the costs of technology and indeed the costs of management. Outsourcing and offshoring are simply two additional margins on which those tradeoffs need to be made.[12] Although it is important to stress that they are not the same thing, they perform similar benefits for firms. Managers should consider the following advantages to both outsourcing and offshoring:[13]

- Reduce operating, development, sales or other costs
- Allow you to focus on your comparative advantage
- Get access to best practices and innovations of specialist firms
- Get access to human capital
- Increase flexibility and scalability of activities
- Get a foothold in the global economy.

It may be the case that if you value domestic jobs over foreign jobs, then the arguments in favour of offshoring should be counterbalanced by this. But why would you think this? Why should jobs in the country you live in be worth more than jobs in other (and typically poorer) ones? Some of those who oppose offshoring like to present it as bad economics and argue that it harms the domestic economy. But yet again there's a gulf between how professional economists and the general public view this. Whilst almost 80% of the general public agreed with the statement 'The "Buy American" policy is good for manufacturing employment' only around 10% of economics experts did.[14] Perhaps it is the economists who are wrong. But perhaps not.

10.2 BALANCE OF PAYMENTS

A country's Balance of Payments (BoP) can look daunting but in reality is merely an application of double-entry book keeping to national accounts. They measure the flow of payments between one country and the rest of the world. International transactions that create an inflow of domestic currency are a credit (+), because they are a source of funds. An outflow of domestic currency is a debit (−), because they are a use of funds. Therefore exports are credits (i.e. a source of foreign exchange), whilst imports are debits (a use of foreign exchange).[15] For simplicity I will assume that we are in the UK and the domestic currency is the pound sterling (£).

The 'balance' stems from the fact that the flow of goods and services across borders *must* be equal to the flow of funds that finance capital accumulation, and it is defined as the following:

$$BoP = \text{Current Account} + \text{Capital Account} \, (+ \text{Financial Account})$$

Traditionally the BoP was simply the relationship between the current and capital accounts; however the IMF uses a separate item. But we can merge the capital and financial account. A typical BoP will look similar to the following:

1. Current Account
   - Trade balance/Net Exports/(X−M)

- Net investment income
- Net transfers received.
2. Capital Account/Financial Account
   - Foreign direct investment (FDI)
   - Portfolio investment
   - Other investment
   - Reserve assets.

By definition we know that 1 = 2, however in practice they don't always add up. Therefore there is usually a final line on a BoP called 'net errors and omissions', which is simply the difference between the two.

Looking at the current account, the first (and usually largest) item is known as the 'trade balance', or 'net exports'. Now that we are thinking about international trade, we can go back to the equation for total spending in an economy, and realise that it is still incomplete. In addition to consumption, investment and government spending, a further source of demand comes from foreign trade. If we export (X) more than we import (M), and have a positive trade balance, this will boost aggregate demand.

$$AD = C + I + G + (X - M)$$

If a country has a trade deficit (which implies a current account deficit),[16] it means that they are importing more than they are exporting. How is it possible to import more than you export? There are really two ways. The first is by drawing down foreign reserves. The second way is to borrow money from overseas. If you think of yourself as a 'country', the only way you can 'import' (consume) more than you 'export' (produce) is either by drawing down your savings, or by borrowing from outside sources. The capital account shows these sources of financing. Whilst FDI is investment in physical infrastructure, 'portfolio investment' tends to be more liquid assets such as government bonds. Some BoP also have a category of 'other investment' which are things like equities (i.e. shares in companies) or corporate bonds. FDI is typically viewed as being more favourable to the recipient country, because it is a more long-term, stable investment. But precisely because indirect investment (also known as 'portfolio investment') is easier to reverse, this may make it more advantageous to the company doing the investing.

There are obviously lots of factors that influence the trade balance, but economists tend to point to three main ones:

- Domestic Income (Y)

   The richer *we* are the more imports we demand. And if M rises then (X−M) *falls*. Therefore there is an inverse relationship between domestic income and the trade balance.
- Foreign income (Y*)

   The richer *foreigners* are the more of our exports they demand. And if X rises then (X−M) *rises*. Therefore there is a positive relationship between foreign income and the trade balance.
- Exchange rate (E)

   If our currency becomes less valuable (depreciates) our exports become cheaper for foreigners to buy, and imported goods become more expensive to us. And if X rises and M falls then (X−M) *rises*. Therefore there is an ambiguous relationship between the exchange rate and the trade balance – it depends on whether we use a direct or indirect quote (we will discuss this in the next section).

If a country has a trade deficit, then it is reasonable to expect that they (i) also have a current account deficit; and (ii) are a net borrower on global markets. Is this a bad thing? Indeed it is typical of rich countries (such as the US and the UK) to import more goods than they export; hence they run current account deficits. But to maintain the balance of payments a current account deficit *must* result in a capital account surplus. You might hear commentators say the following:

> *The US must borrow more than $3 billion per day from foreigners to finance its huge trade deficits.*

But the following is *just as true*:

> *Foreigners must sell the US goods and services worth more than $3 billion per day to finance their huge purchase of US assets.*[17]

People often refer to the 'twin deficits' of a budget deficit (when government spending > government revenue) and a trade deficit (when imports > exports). But it is important to realise that:

- A current account deficit is not necessarily a debt
  If a foreign company such as Sony sells a Playstation 2 for £100 and uses that cash to buy shares in a British company such as Unilever, *there is no debt*.
- Potential political risks are part of a deeper problem
  People may be concerned about foreigners owning large amounts of domestic assets but this gives them an incentive to maintain their value.
- Budget deficits help to create current account deficits
  A trade deficit (or the inflow of foreign investment that *allows* for a trade deficit) off-sets insufficient private (S) and government (T−G) savings. The real problem is therefore the budget deficit, and the current account deficit may just be a symptom.

The main point is that it depends on *why* there is a current account deficit. For emerging markets this might be due to the fact that they are making lots of investments and will experience higher future growth as a result. In which case it may well be perfectly sensible. But as Paul Blustein says, it is true that 'a country can run such a deficit only if foreigners are willing to provide the money used for purchasing imports'.[18] If the current account deficit reflects an underlying indebtedness, then it may well be a problem. But not in and of itself.

10.3 FOREIGN EXCHANGE MARKETS

As with any market the best way to understand changes in a foreign exchange market is to use demand and supply analysis. The equilibrium 'price' and 'quantity' of any currency will be the interaction between demand and supply – the daily balance of expectations. Therefore we need to understand the driving forces on both sides of the market (for simplicity we assume that imports are price-elastic):

1. Demand for £
   a. Foreign consumers who wish to import UK goods and services and need to convert their foreign currency into £.

    b. UK exporters who have sold goods and services for foreign currency and wish to convert this back into £.

    c. Overseas investors/governments who wish to invest in UK assets (e.g. stocks in British companies or UK bonds).

  2. Supply of £

    a. UK consumers who wish to import foreign goods and services need foreign currency and therefore relinquish £.

    b. Foreign companies that have sold goods and services to UK consumers and want to convert their £ into their own currency.

    c. UK investors who want to buy assets in foreign countries.

    d. The domestic money supply will also be a chief driver of the supply of £.

As with any commodity if the demand for £ rises so does its value – it appreciates. If the demand for £ falls then it depreciates. If the supply of £ rises then it becomes less valuable – it depreciates. If the supply of £ falls then it appreciates.

In terms of economic fundamentals just remember the relationship between changes in demand and supply and the changes in value. I'm using 'appreciate' to mean 'become more valuable' and 'depreciate' to mean 'become less valuable'. Whether or not the actual exchange rate goes 'up' or 'down' depends on the type of quote. The reason this is confusing is because we always report the value of a currency in relation to another currency. Therefore the demand for £ may go up, but whether the exchange rate goes up depends on whether we're looking at the number of £ we can get per unit of foreign currency, or the number of units of foreign currency we can get per £.

On 6 September 2012 the ECB announced a new policy of buying troubled assets, and the exchange rate (approximately) changed as follows:

12pm: 1.264 USD/EUR
2pm: 1.257 USD/EUR

In other words, at 12pm €1000 was worth $1264; but by 2pm it was only worth $1257. We can say that the purchasing power of the Euro fell, or that it *depreciated*.[19] By contrast, the Dollar is worth more in terms of the Euro – it has appreciated. But it is important to be careful here. It is also tempting to say that the exchange rate *fell* (from 1.264 to 1.257), but this is only because we are looking at an indirect quote, which is how many units of foreign currency (in this case $) you get per 1 unit of home currency (€). By contrast a direct exchange rate is when you see how many units of home currency you get for 1 unit of foreign currency. Given that these are just two ways to explain the same relationship, it is easy to switch between them. A direct rate is simply the reciprocal of the indirect rate (i.e. it is 1 divided by the indirect rate). In our case this gives the following:

12pm: 0.791 EUR/USD
2pm: 0.796 EUR/USD

Here, at 12pm $1000 was worth €791, but by 2pm it was worth €796. Since you now need more Euros to buy the same amount of dollars, we can see that the Euro has declined in value (it has still *depreciated*). But in this instance the exchange rate has *risen*. It's common for American newspapers to use direct exchange rates, but there can be ambiguity about which currency is the 'home' one in any situation. It is conventional to simply write an exchange rate such that it is greater than 1, which means that in any list of rates there will be a mixture of direct and indirect quotes. For this reason it's better to think in terms of increasing in value (appreciation) or decreasing in value (depreciation) rather than going 'up' or 'down'.

There are four key drivers of foreign exchange rates:

1. Interest rates

    If interest rates fall in the UK, UK bonds become relatively less attractive to investors. This will result in a reduction in the demand for £ (effect 1c), a fall in the quantity of £ being traded and a currency depreciation. The process of borrowing money from countries with low interest rates, and depositing it in countries with higher interest rates, is known as '**the carry trade**', because investors earn a spread (the 'carry'). According to *The Economist*, in all but three of the years from 1979 to 2009 the carry trade offered a positive return.[20]

2. Inflation

    If there is domestic inflation there will be an increase in the supply of £ through channel 2d. Note that the increase in the money supply can be considered to have caused both the price inflation *and* the currency depreciation (these are two sides of the same coin). In addition a higher rate of inflation will reduce the real return on UK assets and reduce the demand for £ through channel 1c. Consequently the amount of £ being traded will increase but the currency will depreciate.

3. The trade balance

    Let's assume that there's an exogenous increase in imports causing the trade deficit to increase. Channel 2a shows how domestic consumers need to acquire foreign currency (and therefore relinquish £), whilst 2b shows how the foreign companies that sell the imported goods will seek to convert the £ into foreign currency. This leads to an increase in the supply of £, an increase in the quantity of £ being traded and a depreciation. Similarly a fall in exports (the other way in which a current account deficit can increase) will lead to a reduction in the demand for £ (foreigners have less need for them) and the value of the £ will fall. Persistent current account deficits cause currencies to depreciate.

4. Economic growth

    Provided the economy is healthy, current account deficits can be sustainable. If investors are confident about the long-term prospects in an economy they will want to invest in it; this increases the demand for £ and causes a currency appreciation.

Perhaps the easiest way to think of the above is to put yourself in the position of an investor, and consider whether each event is likely to encourage you to move money either in or out of the UK. An inflow of funds causes the price to rise (an appreciation in the value of the £), whilst an outflow would cause the price to fall (a depreciation).

Therefore a strong currency tends to be driven by the following:

1. Expectations of higher interest rates
2. Low and stable inflation
3. Trend towards a trade surplus (i.e. higher exports)
4. Healthy economic growth prospects (e.g. rising GDP per capita, low unemployment, high industrial production, low budget deficit).

And of course the opposite of the above will all weaken the currency. Although these are the main 'drivers', there is an infinite list of items that can be said to influence foreign exchange rates. Some of the more common are a reduction in the budget deficit; strong stock market returns; lower tax rates and higher productivity. Traditionally British firms would pay their Chinese suppliers in hard currency (e.g. dollars), but Tesco are an example of one that has sought to pay them in the yuan. Legal changes that would allow trades to be settled in the yuan would alter the demand and supply dynamics of that currency and related ones.[21] But the whole point of having capital markets is for investors to try to work out what other factors will influence market prices. Ultimately investors are not even trying to work out what influences the price, but what people *think* will influence the price.

The key thing to realise is that there are so many factors that influence forex markets it is impossible to isolate the impact of any one change. Therefore we can never be sure how a change in economic fundamentals will affect the exchange rate – this is something we rely upon the market process to tell us. Indeed we can only make theoretical statements about how we'd expect certain changes to impact the exchange rate ceteris paribus.

For example, although we'd normally expect an increase in interest rates to cause a currency to appreciate in value (channel 1c) this isn't necessarily the case. In Chapter 8 we saw that if the UK government raises interest rates it would cause a reduction in AD and slow down the economy. It is conceivable that – in the judgement of some investors – the prospect of reduced growth outweighed the additional return from UK assets. And since the exchange rate is a market price, it will always reflect the balance of expectations. There is no mechanical link between different macroeconomic variables. It depends on how new events are interpreted. As HSBC's David Bloom says,

> the implications of QE on currency are not uniform and are based on market percep-
> tions rather than some mechanistic link.[22]

When the value of a currency is given with respect to another currency it can be hard to gauge absolute movements. For example, bad domestic policy could coincide with an appreciation of the currency if it's being measured against one that has done even worse. There are therefore two important adjustments we can make:

The **Real Exchange Rate** is the price of foreign goods in terms of domestic goods – it shows us the relative prices of *goods*, not *currencies*. As with any 'real' variable it controls for the difference in inflation. If we are based in the UK and are looking at the US we make the following adjustments:

- Take the price of the US good in US dollars (P^*)
- Multiply by the exchange rate (E) to find the price of the US good in UK pounds ($=EP^*$)
- Divide this by the price of UK goods in UK pounds (P) to find the *real* exchange rate (ε)
- Thus $\varepsilon = (EP^*)/P$.

Economists disagree on the causes of real depreciation and appreciation, but it is common for emerging markets to suffer from strong real appreciations in the prelude to a currency crisis. A real appreciation means that domestic goods have become more expensive relative to foreign goods, and that the country has reduced its competitiveness. The fact that exporters' costs are higher than their (foreign) competitors', and domestic firms face more cost inflation than their (foreign) rivals, generates pressure to devalue. The reason for the appreciation may be domestic inflation, or increases in interest rates that intend to generate capital inflows.

TABLE 10.1   Currency changes

People who favour a strong UK currency	People who favour a weak UK currency
British holidaymakers who go abroad	UK companies that wish to export overseas
British expats who live overseas	Foreign consumers who wish to import UK goods and services
UK consumers who wish to import foreign goods and services	UK citizens with foreign earnings
Foreign companies that wish to export to us	The domestic tourism industry

With so many different exchange rates, governments tend to focus on a **trade-weighted index** to judge the value of the domestic currency. For example the nominal effective exchange rate for the Euro is an average rate, weighted by the share of trade done with 21 major trading partners.

But do we want a 'strong currency'? It sounds good, but there are always two sides of the story. Having a 'strong' currency is a mixed blessing – there are winners and losers for all currency movements, as shown in Table 10.1.

If markets are functioning properly the same good should have the same price even if it is in different locations. This is known as 'the law of one price' and rests on the assumption that arbitrage will eliminate any price differentials. This simple theory is the basis of the **purchasing power parity** (PPP) theory of exchange rate determination. PPP implies that over time exchange rates should adjust to ensure that the price of a basket of identical goods costs the same in different countries. If – having taken the market exchange rate – a basket of goods is cheaper in one country than another, it suggests that the currency may be undervalued. Generally speaking, economists think that in the long run foreign currency will be determined by PPP.

Since 1986 *The Economist* magazine has promoted a light-hearted application of PPP by using a single good in its basket: a Big Mac. In June 2012 a Big Mac cost $4.20 in America, but – at market exchange rates – it cost $6.81 in Switzerland and only $2.44 in China. In theory it should cost the same. The fact that it is more expensive in Switzerland implies the Swiss Franc *may* be overvalued relative to the dollar. And the fact it's cheaper in China is evidence that the yuan *may* be undervalued. All else being equal, we would expect the Swiss franc to depreciate relative to the dollar, and the Chinese yuan to appreciate, until their respective purchasing powers were the same. There are several reasons why a Big Mac is a suitable good to use:

- It is available everywhere.
- It is the same product everywhere (in India they don't sell Big Macs, but we can use the Maharaja Mac, made with chicken as a substitute).
- They're produced locally, as opposed to imported.
- It is a reasonably competitive market.

Of course there are some downsides too:

- They can't easily be traded across borders.
- Prices are distorted by differences in the cost of non-traded local inputs (such as rent or wages).

This suggests that the Big Mac index may be more useful when comparing countries at a similar level of economic development, but in reality it should not be useful at all. The fact that it has demonstrated better predictive power than a number of highly complex indices that incorporate a large basket of multiple goods simply demonstrates the difficulty of predicting foreign exchange movements.

The **Balassa-Samuelson effect** is an important offshoot of PPP and suggests that because productivity varies more in countries that have a high amount of traded goods, real wages will be relatively higher, and this will lead to an appreciating real exchange rate.[23]

One of the reasons why foreign exchange can appear daunting is because it ties in closely to other types of financial markets. Currencies can be used in derivative contracts, which are contracts that derive their value from an underlying asset (in this case the currency itself). Investors can use currency derivatives to manage their risk or speculate on changes in the market. There are five main types:

1. Spot transactions – spot rates are the exchange rates that apply to the present moment in time. If you exchange foreign currency at an airport you will be paying the spot rate.
2. Forwards – these are when people agree to exchange currency at some point in the future. Whether or not the forward rate is higher or lower than the spot rate depends on whether the market expects that currency to appreciate or depreciate. They are based on forward contracts, which are agreements to make a future exchange at a fixed price. This means that regardless of what happens to the spot rate, you are locked into an agreement. Contracts are typically for one, three or six months into the future, and offer an opportunity to hedge against potential currency fluctuations.
3. Swaps – if you receive lots of payments in foreign exchange it is possible to 'swap' the stream of foreign currency with someone who is in the opposite situation. For example a Croatian company may receive lots of Serbian dinars and a Serbian company may receive lots of Croatian kuna. Rather than each of them having to buy multiple forward contracts, or indeed expose themselves to currency risk, they can simply agree to swap the currency at a prior agreed rate.
4. Futures – futures contracts relate to a standard volume of currency that is exchanged at a future date. Unlike forward contracts (which tend to be customised to one particular buyer), they are standardised and traded on public markets. This means they are less useful for firms that want to hedge their risk, but more appropriate for firms wishing to speculate on currency changes.
5. Options – these are contracts that give the owner the right to either buy or sell currency at a predefined price at some point in the future. Unlike forward or futures contracts you are not obliged to 'own' the currency once the contract matures, and if it doesn't move in the direction you hope for you can cut your losses and simply pay the premium.

10.4 CURRENCY REGIMES

We previously saw how governments may outsource their monetary authority to a panel of independent economists, as a way to make a credible commitment not to create inflation. We also saw how countries can use a commodity currency, which binds their hands by linking inflation to something with a relatively fixed supply.

Somewhere between these two options, we can think about a country retaining a fiat currency, but tying it to the decisions made in other countries. If this is the case, rather than the exchange rate fluctuating according to the forces of demand and supply (a 'floating exchange rate'), it will be 'fixed' to a designated target.

We said before that a country may have foreign reserves in order to fund a current account deficit. Foreign reserves are a means to pay for imports and pay off creditors. But this was on the assumption that the foreign exchange rate is set by market forces. If a country decides to intervene in the market and 'fix' their exchange rate, then they will need foreign reserves in order to do so. Countries that are operating a fixed exchange rate require **official financing** to maintain the value of the currency. They are able to intervene in the market by selling their own currencies and accumulating foreign exchange reserves. Alternatively, they can buy their own currency and deplete their foreign exchange reserves. This is typically dollars – they account for around 60% of currency reserves.[24]

The main advantage to fixing your exchange rate is if the currency you're fixing yourself to has a stronger reputation than your own. Several countries in Latin America have a history of monetary mismanagement, and it's simply not credible for them to 'promise' to try harder. But by fixing their exchange rate with the dollar they piggyback on the economic reputation of the Federal Reserve. If the currency being fixed to is a well-managed one, then this will serve as an inflation anchor. We might expect confidence in the currency – and the economy itself – to increase, with investors more willing to put their money in. Almost by definition a fixed exchange rate will be more stable and predictable than a floating one. This will help entrepreneurs form expectations, and may increase trade (and indeed may especially increase trade between the countries whose currency is tied). There may also be political capital to be gained from closer economic links.

As ever though, there is a downside. Like any market price exchange rate movements provide information. Instead of seeing the daily balance of expectations, you see only a government policy decision. And since that policy decision is to use monetary policy to hit an exchange rate target, they cannot use monetary policy for other targets. If the economy is in a recession the central bank can no longer change interest rates to boost aggregate demand, since interest rates are already being used as part of the exchange rate target. Countries that fix their currencies give up independent monetary policy of the type discussed in Chapter 8.

In April 1991 the Argentine government announced a policy called 'convertability'. This was an attempt to improve the economy by pegging the value of the peso to the US dollar. They announced that the US dollar would become legal tender in Argentina, and interchangeable with the peso. People would have the freedom to switch currencies, and the Argentinean government was committed to maintain the value. This meant that the central bank needed to keep enough 'hard' currency (i.e. US dollars and gold) in reserve to fully back all of the pesos in circulation. This limited their ability to increase the money supply, because if people became suspicious they would attempt to redeem their pesos for dollars. The government was voluntarily handing over the keys of the printing press to the United States. It is like someone with a gambling addiction deciding to cut up their credit card (or at least giving it to a responsible uncle to look after).

The problem with any fixed exchange rate, though, is that the public (and in particular the markets) may not buy it. If people try to offload pesos this would reduce their value relative to the dollar. To keep the fix the government would have to find other ways to encourage people to want pesos. They'd have to raise interest rates. Generally speaking, economists maintain that we can only ever have two of the following:

- Free capital movements
- Fixed exchange rates
- Independent domestic monetary policy.

If an exchange rate is fixed, then there is a lot of stability. But this stability can be an illusion. If investors are losing confidence then the government will be going to ever-greater lengths to keep the fix. If interest rates are high this will cause a recession, and could be very unpopular. It almost becomes a battle of wills, as investors test just how 'committed' the government is to the fix. If there's sufficient pressure, there will always be a point at which the government decides that the cost of maintaining the fix (in terms of high interest rates) is simply not worth the benefits. In many cases it just comes down to who has deeper pockets.

When the fixed exchange rate is abandoned, we can see dramatic exchange rate movements. Therefore despite offering stability whilst the fixed exchange rate applies, they open the potential for a currency crisis should the fixed rate become too far from where the market thinks it should be. Indeed the definition of a currency crisis is often the abandonment of a fixed exchange rate. As Milton Friedman said, 'under a floating exchange rate there cannot be and never has been a foreign exchange crisis.'[25]

There are varying degrees to which countries that 'fix' their exchange rates though. The general term is a **currency board**, but this is sometimes referred to as a 'peg'. So called because the government chooses an external currency and 'pegs' the value. It could be 1 to 1, or it could be at any specified rate. Usually the peg will be to a trading partner, or a country with a good reputation. It could be pegged to a basket of different currencies. But you do not necessarily need the permission of the country you are pegging to.

It is also possible to have a **currency band**, where instead of choosing a single rate, the government chooses a corridor within which they will keep it. This is almost like a hybrid between a floating and fixed regime, since market sentiment will determine the exchange rate within a particular range, but if it threatens to become either above the ceiling or below the floor the monetary authorities will intervene.

In some cases countries decide to become even more closely tied than a currency board and create a **currency union**. This is such an extreme type of fixed exchange rate that they in fact share a currency. The main arguments in favour of this are similar to the arguments in favour of a currency board, and you could say that since it is even harder to abandon it is even more of a credible commitment. On the other hand, this simply shifts the stakes to another level, because the costs of breaking out of a currency union are even higher than for a currency band. There is a fairly conventional set of assumptions about what constitutes an **optimal currency area**, i.e. the type of characteristics countries should exhibit if they want to share a currency. These are:

- Labour mobility

  Since the labour market is a key part of how the economy responds to shocks, wages need to be flexible and it needs to be possible for people to move within the currency area. This doesn't just refer to things like visa restrictions and employment law, but whether there is a common language and cultural ties.

- Similar shocks

   Since the countries give up their ability to use monetary policy to deal with economic shocks, it is better if they face similar shocks. The greater the differences in the economies, the less likely a common monetary policy will be suitable for all members.
- Fiscal transfers

   If there is a boom in one of the countries, and a recession in the other, and rigidities are preventing labour markets from adjusting, one option is simply using tax money generated in the growing country to boost demand in the one that is suffering. This is where issues such as solidarity come in, because it may be unpopular to simply transfer money from some regions to others.

The economies of California and New York are very different, but most economists think that a common currency is appropriate because US labour markets are reasonably flexible. But given that they face different shocks it isn't unheard of to question whether they should have the same currency. It's also important to realise that fiscal transfers are not a necessary condition for a currency area. America was not a 'transfer union' until after the New Deal. As *The Economist* points out, in the first century of America's existence the federal government only spent about 2% of GDP, which is similar to the European Union's share of GDP today. It's not so much that fiscal transfers are a required part of a currency union, it's that they provide an additional means to help a currency union survive if it starts to run into problems.

We briefly discussed a currency crisis. However this is just one type of financial crisis. William White uses the following forms of financial crises:[26]

1. Banking crisis (B)
2. Currency crisis (C)
3. Sovereign debt crisis (D)
4. Inflation crisis (I)
5. Stock market crisis (+).

Economists Carmen Reinhart and Kenneth Rogoff have done some controversial historical work looking at all types, and they discuss ways in which they feed into each other. For example, they find that banking crises tend to precede and predict sovereign debt crises.[27] And although there are no hard and fast rules to be able to predict financial crises, in their book *This Time is Different* they suggest that the main indicators are (i) asset price inflation; (ii) rising leverage; (iii) large and sustained current account deficits and (iv) slowing growth.[28] When these conditions combine, the outlook for a country looks bleak. Indeed in a 2010 paper they argued (at p. 573),

> *Our main result is that whereas the link between growth and debt seems relatively weak at normal debt levels, median growth rates for countries with public debt over roughly 90 percent of GDP are about one percent lower than otherwise; average (mean) growth rates are several percent lower.*[29]

This reinforced a conventional rule of thumb that when public debt reached 90% of GDP (for developed countries, or 60% for emerging countries) a tipping point was reached, and growth slowed significantly. Due to the direct policy relevance the paper became a famous one, and a graduate student called Thomas Herndon decided to attempt to replicate the results.

TABLE 10.2 Debt ratios

	Public debt (% of GDP)			
	0–30%	**30–60%**	**60–90%**	**90%+**
Reinhart and Rogoff (2010)	4.1%	2.9%	3.4%	−0.1%
Herndon et al. (2013)	4.2%	3.1%	3.2%	2.2%

Real GDP growth by public debt/GDP categories.

It is a common exercise for students to attempt to replicate published articles, but Herndon was unable to generate the same results. It is seen as best practice for economists to make their data public, precisely so that others can replicate it, and Reinhart and Rogoff sent Herndon their original Microsoft Excel file. Herndon then realised that the reason he couldn't replicate it was because of some basic errors. Given the politicised nature of this debate, the fact that a graduate student had 'exposed' these errors became a big story. It caused embarrassment for those who used the 90% tipping point as a justification for austerity.

Table 10.2 compares the original Reinhart and Rogoff figures with the revised ones calculated by Herndon et al.[30] It shows the average amount of real GDP growth depending on how large public debt was, as a percentage of GDP. Herndon et al. agree that once public debt reaches 90% real growth drops considerably. However not as considerably as Reinhart and Rogoff found. Furthermore, Herndon et al. argue that the 90%+ category is too wide, and by breaking it into 90–120% and 120%+ this further reduces the drop-off seen at the 90% threshold.

But it's important to take a step back. The fact that there's a negative correlation between public debt levels and growth is well established. The debate is at what point, if any, it becomes unsustainable. The fact that economists cannot point to a convenient threshold does not make the problem disappear. In the run up to the adoption of the Euro one of the key convergence criteria was that prospective members must have debt to GDP ratios below 60%. The fact that the debate has since shifted to the 90% limit says it all.

NOTES

1. I believe this poem was used by the Anti Corn Law League, who campaigned for free trade in nineteenth-century Britain. The Corn Laws imposed import tariffs on grain and other cereals, resulting in higher prices for basic food such as bread. Whilst British landowners prospered from the lack of competition, it severely affected the living standards of the average working family. The Corn Laws were abolished in 1846.

2. Most of what I know about the story of Josko Joras comes from students that I've taught in Ljubljana. There is an article in English on the 'Ljubljana Life' website called 'Trouble At The Border' [http://www.ljubljana-life.com/ljubljana/border-dispute, accessed 16 September 2013], otherwise you can attempt to translate his page on the Slovenian Wikipedia [http://sl.wikipedia .org/wiki/Jo%C5%A1ko_Joras, accessed 16 September 2013].

3. In his book *The Myth of the Rational Vote* Bryan Caplan uses the 1996 'Survey of Americans and Economists on the Economy' to demonstrate the differences of opinion between the general public (who deem free trade to be bad) and professional economists (who deem it to be good). See Caplan, B. (2007) *The Myth of the Rational Voter*, Princeton. A 2013 study by Paola Sapienza and

Luigi Zingales found that on average there was a 35 percentage point difference between how many professional economists and how many of the general public would agree with various statements about the economy. Sapienza, P. and Zingales, L. (2013) Economic Experts vs. Average Americans, Chicago Booth Research Paper No. 13-11.

4. This story is a retelling of an allegory that I believe was first made by James Ingram in Ingram, J. (1970) *International Economic Problems*, John Wiley & Sons, but the version here is based on one written by Robert Schenk, and is available online [http://ingrimayne.saintjoe.edu/econ/International/InternTrade.html, accessed 16 September 2013].

5. As an example of how long standing and obvious this point is consider the following quote from Samuel Fortrey, writing in 1633: 'Our care should ... be to increase chiefly those things which are of least charge at home, and greatest value abroad ... wherefore, could we employ our lands to anything of more worth, we could not want plenty of corn, though we had none of our own; for what we should increase in the room of it, of greater value by exportation, would not only bring us home as much corn as that land would have yielded, but plenty of money to boot' (quoted in Niehans, J. (1994) *A History of Economic Theory*, Johns Hopkins University Press).

6. Although the origins of the model are in a book written by Bertil Ohlin, his supervisor Eli Heckscher is credited as the co-creator. See Ohlin, B. (1933) *Interregional and International Trade*, Harvard University Press.

7. Stolper, W.F. and Samuelson, P.A. (1941) Protection and Real Wages, *Review of Economic Studies*, **9** (1), 58–73.

8. Rybczynski, T.M. (1955) Factor Endowment and Relative Commodity Prices, *Economica*, **22** (88), 336–341.

9. The economic historian Sudha Shenoy liked to tell the story of her husband who enjoyed eating Dundee marmalade at their home in Australia. Dundee is a small Scottish city that has been making marmalade since the late eighteenth century, despite the cold climate. Local fisherman would trade their Atlantic catch with oranges from farmers in Seville.

10. 'The trouble with outsourcing', *The Economist*, 30 June 2011.

11. See 'On-shoring is the new off-shoring as call centres come back to UK', *HR Zone*, [http://www.hrzone.com/topic/business-lifestyle/shoring-new-shoring-call-centres-come-back-uk/112654, accessed 16 September 2013].

12. In the 2012 US Presidential campaign the difference between outsourcing and offshoring became a major issue. Barack Obama accused Mitt Romney of 'outsourcing American jobs', and mocked his opponent's attempt to draw a distinction between outsourcing and offshoring. See 'Obama Hammers Romney on Outsourcing vs. "Offshoring" Explainer', *ABC News*, 25 June 2012 [http://abcnews.go.com/blogs/politics/2012/06/obama-hammers-romney-on-outsourcing-vs-offshoring-explainer/, accessed 16 September 2013]. But whilst the decision to either outsource or offshore activities can be driven by the same considerations, they are very different things.

13. This list of the advantages of outsourcing and offshoring is based on The Risk Intelligent Approach to Outsourcing and Offshoring, Deloitte Risk Intelligent Series, Issue No. 8.

14. Sapienza and Zingales, Economic Experts (n 3).

15. Moss, D. (2007) *A Concise Guide to Macroeconomics*, Harvard Business School Press, p. 118.

16. For most countries the trade balance and the current account are effectively the same thing, because net investment income and net transfers received will be small. If countries receive a lot of foreign aid, however, this won't be the case and so it is important to know the difference. **Net investment income** is the interest earned by domestic people on foreign investments, less interest earned by foreign people on domestic investments. **Net transfers received** is the aid received from foreign countries less aid.

17. This is a slight variation of a quote attributed to Jack Wenders, by Donald Boudreaux. See Boudreaux, D. (2006) Framing the 'trade deficit', *Cafe Hayek*, 21 March [http://cafehayek.com/2006/03/framing_the_tra.html, accessed 4 October 2013].

18. Blustein, P. (2006) And the money kept rolling in, *Public Affairs*, p. 55.

19. Indeed if the exchange rate fell from 1.264 to 1.257 we could say that it depreciated by (1.264–1.257)/1.264 = 0.55%.
20. 'The weak shall inherit the earth', *The Economist*, 6 October 2012.
21. 'Yuan for the money', *The Economist*, 9 February 2013.
22. 'The weak shall inherit the earth' (n 20).
23. See Samuelson, P.A. (1994) Facets of Balassa-Samuelson Thirty Years Later, *Review of International Economics*, **2** (3), 201–226.
24. 'Yuan for the money' (n 21).
25. Friedman, M. (1998) Markets to the rescue, *Wall Street Journal*, 13 October.
26. White, W. (2010) Comments on 'After the Fall' by C. and V. Reinhart, Symposium on 'Macroeconomic Challenges: The Decade Ahead', Symposium sponsored by the Federal Reserve Bank of Kansas City, Jackson Hole Wyoming, August 2010.
27. Reinhart, C.M. and Rogoff, K.S. (2011b) From Financial Crash to Debt Crisis, *American Economic Review*, **101** (5), 1676–1706.
28. Reinhart, C.M. and Rogoff, K.S. (2009) *This Time is Different: Eight Centuries of Financial Folly*, Princeton University Press.
29. Reinhart, C.M. and Rogoff, K.S. (2010) Growth in a Time of Debt, *American Economic Review: Papers & Proceedings*, **100**, 573–578.
30. Herndon T., Ash, M. and Pollin, R. (2013) Does high public debt consistently stifle economic growth? A critique of Reinhart and Rogoff, University of Massachusetts Amherst Political Economy Research Institute Working Paper.

CHAPTER 11

Behavioural Economics

'*We favour the visible, the embedded, the personal, the narrated, and the tangible; we scorn the abstract.*'

—Nassim Taleb[1]

In his book *Thinking, Fast and Slow* Daniel Kahneman tells the story of his visit to a professional investor, who had just bought tens of millions of dollars of stock in Ford Motor Company. 'When I asked how he made that decision, he replied that he had recently attended an automobile show and had been impressed. "Boy, do they know how to make a car!" was his explanation'.[2] Kahneman points out that the investor preferred to trust his raw emotion, rather than confront what would determine whether he would make a profit, i.e. establish whether the stock was underpriced. 'The question that the executive faced (should I invest in Ford stock?) was difficult, but the answer to an easier and related question (do I like Ford cars?) came readily to his mind and determined his choice.'[3] This chapter aims to do two things. To shed light on the times when we ask the wrong question, and to also explain what economists believe is the right question. We're going to investigate two big questions:

1. Are people rational?
2. Are markets efficient?

Economists may disagree on this issue, but the reason why they may give conflicting answers is because they are defining 'rationality' and 'efficiency' in different ways.[4] Thus far, the concept of 'rationality' that we've used has been a fairly loose one. It simply means that – at the margin – incentives affect people's behaviour. A stricter definition is that people *optimally* use all of the available information at their disposal. This doesn't mean that people are supercomputers and never get things wrong. It just means that they don't make systematic errors. Many people play the lottery, but if they fail to win, this hardly constitutes a 'mistake'. Chances are they were aware it would be unlikely, and made the bet for the thrill of it. Rationality in the loose sense implies that if the odds of winning the lottery increase, then people would be more likely to buy a ticket. Rationality in the strict sense is that – on average – people accurately calculate what the odds are.

The field of behavioural economics has emerged to test some of these assumptions, and finds evidence that people are not 'rational' in the strict sense. In this chapter we will look at some of this evidence, and how it relates to management. We will look at some of the anomalies that managers can suffer from and consider ways to compensate for them. We will also look at the debate about whether capital markets are efficient, focusing on a concept known as the **Efficient Market Hypothesis** (EMH). In short, we will see how much of the financial industry is based on bluff and self-deception. This chapter serves as an antidote to such hubris, and explains why it is so hard to beat the market. When the EMH was originally developed it rested on an assumption that agents were rational. So if our behavioural assumptions are undermined by empirical evidence, does this destroy the claims of financial economics? It is common practice for economists to take one of two positions:

1. Agents are rational and so markets are efficient.
2. Agents are irrational and so markets are inefficient.

Indeed for many people the concepts of agent rationality and market efficiency are so intertwined that evidence of irrationality is viewed as automatically rejecting the efficiency of markets. Not so fast! In this chapter we will look at a middle ground and consider the claim that although agents are *not* 'rational', this doesn't imply that markets are inefficient. Rather, agents are biased and markets have a tendency towards equilibrium.

11.1 BEHAVIOURAL ANOMALIES

Prospect theory stems from psychological studies that attempt to offer a more realistic account of human behaviour than expected utility theory.[5] It studies how real people respond to potential gains and losses in a laboratory setting ('prospect' is used as another word for 'gamble'). In a seminal paper in 1979 Daniel Kahneman and Amos Tversky tested for two famous effects:[6]

- The Certainty Effect – (also known as the 'Allais paradox') finds that people underweigh outcomes that are merely probable compared to those that are certain.
- The Reflection Effect – finds that people are risk averse over gains, but risk-loving over losses.

This launched a field whereby economists conducted experimental research and established a number of interesting findings. These can be referred to as **biases** (a predisposition towards error), and **heuristics** (mental shortcuts). Let's look at some of the more famous ones:

- Excessive optimism
    Studies suggest that people have a tendency to overestimate the likelihood of favourable outcomes. We have a tendency to think that bad things only happen to other people, which might be comforting, but can lead to problems as this IMF paper points out:

    Concerns that foreign investors may be subject to herd behavior, and suffer from excessive optimism, have grown stronger; and even when flows are fundamentally sound, it is recognized that they may contribute to collateral damage, including bubbles and asset booms and busts.[7]

▪ Overconfidence bias

We have a tendency to overestimate our own abilities/ideas. A majority of people think they are better than average drivers, and when students finish an exam they tend to believe that they did better than they actually did.

▪ Hindsight bias

We tend to convince ourselves that things were more obvious than they were, retrospectively. This might be because we have an innate bias for storytelling, and therefore we instinctively attempt to attribute meaning to events even if they're random. For example, imagine we have 10 000 fund managers who make their investment decisions based on the toss of a coin. For any given year, each has a 50–50 chance of making a profit. After four years there will be 625 that have made a profit every year. Randomly. And yet we may expect that these 625 will be lauded as heroes. People will clamour for their thoughts. One of them may be 'fund manager of the year'. But only 312 will win again next year. There's 50% chance the 'fund manager of the year' loses out. Will people say, 'that's reversion to the mean', or 'he got cocky'?

> *In hindsight, people consistently exaggerate what could have been anticipated in foresight. They not only tend to view what has happened as having been inevitable but also to view it as having appeared "relatively inevitable" before it happened. People believe that others* should have *been able to anticipate events much better than was actually the case. They even misremember their own predictions so as to exaggerate in hindsight what they knew in foresight.*[8]

▪ Confirmation bias

This occurs when new evidence makes us increasingly confident, despite our initial beliefs. In a famous study students were asked to give their opinions on the death penalty. They were then given two pieces of evidence, one of which suggested that the death penalty was an effective deterrent, and one saying that it wasn't.[9] You might hope that people would carefully weigh up the evidence and update their beliefs accordingly. In actual fact the students already in favour of the death penalty said that they found the study supporting this view to be the most convincing. And those against thought that the one that confirmed *their* prior beliefs was more compelling. This effect can occur via three main channels:

  ▪ Overemphasising supporting evidence
  ▪ Underemphasising conflicting evidence
  ▪ Misinterpreting ambiguity.

Confirmation bias can also lead to what is known as **belief perseverance**, which occurs when we can stick to a belief despite conflicting evidence. It suggests that if people interpret new information through a mistaken starting assumption, then giving people more information may not lead to better decisions. As Tolstoy said, 'The most difficult subjects can be explained to the most slow-witted man if he has not formed any idea of them already; but the simplest thing cannot be made clear to the most intelligent man if he is firmly persuaded that he knows already, without a shadow of doubt, what is laid before him.'

▪ Attribution bias

We tend to overestimate how much control we have over events. This is also known as 'the illusion of control'. In one experiment some participants were allowed to choose a lottery ticket, whilst others were given one at random. Those who chose their own were more reluctant to swap it.[10]

■ Ownership bias

We tend to place a higher valuation on an asset purely by owning it. In one study students were randomly given tickets to watch a basketball match, and then asked what value they placed on it. Given that the allocation was random, there should not be a difference between the two groups. But those who had been given tickets stated that they were worth 14 times as much as the ones who didn't receive them.[11] If we attach higher values to things once we own them, this has an implication in terms of how markets operate. Economists assume that traders place a value on a particular asset, and if the price goes below it they'll want to buy more, and if the price goes above it they'll be happy to sell. But as *The Economist* says, 'professional market traders are often reluctant to sell investments they already hold, even though they could trade them for assets they would prefer to invest in if starting from scratch.'[12]

■ Representative heuristic

These are judgements based on stereotypes, confusing the fact that just because something is a stereotype does not necessarily make it more likely. For example if you encountered a Chinese professor and had to guess whether he was a professor of Chinese literature, or of psychology, what would you say?[13] The typical answer is the former, due to the fact that you would expect most professors of Chinese literature to actually be Chinese.

But this ignores the base rates. There are far more professors of psychology than of Chinese literature, and so there will be more Chinese professors of psychology than of Chinese literature.

■ Availability heuristic

This is the over-reliance on readily available information. Perhaps the most famous example is the widespread fear of flying, despite the fact that on many measures (such as per journey made, per distance, per time spent travelling) cars are more dangerous. If something is particularly (i) familiar; (ii) important; (iii) personal or (iv) recent we tend to over emphasise its likelihood of occurring.

■ Anchoring heuristic

This is viewing things in relation to an arbitrary point of comparison. In fact, this is an important marketing tool because how something is framed can generate points of comparison that affect people's judgement. The classic example was a 1992 study at Stanford that looked at the impact of a new $429 bread maker. Although it had lots of additional functionality it was very expensive and it didn't sell many units. However the company noticed that sales of the standard $279 model almost doubled. Suddenly it didn't seem as expensive any more.

■ Affect heuristic

This is the over-reliance on intuition/gut feeling/instinct. It can apply to situations where people rely too much on emotion, possibly because of how a problem is phrased. For example a study split people up into two groups and told them about a potential new drug. Group 1 were told that there was a 7% mortality rate. Group 2 told were told that there was a 93% survival rate. Note that this is exactly the same thing. But group 2 were more likely to recommend the treatment.[14] There is even evidence that if people are told that something is '1 in 100' they deem it more likely than if they're told it is '1%', because the former is less abstract.[15]

That's a long list of biases and anomalies, and it may strike you as a bit of a ragbag. And to some extent it is – these are what I consider to be the most important ones, but they are simply psychological phenomena that economists have sought to incorporate. Textbooks are written on this topic alone. Indeed one of them provides a nice summary of why managers in particular need to be aware of these biases,

> *Managers are inclined to choose negative net-present-value projects because they are excessively optimistic about the future prospects of their firms, overconfident about the risks they face, discount information that does not support their views, and exaggerate the extent of the control they wield over final outcomes.*[16]

And also aware of heuristics:

> *Managers are prone to make faulty decisions about uses of funds because they place too much reliance on stereotypical thinking when forming judgments, attach too much emphasis to information that is readily available, become overly fixated on numbers in their analyses, and place too much reliance on intuition.*[17]

The danger of identifying behavioural anomalies is that we might be underestimating the evolutionary reasons for why they might exist.[18] And even when we consider each anomaly in isolation, they may not be so foolish. In an episode of '24', Bill Buchanan, the head of the fictional Counter Terrorism Unit (CTU) was being asked to hand over a prisoner. His colleagues didn't believe the prisoner was of value, and were happy to comply. But Buchanan was reluctant. He didn't want to give away an asset unless he knew its value beforehand.[19] When put in these terms, maybe the ownership bias doesn't seem so irrational. I once caught a bus to Golders Green and needed to find the underground station. Since I didn't have a map I decided to follow where the majority of the passengers were going. In some circumstances, following the crowd (i.e. **herding**) is a sensible strategy. Entrepreneurs are renowned for having more confidence in their abilities than objective data may suggest, and without them we'd have no innovation. Indeed Daniel Kahneman refers to overconfidence as 'the engine of capitalism'.[20] According to *The Economist*, 'inventors and entrepreneurs must often ignore legions of naysayers. That requires self-belief that borders on self-delusion.'[21] But of course the selection bias means that we tend to only see successful entrepreneurs, for whom the self-belief turned out to be valid. What we don't see is the millions of failures, who failed because of their overconfidence. Perhaps pessimism is underrated.

Most of the anomalies we've looked at are 'discovered' in an isolated laboratory setting.[22] But the problem with this is that it can ignore the extent to which (i) in the real world different anomalies can offset each other; (ii) in the real world we have institutions to help us. As John Kay has argued, 'the Wason test[23] is a meaningless card game used by experimental psychologists. Most participants fluff it when it is simply presented as a card game. Faced with the same problem in a practical, social context, most people master it easily.'[24]

Consider the **Winner's Curse**.[25] Let's say you auction off a jar of pennies, and people make bids based on fairly random guesses. The deal is actually rigged in your favour, because if people are guessing randomly we would expect an equal number to overestimate the jar as underestimate. But by the nature of the auction the winning bid will be made by the person who overestimated by the *most*. In other words if several people are bidding for a resource – and it has the same value for them all – the winning bid will be the one that has the highest error term.[26] This phenomenon has a plethora of real world applications:

- Why is it that cities that host the Olympics spend so long paying them off? Well, if we believe that the Olympics confer roughly the same economic benefits on any host city, the challenge is to bid an amount that is marginally less than this expected benefit. But if all potential locations do this some will overestimate the benefits and some will underestimate. The winning city will not be the one that can expect the largest windfall, but the one that overestimated the benefits by the most.
- If a number of oil companies are bidding for the rights to excavate a particular geographical area, they will base their bid on their estimate of the net present value of the oil. If you have the winning bid, instead of celebrating, you should ask yourself why no one else was willing to pay as much!
- Mergers and acquisitions tend to produce lower than expected profits, and again the Winner's Curse offers an explanation.[27] Appealing to notions of 'synergies' is often a cover for the fact that a company overestimated the value of the company they've bought, and we shouldn't be surprised – by the very nature of the auction we expect to see buyer's remorse.

This suggests that institutions are what bridge individual decision making/cognition with outcomes. We need to focus on institutions to determine whether psychological explanations are enough. It is institutions that determine whether human interaction delivers profitable or socially costly activity.

For example, imagine that instead of auctioning off the jar of pennies we simply ask people to *guess* the value of the jar. In this case we would once again expect some people to overestimate and some to underestimate, but the average guess will typically be close to the actual value. This is an example of the **Wisdom of Crowds**.[28] There are plenty of examples where we wouldn't want to rely on the wisdom of crowds (imagine a plane getting into difficulties and the pilot taking a vote on what to do about it),[29] but the amazing insight remains: under the right institutional setting the aggregated information of the crowd can beat expert judgement.

11.2 MARKET EFFICIENCY

Economists have used behavioural economics to explain a number of interesting findings from the stock markets, such as:

- The tendency for stock prices to increase in January
- The tendency for stock prices to fall in October
- The observation that stock returns are often slightly lower on a Monday than on the preceding Friday.

But you don't need to be a hardcore entrepreneur to spot an opportunity here. If stock prices have a tendency to increase in January, and if this is public information, why don't people simply buy shares in December? The Achilles heel of behavioural economics is that although it provides an explanation for some historical events, it is difficult to utilise as a profitable strategy. And so perhaps markets aren't 'efficient', but if there is no systematic way to profit from their inefficiency, it is *as if* they were efficient.

The first building block in the idea that markets are efficient is random walk theory. Despite its name this isn't a theory at all, it's simply an observation that you cannot predict market prices from historical information. According to Eugene Fama the current price reflects all available information.[30] This implies that the driver of stock prices is 'new information'. But note that – *by definition* – any new 'information' will be: (i) as likely good as bad; (ii) unrelated to previous information. According to F.A. Hayek,

> *movements of individual prices must be in some measure unpredictable because their function is to make people adapt to events they cannot know.*[31]

The incredible implication: you can't beat the market!

Not everyone accepts random walk theory, and we can split them into two main groups. The first are **chartists**, who believe that historical information can provide clues about the value of a share that has not already been reflected in the price. But this is really a type of astrology, attempting to infer causal relationships from interesting patterns. There is no link between yesterday's price and today's price – there is just yesterday's market equilibrium, and today's. This might tempt a naïve stock picker to believe that although share prices may fluctuate in a manner that appears like a random walk, over the longer term they will be driven by the **fundamentals** of demand and supply analysis. But Fama's response to this is the following:

> *[T]he challenge of the random-walk theory to the proponent of fundamental analysis is to show that his more complicated procedures are actually more profitable than a simple random selection policy. As in the case of the chartist, the challenge is an empirical one.*[32]

After all, let's remember what market prices are. As previously discussed, they represent the 'daily balance of expectations'. If you believe they are 'wrong', you are claiming to know more than the combined wisdom of the entire market. This isn't impossible, but it is (i) unlikely and (ii) verifiable. As I say to students – if you have a professor claiming that markets aren't efficient (and they give the impression that they understand how), ask to see their bank account! If they say that they get more satisfaction from giving away that information for free than they would from trading on it, ask them to repeat it with a straight face.

Fundamentalists have a tendency to point to volatility as a sign that prices don't stay close to their 'true' value, but this neglects the fact that we only get to see the value of something through the market process. Given that the forces of demand and supply are in constant flux, volatility is not necessarily a sign of 'irrational' deviations from 'true' value: 'markets will be extremely sensitive to new information, leading to both "frenzies", in which demand feeds on itself, and "crashes", in which price drops discontinuously.'[33] As Israel Kizner has said, 'it is in the apparently chaotic sequence of market events that the market's orderliness resides.'[34] We can even tie this into a theory of market regulation. From March to August 2007 Mattel made two recalls of Chinese made toys, and around $2.75 billion was wiped from their market value. At the same time regulators were only beginning to start talking about whether to issue fines or other punishments.[35]

The keystone of market efficiency is the 'efficient market hypothesis',[36] and it has three forms:

- **Weak Form** simply states that the market price reflects all historical information. This is just a restatement of random walk theory.
- **Semi-Strong Form** says that the market price reflects all *public* information.
- **Strong Form** says that the market price reflects all public *and private* information.

What the efficient market hypothesis is getting at is that the key to markets is information, and people being able to act on that information. But note that insider-trading laws actually prevent strong form efficiency from operating, by making it illegal for certain types of private information to be utilised. Some economists, such as Henry Manne, use this as a reason why insider-trading laws actually inhibit market efficiency. He believes that corporate accounting scandals such as Enron were only able to happen because private information was being kept out of the market,

> *I don't think the scandals would ever have erupted if we had allowed insider trading ... because there would be plenty of people in those companies who would know exactly what was going on, and who couldn't resist the temptation to get rich by trading on the information, and the stock market would have reflected those problems months and months earlier than they did under this cockamamie regulatory system we have.*[37]

But even with some information suppressed, there is no greater testament to the power of the efficient market hypothesis than the rise of index funds, such as the Dow Jones, or the FTSE 100. Index funds are useful because:

- They allow us to form general impressions of market movements and measure short-term changes.
- They provide a yardstick to compare managed portfolios.
- They can be used to invest in, as tracker funds.

The basic idea is that if you can't beat the market, why bother trying? Index funds provide a low cost way to invest, and a benchmark that managed portfolios need to beat. People that take EMH seriously will argue, 'it's impossible to beat the market'. But we don't need to go that far. All we need to argue is the following: (i) it is possible to beat the market; however (ii) the expected returns of trying to beat the market are negative and (iii) it is *very* rare to beat the market over time.

(i) It is possible to beat the market

Some people do generate above market returns, so it would be glib (and wrong) to pretend otherwise. The real question is, how do they beat the market? I think it must come down to a combination of four things:

a. Better skill

When we talk about 'skill', we really mean interpretation. This is what successful traders will claim is driving their success. They receive the same information as other people, but they are better able to understand what it means. Or as one successful trader told me, 'price action is like music, whereas economic data is just the component notes'. Some traders have a better ear than others.

b. Greater speed

Better interpretation helps, but this counts for nothing if you don't act on it before others. If it's 'news' that drives markets, getting the news first is imperative. In the 1920s there was an instance where a Merrill Lynch broker bribed the company that printed copies of *Business Week*, in order to get their stories before they hit the stands.[38] The fact that people *don't* bribe printers any more tells you something about the value of the information in such magazines. But market sensitive information is available elsewhere.[39]

Because data doesn't travel at infinite speed, there is evidence that having your Bloomberg terminal geographically closer to their servers gives you a slight informational advantage (and indeed this helps to explain why so many financial firms cluster themselves close to the city).[40] A small number of Thomson Reuters clients paid $6000 per month in order to receive information 2 seconds sooner than the rest of the market.[41]

c. Better luck

When my Uncle Roy won the Australian lottery, it wasn't because he was an expert at lottery theory, or indeed quicker at buying a ticket. He was simply lucky, and we can't discount luck as a source of profit. Even if we see evidence of people that beat the market, it could primarily be down to random effects. Walter Good and Roy Hermansen took 300 students and asked them to guess the outcome of 10 coin tosses. They then recorded the performance of 300 mutual fund managers from 1987–96. They looked at the number of years in which they were in the top 50% of fund managers, and compared this to the simulated ability of students to guess the flip of the coin. The outcome was identical.[42] And therein lies the problem – it is incredibly difficult to distinguish between better skill and luck. The **cross-sectional problem** refers to the fact that if an event is prone to randomness, then at any one moment in time you tend to be observing volatility, rather than return. Imagine you have a bunch of traders who are all just making random guesses. If you decide to see who's doing best on any given day, it will be whoever happens to be at the peak of their 'luck'. This suggests that in some situations the people who are doing 'the best' are actually the last person you'd want to invest with. If there is regression to the mean, continued success implies one of two things: either it is a brilliant trader (and you want to put money *in*), or it is a lucky trader (and you want to take money *out*). But as Nassem Taleb says, 'the larger the sample size, the more likely we'll see a winning streak.'[43] Indeed if there is merit in what I am saying, the worst possible investment advice is to look at last year's results and put your money with the top performer. And yet this is exactly how many people behave!

d. Self-fulfilling prophecy

A separate way in which it may be possible to stay ahead of the market, without having an interpretative, informational or indeed luck advantage, is if your actions aren't independent of how the market moves. It may well be the case that other market participants watch your behaviour (and this may or may not be based on a previous interpretative, informational or luck advantage) and follow suit. If an 'oracle' suggests people buy a share, and people do so, it will become a self-fulfilling prophecy. He is ahead of the market purely on account of the market's willingness to follow.

So it is theoretically possible to beat the market. But how likely is it? In an IFA.com study they compared 1411 mutual funds to the S&P 500 index. They found that 35 of them outperformed the market. So yes, it's possible to beat the market. But how confident are you that your money is with the 2.4% who managed to do so? The logical conclusion of the

EMH is that markets are efficient. But this creates a paradox, because if markets are efficient where do profit opportunities come from? Remember that the existence of profit implies one of two things. It could mean that the market is inefficient, and indeed this is the standard response to the observation of above market returns. But it could also mean that the market is in disequilibrium. It is the latter that solves the paradox. The market is *not* efficient. But any inefficiency is a profit opportunity. Therefore this is a strong incentive for entrepreneurs to eliminate that inefficiency as soon as it is noticed. Prices are just the daily balance of expectation, and the balance will be in constant flux.[44] As long as we're willing to accept that we live in a world of disequilibrium, profit opportunities will exist. It simply implies that they are fleeting moments. A study published by Norges Bank revealed,

> *the existence of numerous short-lived arbitrage opportunities ... The duration of arbitrage opportunities is, on average, high enough to allow agents to exploit deviations from the law of one price, but low enough to explain why such opportunities have gone undetected in much previous research using data at lower frequency.*[45]

However it is important to understand what we mean by 'beats the market'. This isn't the same thing as saying, 'makes a profit', or indeed (in the case of traders that use their own money), 'is very rich'. Many traders are in their office by 7am, and don't get home until after midnight. They spend every waking hour poring over financial information, responding to every new shock. If they nip to the toilet, and there is news, they could get wiped out. I don't know about you, but this isn't the type of lifestyle I'd find appealing. I like having regular lie-ins, and I enjoy making my children their dinner and putting them to sleep. Most Saturdays I switch my phone off for the entire afternoon and evening. Sometimes I wonder how much you'd have to pay me to put in the hours (and take on the stress) that traders operate under – it's probably more than the average salary they receive. Maybe they're being paid a lot because they work hard at an unpleasant job. In the same way that plumbers can generate 'above market returns' by working very hard, so can people in the city. But this is just them receiving the market rate for the value of their labour.

Whenever I teach this class I have a student that says, 'but what about Warren Buffett?' To some extent, this question proves the rule, because it's always the same investor that provides the counter example. And he demonstrates all of the characteristics mentioned above. But there are three responses to the idea that Warren Buffett disproves the EMH. The first is that there's doubt that his company, Berkshire Hathaway, has in fact beaten 'the market'. It depends on which index funds you use as a benchmark. From 1995–2005, for example, Berkshire Hathaway Class A shares delivered a 10.69% annualised market return. An IFA Emerging Markets Value Index delivered 12.90%, and an IFA Index Portfolio 100 delivered 12.08%. Whether you look at a 1 year, 5 year, 10 year or 20 year return, and depending on which index you look at, the claim that Berkshire Hathaway beat the market is ambiguous.[46] The second point is that Buffett isn't a stockpicker. He doesn't sit behind a computer screen trying to outsmart the market. He's an investor. He buys companies and has decision rights over management. And finally, the third reason why Buffett doesn't disprove the idea that diversified index funds are best comes straight from the horse's mouth:

> *Most investors will find the best way to own equities is through an index fund that charges minimal fees. They are sure to beat the net results (after fees and expenses) delivered by the majority of investment professionals.*[47]

(ii) The expected returns of trying to beat the market are negative

According to Hal Varian, if you bought a value-weighted portfolio in 1926, and held it until 2002, it would have generated an annual return of around 10%. 'By contrast, an individual who bought in 1926 but moved his dollars in and out of the market in the same pattern as the average dollar invested in the market would have earned a return of only 8.6 percent a year.'[48]

In fact, if you'd invested $100 per month from November 1998–November 2008 you would have earned a higher nominal return from sticking it under your mattress ($12 000) than investing in equity funds.[49] So why not give it to hedge funds? Well, according to Hedge Fund Research, in 2006 (i.e. in the boom years prior to the collapse of Lehman Brothers) 717 funds ceased to trade, and the average fund lost 1.8% in January of that year.[50,51] So what about unit trusts? According to Trustnet from 2004–2009 only 91 of the 254 UK unit trusts outperformed an index-tracker fund.[52]

According to the *New York Times* investors spend $100bn per year attempting to beat the stock market.[53] However 'after costs and taxes, an indexed investor in a market can beat the average active investor.'[54] Returns are higher for broad, indexed funds than managed ones. So what is the point of spending time and money 'managing' your portfolio when returns are higher for broad, indexed funds? If you are playing roulette and place a £10 bet on black, the expected value is minus £0.53.[55] In other words, you should expect to lose money. Does this make it irrational? Only if your goal is to make money. If you're aware that the chances are you'll lose, but you're willing to bear that cost in exchange for the excitement of gambling, then it's perfectly rational. Economics doesn't tell us whether it is right or wrong to enjoy being exposed to risk. Similarly, just because most people fail to beat the market, doesn't make it wrong to try. But it's important to realise that it only makes sense if you're willing to pay a price for 'enjoying' the *challenge* of trying to beat the market. If your goal is to make money though, there are far better options.

(iii) It is *very* rare to beat the market over time

We looked at some empirical evidence for how rare it is to beat the market, but the longer the timescale the more difficult it becomes. It is true that we can identify people that have 'beaten the market' over a certain period of time. For example John Paulson earned about $4bn betting on a subprime downturn in 2007. This led to a lot of people wanting to invest in his hedge fund, but in 2011,

> [h]is two largest funds, Paulson Advantage and Advantage Plus, lost 36 percent and 52 percent that year, and the red streak has continued into 2012, with Advantage and Advantage Plus down 6.3 percent and 9.3 percent as of the end of May.[56]

Paulson himself highlighted the problem, 'We became overconfident as to the direction of the economy and took a lot of risk.'[57] So yes, it is possible to *have beaten* the market. But that is little use in terms of being able to beat the market in the future. As Burton Malkiel says,

> the problem is, the people who beat it in one period are not the people who beat it in the next period.[58]

In this chapter we have been open-minded about the extent to which behavioural economics contradicts the assumptions of standard economics, and tried to see how managers can benefit from being able to see them at work. And the implications for the finance industry are enormous. But despite these examples of anomalies, they cannot generate a theory that can be profitably applied. After costs, the average investor cannot beat the market. We do not have access to any better estimate of the underlying value of an asset than the market price. Not from historically good traders, and certainly not from regulators. What this suggests is that rationality, and perfect knowledge, are *not* necessary conditions for efficient markets. Indeed markets are institutions that convert people's 'irrational' beliefs into 'rational' outcomes. The greater the degree of 'irrationality', the greater the need for processes that generate the coordination of plans. Behavioural economics doesn't undermine the case for markets; it strengthens it.

NOTES

1. Taleb, N.N. (2001) *Fooled by Randomness*, Random House.
2. Kahneman, D. (2011[2012]) *Thinking, Fast and Slow*, Penguin, p. 12.
3. Kahneman, *Thinking, Fast and Slow* (n 2), p. 12.
4. For a discussion of the different ways in which economists use the term 'rationality' see Cowen, T. (2004) How do economists think about rationality? in Byron, B. (ed.), *Satisficing and Maximizing*, Oxford University Press, pp. 213–236.
5. Expected utility theory is the seemingly obvious claim that people make decisions based on weighing up the combined payoff and probability of all the possible outcomes. For example, if we play a game where I toss a coin and heads means you win £1 and tails means you win 0, we can say that the expected utility is 50p (i.e. 0.5*1+0.5*0). The 'expected value' of this game is 50p and a risk neutral person would be willing to pay 50p to play it. See Mongin, P. (1997) Expected Utility Theory, in Davis, J.B., Hands, D.W. and Maki, U. (eds), *Handbook of Economic Methodology*, Edward Elgar.
6. Kahneman, D. and Tversky, A. (1979) Prospect Theory: An Analysis of Decision under Risk, *Econometrica*, **47** (2), 263–291.
7. Ostry, J.D., Ghosh, A.R., Habermeier, K. et al. (2010) Capital Inflows: The Role of Controls, IMF Staff Position Note, 19 February.
8. Fischhoff, B. (1982) Debiasing, in Kahneman, D., Slovic, P. and Tversky, A. (eds), *Judgement under Uncertainty: Heuristics and biases*, Cambridge University Press, p. 341, my emphasis. This **survivorship bias** is incredibly important. If traders that lose money leave the market, then it is no surprise that the ones who remain have a track record of success. But this success is as much of a warning sign as a signal of competence. As *The Economist* says, the initial success of veteran traders could be due to luck, rather than skill:

   'Successful fund managers attract more clients and thus manage more money. This will keep happening until they have a bad year, when clients will desert them. Their worst result will thus occur when they have the most money to look after.' 'The golden rules of banking', The Economist, *14 July 2012*.

9. Lord, Charles G., Ross, L. and Lepper, M.R. (1979) Biased assimilation and attitude polarization: The effects of prior theories on subsequently considered evidence, *Journal of Personality and Social Psychology*, **37** (11), 2098–2109.
10. Langer, E.J. (1975) The Illusion of Control, *Journal of Personality and Social Psychology*, **32** (2), 311–328.
11. Ariely, D. (2010) *Predictably Irrational*, Harper.

12. 'It's mine, I tell you', *The Economist*, 19 June 2008.

13. Example taken from Bryan Caplan's Graduate Micro II Class, George Mason University, http://econfaculty.gmu.edu/bcaplan/e812/micro9.htm.

14. I am not sure of the original source for this study, but consider the following: 'the impact of dying seems to be greater when it is framed as a mortality rate of 10 percent, than when it is framed as a survival rate of 90 percent' (Peters, E., Finucane, M.L., MacGregor, D.G. and Slovic, P. (2000) The Bearable Lightness of Aging: Judgment and Decision Processes in Older Adults, in Stern, P.C. and Carstensen, L.L. (eds), *The Aging Mind: Opportunities in Cognitive Research*, National Academies Press.

15. Kahan, D.M., Wittlin, M., Peters, E. et al. (2011) The Tragedy of the Risk-Perception Commons: Culture Conflict, Rationality Conflict, and Climate Change, Temple University Legal Studies Research Paper No. 2011-26; Cultural Cognition Project Working Paper No. 89; Yale Law & Economics Research Paper No. 435; Yale Law School, Public Law Working Paper No. 230.

16. Shefrin, H. (2005) *Behavioural Corporate Finance*, McGraw-Hill, p. 10.

17. Shefrin, *Behavioural Corporate Finance* (n 16), p. 10.

18. In the words of William Poundstone (who was paraphrasing comments made in 1954 by Ward Edwards):

> *'it might be "costly" to have self-consistent preferences. The design of the human mind entails complex trade-offs. Survival often requires us to make quick decisions without complete knowledge of the problem. The mind is presumably optimised for mostly accurate hunches and an improvisatory approach that constructs desires and beliefs on the fly' (Poundstone, W. (2010)* Priceless: The hidden psychology of value, *Oneworld, p. 126).*

19. I am not totally sure which episode of '24' this occurred in, but it was around 25 minutes in and occurred in Season 4.

20. Kahneman, D. (2011[2012]) *Thinking, Fast and Slow*, Penguin, p. 255.

21. 'Bah, humbug', *The Economist*, 19 December 2009.

22. Many of these studies have small sample sizes and cannot be replicated. This has led to serious doubts being cast on the validity of the findings, especially since some of the early work on psychological framing effects (i.e. 'priming') turns out to have been fraudulent. *The Economist* says: 'Over the past few years various researchers have made systematic attempts to replicate some of the more widely cited priming experiments. Many of these replications have failed.' ('Trouble at the lab', *The Economist*, 19 October 2013.) Tests for behavioural anomalies more generally are undoubtedly interesting studies, but perhaps they are trivial. Maybe we only really teach them because they are fun and engaging.

23. The Wason Test is when four cards are laid out on a table, each containing a different number or letter, and you are told a particular rule (for example 'if it has a number on one side it has a letter on the other side'). Your task is to work out how many cards you need to turn over in order to establish if the rule is correct.

24. Kay, J. (2008) There are many sensible reasons for irrational behaviour, *Financial Times*, 26 August. Also see Cosmides, L. and Tooby, J. (1992) Cognitive adaptations for social exchange, in Barkow, J., Cosmides, L. and Tooby, J. (eds), *The Adapted Mind: Evolutionary Psychology and the Generation of Culture*, Oxford University Press.

25. Thaler, R.H. (1988) Anomalies: The Winner's Curse, *Journal of Economic Perspectives*, **2** (1), 191–202.

26. Note that the assumption that the underlying value is the same for all bidders is crucial. A good example of this may be bidding for the rights to an oil well, where the value of the asset is almost identical for everyone. The greater the degree to which rivals place different valuations on the same asset, the less applicable is the Winner's Curse.

27. According to McKinsey, 'close to two-thirds of managers overestimate the economies of scale a merger will deliver, often overegging the benefits by more than 25%', see 'Land of the Corporate Giants', *The Economist*, 3 November 2012.

28. Surowiecki, J. (2004) *The Wisdom of Crowds*, Doubleday.

29. Kay, J. (2004) When to ask an expert and when a crowd, *Financial Times*, 31 August.

30. Fama, E.F. (1965) Random Walks in Stock Market Prices, *Financial Analysts Journal*, **21** (5), 55–59. See Malkiel, B.G. (1996) *A Random Walk Down Wall Street*, W.W. Norton.

31. This quote from Hayek was a handwritten note, now stored at the Hoover Institution Archives (140.9).

32. Fama, Random Walks (n 30).

33. Bulow, J. and Klemperer, P. (1994) Rational Frenzies and Crashes, *Journal of Political Economy*, **102** (1), 1–23.

34. Kirzner, I.M. (1996) *The Meaning of Market Process*, Routledge, p. 49.

35. Perry, M. (2007) The market imposes a $2.75 billion fine on Mattel, *Carpe Diem*, 17 August [http://mjperry.blogspot.co.uk/2007/08/market-imposes-275-billion-fine-on.html, accessed 4 October 2013].

36. Fama, E.F. (1970) Efficient Capital Markets: A Review of Theory and Empirical Work, *Journal of Finance*, **25** (2), 383–417.

37. Manne, H. (2004) Legalize Insider Trading, *Capitalism Magazine*, 24 September [http://www.capmag.com/article.asp?ID=3933, accessed 16 September 2013].

38. Kindleberger, C.P. and Aliber, R. (2005) *Manias, Panics and Crashes*, John Wiley & Sons, p. 169.

39. Interestingly, insider-trading laws do not apply to US politicians, giving them an advantage over the rest of the market if sensitive information is presented at closed briefings or other private events. They receive market sensitive information from 'high level, closed briefings or engage in conversations where secrets are disclosed ... That access lets them buy low and sell high ... and they can do it without concern that their remarkable prescience will alert federal investigators of possible wrong doing' (see Woolner, A. (2010) It Isn't Insider Trading When Your Senator Does It, *Bloomberg*, 14 October 2010). Because of this, in 2011 a bill was proposed by Sen. Scott Brown that 'would make it illegal for elected congressional officials, their staffs and executive branch employees to use information about pending bills that's not available to the general public in making investment decisions', (see 'Bill filed to prohibit congressional insider trading' *CNN*, 16 November 2011).

   Interestingly, the portfolios of US Senators 'outperformed the market by an average of 12 per cent a year in the five years to 1998' (Ziobrowski, A.J., Cheng, P., Boyd, J.W. and Ziobrowski, B.J. (2004) Abnormal returns from the Common Stock Investments of the US Senate, *Journal of Financial and Quantitative Analysis*, **39** (4), 661–676). This also provides an incentive for lobbyists and other forms of rent-seeking. Indeed the manner in which the finance industry attempts to get close to new information ties in closely with the concept of Cantillon effects discussed in Chapter 8. The ultimate way to get ahead of the market is to be as close as possible to the source of credit creation. Hence much of the supposed 'profit' of the finance industry can properly be viewed as rent-seeking.

40. There are plenty of nice examples about the importance of seemingly minute informational advantages. The Hibernian Express is a new cable that will be laid underneath the Atlantic Ocean. It is due to cost $300m but will reduce the time it takes to transmit information between London and New York by 6ms. This is less than 10% of the current time, but according to the *Daily Telegraph*, 'a one millisecond advantage could be worth up to $100m (£63m) a year to the bottom line of a large hedge fund.' 'The $300m cable that will save traders milliseconds', *Daily Telegraph*, 11 September 2011.

   Recently it emerged that a savvy Bloomberg employee noticed that many companies used the same URL format when they released annual reports. For example, if the 2011 report was posted to www.kaleidic.org/reports/2011 they were able to guess that the 2012 one would be posted at www.kaleidic.org/reports/2012. Because companies have an obligation to release such information to the whole market simultaneously, rather than begin creating the website and uploading the report at 12pm on launch day, companies will often do this in advance but simply not make the address public. By guessing the URL Bloomberg were able to report figures for many companies slightly ahead of the official release. See Blodget, H. (2010) So THIS is how Bloomberg gets earnings reports hours before they're publicly released, *Business Insider*, 17 December [http://www.businessinsider .com/bloomberg-earnings-news-2010-12, accessed 4 October 2013].

41. 'Reuters feeds the robots two-second scoops' (2013) *Columbia Journalism Review*, 10 July.
42. Good, W.R. and Hermansen, R.W. (1997) *Index Your Way to Investment Success*, New York Institute of Finance.
43. Taleb, N.N. (2001) *Fooled by Randomness*, Random House.
44. Lachmann, L.M. (1976) From Mises to Shackle: An Essay on Austrian Economics and the Kaleidic Society, *Journal of Economic Literature*, **14** (1), 54–62.
45. Akram, Q.F., Rime, D. and Sarnoa, L. (2006) Arbitrage in the Foreign Exchange Market: Turning on the Microscope, Norges Bank Working Paper No. 2005/12.
46. See http://www.ifa.com/pdf/ifa-vs-buffett.pdf, accessed 16 September 2013.
47. Berkshire Hathaway Inc, Chairman's Letter 1996 [http://www.berkshirehathaway.com/letters/1996 .html, accessed 16 September 2013].
48. Varian, H. (2007) The Stock Does Better than the Investor, *New York Times*, 3 May.
49. Albeit bonds would have generated a higher return, see 'When the golden eggs run out', *The Economist*, 4 December 2008.
50. 'Hedge podge', *The Economist*, 16 February 2008.
51. For an application of the Winner's Curse to hedge funds, see 'Rich managers, poor clients', *The Economist*, 7 January 2012.
52. Dillow, C. (2009) Yes, the market is efficient, *Stumbling and Mumbling*, 6 August.
53. Hulbert, M. (2008) Can You Beat the Market? It's a $100 Billion Question, *New York Times*, 9 March.
54. Sharpe, W.F. (2002) Indexed Investing: A Prosaic Way to Beat the Average Investor, Presented at the Spring President's Forum, Monterey Institute of International Studies, 1 May.
55. We can calculate the expected value of betting £10 on black with the following equation:

$$+10 * (18/38) + -10 * (20/38) -10 = -0.526.$$

56. Kolhatkar, S. (2012) John Paulson's very bad year, *Bloomberg Business Week*, 28 June.
57. Kolhatkar, John Paulson's very bad year (n 56).
58. 'Malkiel unleashed: The full interview with Burton Malkiel', *PBS*, 20 June 2003. [http://www.pbs .org/wsw/tvprogram/malkiel_interview.html, accessed 16 September 2013].

CHAPTER 12

Global Prosperity

'Productivity isn't everything, but in the long-run it's almost everything.'
—Paul Krugman[1]

T his chapter asks some broad and fundamental questions about the application of economic theory to the real world, and the role of the economist as a force for making the world a better place. According to some estimates the richest man of all time was Mansa Musa I.[2] He ruled the Malian empire in the fourteenth century and his personal net worth reached $400bn (in 2012 dollars). But how would his living standards compare to the average person today? For a start he died aged 51. The richest American of all time was John D. Rockefeller. But the quality of his house, or his car, would seem deprived by today's standards. In addition, those billionaires lived in an age where income differences were visible. These days, if you bumped into a billionaire you would be unlikely to be able to tell.[3] This chapter will ask how some nations grow rich, and apply the economic way of thinking to politics. The insights on topics such as bureaucracy, rent-seeking and interest groups are directly applicable within a firm, and we will see how public goods and regulation affect managerial decisions. We will also look at how economies can go through periods of rapid transition, and the ways in which the same themes operate in corporate transformation.

12.1 GROWTH THEORY

The first question I ask students when we discuss economic development is the following:

What causes poverty?

This typically leads to a long discussion with a number of explanations offered: war, colonialism, poor geography. But after a while I say that it is really a lot simpler than that. The cause of poverty, I say, is:

Nothing.

Nothing causes poverty. If we think of a subsistence farmer, it is not the presence of bad economic institutions that has likely caused their fate, but the absence of good ones. The mystery of development is not to explain why some nations are poor, but to explain why some nations are *rich*. The biggest challenge of teaching economic development is getting students to realise that *we* are the exception. Poverty is the normal state of affairs.

When we talk about economic growth of a few percent a year it can appear trivial. But these have an exponential effect on living standards and they are a relatively recent phenomenon. Sustained economic growth didn't really occur prior to the eighteenth century, and since then has only happened in a few countries. For much of the world at present GDP per capita is similar to what it was like in Europe prior to the 'Industrial Revolution'. It wasn't until the nineteenth century that some nations began to experience 1% sustained growth per year, and only since the middle of the twentieth century that it has been 2–3%. Although these numbers seem small, they make a big impact. As Stephanie Flanders has pointed out, the economy has grown by about 2.25% per year, on average, from 1970–2010. This means that living standards double every 30 years. But if this growth rate slips to 1.25%, it will take 60 years.[4] If – between the years 1870 and 1990 – the US growth rate had been just 1% less per year than it actually was, then it would have only ended up at the same level of economic development as Mexico.[5]

Whilst around 20% of the world's 6 billion people live on less than $1 a day (adjusted for PPP), anyone reading this chapter will most likely be in the top 1% richest people in the world. Indeed the scale of difference between rich and poor is astounding – the poorest people in a rich country have about three times as much purchasing power as the richest people in a poor country.[6] The basic facts are that we are immensely rich compared to:

- Most of human history
- The majority of the planet.

We have already seen how entrepreneurs convert factors of production (land, labour and capital) into consumer goods and capital goods, and that this accumulation of capital constitutes the wealth of society and the foundation of economic growth. Indeed this is the classical growth model, made famous by Robert Solow. In the same way that a firm's production function is the following:

$$Y = f(L, K)$$

we can model the production function of the economy as a whole:

$$Y = AK^a L^{1-a}$$

In other words output (Y) is a combination of capital (K) and labour (L). The term 'a' is the returns to scale of capital, and if a is less than 1 it means we have diminishing returns to capital (i.e. as we increase the amount of capital being used we cannot indefinitely expect output to increase at the same rate). If the returns to labour are given as '1–a' then there are constant returns to scale for the economy as a whole. The crucial part of the Solow model, however, is A. This variable has been referred to as different things (such as 'multi factor productivity'), but think of it as technology. Or think of it as everything other than capital and labour. Solow used extensive historic data from the US economy to try to understand the links between capital, labour and output. And guess what he found? '87.5% of growth in output in the United States between the years 1909 and 1949 could be ascribed to technological improvements alone.' In other words the one variable in the model that we don't really understand is the one that is driving output!

The main implications of the Solow model are the following:

- Economic policy can affect short-term output, but not long-term growth.
- This is because growth is caused by external factors such as technological progress that leads to capital accumulation.
- We expect high growth rates for poor countries (as they 'catch up' and enjoy high returns on capital) but low growth rates for richer countries (since they experience diminishing returns).

A is also known as the Solow residual, and is testament to our limits of knowledge. In economics you can win a Nobel Prize for demonstrating that our understanding of economic growth is incomplete. But the focus of attention towards productivity and 'technology' took growth theory in an important new direction.

Paul Romer tried to build on Solow's work by bringing some of these external factors inside the model. Partly this was due to the observation that poor countries often don't 'catch up' with richer countries, and whilst many industrialised countries do seem to slow down once they've built a large capital stock, others manage to steam ahead with impressive growth. Rather than treat technology as 'exogenous' he made it 'endogenous' to the model, and this is known as 'endogenous growth theory'.[7] Romer relaxed the assumption of decreasing returns to scale for the factors of production (whilst this is plausible for a firm, it is not necessarily the case for the economy as a whole), and drew attention to the way in which capital and labour are being used.

Traditional growth theory is about increasing output through the *accumulation* of capital – i.e. doing more with more. Endogenous growth theory is about increasing output through the *better direction* of capital – i.e. doing more with less. According to Romer growth is not about the ingredients at your disposal (i.e. the capital stock) but the recipes that can combine these ingredients together. A set of Ikea instructions contains two key sections: a list of the parts that you need (the ingredients) and a step-by-step guide to piecing them together (the recipe). One source of growth is by acquiring more equipment. Another source is combining what you already have in more practical and aesthetically pleasing ways.

Arnold Kling and Nick Schulz refer to this as 'Economics 2.0'.[8] They point out that since having more ingredients is subject to diminishing returns, this explains how many socialist economies failed to convert large capital stocks into higher living standards. Real growth and real development are not down to having more and more ingredients, but better quality recipes. Recipes are essentially ideas and therefore they are costless to reproduce and have unlimited potential. Education and training, and Research and Development not only boost growth but also deliver sustained increases in growth potential.

Kling and Schulz use the analogy of a computer to explain this. A computer is comprised of three main elements. Firstly, there is hardware. This is the physical, tangible equipment such as monitor and keyboard. In economic terms the 'hardware' is the factors of production – the land, labour and capital that we have at our disposal. A computer also has software, which are the programmes that we can run. For the economy these are ideas: the innovation, know-how, science and technology that allow us to find new ways to combine the raw materials. But there's also a third element, which is the operating system. This is the framework that determines how effective the software is. And it is the growth theory of Douglass North that has attempted to study the role of the operating system in an economy. North uses the term 'institutions' to refer to the rules of the game, which are the foundations upon which entrepreneurs mobilise resources. They can be formal (such as laws and regulations) or informal (such as customs and norms). The bottom line is that these three elements – the hardware, software and operating system – all need to be in place for the computer to function. And indeed economic growth depends on the accumulation of capital, better direction of capital, and underlying institutions pioneered by Solow, Romer and North respectively. One reason why economists have done such a poor job making poor countries rich is that it is often historical accident that results in all three being in place. Indeed whilst it is pretty simple for poor countries to have more 'stuff', knowing what to do with it is harder than it appears. And it is not even worth trying to generate wealth without the right institutions. Attitudes towards economic development have broadly followed these stages of growth theory. Economists used to tell the governments of poor countries that growth would come if they invested more in physical infrastructure. Then they urged them to invest in schools and new technologies. Now they emphasise the right legal system and rule of law. But identifying the source of economic growth is far easier than being able to generate it. Even though we know why some countries are rich and some countries are poor, it is naïve in the extreme to think we are able to export this successfully. Any formal institutions must 'stick' with the informal culture that already exists.[9]

We've already seen how the growth of a firm is the result of its capital structure, and therefore growth theory is of direct managerial relevance. Some firms generate growth by accumulating capital resources, others through the better direction of capital.

12.2 HAPPINESS

It's a common complaint that economists focus too much on economic growth, to the detriment of things people really care about. Some accept that living standards have risen during the twentieth century, but say the relevant benchmark should be our immediate neighbours – that we care more about our status relative to other people than to absolute wealth. There are three types of 'good' that exhibit these sorts of 'relative status' properties:

- Positional goods
      Products and services whose value is mostly, if not exclusively, a function of their ranking in desirability in comparison to substitutes.
- Conspicuous consumption
      Goods and services that are acquired mainly for the purpose of displaying income or wealth.
- Invidious consumption
      Consumption of goods and services for the deliberate purpose of inspiring envy in others.

To demonstrate this point Robert Frank asked people to choose whether they'd prefer to live in (a) a 4000-square-foot house in a neighbourhood of 6000-square-foot mansions; or (b) a 3000-square-foot home in a zone of 2000-square-foot bungalows.[10] The typical answer is (b) – people say that they would prefer to lord it over their neighbours rather than have a better house. But is this how people actually behave? Soon after the Frank study was published in a 2007 *New York Times* article, two economists responded on their blogs. Gregory Mankiw argued that market prices should reflect such externalities, and the fact that the quality of the neighbourhood tends to *increase* the price of a house undermines Frank's study.[11] Alex Tabarrok presented data on this, to show that 'the same house is worth more if it is surrounded by more expensive houses'.[12] So although people *say* they would rather have the nicest house in a low quality neighbourhood, *revealed preference* suggests that they actually prefer being surrounded by nicer homes.

The **Easterlin paradox** is the empirical observation that when looking at cross-country survey data the average level of 'happiness' does not seem to correlate with GDP per capita.[13] Indeed lots of research has been done to show that whilst GDP has risen significantly over the last few decades, measures of life satisfaction remain roughly constant. But there are a number of problems with these findings.[14] In terms of methodology, two counter arguments exist:

1. We measure 'happiness' by asking people to estimate how happy they are (typically on a scale of 1–10). For one thing, people tend to answer '7' regardless of their situation. But also think about how difficult it is for 'happiness' to double. Or treble. If people are moderately happy (e.g. 7/10) then it's *impossible* for their happiness to rise by more than 3/10. By contrast we measure GDP on a scale with no upper limit. It's perfectly possible for incomes to double or treble. Purely because 'happiness' has an upper bound, whereas GDP doesn't, we shouldn't expect the former to keep pace with the latter

2. 'Happiness' is found through survey data, and is therefore an *expressed* preference. GDP is a measure of actions taken; therefore it is a *revealed* preference. This is a big difference, and if the responses contradict each other which do we trust? People might say that they don't enjoy commuting to work, but if they continue to do so we should infer that this is preferred to their reasonable alternatives.

There are also philosophical problems with 'happiness' economics. At some fundamental level we only act because we wish to reduce our uneasiness. If we were 'content' we would have no reason to act. There's a famous quote attributed to the jazz pianist Fats Waller – when he was playing an especially difficult piece, and if he was hitting every note, he'd shout 'somebody shoot me while I'm happy!' Perhaps happiness *should* be an unattainable goal.

But there are also empirical counter arguments to 'happiness economics'. Many studies have been done that find people *do* in fact like material prosperity. A 2007 Gallup poll found that from 1980–2007 around 80–90% of Americans said they were 'satisfied' with their personal lives.[15] This number *can't* rise in line with GDP, but surely the high absolute level, and the consistency of it, should be a cause for celebration? Especially when you split the responses up based on three income levels (<$30,000pa; $30,000–$74,999; $75,000+) and see the following:[16]

Very happy: 40%, 50%, 64%

Fairly happy: 48%, 45%, 34%

Not too happy: 11%, 5%, 2%

Indeed if you look at a map of the world material prosperity appears highly correlated with happiness. A study by Angus Deaton shows that 'life satisfaction rises with average income level';[17] Daniel Sacks, Betsy Stevenson and Justin Wolfers show that 'measured subjective well-being grows hand in hand with material living standards'[18] and Betsey Stevenson and Justin Wolfers show that there's no evidence of a satiation point at which this breaks down.[19] As *The Economist* says, 'though some countries seem happier than others, people everywhere report more satisfaction as they grow richer.'[20]

Critics of economists have a point. GDP growth isn't everything. But economists know more than anyone else the limitations of using GDP to make an inference about living standards – the case of the USSR demonstrated this. Firstly, standard growth theory suggests that poorer countries will tend to have higher growth rates than rich ones (because it is easier to catch up to high living standards elsewhere, than to raise those living standards further). So high growth rates may just be an indicator of low initial wealth. Secondly, many economists like to use GDP per capita as a better measure than simply GDP, since this takes into account the size of the population. But there's two ways you can increase GDP per capita – either by increasing GDP, or by reducing 'per capita'. Naïve western academics were amazed by the Soviet Union's high growth rates during the winter months. It's amazing what a famine does for GDP per capita in the short run. The third issue is that GDP doesn't equal satisfaction. You can't eat growth rates. In Soviet Russia managers were incentivised to produce output. In a famous cartoon a manager of a nail factory was given an award for beating his production target, which was measured by weight. In the background you could see a single, giant nail.[21] Output only matters in as much as it generates consumer products that satisfy people's pressing needs. There's no point having high growth rates if you're making the wrong things. The fourth problem with GDP figures is that bureaucrats have an incentive to cheat. It turns out that much of the data in the Soviet Union was fabricated, and there is much uncertainty about figures in China today. It's always dangerous to target a variable that can be manipulated. And finally, the fifth problem is that economists have an incentive to cheat. Economists seemed to genuinely believe Soviet growth figures and David Levy and Sandra Peart use the example of Paul Samuelson's classic textbook.[22] In the 1961 edition Samuelson pointed out that although the US was twice as wealthy as the USSR, the latter's higher growth rate meant that it would overtake the US in 36 years.[23] Three years later the textbook was revised, and sure enough the overtaking time fell to 33 years. And in the 1967 edition, the overtaking time was 28 years. But then something curious happened. The 1970 edition of the textbook predicted that the USSR would overtake the US in 35 years. And so did the 1973 edition. And the starting assumption was still that the US was twice as wealthy as the USSR. What was going on? Basically the evidence was contradicting the growth figures, but instead of questioning why this growth wasn't materialising, Samuelson simply reset the estimate. Indeed in 1980 he was still predicting that in 32 years' time the USSR would overtake the US. And yet in less than a decade it had collapsed.

The USSR taught economists that we should not fetishise growth rates. But we also need to be sure that we do not underestimate the importance of material development. Google's 'GapMinder' is an interactive tool to explore time series data, and reveal the extent to which income per capita strongly correlates with greater life expectancy and lower child mortality. Maybe it's not the 'GDP' figure that's the real problem, but the 'happiness'. As Will Wilkinson has said,

> *While no single variable has a whoppingly large positive impact on average happiness over time, none, other than life expectancy, has a larger effect than GDP per head. If becoming richer does not boost happiness, then, according to the statistics, neither does reducing unemployment, increasing welfare benefits, or ... anything.*[24]

Indeed a lot of happiness research came about during the 'great moderation', where most developed economies were enjoying steady growth. Since the 2008 financial crisis people seem to be less blasé, and realise that it can't be taken for granted. As *The Economist* says, 'there is nothing like a drop in GDP to remind everyone how much this much-maligned metric matters'.[25] Perhaps the 'materialism' of economists is something we should actually be proud of?

> *He who disdains the fall in infant mortality and the gradual disappearance of famines and plagues may cast the first stone upon the materialism of economists.*[26]

In amongst the typical gloom of economic reporting, I wish to emphasise that humanity is thriving.[27] Since 1950 the global population has risen by over 150%. What was the result? Famine? In fact undernourishment in poor countries has *fallen* from 37% to 17%.[28] And global prices fell by 75%. The countries that have embraced economic development have witnessed these gains – infant mortality in China has fallen from 195 to 30 (per 1000 births) over the last half-century. From 1980–2013 the amount of extreme poverty in China fell from 84% to 10%, which equates to about 680m people.[29] For the world as a whole, in 1990 43% of people in developing countries were classified as living in extreme poverty. By 2010 that figure had halved, as almost 1 billion people discovered economic growth.[30]

There was a myth that over the course of the twentieth century, times were getting tougher for people on middle incomes. But the 1997 Annual Report of the Federal Reserve Bank of Dallas presents 'the declining real cost of living in America'. It finds:[31]

- Since 1919 it took less than a third of the time to earn the money needed to buy a 12 item food basket.
- The price per square foot of new housing fell from 7.8 hours of work to 5.6 hours.
- In 1956 50% of new houses had a garage, 28% had two or more bathrooms, 33% had wall insulation, 11% had a dishwasher and 6% had central heating. By 1996 the figures were 86%, 91%, 93%, 93% and 81%.[32]
- In 1901 Americans would spend 76.2% of their income on food, clothing and shelter. In 1995 it was 37.7%.
- In the 1930s if you wanted to fly from coast to coast it would take 2 months' wages and you would be in a non-pressurised cabin without heating or air conditioning, making 10 stops along the way. In 1997 it was 4% of the price, quicker and far more comfortable.

Indeed it's hardly an exaggeration to say that poverty has virtually been eliminated in the rich world. It's led to policymakers redefining 'poverty' as a relative rather than absolute measure. If you look at the US Census 12.6% of Americans were deemed 'poor' in 2005. Of this number over 40% own their own home, and the average home had three bedrooms, one-and-a-half baths, a garage and a porch or patio.[33]

But let's not get complacent. Despite these massive gains plenty of people still live in genuine hardship and they could be escaping it even more quickly. A paper published by Cato created a counterfactual history of India, imagining that their reforms had begun back in 1971.[34] Their findings were that:

- 14.5 million more children would have survived.
- 261 million more people would have become literate.
- 109 million more people would have risen above the poverty line.

12.3 ECONOMIC FREEDOM

But this evidence merely undermines the extent of global inequalities. Consider the following two problems:

1. Lack of calories
2. Lack of capital.

The former refers to starvation. The latter is poverty. These issues have killed much of humanity, both historically and globally today. But if you read newspapers in the UK you're more likely to read about the following problems:

1. Obesity
2. Debt.

Note how the modern problems are due to an abundance of the historical problems. We have solved the two greatest problems facing humanity! In fact we've done it so successfully their *excess* is now our main problem. It's just that we've only done so relatively recently and in some parts of the world. So what's the difference between 'us' and 'them'?

As F. Scott Fitzgerald once wrote, 'Let me tell you about the very rich. They are different from you and me …'[35] Ernest Hemingway was said to have responded, 'Yes, they have more money.' This is trivially true. But as P.T. Bauer pointed out it is logically *untrue* that economic growth requires an influx of capital, because some countries *must* have been able to develop without already being rich.[36] The main question for development economists is how can societies that have solved these problems transfer the solutions to those who haven't? The simple answer is to transfer wealth. To take some of the calories, and some of the capital, from the richer countries and give them to the poorer ones. But this poses (at least) two problems. One is that you cannot take the wealth creation process for granted. This is like the tale of killing the golden goose. If you confiscate wealth, you reduce the incentives to generate it. Arguments about the share of the pie can end up shrinking it. The second problem relates to the process by which we might transfer resources from rich to poor countries. We can think of it as the 'development paradox': we know that foreign aid is ineffective in countries with bad governance, but can be effective in countries with good governance. But countries with good governance have a lower need for foreign aid.

The more subtle answer is that it isn't the resources that need to be transferred, but the institutions. Amartya Sen has pointed out that famines are not typically a result of food shortages. They don't occur because there isn't enough food. They're the result of inadequate institutional mechanisms.[37] Yes, the rich have more money than the poor. But the main difference is that they have economic institutions that generate growth. And this is what typically constitutes 'good' economic policy:

- Private property rights to generate incentives
- Reliable legal framework to correct externalities and constrain predation
- Stable monetary system to maximise information
- Free Trade and the embrace of markets.

This is often seen as being controversial, especially the point about free trade. But amongst economists, it isn't. According to one study, 'the authors generally find consensus within the profession ... consensus is particularly strong for propositions of free international trade and capital flows.'[38] Another study, 'uses survey data to find that 87.5 percent of the members of the American Economic Association agree that "the U.S. should eliminate remaining tariffs and other barriers to trade"'.[39] In another study, when economists were asked whether 'trade agreements between the US and other countries' is a '2 = major reason', '1 = minor reason', or '0 = not a reason at all' for why the economy is not doing better than it is, the average score for economists is 1.87.[40] As famous textbook writer Gregory Mankiw said,

> *Few propositions command as much consensus among professional economists as that open world trade increases economic growth and raises living standards. Smith's insights are now standard fare in Econ 101.*[41]

Recollect that economic calculation requires prices, which stem from exchange, which require property rights. And it is property rights that underpin development. According to Hernando De Soto 'the west' developed capital through the following steps:[42]

- Define the economic potential of assets through securities, title, contract, etc.
- Integrate legal framework into one system.
- Make people accountable through the legal system.
- Make assets fungible, by representing them in a standard form to facilitate interaction and exchange.
- Form networks of people that allow assets to move between agents.
- Protect transactions via the rule of law.

There is very strong evidence to suggest that secure property rights correlate with higher GDP/capita.[43]

This might appear to be a little theoretical, and economists are forced to rely on theory given our inability to conduct experiments. Unlike the physical sciences it's far harder for economists to isolate single variables. But human history has created a number of 'natural' experiments. The starkest, and most illustrative, happened in Korea.[44] From 1910 to 1945 Korea was under Japanese rule. It was economically, culturally and ethnically homogeneous. There were no geographical differences. But after Japan's defeat in World War II, Korea was divided in two, with the USSR controlling the North, and the US the South. This was a completely 'exogenous' separation, approximating an experiment where similar subjects are 'treated' differently. And in this case the 'test' was with regard to alternative economic and political institutions. Communism was applied in the North, and capitalism in the South. Again, this isn't a perfectly controlled experiment. It was capitalism with a large amount of government intervention and early on without democracy. But the outcome was astounding – GDP per capita sharply diverged from 1976,[45] and in 2000 it was 14 times higher in the South than the North. Robert Higgs provides an overview of the 'results' of this '50 year experiment in political economy', and on every measure the role of 'good' economic institutions shines through.[46] As the famous joke about Castro's revolution goes, 'the three successes were education, healthcare and sports. Three failures were breakfast, lunch and dinner.'[47]

This has led a number of think tanks and organisations to attempt to measure 'economic freedom',[48] and they have found that it correlates with:[49]

- Higher GDP per capita
- Higher GDP growth

- Higher life expectancy
- More income for the poorest 10%.

Although the title of this section is 'economic freedom', and I've attempted to emphasise the link to human flourishing, to some extent this phrase is misleading. According to Thomas Sowell,

> One of the last refuges of someone whose pet project or theory has been exposed as economic nonsense is to say: 'Economics is all very well, but there are also non-economic values to consider.' Presumably, these are supposed to be higher and nobler concerns that soar above the level of crass materialism.
>
> Of course there are non-economic values. In fact, there are only non-economic values. Economics is not a value in and of itself. It is only a way of weighing one value against another.[50]

As Sheldon Richman (who was drawing upon Sowell) says, 'there is no *economic* freedom. There is only freedom.'[51]

12.4 PUBLIC CHOICE THEORY

Thus far there's been little discussion of government. Typically economists view government as an outside agent that can intervene and correct for market failures. But even if the market outcome isn't perfect, why should we simply assume that the government alternative is better? There's a famous story of a King who is hiring a new singer for the court. The first one comes in and is truly awful. So the King hires the second one. But how does he know that the second one isn't even worse? Before we make a judgement about alternative institutions, we need to analyse both alternatives. We need to let the second singer sing.

Public Choice theory does exactly this. It applies economic theory to how government operates. For this reason one of the main founders, James Buchanan, referred to it as 'politics without romance'.[52] The main idea is that when people talk about government action they have a tendency to make two assumptions: that governments are omniscient (that they have sufficient information to make successful interventions) and benevolent (they have a pure heart to deliver the intended results). Public Choice theory helps us to challenge both of these.

1. Is government omniscient?

    F.A. Hayek provided the classic example for how markets aggregate and generate knowledge that simply isn't available to central agencies.[53] Prices serve a crucial communicative role in allocating resources, but are denied to policymakers who allocate resources based on hierarchical command. The argument is that rational economic calculation can only take place in market relations. Once we step out of markets, and into central planning, we stumble in the dark

2. Is government benevolent?

    James Buchanan and Gordon Tullock asked why we assume that businessmen act selfishly but politicians act altruistically.[54] They argued that this was inconsistent, and we should use the same behavioural assumptions for people regardless of whether they are operating in markets or politics. Instead of assuming that politicians have pure intentions, assume that they maximise utility subject to constraints.

Public Choice theory is not hardwired to be free market, and it is not saying that policymakers are evil. It simply applies economic logic to the political realm and argues for symmetrical behavioural assumptions. In doing so, it reveals that there are costs of government intervention as well as benefits. It may be true that markets fail, and that in theory government intervention can correct this. But Public Choice theory tells us we should either compare markets in theory with government in theory, or markets in practice with government in practice. Otherwise the analysis is rigged in favour of intervention. Public Choice is about pragmatism, and dealing with the world as it is, not how we wish it were.

Public Choice theory has several important applications, and we'll briefly look at five of them: public goods, bureaucracy, rent-seeking, interest groups and regulation.

○ **Public goods.** In economic terms there are three types of 'market failure' that are used to justify the existence of the state: monopoly, asymmetric information and public goods. We have already looked at the concepts of monopoly and asymmetric information, and these are ways in which governments intervene in markets. The third main example of market failure is about how governments *supplant* markets. As Elinor Ostrom and James Walker said, 'pure public goods have been considered the paradigm case for the necessity of the state.'[55]

Public goods are typically said to have two characteristics. Firstly, they are 'non excludable', meaning that there is no feasible way of excluding people who don't want to pay. And if people don't *have* to pay for something, they probably won't. If consumers free ride on each other, there's no profit motive for firms to produce it, and therefore the good in question will be underprovided by the market, or perhaps not even provided at all.

The second characteristic is being 'non-rivalrous'. This means that additional people can consume the product without increasing the cost of providing it. For example, if I am listening to the radio this doesn't impinge on your ability to do so. And it doesn't increase the costs of the radio station. In economic terms the marginal costs of production are zero. Recollect that in perfect competition price equals marginal cost. Again, we might expect the market to underprovide such goods because private firms will not produce goods for free. But as we've already discussed, perfect competition may not be the right benchmark. Think about a bridge. It doesn't matter whether it's used by 15 000 or 15 001 cars per day; almost all of their costs are fixed ones. Marginal cost is zero. But that doesn't mean they can't find a price. They charge in accordance with customers' marginal valuations, and restrict entry (for example with a toll booth). Crucially, as long as they can exclude non-payers, it can still be profitably provided by the market. Therefore in this case rivalry is irrelevant. Many goods are produced profitably at zero marginal cost (such as movie screenings).

In addition to this, excludability isn't fixed. To some extent it's chosen by the seller. In many supermarkets products like razorblades or batteries (which are small and expensive) are kept in secure boxes, or behind the counter. Whereas fruit and vegetables (reasonably bulky and cheap) are often kept outside the front of the shop. Firms make a deliberate tradeoff between convenience and excludability.[56]

In addition, technology isn't constant. Software companies develop ways of turning non-excludable products into excludable ones (using things like passwords). Often though, they decide that making things freely available is a more profitable strategy, either as a bundle with goods that they do charge for, or as a means of price discrimination. Indeed part of the success of the internet is that it's deliberately non-excludable. Social networks such as Facebook or Twitter could easily 'exclude' people who don't pay a subscription, but they consider higher user numbers to be more profitable than charging those customers who are willing to pay.

The key issue is the institutional framework. We know that in some cases private firms can produce 'public goods', and in some cases there are strong arguments to suggest that they can't. But given that the definition of any good is subjective, there's a danger that when politicians use public good rationale to justify intervention, it isn't because the market would underprovide, but because the market would provide less than the *policymaker* would like. There's a big difference.

The classic example of a public good is a lighthouse. It's non-excludable (it's very hard to ensure that everyone who uses the light is charged for it), and its non-rivalrous (lots of people can use it at the same time). But Ronald Coase wrote an empirical paper suggesting that in actual fact lighthouses had a long history of being provided without central government provision.[57] Public goods aren't set in stone – they are subject to entrepreneurial and technological innovation.

○ **Bureaucracy.** Cyril Northcote Parkinson once did a study of the UK Navy and discovered that even though the Navy was shrinking over time the Admiralty was constantly growing. 'Parkinson's Law' holds that 'work expands to fill the time available for completion' and suggests that bureaucracy can appear to have a life of its own. Bureaucracy isn't a purely political phenomenon, and large corporations can also suffer the costs of too much bureaucracy. We can define them as having four characteristics: (i) large; (ii) accounts for the majority of the employees' income; (iii) hiring and promotion are based on an assessment of the ability to perform an organisational role and (iv) most of the output is not sold on the open market.[58] It means that there's no profit and loss system to judge its effectiveness, and this creates scope for individuals to seek to increase their personal utility, which may be different from the goals of the sponsor. It gives space for them to operate in the dark, since there's no market mechanism to judge performance. In a classic article Roy Wintrobe presents three 'ideal type' examples of bureaucracy:[59]

> The first is 'The Daily Life of a Civil Servant', which tells the story of someone that takes full advantage of agency discretion by shirking and not doing any work.
>
> The second is 'The Servant as Master', which tells how the master steadily becomes dependent on the servant until the servant finally takes over. In economic terms it explains the role of budget maximisation.
>
> The third is 'The Banality of Evil', which looks at the property rights theorem, showing how great evils aren't conducted by sociopaths, but by ordinary people doing what appeared to be normal to them.
>
> All three of these allegories reflect truths about how bureaucracy functions.

We all have colleagues that exhibit these characteristics. The shirkers that do no work. The opportunists that seize power from their superiors. And the disengaged that destroy value without even stopping to think about it.

In Public Choice models we assume that a bureaucrat's utility function contains a mixture of power, money, income, security, etc. and there are several ways they can maximise this:

■ Asymmetric information – the bureaucrat knows the real cost of doing something, but the sponsor doesn't. It may take half an hour to perform a certain task, but they tell them it takes an hour.

■ Agenda control – bureaucrats can affect the outcome of a decision by specifying the alternatives and using framing effects.

- Selective efficiency – if you perform well at something you may be asked to do more of it, so if you underperform at a task you don't want to do, you can control the sponsor's choices.

How can they be controlled?

- Authority – orders and rules.
- Competition – make bureaucrats compete against each other and create an incentive for the true costs to be known (since they will attempt to undercut each other).
- Trust or loyalty – the sponsor can appoint a bureaucrat whose career is tied to their own, or pay higher wages to encourage loyalty.
- Incentives – such as a Beckerian punishment device (i.e. random monitoring and heavy penalties), which explains how it may be rational to impose severe punishment for relatively minor infractions (such as abusing expenses).

○ **Rent-seeking.** Rent-seeking is 'the socially costly pursuit of wealth transfers', and has been identified as a major inhibitor of economic growth. It was pioneered by Gordon Tullock and Anne Krueger, and looks at the social costs of politicians or businessmen pursuing wealth transfers, rather than wealth creation. If you think about a standard monopoly, the traditional 'cost' is the dead weight loss that is generated when output is lower and prices higher than a perfectly competitive alternative. On a graph, this is what's known as a Harberger triangle. But Tullock pointed out that if the monopoly is making profits (the rectangle) they would be willing to pay up to the amount of those profits in order to secure a monopoly. Hence firms lobby government up to the total present value of the expected profit to be granted monopoly status. The resources spent lobbying for this wealth transfer, represent socially costly rent-seeking.[60] It can be applied widely.

There have been plenty of studies to attempt to estimate the costs of rent-seeking. Andrei Shleifer used lawyers as a proxy for rent-seeking, finding that countries with more lawyers have lower growth. Others have taken an accounting approach. Anne Krueger estimated that in India in 1964 around 7% of GNP was devoted to rent-seeking, and in Turkey in 1968 it was 15%. Richard Posner estimated that 3.4% of GNP in the US in 1975 was rent-seeking activity, whilst Ross finds that in Kenya in 1984 it was 38%.

- Rent extraction

  This occurs when governments are lobbied *not* to enact a certain piece of legislation. Private companies will try to block legislation that would harm them, and in this sense governments are being paid to 'do nothing'.[61] Moreover, policymakers can *threaten* legislation in order to generate interest groups from whom they can receive funding.[62]
- Rent dissipation

  This is when the full present value of the potential rent is committed to rent-seeking. If a government licence is expected to generate £5m profit for a company, and they spend £5m on lobbying to attain it, we have rent dissipation. Next time you see a colleague taking your boss out for lunch, consider the costs of rent-seeking.

○ **Interest groups.** Interest groups arise when people wish to demonstrate an intensity of preference. In a typical democracy it may be the case that 90% of the public are indifferent to a particular policy, but 10% feel very strongly. That minority group therefore has an incentive to try to influence the political process to deliver a favourable outcome. Because they are a form of collective action, however, there is an incentive to free ride. Mancur Olson asked how groups can overcome the free rider problem, and came up with three possible ways.[63]

Firstly, they can coerce supply. Licensing requirements are an effective way to get group members to participate, for example, by restricting supply.

Secondly, they can create closed shops. Often trade unions will not *let* anyone free ride. The personal costs of striking are substantial, in terms of the lost wages and the frictions caused with employers. But the collective benefits are large. One way to prevent people from attempting to get the latter, without having to incur the former, is by picketing the employer and not letting people cross the line to work.

Thirdly, there may be a dominant demander. If one member of the group has a significantly higher preference than the others, free riding won't be sufficient to prevent them from acting. We can think of the US as being a dominant demander for NATO and although other countries may free ride on US defence spending, the US has such a large stake they will still act.

If Olson's analysis is accurate, there are a few key characteristics that would make interest groups effective:

- Small – the fewer the people the easier it is to monitor and organize.
- Homogeneous – the more similar the members' preferences, the more likely they'll see benefits from collective action.
- Private benefits – the 'by product theory' says that interest groups can fund their activities by offering private benefits to members at monopoly prices. The problem with this is that it's hard to distinguish between interest groups that provide market services, versus private companies that lobby government. Are the RAC a private company who sell breakdown insurance, or a motorists' lobby group who fund their operations through roadside assistance? It's not clear.

Olson's book *The Rise and Decline of Nations* uses interest group analysis to explain much of world history.[64] The basic idea is that interest groups are effective rent-seekers and therefore welfare destroying. Over time successful interest groups become increasingly powerful, and therefore the economy can't function smoothly. There's a point at which radical change is required to 'break' these dominant groups and reform. This explains why the fastest growing countries after World War II were the ones which had suffered the most destruction – there was an absence of established interest groups to divert resources. In the victors (especially the UK) the interest groups had survived.

This all paints a fairly negative view of interest groups, but what about the original question of whether a lot of weak preferences *should* defeat a few strong preferences? Arthur Bentley thought that law was an expression of force and tension, and that groups express their preference intensity.[65] In 1983 Gary Becker put this into economic language – he used typical rational choice assumptions (i.e. perfect information, free entry and low transaction costs).[66] He also made an assumption that interest groups had solved their dues problems (i.e. he assumes away the free rider problem). If each group campaigns until the marginal benefits (MB) of lobbying equals the marginal cost (MC) of lobbying, and if pressure groups exist on *both sides* of an issue then equilibrium occurs when these two forces offset. In other words MB (positive pressure) = MC (negative pressure). The implications of this approach are as follows:

- Interest groups are really 'pressure groups'.
- They redistribute to their own members at lowest cost to society.
- Interest groups will be optimal in size and 'efficient'.

According to Becker, 'this analysis unifies the view that governments correct market failure and provide efficiently.'[67] So we have two very different views of interest groups. To Olson they are socially inefficient phenomena that disrupt democracy. To Becker they provide efficient solutions. The fact that most lobbying tends to be done by producer groups rather than consumer groups supports the Olson view – such groups have the characteristics (small, homogenous, private benefits) that he predicts.

Also, think about things like the EU Common Agricultural Policy. Or indeed state institutions in India. By Becker's logic these are efficient. But the implication of this logic is that whatever exists must be efficient. By applying economic analysis to politics he merges the two to the extent that whatever is, is efficient. Olson's view, by contrast, provides an explanation for government failure. Brandon Fuller points out an incredible example of interest group activity.[68] It began when several US coat hanger producers complained that Chinese firms were guilty of 'dumping', which is selling a product at below cost. Economists tend to be sceptical of these claims, because if costs are subjective it makes as much sense to say that 'sellers sell at below cost' as 'buyers buy at above value'. It's logically untrue. But even if producers are trying to drive their competitor out of business with low prices, low prices are good for customers! Indeed when a tariff was applied on foreign hangers, this raised the cost to consumers from around $12.95 to $12.96. As you can imagine, this hardly caused a protest. The consumers were a dispersed cost. But across all consumers this amounted to a cost of around $120m. Therefore for US manufacturers it is quite another story. They have a concentrated benefit. Fuller points out that in 2004 there were 564 people working for US hanger manufacturers (with a typical wage of $30,000). If you assume that they would all have lost their jobs in the face of Chinese competition, and divide the cost of the tariff by those jobs, it comes out as costing $212,765 per year. So yes, politicians could brag that they 'saved' over 500 jobs from foreign competition. And the public would barely notice paying an additional penny for their dry cleaning. But at a cost of over $200,000 for every $30,000 job saved!

Why does America still have the 1-cent coin? They cost around 2.4 cents to make,[69] many traders refuse to accept them and people are willing to pay money to convert them to bills.[70] Very rarely does something cost less than 5c, and yet when things cost 99c you are given a cent back in change.[71] When you weigh up the pros and cons, it seems obvious that eliminating the penny would be a good idea. Sebastian Mallaby estimates that it costs the median worker around $3.65 per year,[72] which Greg Mankiw points out is about $1bn for the economy as a whole.[73] So what's stopping us? According to Roger Congleton, one of the main lobbying groups that want to keep the penny is 'Americans for Common Cents'. And they're funded by the zinc industry, which is – surprise surprise – what pennies are made of. Furthermore, here's Alex Tabarrok:

> On the opposite side is representative Jim Kolbe who Sebastian Mallaby calls an Olympian statesman for his opposition to the special interests and dedication to efficiency ... but it's no accident that Kolbe is from Arizona the dominant producer of copper the main ingredient in ... you guessed it ... the nickel.[74]

○ **Regulation.** Regulation is usually advocated on the grounds of consumer protection, but if we accept the implications of interest group theory this seems unlikely. We'd expect small producers to be effective lobbyists, especially individual firms in concentrated industries. We've already seen how the state possesses the power to help an industry, through the power to coerce (they can subsidise via taxation) and through control over entry (they can reduce imports via quotas or tariffs, or increase licensing requirements). Hence the government (i.e. regulators) has powers to create rents, and industries have incentives to rent-seek. The counterintuitive point is that the biggest beneficiary of regulation is often the regulated industry!

Regulatory capture occurs when an agency that is intended to pursue the public interest in fact advances the commercial interest of dominant firms. Imagine that you work for a Big Four auditor (KPMG, Deloitte, PwC, Ernst & Young), and think about who benefits from more regulation?

- Not customers, because this will raise the cost of an audit
- Not mid-tier auditors, because it's more expensive to operate
- Yes, the Big Four may have an increase in costs, but they can spread these costs over a larger amount of output. They already employ lawyers. They are involved in the consultation process. Regulation gives them a competitive edge.

I was once on an easyJet flight when I read the following in their in-flight magazine:

> [T]he same day that we took delivery of our 100th Airbus at easyJet we also called on European governments to remove almost 700 of the oldest, dirtiest aircraft from Europe's skies by banning any aircraft built before 1990 from operating within the European Union after 1st January 2012.

No doubt this law gets reported as an environmental consideration, but the quote above shows that it is part of a concerted attempt by those within the airline industry to reduce competition and use the law to harm their competitors.[75] The Chief Executive of the payday lender Wonga is even more explicit about using regulation to restrict competition: '[W]e want better regulation … as we want to keep the bad guys out.'[76] You may be surprised that moneylenders themselves, and not just consumers' interest groups, are lobbying for more regulation. But this alliance between good intentions and corporate self-interest was known during prohibition as 'Bootleggers and Baptists'. At the time, there were two groups who wanted to make alcohol illegal. Bootleggers – who could make money from controlling the illegal supply – and Baptists – who opposed it on moral grounds. Public Choice helps us realise that a lot of political activity that appears to be Baptist is really Bootleggers. Public Choice says, 'follow the money' – take the romance away and ignore the moral arguments. Instead ask 'whose interests is this legislation in?' and more often than not *that* is who's doing the real lobbying.

If the above is true, it explains where regulation comes from. But it also demonstrates a problem called the **transitional gains trap**.

According to Mark Perry, in 1937 there were 11 787 taxicab medallions in New York City (i.e. licences to operate a taxi).[77] In 2007 there were 13 087. When you consider what's happened to the demand for taxi rides over that 70-year period this shows how effective taxi drivers have been at restricting competition. New medallions are incredibly rare. Indeed when 155 were sold that year the average bid was $309 000. People were willing to pay over three hundred thousand dollars, purely for the right to operate a taxi. Back in 1937, 11 787 may have been viewed as plenty. But by giving away privileges there is immediately an interest group that has a financial stake in preventing de-regulation and free competition. As Gordon Tullock says,

> [O]nce an institution has been set up, it is not automatically reexamined on a regular basis ... this monopoly would remain in existence (and probably largely unnoticed) until such time as positive effort were made to terminate it.[78]

This creates a trap in which the initial benefits have dissipated, but entrenched groups can block reforms – indeed the greater the social benefits that deregulation would create the more vehemently they'd be opposed.

So how does deregulation occur? How do reforms that benefit consumers, rather than producers, ever happen? Industries might seek regulation and capture the regulator to protect their profits, but since this rent-seeking is inefficient over time those profits would probably fall. After all, rent-seeking costs money. Hence deregulation will occur if the regulated firms start making *less* profit than they would in a competitive market. Note that the most efficient firms would be the ones who want to deregulate, which means we should pay even less attention to those who want to remain regulated.

From 1950 to 1986 the US airline industry was quite heavily regulated by the Civil Aviation Board, who forbade price competition. But even though airlines couldn't compete on price, they had an incentive to gain more customers through other means. If you can't cut prices lower than your rivals, you can raise quality instead. Thus US airlines were notorious for their frills – champagne on flights, several flights a day to obscure places, attractive air hostesses etc. This is what's known as 'cost increasing service rivalry', and is the typical offshoot of price controls. The airlines spent so much on increasing quality they competed away all the rents, and therefore it wasn't worth being a regulated industry anymore. Throughout this period their rates of return fell until they were at competitive levels. And guess what, it was the largest (and most efficient) airlines that supported deregulation. According to some estimates deregulation saved consumers around $20bn per year,[79] and ushered in an era of low cost flying bringing air travel within the reach of ordinary people.

This section isn't intended to present the case for anarchy. But if we accept the possibility of market failure, we also need to accept the possibility of government failure. Just because markets 'fail' doesn't mean that intervention is justified. We need to weigh up the costs of market failure with the costs of government failure. We need to compare real world markets with real world government.

The implications for management are immense. Although Public Choice theory originates from a study of government, concepts such as bureaucracy, rent-seeking and interest groups also exist within firms, in the sense that companies are 'islands of conscious power in this ocean of unconscious co-operation'.[80] A recognition of the costs of hierarchy, and of central planning in the economy as a whole, can be applied to companies. If markets deliver the coordination and prosperity we see around us today, there is a major opportunity to harness that internally.

12.5 TRANSITION ECONOMICS

Public choice theory is a way to understand what economics has to say about politics, emphasising the incentives faced in the political realm. Sometimes, however, those incentives can dramatically change. According to Bruce Ackerman a '**constitutional moment**' occurs when there is a political crisis and constitutional changes are made through informal collective action.[81] In addition to understanding the types of deadlock that can occur during 'ordinary' politics, we also need a theory about how and when to pierce through it. A simple way to view this is to distinguish between incentive explanations and ideas. Jeffrey Sachs argues that in 'normal' periods the normal politics of vested interests takes the lead:

> *But when things come apart, when societies are in crisis, when new choices have to be made, when the old structures no longer have legitimacy or no longer have the power, that's when ideas can play a tremendous role.*[82]

Most management studies focus on institutional restructuring, which is analogous to the theory covered in the previous section. But companies are also capable of building meaningful constitutional orders. Therefore we need to look at how constitutional moments occur, and how change is managed. This section will do three things. It will use the collapse of communism in Central and Eastern Europe as a case study of economic transition. It will then put this in the context of the debate about shock therapy versus gradualism. Finally, we will look at how this relates to management.

The first point to make is that the end of communism was remarkably peaceful. In Poland there had been riots in 1956, 1970, 1976 and 1990, just because of price increases. And yet 200 million people went from communism to capitalism, with barely any civil disorder: 'to great positive surprise, no single postcommunist price liberalisation aroused social unrest.'[83] In marked contrast to the 'revolutions' that ousted democracy, the ones in Georgia (November 2003), Ukraine (November 2004) and the Kyrgyz Republic (March 2005) were peaceful and sought to enforce (rather than overthrow) the constitution.[84] Fifteen years after the transition process began, of the 21 communist countries in the region 18 had become market economies, but only 10 had become democracies. Never before had economists played such a central role in social restructuring, and Anders Aslund considers it a success:

> *Market economic reforms have been highly successful, whereas democratisation has only been partially auspicious, and the introduction of the rule of law even less so … At present, we seem to understand how to build a market economy, whereas the ignorance of democracy building and the construction of a legal system are all the more striking.*[85]

Chapter 4 discussed the socialist calculation debate, and explained why we expect market economies to deliver better results than centrally planned ones. In short, it is because there are effective knowledge channels and incentive mechanisms. Or, as Milton and Rose Friedman put it, there are four ways to spend money:[86]

1. You spend your own money on yourself.
2. You spend someone else's money on yourself.
3. You spend your own money on someone else.
4. You spend someone else's money on someone else.

Only in the first case is there both reasonable knowledge (about preferences) and strong incentives (to generate value). You know what you like, and want to pay as little as possible.

By the time you get to the bottom of the list, people are making decisions with no knowledge and little incentive. So we know that socialism will fail, and it is worth emphasising the fact that it did fail. Miserably. Despite starting with the Russian Revolution in 1917, by 1921 Lenin had already launched the 'New Economic Policy' because the economy had collapsed. This involved the privatisation of smaller farms, and granted farmers the ability to sell off surplus production. Some use this U-turn as evidence that socialism was never truly tried, and indeed Lenin was attempting a short cut to socialism that was different to how Marx envisaged it occurring. But the bottom line is that from the onset the socialist experiment was failing. Stalin later reversed these reforms, introducing comprehensive central planning. In 1932 he forced Ukrainian farmers into collective production, and increased their quota by 44%. The result was that 5 million people starved to death.[87]

During the 1930s it is commonly held that the USSR was industrialising. But this isn't quite true. The focus of increased production was the building of arms, and was really a strategy of 'militarisation'. They were making guns, not butter:

> *Contrary to the declared goals of the regime, it was the opposite of a system of production to create abundance for the eventual satisfaction of the needs of the population; it was a system of general squeeze of the population to produce capital goods for the creation of industrial power, in order to produce ever more capital goods with which to produce still further industrial might, and ultimately to produce armaments.*[88]

Following Stalin's death in 1953, the objective became even more explicit about prioritising military strength ahead of consumer goods and higher living standards. This is why it is foolish to use the military strength of a country to infer the underlying living standards. From the West, the military might was seen as an indicator of economic wealth. But although the weapons were real, *that's all they had.* And interestingly, when it came to militarisation – i.e. the things that the central planners wanted – the Soviets understood the socialist calculation problem. The production of military goods was organised differently from consumer goods. According to Pisar Samuel, the military sector was

> *the only sector of the Soviet economy which operates like a market economy, in the sense that the customers pull out of the economic mechanism the kinds of weaponry they want. … The military, like customers in the West … can say 'no, no, no, that isn't what we want.'*[89]

We've already seen the problems with growth figures, and the particular problems that economists had in understanding Soviet ones. And it is convenient now for Western intellectuals to claim that they didn't fully understand the scale of socialist failure. But even in 1963 an article in the *New York Times Book Review* was revealing the truth about Russian economic development.[90] In 1961 the Soviet use of all energy was equal to that of America in 1920. In 1950 the Soviet consumption per employed worker was lower than it had been in 1928. And the standard of living was lower than it had been in the USA around a hundred years earlier. Even Tintin knew what was going on, realising that 'while the Russian people are dying of hunger, immense quantities of wheat are being sent abroad to prove the so-called wealth of the Soviet paradise'.[91] And that was in 1930!

So if central planning was so bad, how did it last so long? There are several factors. Although production was inefficient they started off with lots of natural resources. Russia borrowed a lot of money (including from the US). And the existence of global markets for most of the goods produced in Russia provided a context for understanding relative scarcities, even if the price mechanism wasn't functioning within the country. Indeed an additional reason why the military sector did better than others was because it was subject to foreign competition. Since Russia wasn't completely closed from foreigners, innovations could still spill over. And finally, Russia had a strong culture of 'tolkachi', which loosely translates as 'pullers'. These are entrepreneurs that exist outside of the formal economy, and specialise in correcting the misallocation of resources. The existence of black markets demonstrates the resilience of market activity, and it provided an alternative to the official department stores and supermarkets. People do find ways to escape the state. But the knowledge problem was endemic, as Mikhail Gorbachev recognised:

> [D]uring the final years under Brezhnev, we were planning to create a commis-
> sion ... to solve the problem of women's pantyhose. Imagine a country that flies into
> space, launches Sputniks ... and it can't resolve the problem of women's pantyhose.
> There's no toothpaste, no soap powder, not the basic necessities of life.[92]

The easiest explanation for why it collapsed when it did is bankruptcy. In 1983 Ronald Reagan announced the SDI project (known as 'Star Wars'), which was a space-based missile defence system. It may well have been a bluff, but it escalated the arms race to such an extent Russia knew it simply couldn't keep up. Russia stood at the dawn of transition. As Janos Kornai points out, it had failed. Relative to the US it needed three times as many inputs to get the same level of output (and the quality was lower). Real GNP was never even half what it was in the USA, and on a per capita basis even lower.[93] As Robert Heilbroner conceded,

> The contest between capitalism and socialism is over: capitalism has won.[94]

Just like with Korea, the politics of Eastern Europe represented a natural experiment, when the (relatively) culturally and economically homogenous Germany was split in two. In the East, a command economy. In the west, capitalism. The results of that experiment were spectacular. As John Kay says, 'One third of the way through, it was necessary to build a wall ... , otherwise the inhabitants of one zone would mostly have fled to the other.'[95] In 1989 the wall *did* come down and the disparities were revealed to all. Living standards were noticeably higher in the West.

At the dawn of transition it is easy to underestimate the challenges facing the Russian economy. In Russia, in the winter of 1991 there was just two months of grain left and shops were empty.[96] The economy was completely dysfunctional:

- Many goods had negative economic value. The marginal costs of producing them were higher than the marginal value.
- There were no supply networks other than the state, leading to falling output and shortages.
- Bankrupt public finances were being financed through hyperinflation.
- Entrepreneurs and other wealth creators outside of the formal economy had no incentive to become transparent.

- Interest groups were committed to rent-seeking.
- There was distrust between public officials and the general public.

The problem with interest groups was twofold. Firstly, you had bureaucrats wanting to obstruct reforms in order to retain their positions of authority. And secondly, you had opportunistic businessmen wanting to take advantage of the arbitrage possibilities during transition and to benefit from the privatisation process. These arbitrage opportunities included the following: the fact that prices were fixed domestically but traded at market rates abroad; that raw materials (e.g. grain) could be imported through subsidised prices, but sold as a finished good (e.g. bread) at market prices; and the ability to obtain credit from the state at a fixed interest rate (e.g. 25%) despite inflation of around 2500%. In 1992 direct subsidies accounted for over 10% of Russian GDP, and the opportunities for rent-seeking were enormous.

It was in this context that the debate about the speed of transition took place. There was a consensus amongst economists about the direction required. The 'good' economic policy already discussed was seen as the goal: (i) private property rights, (ii) a reliable legal framework, (iii) a stable monetary system and (iv) free trade. The issue was how to reach it. Some organisations, such as the UN Commission for Europe, argued that market liberalisation should follow the creation of market institutions. The problem with this was that the countries that were slow to liberalise were even slower to build institutions. Maybe they didn't want to reform after all? There was such overwhelming pressure to move towards liberalisation that there was no viable alternative. The bureaucrats saw the tide turning and wanted to be on the right side of history. But how could they retain their positions of authority in a free market economy? By delaying it for as long as possible. According to Oleh Havrylyshyn,

> the proclamations of the political elites in these countries that the society was not ready for the market and gradual evolution was necessary, were not sincere proclamations but masked a hidden agenda.[97]

No doubt some reformers truly believed that gradual reforms were better than fast ones. But policymakers could not take a successful transition for granted. It wasn't so much a choice between shock therapy and gradualism, but between reforms or no reforms. There's a tendency for modern commentators to neglect the fact that Belarus, Turkmenistan and Uzbekistan also entered the transition process. But they ended it as authoritarian dictatorships. With that in mind, 'too fast' is better than 'not at all'. We need to be clear: the reason for the crisis was the failure of state institutions. To rely on them to deliver subtle and steady reforms was naïve at best. As William Lloyd Garrison famously said, 'gradualism in theory is perpetuity in practice.' Ultimately the amount of reforms that had been enacted by 1994–96 pretty much determined how thorough the reforms would be for the next decade. In Anders Aslund's terms, 'the longer the first jump, the farther each country went.'[98]

This emphasis on the window of opportunity is a recurring feature of interviews with policymakers. According to the then Polish Finance Secretary Leszek Balcerowicz,

> The first phase had to be very fast and very comprehensive ... just after breakthrough, there is a short period, which I named the period of extraordinary politics. By definition, people are ready to accept more radical solutions because they are pretty euphoric of freshly regained freedom.[99]

Whilst in the words of the then Prime Minister of Estonia, Mart Laar,

That window of opportunity does not last long. It quickly gives way to the more mundane politics of contending parties and interest groups, which is normal in established democracies.[100]

According to Peter Boettke, economic shock therapy stems from the need to make real time reforms in a world of opportunism and distrust. He lists four key aspects:[101]

1. Understand the current position.
2. Understand the informal institutions that are currently at play.
3. Design reforms that address both the knowledge problem and incentive problem.
4. Send credible signals that policymakers are committed to reforms.

He also points out that the use of the term 'shock therapy' to describe radical transition is inappropriate. Shock therapy originated as a prelude to medical treatment. It was used on patients suffering mental illness because they were considered so far from recovery that they needed a drastic measure to basically reset the brain. It is an intervention, not a cure. By contrast, the economic policies being discussed now were not intending to 'shock' the economy. The collapse of communism was the 'shock'. These economic policies were intended to rebuild it – they were a proffered cure. And because the structural inefficiencies were so deep rooted, effective transition could only take place with an immediate step into a market context.[102]

The most famous example of 'shock therapy' is the Balcerowicz Program, which was designed for Poland but became a standard for radical and comprehensive reforms. Anders Aslund summarises it as follows:[103]

1. Macroeconomic stabilisation
    End hyperinflation through fiscal discipline and sound monetary policy. This involves the creation of a ministry of finance and an independent central bank. Allow foreign currency to be fully convertible to enable foreign trade.
2. Deregulation
    Allow prices to derive from supply and demand. Cut subsidies, liberalise trade and break up monopolies. Given the existence of shortages free trade is even more important as a means of increasing the availability of goods.
3. Privatisation
    Make it easy to start new businesses, and sell large state owned companies to the private sector.
4. Social safety net
    Provide assistance for workers that lose their jobs, and pensioners who lose their wealth due to the inflation.

The countries that embraced this programme of reforms most were Poland, Czech Republic, Estonia, Latvia and Lithuania. The results were outstanding. Although inequality rose in all countries, other indicators of living standards – such as infant mortality and life expectancy – improved. These reforms were popular. Generally speaking, governments that adopted radical policies did better in elections than gradualist ones,[104] and opinion polls suggested that if anything people thought the pace of change was too slow.[105] The GDP figures showed an initial decline, but growth rebounded quickly. This is to be expected, and not necessarily bad.

In the Soviet system you get paid for how much you produce. So there's an incentive to overstate your economic activity. In a market economy you get *taxed* on what you produce. Therefore there is an incentive to underreport your activity. This is one reason why we might expect official GDP to be lower as you move into a capitalist system. In addition to this, lots of the production prior to 1992 was destroying value. If the 'lost output' is for goods that have no consumer demand, you *want* to see GDP fall.[106] In addition, Andrei Shleifer and Daniel Treisman point out that the biggest fall in output tends to occur in the countries that reformed the most. This may simply be because the figures became more accurate, and therefore it's hard to make pre- and post-reform comparisons.[107]

Some people are surprised to see social welfare occupy such a prominent role in the plan for 'shock therapy'. However it is to be expected that unemployment will rise during a transition process. This isn't because existing jobs suddenly become redundant, but because they are revealed to already be redundant. Consequently a new social safety net was part of the programme. According to the World Bank health expenditure rose in real terms – from 4% of GDP in 1991 to 6% in 2003.[108] The education system was transformed, with subjects such as economics being offered for the first time and the number of university students doubled from 1989 to 1999.[109] In fact, it could be argued that some of the social spending was impeding transition. In Russia and the Ukraine only 10% of social transfers ended up with the poorest 20% of the population.[110] This suggests that the better off were better rent-seekers than the needy.

Recollect that credibility plays an important role in the transition process. Many attempts at reform had occurred previously, and it cannot be taken for granted that it will be a success. Khrushchev's reforms were treated as a 'big lie', and Gorbachev had been associated with 'indecision and inconsistency'.[111] The Russian government in 1992 was claiming that the country would become a democratic market economy, but the reality suggested otherwise. Black markets still existed. Investors were still moving their capital overseas. In short, Boris Yeltsin wasn't a credible reformer.[112] For example, price liberalisation began in January 1992, but by March Yeltsin was condemning 'profiteering' and placing restrictions on the amounts being sold.[113] Faced with mounting budget deficits the economic advice given to Russia was to slash government spending and sell off assets. Instead, they monetised the debt. Therefore the hyperinflation wasn't the result of shock therapy, but the fact that it wasn't being employed. As Jeffrey Sachs – one of the key World Bank advisors at the time – said, 'The advice that I gave: Eliminate price controls, stop subsidies to loss-making state enterprises, make the currency convertible and open the economy to trade.'[114] He points out that these measures worked in Poland, Estonia, Slovenia and elsewhere. They curtailed hyperinflation and generated growth. In his opinion 'The same advice would have worked in Russia, but it was not followed.'[115]

With regard to privatisation, this was one of the most crucial aspects of the Balcerowicz programme. To some extent the transition from socialism to capitalism *is* simply an exercise in privatisation. And indeed the scale of privatisation across Central and Eastern Europe was staggering. In less than a decade over 150 000 large and medium enterprises, hundreds of thousands of small firms and millions of apartments were released from the grasp of the state.[116] In a presentation for the Peterson Institute, Anders Aslund provides compelling evidence to show that privatisation is correlated with more democracy and less corruption.[117] He says,

> *The more partial and slower the reforms were, the greater the distortion and the larger the rents. The most prominent source of rent seeking in the public mind was privatization, but rent seeking peaked in 1992 when privatization had barely started.*[118]

This isn't to say that privatisation wasn't without problems. But they occurred mostly where it was slow and corrupt. Although many think that it was done to the benefit of outsiders, a lot of vouchers were granted to employees. And this isn't necessarily the best way to instigate change. Robert Skidelsky explains the problem:

> *As a result of privatization, managers and workers ended up owning about 70 per cent or more of each company, with managers obtaining far more than they got in closed subscriptions ... Workers and management collude to maintain their existing position with subsidies from the central bank. In a typical large-firm privatisation, only 14% of shares are owned by outsiders.*[119]

The question though isn't whether or not privatisation was perfect, but whether corrupt privatisation was better than no privatisation. It should be expected that a privatisation process will be flawed. After all, if we knew how much the assets were worth, and how they should be managed, there would be no need to privatise in the first place. Although conventional wisdom says that it was just a racket to make some politically connected 'oligarchs' rich at the expense of everyone else, there's more to it than that. The oligarchs prospered because they had a unique skill set. They had sound management skills and the ability to run a large company. But they also had knowledge of the local norms and the country-specific situation. Lots of foreign companies entered Russia in the mid-1990s and were stung by the situation they faced. But oligarchs didn't create this situation. As Grigory Yavlinsky said, 'business is people who are playing the game which the state is offering them.'[120] If the rules are bad, the problem is with policymakers. The oligarchs performed an important role in the economy at an important time.[121]

I haven't tried to draw too explicit a connection between the transition process and corporate transformation, but the relevance should be obvious. We can view the dissolution of the USSR as a large corporate unravelling, and use the same toolkit to learn about issues such as entrenched bureaucracies, interest group deadlock, shock therapy and the importance of 'constitutional moments' that engage the people who participate in radical change. The key insight is that successful transition isn't a result of putting better people in charge. It's about creating the conditions required for markets to operate. You solve the knowledge and incentive problems by replacing hierarchies with markets.

This book has been about economics, and has attempted to provide a fair reflection of the field. Economics is a positive science – the logic is independent of ethical or moral conclusions. When done well, it can help to *inform* our moral opinions, but there is always a danger that our prior beliefs shape how we approach the discipline. I'm sure my own belief in the beauty and power of markets is evident, but I also hope that I have given a fair account of the theories and schools of thought that I don't find convincing. And I also hope that I've been clear about where there is a reasonable degree of consensus amongst economists, so that it doesn't appear as if I'm presenting 'my' opinions. In this chapter in particular, we have looked at topics that touch upon far more disciplines than economics. Therefore it's only honest to be explicit about some of the issues that we've left off the table. I've put to one side the pre-institutional determinants of growth. There may well be crucial differences between countries that explain economic growth prior to the economic institutions I've mentioned. I'd recommend three books that look at this in more detail. In *Guns, Germs and Steel* Jared Diamond makes the case that geography matters, and in particular that development is due to an uneven distribution of domesticable plants and animals.[122] I also recommend *The Wealth and Poverty of Nations*, by David Landes. He asks what was special about England that meant it led the Industrial Revolution, and focuses on issues such as culture, climate and the role of science.[123] Deirdre McCloskey's *The Bourgeois Virtues* argues that the Industrial Revolution was due to respect for innovation and the culture of commerce.[124]

Economics is supposed to be fun. It is illuminating. It helps us to see the world in a different way. But it is important, because the stakes are high. In the words of Israel Kirzner:

'Economics is not an intellectual game. Economics is deadly serious. The very future of mankind – of civilization – depends … upon [the] widespread understanding of, and respect for, the principles of economics …'[125]

NOTES

1. Krugman, P. (1990) *The Age of Diminishing Expectations: U.S. Economics Policy in the 1990s*, MIT Press.
2. Warner, B. (2012) The 25 Richest People Who Ever Lived – Inflation Adjusted, Celebrity Net Worth, 13 October [http://www.celebritynetworth.com/articles/entertainment-articles/25-richest-people-lived-inflation-adjusted/#!/1-mansa-musa-net-worth_1019/ accessed 25 September 2013].
3. Perhaps we have mass marketing to thank for this, as Andy Warhol implies:
   'What's great about this country is that America started the tradition where the richest consumers buy essentially the same things as the poorest. You can be watching TV and see Coca-Cola, and you know that the President drinks Coke, Liz Taylor drinks Coke, and just think, you can drink Coke, too. A Coke is a Coke and no amount of money can get you a better Coke than the one the bum on the corner is drinking. All the Cokes are the same and all the Cokes are good. Liz Taylor knows it, the President knows it, the bum knows it, and you know it.'
   Warhol, A. (1975) *The Philosophy of Andy Warhol (From A to B and Back Again)*, Harvest (cited by Kottke, J. (2010) Andy Warhol on Coca-Cola, *Kottke.org*, 18 October).
4. Flanders, S. (2011) The search for growth, *BBC News*, 15 March 2011, [http://www.bbc.co.uk/blogs/thereporters/stephanieflanders/2011/03/the_search_for_growth.html, accessed 24 September 2013].
5. Cowen, T. (2002) Does the welfare state help the poor? in Frankel-Paul, E., Miller, F. and Paul, J., *Should Differences in Income and Wealth Matter?* Cambridge University Press.
6. The assumptions used are that 'poor' means 'bottom 10%', 'rich' means 'top 10%', and we care only about consumption. The figures are valid for 2004 at PPP. See Rodrik, D. (2007) And the winner is …, *Dani Rodrik's Weblog*, 5 May [http://rodrik.typepad.com/dani_rodriks_weblog/2007/05/and_the_winner_.html, accessed September 2013].
7. Romer, P.M. (1994) The Origins of Endogenous Growth, *The Journal of Economic Perspectives*, **8** (1), 3–22.

8. Kling, A. and Schulz, N. (2009) *From Poverty to Prosperity: Intangible assets, hidden liabilities and the lasting triumph over scarcity*, Encounter.
9. Boettke, P.J. and Coyne, C.J. and Leeson, P.T. (2008) Institutional Stickiness and the New Development Economics, *American Journal of Economics and Sociology*, **67** (2), 331–358.
10. Gross, D. (2007) Thy Neighbor's Stash, *New York Times*, 5 August.
11. Mankiw, N.G. (2007) Do people dislike being around the rich?, *Greg Mankiw's Blog*, 4 August [http://gregmankiw.blogspot.co.uk/2007/08/do-people-dislike-being-around-rich.html, accessed 24 September 2013].
12. Tabarrok, A. (2007) Home envy, *Marginal Revolution*, 6 August [http://marginalrevolution.com/marginalrevolution/2007/08/home-envy.html, accessed 24 September 2013].
13. Easterlin, R.A. (1974) Does Economic Growth Improve the Human Lot? in David, P.A. and Reder, M.W. (eds), *Nations and Households in Economic Growth: Essays in Honor of Moses Abramovitz*, Academic Press, Inc.
14. See Jones, H. and Ormerod, P. (2007) *Happiness, Economics and Public Policy*, Institute of Economic Affairs.
15. One reason why happiness didn't seem to rise with GDP is because in 1964 the survey question changed. The highest answer is now 'completely satisfied'. Previously it was 'Although I am not innumerably satisfied, I am generally satisfied with life now.' See Leonhardt, D. (2008) Maybe money does buy happiness after all, *New York Times*, 16 April.

    Carroll, J. (2007) Most Americans 'Very Satisfied' With Their Personal Lives, *Gallup Wellbeing*, 31 December [http://www.gallup.com/poll/103483/Most-Americans-Very-Satisfied-Their-Personal-Lives.aspx, accessed 24 September 2013].
16. Carroll, J., Most Americans (n 15).
17. Deaton, A. (2008) Worldwide, Residents of Richer Nations More Satisfied, *Gallup Wellbeing*, 27 February [http://www.gallup.com/poll/104608/worldwide-residents-richer-nations-more-satisfied.aspx, accessed 24 September 2013].
18. Sacks, D.W., Stevenson, B., and Wolfers, J. (2010) Subjective wellbeing, income, economic development, and growth, NBER Working Paper No. 16441.
19. Stevenson, B., and Wolfers, J. (2013) Subjective wellbeing and income – is there any evidence of satiation? NBER Working Paper No. 18992.
20. 'Money can buy happiness', *The Economist*, 2 May 2013.
21. See Roberts, P.C. (2002) My time with Soviet economics, *The Independent Review*, **7** (2).
22. Levy, D.M. and Peart, S.J. (2011) Soviet growth and American textbooks: An endogenous past, *Journal of Economic Behavior & Organization*, **78** (1–2), 110–125.
23. I'm using their 'max-max' measure, which assumed that they both grow at the maximum forecast rate. The basic point remains if you use other scenarios.
24. Wilkinson, W. (2006) Growth is good, *Prospect Magazine*, 21 October.
25. 'The joyless of the jobless', *The Economist*, 27 November 2010.
26. Mises, L.v. (1949[1996]) *Human Action: A Treatise of Economics*, Fox & Wiles, p. 193.
27. See Jacoby, J. (2007) A World Full of Good News, *The Boston Globe*, 13 May.
28. I don't like using the terms 'developed' and 'developing' countries. The whole point of 'development' is that rich countries are the ones that are 'developing' and poor countries aren't!
29. 'Towards the end of poverty', *The Economist*, 1 June 2013.
30. 'Towards the end of poverty' (n 29).
31. Time Well Spent The Declining Real Cost of Living in America, 1997 Annual Report, Federal Reserve Bank of Dallas [http://dallasfed.org/assets/documents/fed/annual/1999/ar97.pdf, accessed 24 September 2013].
32. If you think these sorts of household appliances are flippant, see Hans Rosling's TED talk about the social impact of washing machines: http://www.ted.com/talks/hans_rosling_and_the_magic_washing_machine.html [accessed 24 September 2013].

In addition, it's not only that the penetration of consumption goods has increased, but also they are spreading at a faster rate. Computers existed in the 1960s, but it was only in the 1990s that people were likely to own one. As Alexis Madrigal says, 'more time was spent going from zero to one percent penetration than from one to 50'. But now things – especially consumer technology – tend to be available to all more quickly. See Madrigal, A.C. (2012) Most people didn't have A/C until 1973 and other strange tech timelines, *The Atlantic*, 27 July.

33. Rector, R.E. (2007) How Poor Are America's Poor? Examining the 'Plague' of Poverty in America? Heritage Foundation Backgrounder #2064.

34. Swaminathan S. Anklesaria Aiyar (2009) Socialism Kills The Human Cost of Delayed Economic Reform in India, CATO Institute, 21 October.

35. This quote appears in Fitzgerald, F.S. (1926) *The Rich Boy*, but it is often misquoted as 'The rich are different to you and me'.

36. Bauer, P.T. (2004) *From Subsistence to Exchange and Other Essays*, Princeton University Press. It is important to see a distinction here between government-to-government transfers of capital, and the flow of capital due to the profit seeking activity of private foreign investment. See Mises, L.v. (1979[2006]) *Economic Policy*, Ludwig von Mises Institute (3rd edition).

37. Sen, A. (1981) *Poverty and Famines: An Essay on Entitlements and Deprivation*, Oxford, Clarendon Press.

38. Fuller, D. and Geide-Stevenson, D. (2003) Consensus among economists: Revisited. *Journal of Economic Education*, **34**, 369–387.

39. Whaples, R. (2006) Do Economists Agree on Anything? Yes! *The Economists' Voice*, **3** (9), 1–6.

40. Caplan, B. (2002) Systematically Biased Beliefs About Economics: Robust Evidence of Judgmental Anomalies from the Survey of Americans and Economists on the Economy, *Economic Journal*, **112** (479), 433–458.

41. Mankiw, N.G. (2006) Outsourcing Redux, *Greg Mankiw's Blog*, 7 May [http://gregmankiw. blogspot.com/2006/05/outsourcing-redux.html, accessed September 2013].

42. De Soto, H. (2000) *The Mystery of Capital: Why Capitalism Triumphs in the West and Fails Everywhere Else*, Basic Books, pp. 49–62.

43. Acemoglu, D., Johnson, S. and Robinson, J. (2005) Institutions as the Fundamental Cause of Long-Run Growth, in Aghion, P. and Durlauf, S. (eds), *Handbook of Economic Growth*, North Pole.

44. Acemoglu, Johnson and Robinson, Institutions as the Fundamental Cause (n 43).

45. Acemoglu, Johnson and Robinson, Institutions as the Fundamental Cause (n 43) (see Figure 3).

46. Higgs, R. (2000) Results of a Fifty-Year Experiment in Political Economy, *The Independent Review* **5** (1). For China vs. Taiwan see Higgs, R. (2001) Results of Another Fifty-Year Experiment in Political Economy, *The Independent Review*, **5** (4). For Estonia vs. Finland see Higgs, R. (2007) Results of Still Another Fifty-Year Experiment in Political Economy, *The Independent Review*, **12** (1).

47. Jokes don't require citations, but see Anderson, K. (2011) Craft an attention-grabbing message, Harvard Business Review Blog Network, 29 December. Although America is often considered to be a young country, Galileo was offered a chair at Harvard University (see Micklethwaite, J. and Wooldridge, A. (2004) *The Right Nation: Conservative Power in America*, Penguin).

48. For example, Economic Freedom of the World, Fraser Institute, [http://www.freetheworld.com/, accessed 24 September 2013] and Index of Economic Freedom, Wall Street Journal/Heritage Foundation [http://www.heritage.org/index/, accessed 24 September 2013].

49. Lawson, R.A. (2007) Economic Freedom, *The Concise Encyclopaedia of Economics* (2nd edition) [http://www.econlib.org/library/Enc/EconomicFreedom.html, accessed 24 September 2013].

50. Sowell, T. (2007) *Basic Economics: A Common Sense Guide to the Economy*, Basic Books.

51. Richman, S. (2012) There's No Such Thing as Economic Freedom. There is only freedom, *The Freeman*, 8 June [http://www.fee.org/the_freeman/detail/theres-no-such-thing-as-economic-freedom, accessed 25 September 2013].

52. Buchanan, J.M. (1979) Politics without Romance: A Sketch of Positive Public Choice Theory and Its Normative Implications, Inaugural Lecture, Institute for Advanced Studies, Vienna, Austria, *IHS Journal, Zeitschrift des Instituts für Höhere Studien*, **3**, B1–B11.

53. Hayek, F.A. (1945) The Use of Knowledge in Society, *American Economic Review*, **35** (4), 519–530.

54. Buchanan, J.M. and Tullock, G. (1962) *The Calculus of Consent*, University of Michigan Press.

55. Ostrom, E. and Walker, J. (1997) *Neither markets nor states: linking transformation processes in collective-action arenas*, in Mueller, D.C. (ed.) *Perspectives on Public Choice*, Cambridge University Press, p. 35.

56. The US federal government shutdown in October 2013 led to the restriction of access to various national parks. For example, the World War II memorial in Washington DC was barricaded to prevent people from visiting it (despite it being on open land with minimal supervision required). Note the irony – these sorts of monuments are publicly operated on the grounds that they are non-excludable, and yet when the administration wanted to signal to the public the importance of securing a budget, they easily blocked admission. See World War II memorial becomes shutdown central, *Wall Street Journal Blogs*, 2 October 2013 [http://blogs.wsj.com/washwire/2013/10/02/world-war-ii-memorial-becomes-shutdown-central/, accessed 25 November 2013].

57. See Coase, R.H. (1974) The Lighthouse in Economics, *Journal of Law and Economics*, **17** (2), 357–376. Coase provided historical evidence to show that lighthouses have been provided by private organisations, and his main aim was to say, 'economists should not use the lighthouse as an example of a service which could only be provided by government'. However, this doesn't mean that government played no role in the provision of lighthouses. Peter Klein argues that Coase's main insight was that 'public goods can be financed through user fees, rather than general tax revenue' (Klein, P.G. (2006) Was Coase Right about the Lighthouse?, *Organisations and Markets*, 24 October [http://organizationsandmarkets.com/2006/10/24/was-coase-right-about-the-lighthouse/, accessed 25 November 2013]). Also see van Zandt, D. (1993) The lessons of the lighthouse: 'Government' or 'private' provision of goods, *Journal of Legal Studies*, **22** (1), 47–72 and Bertrand, E. (2006) The Coasean Analysis of Lighthouse Financing: Myths and Realities, *Cambridge Journal of Economics*, **30** (3), 389–402.

58. Downs, A. (1965) A Theory of Bureaucracy, *American Economic Review*, **55** (1/2), 439–446.

59. Wintrobe, R. (1997) Modern bureaucratic theory, in Mueller, D.C., *Perspectives on Public Choice: A Handbook*, Cambridge University Press.

60. Note that bribery is often used as an example of rent-seeking, but the definition of rent-seeking is the pursuit of a wealth transfer. A bribe is a wealth transfer; therefore it cannot be considered rent-seeking. However spending resources to be in a position that will allow you to receive bribes is rent-seeking.

61. McChesney, F.S. (1997) *Money for Nothing: Politicians, Rent Extraction and Political Extortion*, Harvard University Press.

62. McChesney, F.S. (1987) Rent extraction and rent creation in the economy theory of regulation, *Journal of Legal Studies*, **16** (1), 101–118.

63. Olson, M. (1965[1971]) *The Logic of Collective Action*, Harvard University Press.

64. Olson, M. (1962) *The Rise and Decline of Nations*, Yale University Press.

65. Bentley, A. (2008[1908]) *The Process of Government: A Study of Social Pressures*, Transactions Publishers.

66. Becker, G.S. (1983) A Theory of Competition among Pressure Groups for Political Influence, *Quarterly Journal of Economics*, **98** (3), 371–400.

67. Becker, A Theory of Competition (n 66).

68. Fuller, B. (2008) The Hanger Hang-Up, *Aplia Econ Blog*, 21 May [http://econblog.aplia.com/2008/05/hanger-hang-up.html, accessed 24 September 2013].

69. 'Making no cents', *The Economist*, 12 May 2012.

70. 'The penny drops', *The Economist*, 2 March 2013.

71. One of the reasons for requiring the shopkeeper to provide change is because it forces them to open the till, and therefore reduces corruption and stealing. It's a monitoring device.

72. Mallaby, S. (2006) The Penny Stops Here, *Washington Post*, 25 September 2006 [http://www.washingtonpost.com/wp-dyn/content/article/2006/09/24/AR2006092400946.html, accessed 24 September 2013].

73. Mankiw, N.G. (2006) How to make $1 billion, *Greg Mankiw's Blog*, 25 September [http://gregmankiw.blogspot.co.uk/2006/09/how-to-make-1-billion.html, accessed 24 September 2013].

74. Tabarrok, A. (2006) Penny Politics, *Marginal Revolution*, 26 September [http://marginalrevolution.com/marginalrevolution/2006/09/penny_politics.html, accessed 24 September 2013].

75. As another example, the English Premier League introduced a rule to say that managers have to possess the UEFA 'A' Pro License. The effects of this are that the supply of managers will shrink, so remaining managers will be able to command higher wages. Managers that don't have the badge are worse off, because they can't get a job. Managers that do have the licence see an increase in wages through a reduction in competition. It won't be a surprise to learn that the League Managers Association campaigned for the rule change.

76. Quinn, J. (2013) Wonga calls for tougher rules on payday loans, *Daily Telegraph*, 29 June.

77. Perry, M. (2007) Taxi Cartel Membership Has Its Privileges: Returns That Have Outperformed Every Major Index, *Carpe Diem*, 3 November [http://mjperry.blogspot.com/2007/11/taxi-cartel-membership-has-its.html, accessed 24 September 2013].

78. Tullock, G. (1975) The Transitional Gains Trap, *Bell Journal of Economics and Management Science*, **6** (2), 671–678.

79. 'Alfred Kahn', *The Economist*, 22 January 2011.

80. Robertson, D.H. (1923) *Control of Industry*, Nisbet & Co.

81. Ackerman, B. (1991) *We the People: Foundations*, Harvard University Press; Ackerman, B. (1998) *We The People: Transformations*, Harvard University Press.

82. Sachs, Jeffrey, Interview with PBS Commanding Heights, conducted 15 June 2000.

83. Aslund, A. (2007) *How Capitalism was Built: The Transformation of Central and Eastern Europe, Russia, the Caucasus, and Central Asia*, Cambridge University Press.

84. This is not to say that the entire transition process occurred without violence. There was obviously a war in Yugoslavia, Armenia and Azerbaijan; civil wars in Tajikstan and Georgia; and violent secessions in Georgia, Moldova and Chechnya.

85. Aslund, *How Capitalism was Built* (n 83), pp. 305 and 311.

86. Friedman, M. and Friedman, R. (1980) *Free to Choose*, Harcourt.

87. Conquest, R. (1986) *The Harvest of Sorrow*, Oxford University Press.

88. Malia, M. (1994) *The Soviet Tragedy: A History of Socialism in Russia 1917–1991*, Free Press, p. 209.

89. Smith, H. (1974) *The Russians*, Ballantine, pp. 312–313.

90. Gass, O. (1963) Russian economic development, *New York Review of Books*, **1** (1).

91. Herge (1930) *Tintin in the Land of the Soviets*, Le Petit Vingtième.

92. Gorbachev, M., Interview with PBS Commanding Heights, conducted 4 April 2001.

93. Skidelsky, R. (1997) *The Road from Serfdom*, Penguin; Kornai, J. (1992) *The Socialist System: The Political Economy of Communism*, Princeton University Press, pp. 362, 315.

94. Heilbroner, R. (1989) Reflections, 'The Triumph of Capitalism', *The New Yorker*, 23 January, p. 98.

95. Kay, J. (1997) A German lesson, *Financial Times*, 3 January.

96. 'Yegor Gaidar', *The Economist*, 19 December 2009.

97. Havrylyshyn, O. (2006) *Divergent Paths in Post-Communist Transformation: Capitalism for All or Capitalism for the Few?* Palgrave Macmillan, p. 272.

98. Aslund, *How Capitalism was Built* (n 83), p. 84.

99. Balcerowicz, L., Interview with PBS Commanding Heights, conducted 12 November 2000.

100. Laar, M. (2007) *The Estonian Economic Miracle*, Heritage Foundation, p. 3.

101. Boettke, P. (1999) The Russian Crisis, *American Journal of Economics and Sociology*, **58** (3), 371–384.
102. Boettke, The Russian Crisis (n 101).
103. Aslund, *How Capitalism was Built* (n 83), p. 33. Balcerowicz, L. (1995) *Socialism, Capitalism, Transformation*, Central European University Press.
104. Aslund, *How Capitalism was Built* (n 83), p. 217.
105. Aslund, *How Capitalism was Built* (n 83), p. 233.
106. Shleifer, A. and Treisman, D. (2005) A Normal Country: Russia After Communism, *Journal of Economic Perspectives*, **19** (1), 151–174.
107. Shleifer and Treisman, A Normal Country (n 106).
108. Aslund, *How Capitalism was Built* (n 83), p. 190.
109. Aslund, *How Capitalism was Built* (n 83), p. 195.
110. Aslund, *How Capitalism was Built* (n 83), p. 198.
111. Goldman, M. (1991) *What Went Wrong with Perestroika?* Norton.
112. During a 1995 stay at the White House, Yeltsin was found by secret service half naked and totally drunk trying to hail a taxi. When questioned he said that he was trying to get a pizza. See Thompson, P. (2009) Drunk Boris Yeltsin was found outside White House in underpants trying to hail cab 'because he wanted some pizza', *Daily Mail*, 22 September.
113. Boettke, P. (1993) Yeltsin's shock therapy applied too little voltage, *Orange County Register*, 31 January.
114. Sachs, J. (1998) The Dismal Decade, *Los Angeles Times*, 22 November.
115. Sachs, The Dismal Decade (n 114).
116. Aslund, *How Capitalism was Built* (n 83).
117. Aslund, A. (2007) How Capitalism was Built, Peterson Institute for International Economics, Washington DC, 19 September.
118. Aslund, *How Capitalism was Built* (n 83), pp. 51–52.
119. Skidelsky, R. (1997) *The Road from Serfdom*, Penguin, p. 156.
120. Yavlinsky, Y., Interview with PBS Commanding Heights, conducted 9 October 2000.
121. Oligarchs have a very bad reputation amongst the general public, but the biggest scandals tend to either be overstated or contrary to the economic advice. The infamous 'loan for shares' scandal, for example, had little to do with transition policy. The idea was for Russian businessmen to give the government loans in exchange for shares in strategic assets. Given that most of the economically viable industries were not part of the early privatisation plans, entrepreneurs were keen to own them. Many of the companies ended up being bought back by the people giving the loans, making them very wealthy. But this scheme was proposed in 1995, just one year before a general election. At the time there was a real chance that communists might return to power, and Yeltsin was desperate to solidify support (and improve public finances). As his advisor Anatoly Chubais said, 'tomorrow I would do the same, if only for winning the battle with the Communists, which it was at the time' [Chubais, A., Interview with PBS Commanding Heights, conducted 12 December 2000].

    Norilsk Nickel was a state owned mining company, which was privatised in 1997. One of the entrepreneurs that bought out the company, Vladimir Potanin, became a famous oligarch. But within a year they had paid all salary debt, restructured several billion dollars' worth of outstanding debt, and implemented a crisis management process. Despite having had no reinvestment in over 20 years, in the early 2000s more than $1bn was put into the company [Vladimir Potanin, Interview with PBS Commanding Heights, conducted 6 October 2000, and Boris Jordan, Interview with PBS Commanding Heights, conducted 3 October 2000].

    Another example is the oil and gas company Yukos. It was set up in 1993 and produced 20% of Russia's oil (which amounted to about 2% of global output). A minority stake was privatised for $310 million, but by 2003 it had a market capitalisation of $45 billion. This is often treated as evidence of the nation's wealth being handed over to the rich. But this ignores the extent to which the value is a result of managerial decisions. And debate about 'who benefited' focuses only on the incentive function of markets. Rather than squabble about desert, we also need to recognise the knowledge function, and the importance of having a reasonable estimate of what the company is actually worth. By 2000 it had an annual tax bill of $6 billion, so it isn't as if the 'public' didn't share in the turnaround. In 2007 the company was dissolved following tax issues with the Russian government, and the Chairman and CEO Mikhail Khordokovsky was exiled to Siberia. According to *The Economist*, he 'financed boarding schools for orphans, computer classes for village schools and civil-society programmes for journalists and politicians' ['Modernising Russia', *The Economist*, 13 March 2010]. It is conceivable that his treatment by Putin had an element of political motivation. It is debatable whether these examples demonstrate that the oligarchs had too much power, or too little.

The oligarchs that profiteered from transition only did so whilst the window of transition was open, after which they consolidated and reinvested. According to Andrei Shleifer and Daniel Treisman, 'the audited financial statements of these companies suggest that their assets have grown dramatically, especially since 1998 … and the major oligarchs have been investing hundreds of millions of dollars annually in their companies … in contrast, the greatest asset-stripping scandals occurred in companies that remained under state control' [Shleifer and Treisman, A Normal Country, p. 29].

122. Diamond, J. (1997) *Guns, Germs and Steel*, W.W. Norton.
123. Landes, D.S. (1998) *The Wealth and Poverty of Nations*, W.W. Norton.
124. McCloskey, D.N. (2006) *The Bourgeois Virtues*, University of Chicago Press.
125. Comments made during the acceptance speech of his lifetime achievement award from the Society for the Development of Austrian Economics. For a transcript see Sautet, F. (2006) Lifetime Achievement Award to Professor Israel M. Kirzner, Coordination Problem, 22 November [http://austrian economics.typepad.com/weblog/2006/11/lifetime_achiev.html, accessed 25 September 2013].

Bibliography

AUTHORED BOOKS, ARTICLES, WORKING PAPERS, SPEECHES AND BLOGS

Acemoglu, D., Johnson, S. and Robinson, J. (2005) Institutions as the Fundamental Cause of Long-Run Growth, in Aghion, P. and Durlauf, S. (eds), *Handbook of Economic Growth*, North Pole.

Ackerman, B. (1991) *We the People: Foundations*, Harvard University Press.

Ackerman, B. (1998) *We the People: Transformations*, Harvard University Press.

Adams, S. (1995) The Dilbert Principle, *Wall Street Journal*, 22 May [http://voxmagister.ifsociety.org/dilbert_principle.htm, accessed 17 December 2013].

Akram, Q.F., Rime, D. and Sarnoa, L. (2006) Arbitrage in the Foreign Exchange Market: Turning on the Microscope, Norges Bank Working Paper No. 2005/12.

Albergotti, R. and Wang, S. (2009) Is it time to retire the football helmet?, *Wall Street Journal*, 11 November [http://online.wsj.com/article/SB10001424052748704402404574527881984299454.html accessed 24 September 2013].

Alchian, A. and Allen, W.R. (1964) *University Economics*, Belmont.

Alesina, A. (2010) Fiscal adjustments: What do we know and what are we doing?, Mercatus Center Working Paper No. 10-61.

Alesina, A. and Ardagna, S. (2009) Large changes in fiscal policy: taxes versus spending, NBER Working Paper No. 15438, October.

Alesina, A. and Ardagna, S. (2010) 'Large changes in fiscal policy: taxes versus spending', *Tax Policy and the Economy*, Volume 24, The University of Chicago Press, pp. 35–68.

Alesina, A., Carloni, D. and Lecce, G. (2011) The electoral consequences of large fiscal adjustments, NBER Working Paper No. 17655, December 2011.

Anderson, K. (2011) Craft an attention-grabbing message, *Harvard Business Review Blog Network*, 29 December.

Ariely, D. (2010) *Predictably Irrational*, Harper.

Arnold, R.A. (2013) *Macroeconomics*, Cengage (11th edition).

Aslund, A. (2007) *How Capitalism was Built*, Peterson Institute for International Economics, Washington DC, 19 September.

Aslund, A. (2007) *How Capitalism was Built: The Transformation of Central and Eastern Europe, Russia, the Caucasus, and Central Asia*, Cambridge University Press.

Balcerowicz, L. (1995) *Socialism, Capitalism, Transformation*, Central European University Press.

Barro, R. (1974) Are Bonds Net Wealth?, *Journal of Political Economy*, **82** (6), 1095–1117.

Barro, R. (2009) Government Spending is No Free Lunch, *Wall Street Journal*, **22** January.

Bartlett, B. (2000) Thank you Federal Reserve, *American Enterprise*, pp. 20–23.

Bastiat, F. (1850) *That Which Is Seen, and That Which Is Not Seen*, Impr. de F. Pérez.

Bauer, P.T. (2004) *From Subsistence to Exchange and Other Essays*, Princeton University Press.

Becker, G.S. (1983) A Theory of Competition among Pressure Groups for Political Influence, *Quarterly Journal of Economics*, **98** (3), 371–400.

Becker, G.S. (1992) The economic way of looking at life, Nobel Lecture [http://www.nobelprize.org/nobel_prizes/economic-sciences/laureates/1992/becker-lecture.pdf accessed 24 September, 2013].

Bennett, A. (1999) *The Lady in the Van*, Profile Books.

Bentley, A. (2008[1908]) *The Process of Government: A Study of Social Pressures*, Transactions Publishers.

Bentolila, S., Dolado, J. and Jimeno, J.F. (2012) The Spanish labour market: A very costly insider-outsider divide, *VoxEU.org*, 20 January [http://www.voxeu.org/article/jobless-spain-what-can-be-done-about-insider-outsider-divide, accessed 3 October 2013].

Beowulf (2011) Coin Seigniorage and the Irrelevance of the Debt Limit, 3 January [http://my.firedoglake.com/beowulf/2011/01/03/coin-seigniorage-and-the-irrelevance-of-the-debt-limit/, accessed 29 September 2013].

Berg, J.E., Nelson, F.D. and Rietz, T.A. (2008) Prediction market accuracy in the long run, *International Journal of Forecasting*, **24** (2), 285–300.

Bergh, A. and Karlsson, M. (2010) Government size and growth: Accounting for economic freedom and globalization, *Public Choice*, **142** (1–2), 195–213.

Bernanke, B. (2002) Deflation: Making sure 'it' doesn't happen here, Remarks at the National Economists Club, Washington DC, 21 November [http://www.federalreserve.gov/boarddocs/speeches/2002/20021121/, accessed September 2013].

Bernanke, B. (2002) FRB Speech: Remarks by Governor Ben S. Bernanke, At the conference to honor Milton Friedman, University of Chicago, 8 November.

Bernanke, B. (2004) Money, Gold, and the Great Depression, H. Parker Willis Lecture in Economic Policy, Washington and Lee University, Lexington, Virginia, 2 March [http://www.federalreserve.gov/boarddocs/speeches/2004/200403022/, accessed 30 September 2013].

Bernanke, B. (2006) Panel Discussion: Comments on the Outlook for the U.S. Economy and Monetary Policy, at the International Monetary Conference, Washington, DC, 5 June.

Bernanke, B. and Gertler, M. (1989) Agency costs, net worth, and business fluctuations, *American Economic Review*, **79** (1), 14–31.

Bernholz, P. (2006) *Monetary Regimes and Inflation: History, economics and political relationships*, Edward Elgar.

Bertrand, E. (2006) The Coasean Analysis of Lighthouse Financing: Myths and Realities, *Cambridge Journal of Economics*, **30** (3), 389–402.

Bewley, T.F. (2002) *Why Wages Don't Fall During a Recession*, Harvard University Press.

Binmore, K. and Klemperer, P. (2001) The biggest auction ever: the sale of British 3G telecom licenses [http://papers.ssrn.com/sol3/papers.cfm?abstract_id=297879, accessed 30 September 2013].

Blanchard, O., Griffiths, M. and Gruss, B. (2013) Boom, Bust, Recovery Forensics of the Latvian Crisis, Fall 2013 Brookings Panel on Economic Activity, 19–20 September 2013.

Blanchard, O.J. and Summers, L.H. (1987) Hysteresis in unemployment, *European Economic Review*, **31** (1–2), 288–295.

Blaug, M. (1995) *The Quantity Theory of Money: From Locke to Keynes and Friedman*, Edward Elgar.

Blodget, H. (2010) So THIS is how Bloomberg gets earnings reports hours before they're publicly released, *Business Insider*, 17 December [http://www.businessinsider.com/bloomberg-earnings-news-2010-12, accessed 4 October 2013].

Blustein, P. (2005) *And the Money Kept Rolling In*, Public Affairs.

Boettke, P.J. (1989) Austrian Institutionalism: A Reply, *Research in the History of Economic Thought and Methodology*, **6**, 181–202.

Boettke, P.J. (1990) *The Political Economy of Soviet Socialism: The Formative Years*, 1918–1928, Kluwer.

Boettke, P.J. (1993) *Why Perestroika Failed: The Politics and Economics of Socialist Transformation*, Routledge.

Boettke, P.J. (1993) Yeltsin's shock therapy applied too little voltage, *Orange County Register*, 31 January.

Boettke, P.J. (1999) The Russian Crisis, *American Journal of Economics and Sociology*, **58** (3), 371–384.

Boettke, P.J., Coyne, C.J. and Leeson, P.T. (2008) Institutional Stickiness and the New Development Economics, *American Journal of Economics and Sociology*, **67** (2), 331–358.

Booth, P. (2012) Thirty years of fiscal drag, *Institute of Economic Affairs Blog*, 16 May [http://www.iea.org.uk/blog/thirty-years-of-fiscal-drag, accessed September 2013].

Booth, P. (ed.) (2006) Were 364 economists all wrong? Institute of Economic Affairs.

Boudreaux, D. (2006) Framing the 'trade deficit', *Cafe Hayek*, 21 March [http://cafehayek.com/2006/03/framing_the_tra.html, accessed 4 October 2013].

Boulding, K. (1966) The economics of knowledge and the knowledge of economics, *American Economic Review, Papers and Proceedings*, **56**, 1–13.

Boulding, K.E. (1986) Proceedings of the 7th Friends Association for Higher Education Conference, Malone College.

Bradsher, K. (2008) China Shuns Investments in West's Finance Sector, *New York Times*, 3 December.

Broadbent, B. and Daly, K. (2010) Limiting the Fall-Out from Fiscal Adjustment, Goldman Sachs Global Economics Paper No. 195, 14 April.

Buchanan, J. (1969) *Cost and Choice: An enquiry in economic theory*, University of Chicago Press.

Buchanan, J. and Wagner, R.E. (1977) *Democracy in Deficit: The political legacy of Lord Keynes*, Academic Press Inc.

Buchanan, J.M. (1979) Politics without Romance: A Sketch of Positive Public Choice Theory and Its Normative Implications, Inaugural Lecture, Institute for Advanced Studies, Vienna, Austria, *IHS Journal, Zeitschrift des Instituts für Höhere Studien*, **3**, B1–B11.

Buchanan, J.M. and Tullock, G. (1962) *The Calculus of Consent*, University of Michigan Press.

Bulow, J. and Klemperer, P. (1994) Rational Frenzies and Crashes, *Journal of Political Economy*, **102** (1), 1–23.

Burn-Callander, R. (2013) UK workers waste a year of their lives in useless meetings, *Management Today*, 18 March.

Burns, A.F. and Mitchell, W.C. (1946) *Measuring Business Cycles*, National Bureau of Economic Research.

Byard, R.W., Cala, A., Ritchey, D. and Woodford, N. (2011) Bicycle helmets and accidental asphyxia in childhood, *Medical Journal of Australia*, **194** (1), 49.

Caplan, B. (2002) Systematically Biased Beliefs About Economics: Robust Evidence of Judgmental Anomalies from the Survey of Americans and Economists on the Economy, *Economic Journal*, **112** (479), 433–458.

Caplan, B. (2007) *The Myth of the Rational Voter*, Princeton.

Caplan, B. (2013) The myopic empiricism of the minimum wage, *EconLog*, 12 March [http://econlog.econlib.org/archives/2013/03/the_vice_of_sel.html, accessed 3 October 2013].

Caplan, B. (2013) Why Don't Wages Fall During a Recession?: Q&A With Me Channeling Truman Bewley, *EconLog*, 23 September [http://econlog.econlib.org/archives/2013/09/why_dont_wages.html. accessed 23 September 2013].

Card, D. and Krueger, A.B. (1994) *Myth and Measurement: The new economics of the minimum wage*, Princeton University Press.

Carroll, J. (2007) Most Americans 'Very Satisfied' With Their Personal Lives, Gallup Well-being, 31 December [http://www.gallup.com/poll/103483/Most-Americans-Very-Satisfied-Their-Personal-Lives.aspx, accessed 24 September 2013].

Chapman, S. (2007) In a world of options for consumers, fear of mergers is misplaced, *Baltimore Sun*, 26 June.

Clark, T. (2007) Don't Fear Starbucks, *Slate.com*, 28 December.

Coase, R.H. (1937) The Nature of the Firm, *Economica* **4** (16), 386–405.

Coase, R.H. (1974) The Lighthouse in Economics, *Journal of Law and Economics*, **17** (2), 357–376.

Coase, R.H., 'Biographical', NobelPrize.org [http://www.nobelprize.org/nobel_prizes/economic-sciences/laureates/1991/coase-bio.html, accessed 7 October 2013].

Cochrane, J.H. (2009) Fiscal Stimulus, Fiscal Inflation, or Fiscal Fallacies?, Unpublished manuscript, 27 February [http://faculty.chicagobooth.edu/john.cochrane/research/papers/fiscal2.htm, accessed 7 October 2013].

Cole, H.L. and Ohanian, L.E. (2004) New Deal Policies and the Persistence of the Great Depression: A General Equilibrium Analysis, *Journal of Political Economy*, **112**, 813.

Coles, P., Lakhani, K. and McAfee, A. (2007) Prediction Markets at Google, Harvard Business School Case No. 9-607-088, 20 August.

Commons, J. R. (1931) Institutional Economics, *American Economic Review*, **21**, 648–657.

Conquest, R. (1986) *The Harvest of Sorrow*, Oxford University Press.

Conway, E. (2013) Making sense of Britain's lopsided recovery, *Sky News*, [http://news.sky.com/story/1018975/making-sense-of-britains-lopsided-recovery, accessed 23 September 2013].

Cosmides, L. and Tooby, J. (1992) Cognitive adaptations for social exchange, in Barkow, J., Cosmides, L. and Tooby, J. (eds), *The Adapted Mind: Evolutionary Psychology and the Generation of Culture*, Oxford University Press.

Cowen, T. (1995) A Review of G.C. Archibald's Information, Incentives, and the Economics of Control, *Journal of International and Comparative Economics*, **4**, 243–249.

Cowen, T. (1997) *Risk and Business Cycles*, Routledge.

Cowen, T. (2002) Does the welfare state help the poor? in Frankel-Paul, E., Miller, F. and Paul, J., *Should Differences in Income and Wealth Matter?*, Cambridge University Press.

Cowen, T. (2004) How do economists think about rationality? in Byron, B. (ed.), *Satisficing and Maximizing*, Oxford University Press.

Cowen, T. (2012) *An Economist Gets Lunch*, E.P. Dutton & Co.

Cowen, T. and Tabarrok, A. (1995) Good grapes and bad lobsters: Applying the Alchian and Allen Theorem, *Economic Inquiry*, **33**, 253–256.

Cowen, T. and Tabarrok, A. (2012) *Modern Principles: Macroeconomics*, Worth (2nd edition).

Coyne, C.J. (2006) Reconstructing Weak and Failed States: Foreign Intervention and the Nirvana Fallacy, *Foreign Policy Analysis*, **2**, 343–361.

Curtis, P. (2010) How Nick Clegg got it wrong on debt, *The Guardian Politics Blog*, 9 May [http://www.theguardian.com/politics/reality-check-with-polly-curtis/2012/may/09/nickclegg-davidcameron, accessed 26 September 2013].

De Soto, H. (2000) *The Mystery of Capital: Why Capitalism Triumphs in the West and Fails Everywhere Else*, Basic Books.

Deaton, A. (2008) Worldwide, Residents of Richer Nations More Satisfied, Gallup Wellbeing, 27 February [http://www.gallup.com/poll/104608/worldwide-residents-richer-nations-more-satisfied.aspx, accessed 24 September 2013].

Diamond, J. (1997) *Guns, Germs and Steel*, W.W. Norton.

Dillow, C. (2007) Splitting the home office and transaction costs, *Stumbling and Mumbling*, 24 January [http://stumblingandmumbling.typepad.com/stumbling_and_mumbling/2007/01/splitting_the_h.html, accessed 7 October 2013].

Dillow, C. (2009) Yes, the market is efficient, *Stumbling and Mumbling*, 6 August.

Dillow, C. (2011) How bonuses backfire, *Stumbling and Mumbling*, 19 September and Dillow, C. (2011) How bonuses backfire, *Stumbling and Mumbling*, 1 March.

Dillow, C. (2012) Unemployment: a river not a pool, *Stumbling and Mumbling*, 16 May [http://stumblingandmumbling.typepad.com/stumbling_and_mumbling/2012/05/unemployment-a-river-not-a-pool.html, accessed 23 September 2013].

Dohmen, T.J. (2008) Do professionals choke under pressure?, *Journal of Economic Behavior & Organization*, **65** (3–4), 636–653.

Doornik, K. and Roberts, J. (2011) Nokia corporation: Innovation and efficiency in a high-growth global firm, Stanford University Graduate School of Business, Case No. S-IB-23, February 2011, p. 2.

Doucet, L. (2013) Syria's battle for bread, *BBC News*, 16 December [http://www.bbc.co.uk/news/world-middle-east-25397140, accessed 20 December 2013].

Dowd, K. (1989) *The State and the Monetary System*, Hemel Hempstead: Philip Allan, and New York: St Martin's Press.

Downs, A. (1965) A Theory of Bureaucracy, *American Economic Review*, **55** (1/2), 439–446.

Drucker, P. (1995) The Information Executives Truly Need, *Harvard Business Review*, **73** (1), 54–62.

Dustmann, C., Frattini, T. and Halls, C. (2009) Assessing the fiscal costs and benefits of A8 migration to the UK, Centre for Research and Analysis of Migration, Discussion Paper 18/09, July.

Easterlin, R.A. (1974) Does Economic Growth Improve the Human Lot? in David, P.A. and Reder, M.W. (eds), *Nations and Households in Economic Growth: Essays in Honor of Moses Abramovitz*, Academic Press, Inc.

Ellicott, C. (2012) Steel yourselves for the smaller new 5p and 10p that will save Treasury £8 million a year, *Daily Mail*, 23 January 2012.

Ellis, B., Marissa Mayer's first-year pay: $6 million, *CNN Money*, 1 May 2013 [http://money.cnn.com/2013/04/30/technology/marissa-mayer-pay/ accessed 17 November 2013].

Elster, J. (1982) Marxism, Functionalism and Game Theory, *Theory and Society*, **11**, 453.

Evans, A.J. (2010) Only Individuals Choose, in Boettke, P.J. (ed.) *Handbook on Contemporary Austrian Economics*, Edward Elgar.

Evans, A.J., Sola, D. and Poenaru, A. (2008) *Enterprising Britain: Building the enterprise capital of the world*, independent report for the Conservative Party.

Fackler, M. (2009) Japan's big-works stimulus is a lesson, *New York Times*, 5 February.

Fainaru-Wada, M. and Fainaru, S. (2013) *League of Denial: The NFL, Concussions and the Battle for Truth*, Crown Archetype.

Fama, E.F. (1965) Random Walks in Stock Market Prices, *Financial Analysts Journal*, **21** (5), 55–59.

Fama, E.F. (1970) Efficient Capital Markets: A Review of Theory and Empirical Work, *Journal of Finance*, **25** (2), 383–417.

Farrow, P. (2008) Interest rates: How do gilts work and where can I buy them? *The Daily Telegraph*, 7 November.

Faulks, S. (2007) *Engleby*, Hutchinson.

Feldmann, H. (2010) Government size and unemployment: Evidence from industrial countries, *Public Choice*, **127** (3–4), 451–467.

Ferguson, M.F. and Witte, H.D. (2006) Congress and the Stock Market (13 March). Available at SSRN: http://ssrn.com/abstract=687211.

Ferguson, N. (2008) Wall Street Lays Another Egg, *Vanity Fair*, December.

Ferguson, N. (2013) An open letter to the Harvard community, *The Harvard Crimson*, 7 May [http://www.thecrimson.com/article/2013/5/7/Ferguson-Apology-Keynes/, accessed 30 September 2013].

Ferguson, N. (2013) An unqualified apology, *NiallFerguson.com*, 5 April [http://www.niallferguson.com/blog/an-unqualified-apology, accessed 30 September 2013].

Fischhoff, B. (1982) Debiasing, in Kahneman, D., Slovic, P. and Tversky, A. (eds), *Judgement under Uncertainty: Heuristics and biases*, Cambridge University Press.

Fisman, R. and Sullivan, T. (2013) *The Org. The Underlying Logic of the Office*, Twelve Books.

Fitzgerald, F.S. (1926) *The Rich Boy*.

Flanders, S. (2009) It might not be you, *Stephanomics Blog*, 23 February.

Flanders, S. (2011) The search for growth, *BBC News*, 15 March 2011, [http://www.bbc.co.uk/blogs/thereporters/stephanieflanders/2011/03/the_search_for_growth.html, accessed 24 September 2013].

Florio, M. (2013) Meriweather returns with a bang, *NBC Sports*, 28 October [http://profootballtalk.nbcsports.com/2013/10/28/meriweather-returns-with-a-bang/ accessed 17 November 2013].

Foldvary, F.E. and Klein, D.B. (2003) *The Half Life of Policy Rationales*, New York University Press.

Forsyth, J.E., Gupta, A., Haldar, S. and Marn, M.V. (2000) Shedding the commodity mind-set, *McKinsey Quarterly*, **4**, 79–85.

Foss, N.J. and Klein, P.G. (2012) *Organizing Entrepreneurial Judgment*, Cambridge University Press.

Friedberg, R.M. (2001) The impact of mass migration on the Israeli labour market, *Quarterly Journal of Economics*, **1116** (4), 1373–1408.

Friedman, J. (2010) Capitalism and the crisis, in Friedman, J. (ed.) *What Caused the Financial Crisis?* University of Pennsylvania Press, p. 45.

Friedman, M. (ed.) (1956) *Studies in the Quantity Theory of Money*, The University of Chicago Press.

Friedman, M. (1957) *A Theory of the Consumption Function*, Princeton University Press.

Friedman, M. (1963) *Inflation: Causes and Consequences*, Asia Publishing.

Friedman, M. (1970) The Counter-Revolution in Monetary Theory, IEA Occasional Paper, no. 33.

Friedman, M. (1998) Markets to the rescue, *Wall Street Journal*, 13 October.

Friedman, M. and Friedman, R. (1980) *Free to Choose*, Harcourt.

Friedman, M. and Schwartz, A.J. (1963) *A Monetary History of the United States*, Princeton University Press.

Froeb, L.M. and McCann, B.T. (2008) *Managerial Economics*, Thomson South Western (2nd edition).

Froeb, L.M., McCann, B.T., Ward, M.R. and Shor, M. (2013) *Managerial Economics*, Thomson South Western (3rd edition).

Froeb, L.M. and McCann, B.T. (2008) *Managerial Economics*, Cengage learning (1st edition).

Fuller, B. (2008) The Hanger Hang-Up, *Aplia Econ Blog*, 21 May [http://econblog.aplia.com/2008/05/hanger-hang-up.html, accessed 24 September 2013].

Fuller, D. and Geide-Stevenson, D. (2003) Consensus among economists: Revisited. *Journal of Economic Education*, **34**, 369–387.

Gallagher, P. (2013) Hats on for cyclists? With deaths at a five-year high – calls for helmets to be made compulsory are getting louder. But not everyone agrees, *The Independent*, 4 August.

Garrison, R. (2001) *Time and Money*, Routledge.

Garrison, R.W. (1985) Predictable behaviour: Comment, *American Economic Review*, **75** (3), 76–78.

Garrison, R.W. (1997) The Austrian theory of the business cycle, in Glasner, D. (ed.) *Business Cycles and Depressions*, Garland Publishing.

Gass, O. (1963) Russian economic development, *New York Review of Books*, **1** (1).

Geroski, P. and Gregg, P.A. (1997) *Coping with Recession*, Cambridge University Press. Cited by Dillow, C. (2005) Geroski on recession, *Stumbling and Mumbling*, 31 August [http://stumblingandmumbling.typepad.com/stumbling_and_mumbling/2005/08/geroski_on_rece.html, accessed 23 September 2013].

Ghemawat, P. (2011) *World 3.0: Global Prosperity and How to Achieve It*, Harvard Business School Press.

Giavazzi, F. and Pagano, M. (1990) Can fiscal contractions be expansionary? Tales of two small European countries, NBER Working Paper 3372.

Gibson, Warren, C. (2011) Unemployment: What is it?, *The Freeman*, November.

Gneezy, U. and Rustichini, A. (2000) A Fine is a Price, *The Journal of Legal Studies*, **29** (1), 1–17.

Goff, S. and Jenkins, P. (2013) Job half done for Lloyds' chief António Horta-Osório, *Financial Times*, 13 October.

Goldman, M. (1991) *What Went Wrong with Perestroika?* Norton.

Good, W.R. and Hermansen, R.W. (1997) *Index Your Way to Investment Success*, New York Institute of Finance.

Greenwood, J. (2006) Monetary policy and the Bank of Japan, in Booth, P. and Matthews, K. (eds), *Issues in Monetary Policy*, John Wiley & Sons.

Gross, D. (2007) Thy Neighbor's Stash, *New York Times*, 5 August.

Grote, D. (2009) Gilt yields plunge as Bank of England prepares to splurge 'new' cash, *City Wire*, 10 March.

Gurri, A. (2011) Create value not jobs, 4 December [http://adamgurri.com/?p=78, accessed 23 September 2013].

Gwartney, J.D., Stroup, R.L., Sobel, R.S. and Macpherson, D.A. (2010) *Economics: Private and Public Choice*, Cengage Learning.

Hanke, S.H. (2009) R.I.P. Zimbabwean dollar, Cato Institute, 5 February [for a collection of articles in the Zimbabwe hyperinflation see http://www.cato.org/zimbabwe, accessed 25 November 2013].

Harford, T. (2007) Minibar Economics: Why you should stay at hotels that overcharge for drinks and Wi-Fi access, *Slate*, 17 February, [http://www.slate.com/articles/arts/the_undercover_economist/2007/02/minibar_economics.html, accessed 19 September 2013].

Harford, T. (2008) Why a tax cut just isn't fair on teenagers, *Financial Times*, 31 May.

Harford, T. (2009) Some recession experiences are more equal than others, *Financial Times*, 21 February.

Harper, F.A. (1957) *Why Wages Rise*, Foundation for Economic Education.

Harris, J. (2011) King lifts lid on inflation error, *City AM*, 17 February.

Harvey, C.R. (1986) *Recovering Expectations of Consumption Growth from an Equilibrium Model of the Term Structure of Interest Rates*, University of Chicago Dissertation [http://faculty.fuqua.duke.edu/~charvey/Research/Thesis/Thesis.htm, accessed 26 September 2013].

Havrylyshyn, O. (2006) *Divergent Paths in Post-Communist Transformation: Capitalism for All or Capitalism for the Few?* Palgrave Macmillan.

Hayek, F.A. (1931[2008]) *Prices and Production*, Mises Institute.

Hayek, F.A. (1931) Reflections on the Pure Theory of Money of Mr J. M. Keynes, *Economica*, **33**, 270–295.

Hayek, F.A. (1945) The Use of Knowledge in Society, *American Economic Review*, **35** (4), 519–530.

Hayek, F.A. (1948[1980]) The Meaning of Competition, in *Individualism and Economic Order*, University of Chicago Press.

Heath, A. (2012) QE not the answer to UK's problems, *City AM*, 10 February 2012.

Heilbroner, R. (1989) Reflections, 'The Triumph of Capitalism', *The New Yorker*, 23 January, p. 98.

Henderson, D. (2001) *The Joy of Freedom*, Prentice Hall.

Henderson, D. (2010) Canada's budget triumph, Mercatus Center Working Paper, 30 September.

Henderson, D.R. (2010) GDP fetishism, *Library of Economics and Liberty*, 1 March.

Henry Ford's $5-a-Day Revolution, Ford News Center, [http://corporate.ford.com/news-center/press-releases-detail/677-5-dollar-a-day, accessed 22 November 2013].

Herge (1930) *Tintin in the Land of the Soviets*, Le Petit Vingtième.

Herndon, T., Ash, M. and Pollin, R. (2013) Does high public debt consistently stifle economic growth? A critique of Reinhart and Rogoff, University of Massachusetts Amherst Political Economy Research Institute Working Paper.

Higgs, R. (1992) Wartime Prosperity? A Reassessment of the U.S. Economy in the 1940s, *The Journal of Economic History*, **52** (1), 41–60.

Higgs, R. (1997) Regime uncertainty: why the Great Depression lasted so long and why prosperity resumed after the war, *The Independent Review*, **1** (4), 561–590.

Higgs, R. (2000) Results of a Fifty-Year Experiment in Political Economy, *The Independent Review*, **5** (1).

Higgs, R. (2001) Results of Another Fifty-Year Experiment in Political Economy, *The Independent Review*, **5** (4).

Higgs, R. (2007) Results of Still Another Fifty-Year Experiment in Political Economy, *The Independent Review*, **12** (1).

Hijzen, A., Upward, R. and Wright, P. (2007) *Job Creation, Job Destruction and the Role of Small Firms: Firm-Level Evidence for the UK*, Globalisation and Economic Policy Research Centre, University of Nottingham, February 2007.

Horwitz, S. (1990) A subjectivist approach to the demand for money, *Journal des Economistes et des Etudes Humaines*, **1** (4), 459–471.

Horwitz, S. (2003) The Costs of Inflation Revisited, *Review of Austrian Economics*, **16** (1), 77–95.

Horwitz, S. (2009) Wal-Mart to the rescue: Private enterprise's response to Hurricane Katrina, *The Independent Review*, **13** (4), 511–528.

Hughes, T.P. (2004) *American Genesis: A Century of Invention and Technological Enthusiasm, 1870–1970*, University of Chicago Press.

Hulbert, M. (2008) Can You Beat the Market? It's a $100 Billion Question, *New York Times*, 9 March.

Hummel, J.R. (1996) *Emancipating Slaves, Enslaving Free Men*, Open Court.

Ingram, J. (1970) *International Economic Problems*, John Wiley & Sons, (see version written by Robert Schenk, available online [http://ingrimayne.saintjoe.edu/econ/International/InternTrade.html, accessed 16 September 2013]).

Ito, T. and Mishkin, F. (2004) Two decades of Japanese monetary policy and the deflation problem, NBER Working Paper No. 10878.

Jacoby, J. (2007) A World Full of Good News, *The Boston Globe*, 13 May.

James, D.N. (2002) The Trouble I've Seen, *Harvard Business Review*, **80** (3), 42–49.

Jensen, M.C. and Meckling, W.H. (1976) Theory of the firm: managerial behaviour, agency costs and ownership structure, *Journal of Financial Economics*, **3** (4), 305–360.

Jones, H. and Ormerod, P. (2007) *Happiness, Economics and Public Policy*, Institute of Economic Affairs.

Kahan, D.M., Wittlin, M., Peters, E. et al (2011) The Tragedy of the Risk-Perception Commons: Culture Conflict, Rationality Conflict, and Climate Change, Temple University Legal Studies Research Paper No. 2011-26; Cultural Cognition Project Working Paper No. 89; Yale Law & Economics Research Paper No. 435; Yale Law School, Public Law Working Paper No. 230.

Kahneman, D. (2011[2012]) *Thinking, Fast and Slow*, Penguin.

Kahneman, D. and Tversky, A. (1979) Prospect Theory: An Analysis of Decision under Risk, *Econometrica*, **47** (2), 263–291.

Kapuscinski, R. (1994) *Imperium*, Granta (English translation).

Kay, J. (1997) A German lesson, *Financial Times*, 3 January.

Kay, J. (2004) When to ask an expert and when a crowd, *Financial Times*, 31 August.

Kay, J. (2008) There are many sensible reasons for irrational behaviour, *Financial Times*, 26 August.

Kestenbaum, D. (2012) Why coke cost a nickel for 70 years, *NPR*, 15 November [http://www.npr.org/blogs/money/2012/11/15/165143816/why-coke-cost-a-nickel-for-70-years, accessed 29 September 2013].

Keynes, J.M. (1922) Introduction to the Cambridge Economic Handbook Series, in Robertson, D.H., *Money*, Cambridge University Press.

Keynes, J.M. (1924) *Tract on Monetary Reform*, Macmillan.

Keynes, J.M. (1936[1973]) *The General Theory of Employment, Interest and Money*, Cambridge University Press.

Keynes, J.M. (1937) The General Theory of Employment, *The Quarterly Journal of Economics*, **51** (2), 209–223.

Keynes, J.M. (1942) *Collected Writings*, vol. XXVII.

Kindleberger, C.P. (1978) *Manias, Panics, and Crashes: A History of Financial Crises*, Macmillan.

Kindleberger, C.P. and Aliber, R. (2005) *Manias, Panics and Crashes*, John Wiley & Sons.

Kirzner, I.M. (1973) *Competition and Entrepreneurship*, University of Chicago Press.

Kirzner, I.M. (1982) Competition, Regulation, and the Market Process: An 'Austrian' Perspective, *Cato Policy Analysis* **18**.

Kirzner, I.M. (1996) *The Meaning of Market Process*, Routledge.

Kitch, E.W. (1983) The fire of truth: a remembrance of law and economics at Chicago, 1932–1970, *Journal of Law and Economics*, **26** (1), 163–234.

Klein, D.B. (2005) The People's Romance: Why People Love Government (as Much as They Do), *The Independent Review*, **10** (1), 5–37.

Klein, P.G. (2006) Was Coase Right about the Lighthouse?, *Organisations and Markets*, 24 October [http://organizationsandmarkets.com/2006/10/24/was-coase-right-about-the-lighthouse/, accessed 25 November 2013]).

Kling, A. (2008) Lectures on macroeconomics [http://arnoldkling.com/econ/macrolectures.html, accessed 4 October 2013].

Kling, A. (2009) The recalculation model, simplified, *EconLog*, 6 September [http://econlog.econlib. org/archives/2009/09/the_recalculati.html, accessed 23 September 2013].

Kling, A. (2009) What Makes Health Care Different? *EconLog*, 22 July 2009 [http://econlog.econlib. org/archives/2009/07/what_makes_heal.html, accessed 17 November 2013].

Kling, A. and Schulz, N. (2009) *From Poverty to Prosperity: Intangible assets, hidden liabilities and the lasting triumph over scarcity*, Encounter.

Knight, F. (1921[2006]) *Risk, Uncertainty and Profit*, Dover.

Koch, C.G. (2006) *The Science of Success*, John Wiley & Sons.

Kolhatkar, S. (2012) John Paulson's very bad year, *Bloomberg Business Week*, 28 June.

Kornai, J. (1992) *The Socialist System: The Political Economy of Communism*, Princeton University Press.

Kotlikoff, L.J. (2010) *Jimmy Stewart Is Dead: Ending the World's Ongoing Financial Plague with Limited Purpose Banking*, John Wiley & Sons.

Krauss, C. (2011) Filling Stations Fret Over Price Creep, *New York Times*, 9 March [http://green. blogs.nytimes.com/2011/03/09/filling-stations-fret-over-price-creep, accessed 29 September 2013].

Krugman, P. (1990) *The Age of Diminishing Expectations: U.S. Economics Policy in the 1990s*, MIT Press.

Kuznets, S. (1934) National Income, 1929–1932. 73rd US Congress, 2d session, Senate document no. 124, p. 7.

Kydland, F.E. and Prescott, C. (1982) Time to build and aggregate fluctuations, *Econometrics*, **50**, 1345–1370.

Laar, M. (2007) *The Estonian Economic Miracle*, Heritage Foundation.

Lachmann, L. (1976) From Mises to Shackle: An Essay on Austrian Economics and the Kaleidic Society, *Journal of Economic Literature*, **14** (1), 54–62.

Lachmann, L.M. (1956 [1978]) *Capital and its Structure*, Sheed Andrews and McMeel.

Lachmann, L.M. (1976) From Mises to Shackle: An Essay on Austrian Economics and the Kaleidic Society, *Journal of Economic Literature*, **14** (1), 54–62.

Laffer, A. (2004) The Laffer curve: past present and future, *Heritage Backgrounder*, 1 June.

Landes, D.S. (1998) *The Wealth and Poverty of Nations*, W.W. Norton.

Landsburg, S.E. (1998) Taken to the Cleaners? *Slate.com*, 3 July. [http://www.slate.com/articles/ arts/everyday_economics/1998/07/taken_to_the_cleaners.html, accessed 19 September 2013].

Langer, E.J. (1975) The Illusion of Control, *Journal of Personality and Social Psychology*, **32** (2), 311–328.

Lawson, R.A. (2007) Economic Freedom, *The Concise Encyclopaedia of Economics* (2nd edition) [http://www.econlib.org/library/Enc/EconomicFreedom.html, accessed 24 September 2013].

Lemos, S. and Portes, J. (2008) New Labour? The Impact of Migration from Central and Eastern European Countries on the UK Labour Market, IZA Discussion Paper No. 3756, October.

Leonard, T. (2005) Protecting family and race: The Progressive case for regulating women's work, *American Journal of Economics and Sociology*, **64** (3), 757–791.

Leonhardt, D. (2008) Maybe money does buy happiness after all, *New York Times*, 16 April.

Levy, D.M. and Peart, S.J. (2011) Soviet growth and American textbooks: An endogenous past, *Journal of Economic Behavior & Organization*, **78** (1–2), 110–125.

Lewin, P. (1999) *Capital in Disequilibrium*, Routledge.

Lewin, P. (2012) Austrian capital theory: why it matters, *The Freeman*, 30 May [http://www.fee.org/ the_freeman/detail/austrian-capital-theory-why-it-matters, accessed 26 November 2013].

Lilico, A. (2012) Why does cutting government spending mean faster growth?, *The Daily Telegraph*, 29 April.

Lilico, A., Holmes, E. and Sameen, H. (2009) Controlling spending and government deficits, *Policy Exchange*, November.

Lipset, S.M. and Schneider, W. (1987) *The Confidence Gap: Business, labour and government in the public mind*, Johns Hopkins University Press.

Lord, Charles G., Ross, L. and Lepper, M.R. (1979) Biased assimilation and attitude polarization: The effects of prior theories on subsequently considered evidence, *Journal of Personality and Social Psychology*, **37** (11), 2098–2109.

Lucas, R.E. (1976) Econometric Policy Evaluation: A Critique, *Carnegie-Rochester Conference Series on Public Policy*, **1**, 19–46.

Madrigal, A.C. (2012) Most people didn't have A/C until 1973 and other strange tech timelines, *The Atlantic*, 27 July.

Maital, S. (2011) *Executive Economics: Ten Essential Tools for Managers*, Free Press.

Malia, M. (1994) *The Soviet Tragedy: A History of Socialism in Russia 1917–1991*, Free Press.

Malkiel, B.G. (1996) *A Random Walk Down Wall Street*, W.W. Norton.

Mallaby, S. (2006) The Penny Stops Here, *Washington Post*, 25 September 2006 [http://www.washingtonpost.com/wp-dyn/content/article/2006/09/24/AR2006092400946.html, accessed 24 September 2013].

Malone, T.W. (2004) Bringing the market inside, *Harvard Business Review*, April.

Mankiw, N.G. (2006) How to make $1 billion, *Greg Mankiw's Blog*, 25 September [http://gregmankiw.blogspot.co.uk/2006/09/how-to-make-1-billion.html, accessed 24 September 2013].

Mankiw, N.G. (2006) *Macroeconomics*, Worth Publishers (6th edition).

Mankiw, N.G. (2006) Outsourcing Redux, *Greg Mankiw's Blog*, 7 May [http://gregmankiw.blogspot.com/2006/05/outsourcing-redux.html, accessed September 2013].

Mankiw, N.G. (2006) Who pays the corporate income tax? *Greg Mankiw's Blog*, 24 August.

Mankiw, N.G. (2007) Do people dislike being around the rich?, *Greg Mankiw's Blog*, 4 August [http://gregmankiw.blogspot.co.uk/2007/08/do-people-dislike-being-around-rich.html, accessed 24 September 2013].

Mankiw, N.G. (2009) Shiller on animal spirits, *Greg Mankiw's Blog*, 27 January [http://gregmankiw.blogspot.com/2009/01/shiller-on-animal-spirits.html, accessed 30 September 2013].

Manne, H. (2004) Legalize Insider Trading, *Capitalism Magazine*, 24 September [http://www.capmag.com/article.asp?ID=3933, accessed 16 September 2013].

Margolis, J. (2011) So what's new? *Business life* [BA in-flight magazine], March, p. 16.

Marn, M.V., Roegner, E.V. and Zawada, C.C. (2003) Pricing new products, *The McKinsey Quarterly*, **3**.

Mathews, J. (2006) *Strategising Disequilibrium and Profit*, Stanford Business Books.

McChesney, F.S. (1987) Rent extraction and rent creation in the economy theory of regulation, *Journal of Legal Studies*, **16** (1), 101–118.

McChesney, F.S. (1997) *Money for Nothing: Politicians, Rent Extraction and Political Extortion*, Harvard University Press.

McCloskey, D.N. (2006) *The Bourgeois Virtues*, University of Chicago Press.

McCracken, H. (2012) Apple's Phil Schiller on the State of the Mac, *Time's Technologizer blog*, 26 October.

McInerney, J. (1984) *Bright Lights, Big City*, Vintage.

Menger, C. (1892) On the Origins of Money, *Economic Journal*, **2**, 239–255.

Micklethwaite, J. and Wooldridge, A. (2004) *The Right Nation: Conservative Power in America*, Penguin.

Mill, J.S. (1848) *Principles of Political Economy, with Some of Their Applications to Social Philosophy*.

Mises, L.v. (1912[1953]) *The Theory of Money and Credit*, Yale University Press.

Mises, L.v. (1912[1981]) *The Theory of Money and Credit*, Liberty Fund.

Mises, L.v. (1920[1990]) *Economic Calculation in the Socialist Commonwealth*, Ludwig von Mises Institute.

Mises, L.v. (1934[1981]) *The Theory of Money and Credit*, Liberty Fund.

Mises, L.v. (1936[1981]) *Socialism*, Liberty Fund.

Mises, L.v. (1949[1996]) *Human Action: A Treatise on Economics*, Fox & Wiles.

Mises, L.v. (1979[2006]) *Economic Policy*, Ludwig von Mises Institute (3rd edition).

Mohammed, R. (2003) The Problem with Price Gouging Laws, *HBR Blog Network*, 23 July.

Mongin, P. (1997) Expected Utility Theory, in Davis, J.B., Hands, D.W. and Maki, U. (eds), *Handbook of Economic Methodology*, Edward Elgar.

Moss, D.A. (2007) *A Concise Guide to Macroeconomics*, Harvard Business School Press.

Moss, V. (2009) London Summit 2009: Alistair Darling vows to do whatever it takes to beat economic crisis, *Daily Mirror*, 15 March [http://www.mirror.co.uk/news/uk-news/london-summit-2009-alistair-darling-382642, accessed 30 September 2013].

Nelson, C.R. and Plosser, C.I. (1982) Trends and random walks in macroeconomic time series. Some evidence and implications, *Journal of Monetary Economics*, **10**, 139–162.

Nelson, R.R. and Winter, S.G. (1982) *An Evolutionary Theory of Economic Change*, Harvard University Press.

Neumark, D. and Wascher, W.L. (2008) *Minimum Wages*, MIT Press.

Niehans, J. (1994) *A History of Economic Theory*, Johns Hopkins University Press.

Northrup, L. (2013) Time Warner boosts my speed, cuts my bill: I just happen to live near Google Fiber, *Consumerist.com*, 30 January.

Nutter, G.W. (1962) *The Growth of Industrial Production in the Soviet Union*, Princeton University Press.

O'Driscoll, G. (2011) Keynesian death spiral, *Think Markets*, 4 August [http://thinkmarkets.wordpress.com/2011/08/04/%E2%80%9Ckeynesian-death-spiral%E2%80%9D/, accessed 30 September 2013].

O'Driscoll, G.P. and Rizzo, M.J. (1985) *The Economics of Time and Ignorance*, Routledge.

Ohlin, B. (1933) *Interregional and International Trade*, Harvard University Press.

Oliver, R. and Shor, M. (2003) Digital Redemption of Coupons: Satisfying and Dissatisfying Effects on Promotion Codes, *Journal of Product and Brand Management*, **12** (2), 121–134.

Olson, M. (1962) *The Rise and Decline of Nations*, Yale University Press.

Olson, M. (1965[1971]) *The Logic of Collective Action*, Harvard University Press.

Oppers, S.E. (2002) The Austrian Theory of Business Cycles: Old Lessons for Modern Economic Policy? IMF Working Paper.

Orange, R. (2011) Turkmenistan rebuilds giant rotating golden statue, *Daily Telegraph*, 24 May.

Ormerod, P. (2011) 'Expansionary fiscal contraction', *IEA Blog*, 9 November [http://www.iea.org.uk/blog/expansionary-fiscal-contraction, accessed 30 September 2013].

Ostrom, E. and Walker, J. (1997) Neither markets nor states: linking transformation processes in collective-action arenas, in Mueller, D.C. (ed.), *Perspectives on Public Choice*, Cambridge University Press.

Ostry, J.D., Ghosh, A.R., Habermeier, K. et al (2010) Capital Inflows: The Role of Controls, IMF Staff Position Note, 19 February.

Owyang, M.T., Ramey, V.A. and Zubairy, S. (2013) Are government spending multipliers greater during periods of slack? Evidence from 20th century historical data, NBER Working Paper No. 18769.

Padovano, F. and Galli, E. (2001) Tax rates and economic growth in the OECD countries (1950–1990), *Economic Enquiry*, **39** (1), 44–57.

Panic, I.K. (2013) Talent is a gift from god (an interview with Lazar Ristovski), *Air Serbia Review*, December.

Paulson, H.M. (2010) *On the Brink*, Hachette.

Peltzman, S. (2004) Regulation and the Natural Progress of Opulence, American Enterprise Institute, vii. [http://www.aei.org/files/2005/05/16/files/2005/05/16/Peltzman-Lecture.pdf, accessed 24 September 2013].

Pennington, M. (2011) *Robust Political Economy*, Edward Elgar.

Penrose, E.T. (1959) *The Theory of the Growth of the Firm*, John Wiley & Sons.

Perry, M. (2007) Taxi Cartel Membership Has Its Privileges: Returns That Have Outperformed Every Major Index, *Carpe Diem*, 3 November [http://mjperry.blogspot.com/2007/11/taxi-cartel-membership-has-its.html, accessed 24 September 2013].

Perry, M. (2007) The market imposes a $2.75 billion fine on Mattel, *Carpe Diem*, 17 August [http://mjperry.blogspot.co.uk/2007/08/market-imposes-275-billion-fine-on.html, accessed 4 October 2013].

Peters, E., Finucane, M.L., MacGregor, D.G. and Slovic, P. (2000) The Bearable Lightness of Aging: Judgment and Decision Processes in Older Adults, in Stern, P.C. and Carstensen, L.L. (eds), *The Aging Mind: Opportunities in Cognitive Research*, National Academies Press.

Phillips, A.W. (1958) The Relation between Unemployment and the Rate of Change of Money Wage Rates in the United Kingdom, 1861–1957, *Economica*, **25** (100), 283–299.

Piccone, P. (1994) From the New Left to the New Populism, *Telos*, **101**, 173–208.

Pirie, M. (2012) *Economics Made Simple: How Money, Trade and Markets Really Work*, Harriman.

Portes, J. (2012) Why Ed Miliband shouldn't apologise for making the right decision on Eastern European migration, National Institute of Economic and Social Research blog, 22 June [http://niesr.ac.uk/blog/why-ed-miliband-shouldnt-apologise-making-right-decision-eastern-european-migration #.UkNmXGRAR9Y, accessed 22 September 2013].

Poundstone, W. (2010) *Priceless: The hidden psychology of value*, Oneworld.

Powell, B. (2007) 'Japan', *The Concise Encyclopedia of Economics*.

Powell, B. (2014) *Sweatshops: Improving Lives and Economic Growth*, Cambridge University Press.

Powell, B. and Skarbek, D. (2006) Sweatshops and third-world living standards: are the jobs worth the sweat?, *Journal of Labor Research*, **17** (2), 263–274.

Powell, B. and Zwolinski, M. (2012) The Ethical and Economic Case Against Sweatshop Labor: A Critical Assessment, *Journal of Business Ethics*, **107** (4), 449–472.

Powell, B., Ford, R. and Nowrasteh, A. (2008) Somalia after state collapse: Chaos or improvement?, *Journal of Economic Behaviour & Organisation*, **67** (3–4), 657–670.

Quinn, J. (2013) Wonga calls for tougher rules on payday loans, *Daily Telegraph*, 29 June.

Raff, D. (1988) Wage determination theory and the five-dollar day at Ford, *Journal of Economic History*, **48** (02), 387–399.

Rector, R.E. (2007) How Poor Are America's Poor? Examining the 'Plague' of Poverty in America? *Heritage Foundation Backgrounder* #2064.

Reed, L.W. (1998) Great myths of the great depression, *The Freeman*, 1 August [http://www.fee.org/the_freeman/detail/great-myths-of-the-great-depression accessed 30 September 2013].

Reinhart, C.M. and Rogoff, K.S. (2009) *This Time is Different: Eight Centuries of Financial Folly*, Princeton University Press.

Reinhart, C.M. and Rogoff, K.S. (2010) Growth in a Time of Debt, *American Economic Review: Papers & Proceedings*, **100**, 573–578.

Reinhart, C.M. and Rogoff, K.S. (2011) From Financial Crash to Debt Crisis, *American Economic Review*, **101** (5), 1676–1706.

Reinhart, C.M. and Rogoff, K.S. (2011) The forgotten history of domestic debt, *Economic Journal*, **121** (552), 319–350.

Rhoads, J. (2010) Adam Smith's four principles of taxation, *Greater Boston Tea Party Blog*, 10 April [http://greaterbostonteaparty.com/?p=220, accessed 26 September 2013].

Richman, S. (2012) There's No Such Thing as Economic Freedom. There is only freedom, *The Freeman*, 8 June [http://www.fee.org/the_freeman/detail/theres-no-such-thing-as-economic-freedom, accessed 25 September 2013].

Rizzo, M. (2010) 'In the long run, we are all dead': What did Keynes really mean?, *Think Markets*, 28 June [http://thinkmarkets.wordpress.com/2010/06/28/%E2%80%9Cin-the-long-run-we-are-all-dead%E2%80%9D-what-does-it-mean/, accessed 30 September 2013].

Roberts, P.C. (2002) My time with Soviet economics, *The Independent Review*, **7** (2).

Robertson, D.H. (1923) *Control of Industry*, Nisbet & Co.

Robinson, D.L. (2006) No clear evidence from countries that have enforced the wearing of helmets, *BMJ*, **332** (7543), 722–725.

Rockoff, H. (2007) 'Price Controls', *Concise Encyclopaedia of Economics* (2nd edition) [http://www.econlib.org/library/Enc/PriceControls.html, accessed 17 September 2013].

Rodrik, D. (2007) And the winner is ..., *Dani Rodrik's Weblog*, 5 May [http://rodrik.typepad.com/dani_rodriks_weblog/2007/05/and_the_winner_.html, accessed September 2013].

Romer, C. and Romer, D.H. (2010) The macroeconomic effects of tax changes: estimates based on a new measure of fiscal shocks, *American Economic Review*, **100**, 763–801.

Romer, C.D. (1991) What Ended the Great Depression?, *The Journal of Economic History*, **52** (4), 757–784.

Romer, P.M. (1994) The Origins of Endogenous Growth, *The Journal of Economic Perspectives*, **8** (1), 3–22.

Rosegrant, S. (2007) Wal-Mart's Response to Hurricane Katrina: Striving for a Public Private Partnership. Kennedy School of Government Case Program C16-07-1876.0, Case Studies in Public Policy and Management. Cambridge, MA: Kennedy School of Government.

Rosling, H. TED talk about the social impact of washing machines: http://www.ted.com/talks/hans_rosling_and_the_magic_washing_machine.html [accessed 24 September 2013].

Rothbard, M.N. (1962) The Case for the 100 Percent Gold Dollar, in Yeager, L.B. (ed.), *In Search of a Monetary Constitution*, Harvard University Press.

Rothbard, M.N. (1963[2005]) *What Has Government Done to our Money?* Mises Institute.

Rothbard, M.N. (1970[2009]) Power and Market, in *Man, Economy and State with Power and Market*, Mises Institute.

Rumsfeld, D. (2010) *Known and Unknown*, Penguin.

Rybczynski, T.M. (1955) Factor Endowment and Relative Commodity Prices, *Economica*, **22** (88), 336–341.

Rzonca, A. and Cizkowicz, P. (2005) Non-Keynesian effects of fiscal contraction in new member states, European Central Bank Working Paper Series No. 519.

Sachs, J. (1998) The Dismal Decade, *Los Angeles Times*, 22 November.

Sacks, D.W., Stevenson, B. and Wolfers, J. (2010) Subjective wellbeing, income, economic development, and growth, NBER Working Paper No. 16441.

Saez, E., Slemrod, J.B. and Giertz, S.H. (2012) The Elasticity of Taxable Income with Respect to Marginal Tax Rates: A Critical Review, *Journal of Economic Literature*, **50** (1), 3–50.

Salmon, F. (2011) How the New York Times Paywall is Working, *Wired.com*, 14 August.

Samuelson, P.A. (1994) Facets of Balassa-Samuelson Thirty Years Later, *Review of International Economics* **2** (3), 201–226.

Sapienza, P. and Zingales, L. (2013) Economic Experts vs. Average Americans, Chicago Booth Research Paper No. 13-11.

Sargent, T. and Wallace, N. (1976) Rational Expectations and the Theory of Economic Policy, *Journal of Monetary Economics*, **2** (2), 169–183.

Sautet, F. (2006) Lifetime Achievement Award to Professor Israel M. Kirzner, Coordination Problem, 22 November [http://austrianeconomists.typepad.com/weblog/2006/11/lifetime_achiev.html, accessed 25 September 2013].

Sautet, F. (2010) The competitive market is a process of entrepreneurial discovery, in Boettke, P.J. (ed.), *Handbook on Contemporary Austrian Economics*, Edward Elgar.

Schuler, K. (1992) The world history of free banking: an overview, in Dowd, K. (ed.) *The Experience of Free Banking*, Routledge.

Schumpeter, J.A. (1934) *The Theory of Economic Development*, Transaction, [first published in 1911 as Theorie der wirtschaftlichen Entwicklung].

Schumpeter, J.A. (1942 [1950]) *Capitalism, Socialism, and Democracy*, Harper and Brothers.

Schurenberg, E. (2012) What's an entrepreneur? The best answer ever, *Inc.Com*, 9 January [http://www.inc.com/eric-schurenberg/the-best-definition-of-entepreneurship.html, accessed 19 September 2013].

Selgin, G. (1988) *The Theory of Free Banking: Money Supply under Competitive Note Issue*, Rowman and Littlefield.

Selgin, G. (2013) Those dishonest goldsmiths, *Financial History Review*, **19** (3), 269–288.

Sen, A. (1981) *Poverty and Famines: An Essay on Entitlements and Deprivation*, Oxford, Clarendon Press.

Senge, P.M. (1990) *The Fifth Discipline*, Doubleday/Currency.

Shackle, G.L.S. (1992) *Epistemics and Economics*, Transaction.

Shales, A. (2009) FDR Was a Great Leader, But His Economic Plan Isn't One to Follow, *The Washington Post*, 1 February.

Sharpe, W.F. (2002) Indexed Investing: A Prosaic Way to Beat the Average Investor, Presented at the Spring President's Forum, Monterey Institute of International Studies, 1 May.

Shefrin, H. (2005) *Behavioural Corporate Finance*, McGraw-Hill.

Shleifer, A. and Treisman, D. (2005) A Normal Country: Russia After Communism, *Journal of Economic Perspectives*, **19** (1), 151–174.

Silverman, R.E. (2012) No more angling for the best seat; more meetings are stand up jobs, *Wall Street Journal*, 2 February.

Sinclair, M. (2012) The rich, the poor and the middle pay a lot of tax. *Tax Payers' Alliance Blog*, 16 April [http://www.taxpayersalliance.com/economics/2012/04/rich-poor-middle-pay-lot-tax.html, accessed 26 September 2013].

Skidelsky, R. (1997) *The Road from Serfdom*, Penguin.

Smith, A. (1776 [1976]) *An Inquiry into the Nature and Causes of the Wealth of Nations*, University of Chicago Press.

Smith, H. (1974) *The Russians*, Ballantine.

Smith, M.D. and Ward, T.J. (2013) If I hit Rob Gronkowski high, I would have been fined, *NBC Sports*, 9 December [http://profootballtalk.nbcsports.com/2013/12/09/t-j-ward-if-i-hit-rob-gronkowski-high-i-would-have-been-fined/, accessed 20 December 2013].

Snider, J.H. (2007) The Art of Spectrum Lobbying, *New America Foundation*, August.

Sowell, T. (2007) *Basic Economics: A Common Sense Guide to the Economy*, Basic Books.

Spence, M. (1973) Job market signalling, *The Quarterly Journal of Economics*, **87** (3), 355–374.

Stevenson, B. and Wolfers, J. (2012) Crowds are this election's real winners, *Bloomberg*, 19 November.

Stevenson, B. and Wolfers, J. (2013) Subjective wellbeing and income – is there any evidence of satiation? NBER Working Paper No. 18992.

Stibel, J. (2012) Don't divest just because the economy is rotten, *HBR Blog Network*, 18 February [http://blogs.hbr.org/2011/02/dont-divest-just-because-the-e/, accessed September 2013].

Stolper, W.F. and Samuelson, P.A. (1941) Protection and Real Wages, *Review of Economic Studies*, **9** (1), 58–73.

Stossel, J. and Binkley, G. (2006) MYTH: Price-Gouging is Bad, *ABC News*, 12 May [http://abcnews.go.com/2020/Stossel/story?id=1954352, accessed 17 November 2013].

Stringham, E. (2006) *Anarchy, State and Public Choice*, Edward Elgar.

Sumner, S. (2008) Score-Keeping with Selgin, *Cato Unbound*, 28 September [http://www.cato-unbound.org/2009/09/28/scott-sumner/score-keeping-with-selgin/, accessed 29 September 2013].

Sumner, S. (2013) Money matters, *The Money Illusion*, 16 March [http://www.themoneyillusion.com/?p=20114, accessed 6 October 2013].

Surowiecki, J. (2004) *The Wisdom of Crowds*, Doubleday.

Swaminathan, S. Anklesaria Aiyar (2009) Socialism Kills: The Human Cost of Delayed Economic Reform in India, CATO Institute, 21 October.

Tabarrok, A. (2006) Penny Politics, *Marginal Revolution*, 26 September [http://marginalrevolution.com/marginalrevolution/2006/09/penny_politics.html, accessed 24 September 2013].

Tabarrok, A. (2007) Home envy, *Marginal Revolution*, 6 August [http://marginalrevolution.com/marginalrevolution/2007/08/home-envy.html, accessed 24 September 2013].

Tabarrok, A. (2011) Not from the onion, *Marginal Revolution*, 5 November.

Tabarrok, A. (2011) Rewarding altruism: blood for money, *Marginal Revolution*, 7 December [http://marginalrevolution.com/marginalrevolution/2011/12/rewarding-altruism-blood-for-money.html accessed 24 September 2013].

Taleb, N.N. (2001) *Fooled by Randomness*, Random House.

Tanzi, V. (2005) The economic role of the state in the 21st century, *Cato Journal*, **25** (3), 617–638.

Tanzi, V. and Schuknecht, L. (2000) *Public Spending in the 20th Century*, Cambridge University Press.

Thaler, R.H. (1988) Anomalies: The Winner's Curse, *Journal of Economic Perspectives*, **2** (1), 191–202.

Thompson, P. (2009) Drunk Boris Yeltsin was found outside White House in underpants trying to hail cab 'because he wanted some pizza', *Daily Mail*, 22 September.

Tobin, J. (1998) Monetary policy: recent theory and practice, Cowles Foundation Discussion Paper No. 1187 [http://cowles.econ.yale.edu/P/cd/d11b/d1187.pdf, accessed 6 October 2013].

Tullock, G. (1975) The Transitional Gains Trap, *Bell Journal of Economics and Management Science*, **6** (2), 671–678.

Twaronite, L. and Kitchen, M. (2011) Japan's economy slips back into recession, *Market Watch* [http://www.marketwatch.com/story/japans-economy-shrinks-sharply-in-january-march-2011-05-18, accessed 6 October 2013].

van Zandt, D. (1993) The lessons of the lighthouse: 'Government' or 'private' provision of goods, *Journal of Legal Studies*, **22** (1), 47–72.

Varian, H. (2007) The Stock Does Better than the Investor, *New York Times*, 3 May.

Vihanto, M. (1992) Competition between local governments as a discovery procedure, *Journal of Institutional and Theoretical Economics*, **148**, 411–436.

Wallop, H. (2013) 'Extreme couponing': How I did whole Christmas shop for 4p, *Daily Telegraph*, 20 December.

Warhol, A. (1975) *The Philosophy of Andy Warhol (From A to B and Back Again)*, Harvest (cited by Kottke, J. (2010) Andy Warhol on Coca-Cola, *Kottke.org*, 18 October).

Warner, B. (2012) The 25 Richest People Who Ever Lived – Inflation Adjusted, Celebrity Net Worth, 13 October [http://www.celebritynetworth.com/articles/entertainment-articles/25-richest-people-lived-inflation-adjusted/#!/1-mansa-musa-net-worth_1019/ accessed 25 September 2013].

Wennekers, S. and Thurik, R. (1999) Linking entrepreneurship and economic growth, *Small Business Economics*, **13** (1), 27–55.

Wessin, R.R. and Porter, D. (2007) The Cassini Resource Exchange, *Ask Magazine*, **16**, 14–18.

Whaples, R. (2006) Do Economists Agree on Anything? Yes! *The Economists' Voice*, **3** (9), 1–6.

White, L.H. (1989) *Competition and Currency*, New York University Press.

White, W. (2010) Comments on 'After the Fall' by C. and V. Reinhart, Symposium on 'Macroeconomic Challenges: The Decade Ahead', Symposium sponsored by the Federal Reserve Bank of Kansas City, Jackson Hole Wyoming, August 2010.

Whittington-Egan, R. (1985) *Liverpool Characters and Eccentrics*, The Galley Press.

Wilkinson, W. (2006) Growth is good, *Prospect Magazine*, 21 October.

Will, G. (2007) Lovin' It All Over, *Washington Post*, 27 December.

Williams, W.E. (1989) *South Africa's War Against Capitalism*, Praeger.

Williamson, O.E. (1979) Transaction-Cost Economics: The governance of contractual relations, *Journal of Law and Economics*, **22** (2), 233–262.

Winter, E. (2007) *Incentive Reversal*, The Center for the Study of Rationality and the Economics Department, The Hebrew University of Jerusalem [http://www.dklevine.com/archive/refs4843644000000000241.pdf accessed September 2013].

Wintrobe, R. (1997) Modern bureaucratic theory, in Mueller, D.C., *Perspectives on Public Choice: A Handbook*, Cambridge University Press.

Wolf, M. (2009) Central banks should target more than just inflation, *Financial Times*, 5 May.

Womack, J.P., Jones, D.T. and Roos, D. (1990) *The Machine that Changed the World*, Harper Perennial.

Woolner, A. (2010) It Isn't Insider Trading When Your Senator Does It, *Bloomberg*, 14 October 2010.

Yeager, L.B. (1968) Essential properties of the medium of exchange, *Kyklos*, **21** (1), 45–69.

Ziobrowski, A.J., Cheng, P., Boyd, J.W. and Ziobrowski, B.J. (2004) Abnormal returns from the Common Stock Investments of the US Senate, *Journal of Financial and Quantitative Analysis*, **39** (4), 661–676.

Zola, E. (1883 [2008]) *The Ladies Paradise* (originally published as *Au Bonheur des Dames*), Oxford University Press.

ECONOMIST ARTICLES

'A contagious Irish disease?', *The Economist*, 25 November 2010.

'A nation of shoppers', *The Economist*, 21 May 2011.

'A toll on the common man', *The Economist*, 1 July 2006.

'Accentuate the negative', *The Economist*, 4 November 2010.

'Alfred Kahn', *The Economist*, 22 January 2011.

'And for my next trick', *The Economist*, 6 November 2010.

'Bah, humbug', *The Economist*, 19 December 2009.

'Brewed force', *The Economist*, 17 December 2011.

'Clock-watchers no more', *The Economist*, 16 May 2009.

'Cut or loose', *The Economist*, 16 July 2011.

'Enter the quiet giant', *The Economist*, 19 June 2008.

'European bond spreads', *The Economist*, 27 March 2010.

'Europe's three great delusions', *The Economist*, 22 May 2010.

'Far from the meddling crowd', *The Economist*, 30 October 2010.

'Go for the churn', *The Economist*, 11 February 2012.

'Guts and glory', *The Economist*, 9 October 2010.

'Hedge podge', *The Economist*, 16 February 2008.

'How to taper safely', *The Economist*, 14 September 2013.

'In a spin', *The Economist*, 29 December 2010.

'It's mine, I tell you', *The Economist*, 19 June 2008.

'Kerry Packer', *The Economist*, 5 January 2006.

'Land of the Corporate Giants', *The Economist*, 3 November 2012.

'Looking good by doing good', *The Economist*, 17 January 2009.

'Making no cents', *The Economist*, 12 May 2012.

'Matchmakers and trustbusters', *The Economist*, 8 December 2005.

'Modernising Russia', *The Economist*, 13 March 2010.

'Money can buy happiness', *The Economist*, 2 May 2013.

'Much ado about multipliers', *The Economist*, 24 September 2009.

'Of businessmen and ballerinas', *The Economist*, 9 February 2013.

'One to ten', *The Economist*, 7 July 2012.

'Paper chains', *The Economist*, 19 August 2010.

'Portrait of the artist as an entrepreneur', *The Economist*, 17 December 2011.

'Rich managers, poor clients', *The Economist*, 7 January 2012.

'Riding the tiger', *The Economist*, 9 October 2010.

'Rules for fools', *The Economist*, 14 May 2011.

'Serviceable', *The Economist*, 5 January 2013.

'Shock treatment', *The Economist*, 15 November 2007.

'Soft landing at Longbridge', *The Economist*, 10 March 2006.

'Sticking pins into an icon', *The Economist*, 19 June 2007.

'The Big Bear', *The Economist*, 18 October 2008.

'The bottom of the pyramid', *The Economist*, 25 June 2011.

'The crowd within', *The Economist*, 28 June 2008.

'The golden rules of banking', *The Economist*, 14 July 2012.
'The joyless of the jobless', *The Economist*, 27 November 2010.
'The meaning of Bill Gates', *The Economist*, 26 June 2008.
'The meaning of iPod', *The Economist*, 10 June 2004
'The new green', *The Economist*, 8 September 2012.
'The new young Turks', *The Economist*, 8 June 2013.
'The penny drops', *The Economist*, 2 March 2013.
'The price of cooking the books', *The Economist*, 25 February 2012.
'The reform club', *The Economist*, 22 September 2012.
'The silence of Mammon', *The Economist*, 19 December 2009.
'The transience of power', *The Economist*, 16 March 2013.
'The trouble with outsourcing', *The Economist*, 30 June 2011.
'The weak shall inherit the earth', *The Economist*, 6 October 2012.
'Thriving on adversity', *The Economist*, 3 October 2009.
'Towards the end of poverty', *The Economist*, 1 June 2013.
'Trouble at the lab', *The Economist*, 19 October 2013.
'Upwardly mobile Africa', *The Economist*, 22 December 2012.
'Wanted: chief firefighter', *The Economist*, 4 June 2011.
'When the golden eggs run out', *The Economist*, 4 December 2008.
'Wonder drug', *The Economist*, 11 December 2010.
'Yegor Gaidar', *The Economist*, 19 December 2009.
'Yuan for the money', *The Economist*, 9 February 2013.

UNAUTHORED AND MISCELLANEOUS

'7 ways people woke up, pre-alarm clock' *Mental Floss*, [http://mentalfloss.com/article/24117/7-ways-people-woke-pre-alarm-clock, accessed 23 September 2013].
Address and Question and Answer Period at the Economic Club of New York, 14 December 1962.
'Aldi splashes out $1b on upgrade', *Sydney Morning Herald*, 14 March 2009.
Berkshire Hathaway Inc, Chairman's Letter 1996 [http://www.berkshirehathaway.com/letters/1996.html, accessed 16 September 2013].
'Bill filed to prohibit congressional insider trading', *CNN*, 16 November 2011.
'Britain's fastest growing jobs', *Daily Telegraph* [http://www.telegraph.co.uk/finance/jobs/10307542/Britains-fastest-growing-jobs.html?frame=2670830, accessed 23 September 2013].
Bryan Caplan's Graduate Micro II Class, George Mason University, http://econfaculty.gmu.edu/bcaplan/e812/micro9.htm.
Budget 2011, HM Treasury.
'Chile mining accident (2010)', *New York Times*, 12 October 2011 [http://topics.nytimes.com/top/reference/timestopics/subjects/c/chile_mining_accident_2010/, accessed 25 November 2013].
'Composer and behavioural finance experts create "reality" opera based on open outcry stock trading floor', 6 December 2012 [http://www.multivu.com/mnr/58659-barclays-opera, accessed 17 September 2013].
'Damage Situation and Police Countermeasures associated with 2011 Tohoku district – off the Pacific Ocean Earthquake', *National Police Agency of Japan* [http://www.npa.go.jp/archive/keibi/biki/higaijokyo_e.pdf, accessed 6 October 2013].
'Dutchman Helps to Liquidate Dying Churches', *Der Spiegel*, 22 December 2011.
Economic Freedom of the World, Fraser Institute, [http://www.freetheworld.com/, accessed 24 September 2013] and Index of Economic Freedom, Wall Street Journal/Heritage Foundation [http://www.heritage.org/index/, accessed 24 September 2013].

Gross Public Income – United Kingdom 1801–1980, in Mitchel, B.R. (1988) *British Historical Statistics,* Cambridge University Press.

'Helicopter money and supply siders', *Financial Times*, 6 February 2013.

http://biz.yahoo.com/p/sum_qpmd.html [accessed 4 October 2013].

http://www.competition-commission.org.uk/about_us/, accessed 21 September 2013.

http://www.ifa.com/pdf/ifa-vs-buffett.pdf, accessed 16 September 2013.

http://www.rate.co.uk/tax/incometax9500.html, accessed 29 September 2013.

http://www.reddit.com/r/AskReddit/comments/1a5rkq/subway_employees_of_reddit_whats_the_most/, accessed September 2013.

http://www.tax-news.com/news/UK_Treasury_Set_To_Benefit_From_Bracket_Creep____15495.html, accessed 29 September 2013.

https://www.frbatlanta.org/research/inflationproject/stickyprice/, accessed 30 September 2013.

'Is this the end of the Concorde dream?', *Daily Telegraph*, 16 August 2000.

'Japan Earthquake - Tsunami Fast Facts', *CNN*, 20 September 2013 [http://edition.cnn.com/2013/07/17/world/asia/japan-earthquake—tsunami-fast-facts/index.html, accessed 6 October 2013].

'Japan exits recession triggered by March earthquake' *Daily Telegraph*, 14 November 2011 [http://www.telegraph.co.uk/finance/economics/8887894/Japan-exits-recession-triggered-by-March-earthquake.html, accessed 6 October 2013].

'KFC revamp and promotions help Restaurant Brands dish up rise in sales' *New Zealand Herald*, 3 March 2009.

'Ljubljana Life' website called 'Trouble At The Border' [http://www.ljubljana-life.com/ljubljana/border-dispute, accessed 16 September 2013], otherwise you can attempt to translate his page on the Slovenian Wikipedia [http://sl.wikipedia.org/wiki/Jo%C5%A1ko_Joras, accessed 16 September 2013].

'Malkiel unleashed: The full interview with Burton Malkiel', *PBS*, 20 June 2003. [http://www.pbs.org/wsw/tvprogram/malkiel_interview.html, accessed 16 September 2013].

'Millennium Dome Collection' website, http://www.dome2000.com, accessed 23 September 2013.

Minutes of the Monetary Policy Committee Meeting, 4 and 5 February 2009, 18 February 2009.

'New USGS number puts Japan quake at 4th largest' *CBS News*, 14 March 2011. [http://www.webcitation.org/5xgjFTgf4, accessed 6 October 2013].

'Obama Hammers Romney on Outsourcing vs. "Offshoring" Explainer', *ABC News*, 25 June 2012 [http://abcnews.go.com/blogs/politics/2012/06/obama-hammers-romney-on-outsourcing-vs-offshoring-explainer/, accessed 16 September 2013].

'On-shoring is the new off-shoring as call centres come back to UK', *HR Zone* [http://www.hrzone.com/topic/business-lifestyle/shoring-new-shoring-call-centres-come-back-uk/112654, accessed 16 September 2013].

Population Estimates for UK, England and Wales, Scotland and Northern Ireland, Office for National Statistics, 8 August 2013.

Private correspondence with Claire Moorhead, Treasurer for The Friends of Williamson's Tunnels.

'Public Attitudes to Banking', The Cobden Centre, June 2010.

'Recession puts groups in mood to expand', *Financial Times*, 15 June 2009.

Reported Road Casualties, Great Britain 2011, Department for Transport [https://www.gov.uk/government/uploads/system/uploads/attachment_data/file/9280/rrcgb2011-complete.pdf, accessed 7 October 2013.]

'Reuters feeds the robots two-second scoops', (2013) *Columbia Journalism Review*, 10 July.

Revolver, Parlophone Records, 1966.

Royal Mint Annual Report, 2010–11. [http://www.royalmint.com/~/media/Files/AnnualReports/ar20102011.ashx, accessed, 29 September 2013].

'Secrets from the potato chip factory', http://vimeo.com/62709769.

'Smartphones enter the nation's basket', *Metro*, 16 March 2011.

Tax Matters: Reforming the Tax System, The Report of the Tax Reform Commission, October 2006.

'The $300m cable that will save traders milliseconds', *Daily Telegraph*, 11 September 2011.

The Jobs of Yesteryear: Obsolete Occupations, *NPR*, 5 March 2010 [http://www.npr.org/templates/ story/story.php?storyId=124251060, accessed 23 September 2013].

'The Price Impact of Wal-Mart: An Update Through 2006', *Global Insight*.

The Risk Intelligent Approach to Outsourcing and Offshoring, Deloitte Risk Intelligent Series, Issue No. 8.

The Single Income Tax, 2020 Tax Commission, May 2012.

Time Well Spent: The Declining Real Cost of Living in America, 1997 Annual Report, Federal Reserve Bank of Dallas [http://dallasfed.org/assets/documents/fed/annual/1999/ar97.pdf, accessed 24 September 2013].

'UK falls behind Brazil in manufacturing', *Financial Times*, 21 March 2011.

Wall Street Journal Blogs, 2 October 2013 [http://blogs.wsj.com/washwire/2013/10/02/world-war-ii-memorial-becomes-shutdown-central/, accessed 25 November 2013].

'West Ham Olympic Stadium move "a mistake" Richard Caborn', BBC Sport, 22 March 2013 [http://www.bbc.co.uk/sport/0/football/21897902, accessed 23 September 2013].

Winding-up The New Millennium Experience Company Limited', Report by the comptroller and auditor general, 17 April 2002. [http://www.nao.org.uk/wp-content/uploads/2002/04/0102749.pdf, accessed 23 September 2013].

Would You Give Up The Internet For 1 Million Dollars? TFAS Video, You Tube, [http://www.youtube.com/watch?v=0FB0EhPM_M4 accessed 24 September 2013].

INTERVIEWS

Balcerowicz, L., Interview with PBS Commanding Heights, conducted 12 November 2000.

Chubais, A., Interview with PBS Commanding Heights, conducted 12 December 2000.

Gorbachev, M., Interview with PBS Commanding Heights, conducted 4 April 2001.

Jordan, B., Interview with PBS Commanding Heights, conducted 3 October 2000.

Potanin, V., Interview with PBS Commanding Heights, conducted 6 October 2000

Sachs, J., Interview with PBS Commanding Heights, conducted 15 June 2000.

Yavlinsky, Y., Interview with PBS Commanding Heights, conducted 9 October 2000.

Index

Note: Page numbers in **bold** denote tables.